Eighteenth-Century
English Literature

Cultural History of Literature

Ann Hallamore Caesar and Michael Caesar *Modern Italian Literature*
Christopher Cannon *Middle English Literature*
Sandra Clark *Renaissance Drama*
Glenda Dicker/sun *African American Theatre*
Alison Finch *French Literature*
Roger Luckhurst *Science Fiction*
Katie Normington *Medieval English Drama*
Lynne Pearce *Romance Writing*
Charles J. Rzepka *Detective Fiction*
Jason Scott-Warren *Early Modern English Literature*
Charlotte Sussman *Eighteenth-Century English Literature*
Mary Trotter *Modern Irish Theatre*
Andrew Baruch Wachtel and Ilya Vinitsky *Russian Literature*
Andrew J. Webber *The European Avant-Garde*
Tim Whitmarsh *Ancient Greek Literature*

Eighteenth-Century English Literature

1660–1789

CHARLOTTE SUSSMAN

polity

First published in 2012 by Polity Press

Polity Press
65 Bridge Street
Cambridge CB2 1UR, UK

Polity Press
350 Main Street
Malden, MA 02148, USA

ISBN-13: 978-0-7456-2514-0
ISBN-13: 978-0-7456-2515-7(pb)

A catalogue record for this book is available from the British Library.

Typeset in 11.25 on 13 pt Dante
by Toppan Best-set Premedia Limited
Printed and bound in Great Britain by the MPG Books Group

The publisher has used its best endeavours to ensure that the URLs for external websites referred to in this book are correct and active at the time of going to press. However, the publisher has no responsibility for the websites and can make no guarantee that a site will remain live or that the content is or will remain appropriate.

Every effort has been made to trace all copyright holders, but if any have been inadvertently overlooked the publisher will be pleased to include any necessary credits in any subsequent reprint or edition.

For further information on Polity, visit our website: www.politybooks.com

Contents

Acknowledgements

This book has been many years in the making, and more people than I can name, both inside and outside of academia, have helped me along the way. Thank you all. In particular, I'd like to thank Andrea Drugan, Neil de Cort and everyone at Polity over the years for their extraordinary patience with this project. I am perhaps even more grateful to Gail Ferguson for her equal patience and for her fine editing skills. The opportunity to teach eighteenth-century literature at the University of Colorado and Duke University made this book what it is, and I would like to thank my students for not only showing me what answers needed to be given, but also what questions needed to be asked. I have also been fortunate to have wonderful colleagues at both institutions, including Jillian Heydt-Stevenson, Katherine Eggert, Srinivas Aravamudan and Kathy Psomiades. I need to single out John Allen Stevenson, however, both for teaching me far more about teaching eighteenth-century literature than I ever imagined there was to learn, and for being such an exceedingly wise and generous senior colleague while I was at CU-Boulder. Sarah Peterson Pittock, who was my research assistant then, and is an established teacher in her own right now, made this book infinitely better than it would have been without her help. Finally, this book is dedicated to my sons, Henry and Jacob Green, who teach me something new every day, most especially about joy.

Introduction

Two concurrent and unprecedented historical developments shaped eighteenth-century literature and culture. As print technology grew more sophisticated and literacy rates rose, hitherto unknown possibilities emerged for both public interaction and the private articulation of selfhood. The period between 1660 and 1789 can be understood, on one level, as a time when the relationships between persons and communities were being worked out afresh, finally coalescing into the unstable formations we now call "the reading public," "the nuclear family," and "individuality." At the same time, England's colonial expansion into the Americas, mercantile penetration of the Far East, and assimilation of the "internal colonies" of Scotland and Ireland resulted in extraordinary riches flowing into the metropolis, riches that fostered a variety of new urban entertainments and commodities, as well as an anxiety about England's susceptibility to luxury. This period, therefore, can also be understood as a time when England formed a new kind of national identity in the face of its international triumphs and defeats. "Britishness" was remade, during this era, in response to a variety of influences – from Scotland and Ireland, from Africa, from China, and from the New World.

But how did these social, political, and economic developments shape a literary period? This book chooses to start its investigation of that subject forty years before the eighteenth century technically began, in 1660, and ends eleven years before it officially ended, in 1789. There is nothing unusual about that: these dates are the traditional bookends of the field known as "eighteenth-century literature," but it is worth pausing over this misalignment of literary era and chronological century for a moment, to examine why these dates have been deemed so important. The first – 1660 – is often considered the moment when the Renaissance turned into the Enlightenment, and it marks a political event: the Restoration of the Stuart monarchy. After almost twenty years of civil war, England's period without a king, its "Interregnum," came to an end; for this reason, the years between 1660 and 1689 are called, by both literary scholars and historians, "the

Restoration." Yet the date signals a shift in cultural practices as well. When Charles II ascended the throne, he reopened London's theaters, allowing actresses on stage for the first time. He also curtailed religious freedom, while at the same time loosening restrictions on scientific inquiry. And, he personally set the tone for an era of ribald humor, licentious depictions of sexual relations, and exuberant wit. The latter date – 1789 – is also both a political and cultural landmark. That year witnessed the beginning of the French Revolution – an event that had dramatic consequences for Britain's self-understanding; it also saw the publication of William Blake's *Songs of Innocence and Experience*, an event that heralded the dawn of a new literary period – the Romantic era. By covering only material written between these two dates, I am tacitly suggesting that eighteenth-century literature can be distinguished, on the one hand, from Renaissance or Early Modern literature, and, on the other, from Romantic-era literature.

Such distinctions will always be somewhat artificial. *Paradise Lost*, for instance, was written in 1667, but it is hardly ever considered a piece of "Restoration literature" (and is not in this book). Robert Burns's *Poems, Chiefly in the Scottish Dialect* was published in 1786, but it is as often included in the canon of Romanticism as it is read in surveys of eighteenth-century literature (and it *is* included in this book). Literary periodization can be a tricky, if fascinating, issue. Nevertheless, I have organized this book around important cultural changes that seem central and specific to Britain between 1660 and 1789. During this period, many of the things we take for granted about modern life suddenly took shape: the novel began to dominate the literary marketplace; people entertained the possibility that all human beings were created equal; philosophers proposed that reason could triumph over superstition; ministers became more powerful than kings; and the consumer emerged as a political force.

Many important political events happened between those two dates as well. I have already noted the counterrevolution of 1660, but 28 years later counterrevolution shifted England's governmental structure yet again. The Glorious Revolution of 1688 deposed the autocratic James II (Charles II's brother, who had succeeded him) in favor of William of Orange, who was married to James's daughter Mary. Summarizing a complicated situation, we might say that William was brought in because he was willing to reign as a constitutional monarch, and because he supported Protestantism (in the form of the Church of England) – in contrast to the crypto-Catholic Stuarts. The Act of Settlement of 1701 ensured that all future monarchs of England would uphold these principles. When William died, James's other daughter, Anne, took the throne. She was the last Stuart to reign in

England. At her death, the Act of Settlement necessitated bringing in the closest Protestant relation to succeed her. This turned out to be George of Hanover; and so for the rest of the eighteenth century England was ruled by Hanoverian kings. The first of these, George I (1714–1727), spoke little English, but his successors, George II (1727–1760) and George III (1760–1820), assimilated well to their adoptive country. They were innocuous enough kings – as uninterested in the flamboyant court life of the Stuarts as they were in the theory of divine right.

Their reigns influenced the flavor of later eighteenth-century literature in that most writers felt little interest in court patronage or influence, focusing their attention on the more vibrant arenas of the market, public entertainment, and parliamentary politics. Indeed, when one thinks of "politics" during most of the eighteenth century, one thinks of the newly complex interaction between parliament and the public sphere, rather than the struggle for monarchical patronage and the court rivalries that arguably characterized the Early Modern era and the Restoration. Even so, it is important to remember how small the franchise was throughout the eighteenth century – restricted to adult men who owned land worth at least 40 shillings (historians estimate that on the eve of the Great Reform Act of 1832, only 200,000 people in Great Britain could vote for their Member of Parliament). Thus, while the governmental structure of the later eighteenth century was remarkably stable, the first part of the period saw a remarkable number of reversals. It is useful to remember that Restoration writers like John Dryden, Katherine Philips, or Aphra Behn experienced three abrupt changes in regime during their lifetimes, and had to adapt their creative and political practices accordingly.

Although the British governmental system remained unchanged after 1688, it did not go unchallenged. Despite being deposed, the heirs to the Stuart monarchy did not simply disappear. On the contrary, they plotted in exile, and mounted two serious attempts to retake the throne during the eighteenth century – the so-called Jacobite revolts of 1715 and 1745. Both of these rebellions (or "risings" to their partisans) originated in Scotland, where sympathy for the Stuarts ran deep. In 1715, the "Old Pretender" (the former James II) conspired with the Earl of Mar to raise the Scottish clans. An army made up of these groups took the Scottish city of Perth, and marched into northern England. But the support they expected from English sympathizers never materialized, and they were defeated by government forces at the Battle of Preston, the Old Pretender abandoning the effort long before its close. The second revolt, in 1745, was more serious. This one took place under the auspices of the "Young

Pretender" – Charles Edward Stuart, or "Bonnie Prince Charlie." This time, Jacobite forces were able to take Edinburgh (though not the castle) after the success of the Battle of Preston Pans, and advanced to the town of Derby in northern England, only 125 miles from London itself. At this point, however, it became clear that the promised English support was, once again, not there, and that the capital was heavily defended. In the face of all this, Charles and his commanders made the strategic decision to retreat to Scotland. After a series of scattered skirmishes, the Jacobite forces were finally routed at the devastating battle of Culloden. Charles abandoned his remaining troops and escaped back to France, disguised as Flora McDonald's lady's maid. With this defeat, and the subsequent draconian punishments the English government imposed on the Highland clans, the Jacobite threat to the Hanoverian dynasty was effectively eliminated. Historians have argued recently that Jacobite sympathies were more widespread in England than the simple recitation of their defeats would indicate. But it is clear that most Britons valued the continued stability of the Hanoverian regime, whatever its faults, over the possibility of more political upheaval.

Although they were primarily internal conflicts, the Jacobite revolts featured significant French involvement. Indeed, most of England's wars during the eighteenth century took place on a pan-European, and often transatlantic, stage, evidence of the "global" sweep of culture and politics during the era. In the first decades of the eighteenth century, Britain was embroiled in the War of Spanish Succession, joining with European powers, such as the Dutch Republic and the Duchy of Savoy, to prevent the possible unification of Spain and France under a single Bourbon monarch. The war also played out on North American soil, as English colonists fought French colonists in "Queen Anne's War." Britain was on the winning side in the this war, and, importantly, was awarded the Assiento – a contract for a monopoly of the slavery trade to the New World – as part of the Treaty of Utrecht that ended it. A similarly sprawling war – called the Seven Years' War – reoccupied Britain during the middle years of the century (1756–1763). Once again, Britain and the European powers divided into sides – Prussia, Portugal and some of the smaller German states sided with Britain, while Austria, France, Russia, Sweden, Saxony and eventually Spain lined up against them. After a good deal of bloody conflict, the war ended with the signing of the Treaty of Paris, without much change in the existing power relations between nations. This war, too, had battlefields in North America where it is known as the French and Indian War (since it was fought by British colonists against the French and

their Native American allies). The end of this war had significant consequences for Britain's empire. On the one hand, it ousted the French as one
of the important colonial powers in the region (they gave up much of their
American territory in the Treaty of Paris, along with some sugar producing
colonies). On the other hand, the war was hugely expensive, and the British
crown instituted a number of colonial tax policies in its wake in an attempt
to get the colonies to pay for a war that had been fought to protect them.
The war's aftermath left many British subjects wondering about the value
of such expensive foreign conflicts and many British colonists enraged over
the injustice of edicts like the Stamp Tax and the Tea Tax.

We might say then, that these earlier conflicts, though largely forgotten
today, set the stage for the American War of Independence (1776–1783) –
the conflict that brought about the end of what has been called Britain's
first empire. After years of growing unrest with Britain's policies with
regard to its North American territories, the thirteen colonies declared
their independence from Britain and their own status as a new nation – the
United States of America – in 1776. France allied itself officially with the
colonists in 1778, and the war came to an end – with Britain acknowledging
the new country – in 1783. Britain still had colonial holdings in the Americas
– the vast lands in Canada that were one of the "prizes" of the Seven Years'
War, as well as the immensely profitable sugar colonies of the Caribbean
– but the balance of power in the region had shifted for ever.

These military and imperial endeavors cannot be disentangled from the
structural changes simultaneously occurring in Britain's economy. John
Brewer has demonstrated that Britain was only able to wage these wars by
drastically increasing taxation, developing new modes of deficit financing
(i.e., a standing national debt), and, as a result, instituting a modern form
of governmental bureaucracy. The resulting "fiscal-military state" was an
important element of Britain's modernity.[1]

Central to these developments was the establishment of the Bank of
England in 1694, which William III chartered to fund his war with France.
The first national, central bank of its kind, the Bank of England functioned
as the crown's banker and lender, allowing many of the developments
Brewer describes.[2] The growing number of joint stock companies founded
by royal charter during the Restoration also shaped the economic climate
of the age, and provide further evidence of the "global" nature of the
British economy during the eighteenth century. While England's first joint
stock companies had been formed at the beginning of the seventeenth
century (the Virginia Company, founded in 1606, for instance, helped make
early colonization of the New World possible), the Stuart monarchs issued

charters for several important ones in the 1660s and 1670s: the Royal African Company, chartered in 1660, held the monopoly on Britain's slave trade until 1698 (when it shifted its attention to ivory and gold dust); and the Hudson Bay Company, chartered in 1670, controlled the extremely profitable fur trade in what is now Canada. Another of these entities, the South Sea Company, triggered one of the first modern financial crises in 1720. "The South Sea Bubble," as it was called, resulted from wildly inflated share prices, and a widespread interest in investing. When share prices plummeted, many, including the composer Handel, were ruined.

Rather than simply moving through a chronological survey of works and authors, this book is organized into ten thematic chapters, each one dealing with a significant development in eighteenth-century English culture and its effect on literature. Each chapter, however, explores its theme chronologically in order to illustrate how the issue changed over time. The book begins with a survey of how England's national identity developed over the course of the eighteenth century. A central aspect of national life during the period was the rapid rise of print culture, something that facilitated the new concept of the public sphere, and the second chapter takes on these conjoined issues. A chapter on the city follows, detailing the significance of the rapid urbanization of England during this period; the following chapter investigates contrasting representations of the countryside. The fifth chapter again turns away from these broader social formations and towards the individual, examining changes in ideas of selfhood and personal identity. The eighteenth century has long been associated with increasing secularism, but the next chapter, on religious experience, makes a case for the centrality of spiritual beliefs during this time, even if their expression differed from that of previous historical periods. The book then turns to questions of sex and gender roles in a discussion of representations of female sexuality and the emerging ideal of domesticity. A chapter on wit and sensibility examines two important aspects of the "history of manners" during the eighteenth century, charting representations of social interaction. The two final chapters turn towards the "peripheries" of British culture, arenas that may have been far removed from those who wrote about them, but were never marginal in terms of their significance for British culture and literature: one looks at the growing importance of trade and travel, both economically and in terms of the development of literary genres; a final chapter examines Britain's changing understanding of its involvement in slavery and colonialism during this time. Although these topics are separated into ten chapters, I do not want to give readers the impression that these themes are truly discrete. The massive changes that characterized the eighteenth century were interdependent. Thus, the transformation of London into a world city could not have happened without the influx of wealth from both England's far-flung trading empire and its sugar-producing colonies; nor could London have grown to the degree it did without the mass migration of people from the country to the city occasioned by the agricultural revolution and the enclosure movement. The idea of a public sphere is perhaps impossible without new ideas about individuality and identity.

To describe a book as a cultural history of English literature implies, none too subtly, that literature and the culture in which it is written interact on some fundamental level. Nevertheless, it is hard to explain exactly how that interaction works. We know that literature never simply reflects the world around it; and yet we also know that literature is never completely unmarked by the context in which it is written. This book aims to give readers a broader sense of that context – to alert them to some of the social, economic, and cultural trends to which important works of eighteenth-century literature may have been responding: to urge them, to put it very simply, to see that literature as a window onto another time, one that allows us to see the vibrancy and tumult of the era not as something suspended in a kind of historical amber, but as something that can still touch us today. And yet, we need to acknowledge the implications of that metaphor: a window is always a precisely framed view of things, glimpsed through a particular texture of glass. Eighteenth-century literature is no camera's eye on the world around it. Each work shapes what we see; together they give us a plethora of distinctive, idiosyncratic, "interested" (to use the eighteenth-century terminology) accounts of what was happening around them. Indeed, many scholars have argued that literature shaped the culture around it as much as the culture shaped it. To mention just two such arguments discussed in the following chapters: "prospect poetry" may have taught its readers how to view landscapes as private property; and the domestic novel may have inculcated in its readers an idea of the proper relationship between the private and public spheres. Finally, we also need to remember that most eighteenth-century literature did not see itself as divorced from the project of cultural formation. It was far more comfortable than twentieth-century literature with its own didactic force – as we can see in works ranging from Pope's satires to Richardson's novels. Most writers did not view themselves as standing outside society, pursuing their own creative impulses, but as active, necessary spokespeople for their beliefs, there to encourage virtue and crack the whip on vice, or even to take a public stand on political issues, such as the slave trade. That sense of the intense social involvement of eighteenth-century literature is one of the most important things I hope readers will take away from this book.

Of course, literature responds not only to the world around it, but also to its precursors. Eighteenth-century mock epic, for example, engages not only with the foibles and vices of eighteenth-century England, but with the complex legacy of the epic itself. As this book is primarily focused on eighteenth-century literature's relationship with its historical milieu, I have rarely had space to deal with the question of generic history, of the genealogy of form. Nevertheless, I would urge readers to be aware of eighteenth-century literature's consciousness of its place in that history, to note that some of its meaning, some of its resonance, derives from the transhistorical framework of genre.

The field of eighteenth-century studies has changed dramatically over the past twenty years as scholars have challenged the stability and certainties of the "Age of Reason." Always interdisciplinary, the field has become both more inclusive – of writing by women, the colonized, and the laboring classes – and more self-conscious of its own assumptions and methodologies. Even in the (admittedly lengthy amount of) time I have spent writing this book, avenues of inquiry have evolved. Readers have begun to look outside the traditional canon to less well-known writers. Perhaps most urgently, as I complete this book, readers have begun to explore the global, and more specifically, the transatlantic nature of eighteenth-century culture and literature.

This book aims to introduce readers to broad, ongoing literary and historical debates, and to the difficulties of understanding the relationship between literature and history. I hope that each chapter will give the reader a sense of what issues are at stake in the literary texts and suggest questions that productively might be asked about them. I hope it will foster discussion and analysis, rather than pat understanding or facile explanations. Ideally, this book is not a package of information to be absorbed but rather an introduction that will show readers that eighteenth-century literature is a vibrant and complex field of research – one with which they can all engage critically.

National Identity and
a National Literature

Introduction

[S]hould it ever be the case of the English, in the progress of their refinements to arrive at the same polish that distinguishes the French, if we did not lose the *politesse de coeur*, which inclines men more to humane actions than courteous ones – we should at least lose that distinct variety and originality of character which distinguishes them, not only from each other, but from all the world besides...The English, like ancient medals, kept more apart, and passing but few people's hands, preserve the first sharpnesses that the fine hand of nature has given them – they are not so pleasant to feel – but in return, the legend is so visible, that at first look you see whose image and superscription they bear.

Laurence Sterne, 1768[1]

Just who were the British? Did they even exist?[2]

Speaking to a French acquaintance, Yorick, the protagonist of Sterne's *A Sentimental Journey*, encapsulates some of the characteristics of English national identity during the eighteenth century. The English are unpolished but humane, sincere, and straightforward, if not always polite. Some of their qualities are paradoxical; the English are all original and various, distinguished not just from other nations, but from each other. Their very lack of a uniform character constitutes their collective identity.[3] How difficult then to summarize a national identity that includes not just the English, but also the inhabitants of an ever-expanding Britain. (Indeed, Sterne himself was Irish, although Yorick is English.) If we look across the wide spectrum of the British population, can we find a uniform national identity? Or, conversely, can we say that there were no self-identified characteristics that unified the inhabitants of Great Britain and its settler colonies? These were questions that animated British writers during the eighteenth century, when the manifestations of national identity were a favorite subject of literature and the other arts.

National identity is a relatively new invention, a concept that may not have existed at all in Britain before the eighteenth century, or even during it. As Benedict Anderson has shown, national identity is an abstract idea. Men and women from diverse social backgrounds, who live in very different physical conditions, and who may even speak different languages, see themselves as belonging to an aggregate of others, most of whom they have never met. There is no necessary physical or linguistic marker of national identity; it is an identification based on internal self-conviction. Of course, national characteristics were assigned to the British by outside observers. But, to the British themselves, the definitions that mattered were self-conceived. In order to have national identity, they needed to image themselves as belonging to a nation, a culturally unified territory of long standing, rather than viewing themselves as simply the subject of monarchy or government.

Nationalism is often distinguished from patriotism, although the two are closely connected. Gerald Newman, for example, defines patriotism as "a mere primitive feeling of loyalty": "in some way connected with military matters, the patriotic sentiment should be regarded as primarily an attachment to the country's prestige in a context of foreign relations; to its arms, flags and power in the international sphere." Patriotism thus involves a fervent, often aggressive belief in the superiority of one's country to all others. Nationalism, as Newman writes, must function "in peace as well as war."[4] The emotions of national identity are often organized around symbols – a flag, a song, or a particular national hero – although the meanings of those symbols may differ over time, or from person to person. The fact that both the British national anthem "God Save the King [or Queen]" and the great nationalist hymn "Rule Britannia" were composed during the eighteenth century is an index of how important the codification of national identity was during the period.

National identity presumes not simply the achievements of the nation in the present, but the persistence of the nation through time. National identity is thus always concerned with history. Yet, that history is perpetually under construction, both by the recovery of appropriate ancestors and exemplary moments for the nation, and by the forgetting of divisive or embarrassing people and events. As Ernest Renan argues, the nation exists by "the possession in common of a rich legacy of memories," while at the same time, "forgetting, ... even ... historical error, is a crucial factor in the creation of a nation."[5] As Homi Bhabha points out about this formulation, "being obliged to forget becomes the basis of remembering the nation, peopling it anew, imagining the possibility of contending and liberating forms of cultural identification."[6] Literature, as it offers compelling and coherent narratives of national endeavor, has a vital role in this continual, imaginative reconstruction of the nation's past and present.

During the eighteenth century, however, many obstacles stood in the way of Britons imagining themselves to be a coherent nation. For one thing, the countries that made up Great Britain had either only recently been joined together politically or were in the slow process of political assimilation during the eighteenth century. England was formally joined to Wales in 1536, but union with Scotland took place only in 1707, and Scotland retained its own legal system and parliament throughout the period. Ireland's status was even more volatile and difficult to understand. A virtual colony through most of the century, only the Anglo-Irish had any political representation in the British parliament (most inhabitants of Ireland could not vote because they were Catholic). Ireland was granted its own parliament in 1785 ("Grattan's Parliament"), but this was dissolved at the Union of Ireland with the rest of Britain in 1801. During the period, many of the inhabitants of these regions still spoke their own languages: Welsh, Gaelic, or Scots Gaelic (Erse). Within England itself, other divides presented themselves, such as those between country and city, or between north and south. When Defoe wrote *The True-Born Englishman*, he emphasized these internal differences, as manifestations of Britain's history of conquest by foreign powers.

> In eager rapes, and furious lust begot,
> Betwixt a painted Briton and a Scot:
> Whose gend'ring offspring quickly learnt to bow,
> And yoke their heifers to the Roman plough:
> From whence a mongrel half-bred race there came,
> With neither name nor nation, speech nor fame
> In whose hot veins now mixtures quickly ran,
> Infus'd betwixt a Saxon and a Dane.
> While their rank daughters, to their parents just,
> Receiv'd all nations with promiscuous lust.
> This nauseous brood directly did contain
> The well-extracted blood of Englishmen... (ll. 281–92)

Culturally heterogeneous, the inhabitants of Great Britain had fewer reasons than one might expect to imagine themselves as part of the same nation.

In the face of all these divisions, however, members of these disparate groups still often thought of themselves as a unified whole, and viewed their country with pride and self-satisfaction. They celebrated their accomplishments, both man-made and geographical. Oliver Goldsmith declared, for example, in "The Comparative View of Races and Nations" (1760): "Hail Britain, happiest of countries! Happy in thy climate, fertility, situation and commerce; but still happier in the peculiar nature of thy laws and government."[7] Religion also played a significant role in British national identity, particularly after the Act of Settlement of 1701. This act excluded the heirs of the last Catholic king, James II, and stipulated that all future monarchs would be members of the Church of England. Thus Protestantism, particularly Anglicanism, became part of British national identity, both legally and culturally. Catholics and members of other religions, including Jews and dissenters from the Church of England, were denied most of the rights of other citizens throughout the period.[8] Both anti-Catholicism and anti-Semitism played a significant role in defining Britishness.

National identity also manifested itself in a variety of physical practices, including food consumption. A character in Frances Burney's novel *The Wanderer* (1814), for instance, describes what he believes to be a gracious invitation to some new French acquaintances thus:

> You won't think me wanting to my country, if for the honour of old England, I give these poor half-starved souls a hearty meal of good roast beef, with a bumper of Dorchester ale and Devonshire cyder? Things which I conclude they have never yet tasted from their birth to this hour; their own washy diet of soup meager and salad, with which I would not fatten a sparrow, being what they are more naturally born to.[9]

The idea of roast beef as the national food had already been enshrined by Hogarth's engraving, "The Roast Beef of Old England." As both these examples make clear, national characteristics stood in the sharpest relief when juxtaposed to the shortcomings of other nations, especially France. In her influential study of national identity, *Britons: Forging the Nation, 1707–1837*, Linda Colley argues strongly that the British "came to define themselves as a single people not because of any political or cultural consensus at home, but rather in reaction to the Other beyond their shores."[10] The many wars between France and England during the century helped cement a sense of national unity.

And yet we should not assume that there was a single formation of national identity to which all Britons subscribed during the period. Indeed, the period was marked by conflict between different ideas of where national identity came from, and who deserved to belong to the nation. These conflicts played out around religion, as both the press and the government debated whether to extend the rights of British citizens to Catholics, Jews, and dissenters. Conflict also arose around the question of colonial expansion and the rights of the inhabitants of the British colonies. For most of the century, the growth of the British Empire was a source of national pride. At the end of the century, however, both the American War of Independence and the debates over slavery challenged belief in national coherence. As Kathleen Wilson argues:

> Within Britain itself, from the perspective of the metropole, the Welsh, and, more gradually, the Scots become naturalized as British, the Irish, Jews and Africans perhaps never do; beyond the British isles, the claims of people of different races and cultures to British rights and liberties were even more remote and contingent, and Britishness was conferred or denied not only in relation to the numbers of white British settlers in residence, but also to the degree of acceptance by colonial peoples of English hegemony and the legitimacy of British rule.[11]

Often, then, national identity can be viewed as more of a desire to belong to a national whole, a willful dismissing of the material, economic, and cultural divisions that separate the inhabitants of a nation, than as a natural, or organic formation.

This section is a survey of some of the literary projects that helped build national identity by offering visions of Britain that attempted to smooth over these divisions, or subsume them into representations of the nation with which Britons could identify with pride. Towards this end, literature worked to find a "common" language that all literate inhabitants might share.[12] The section also traces the changes in the sources writers sought for that identity – from classical analogies to indigenous roots. While writers of the neoclassical, or Augustan, era of the early eighteenth century looked for a definition of English greatness in comparison to the glories of the Roman Empire, later writers searched for a national identity that would be geographically rooted in British soil.

> In this transposition of terms, an important event in literary culture occurred. Critics established English antiquity as the moment of literary achievement against which all subsequent writing would be measured. A national canon formed on the precedent example of the classical canon took shape. This canon was necessarily old and carried with it much of the aura of antiquity: difficulty, rarity, sublimity, masculinity.[13]

Thus, as the century ended, the project of formulating a national canon gave rise to a number of collections and evaluations of English writers of the preceding hundred years, including Samuel Johnson's *Lives of the*

English Poets (1781) and Anna Barbauld's fifty-volume set of *The British Novelists* (1810).

The works discussed in this segment emphasize that even as British culture, and its literary forms, experienced extensive change and innovation during the period, the search for national identity in eighteenth-century Britain was concerned centrally with the uses of history. From Dryden to the author of the Ossian poems, writers give a variety of answers to the question of which past Britain would choose, and what use would be made of that past. Finally, we might speculate that, as more traditional forms of community dissolved during the period, the nation offered an alternative and satisfying way of formulating individual identity in relation to a group. As Antony Easthope writes, "As the particular mode of collective identity made available by modernity, national identity is caught up in the new forms of subjectivity; it is desired with special intensity; and that desire overlooks the fact that it is *more* manifestly an effect of construction."[14] The fervency with which the authors in this section devote themselves to uncovering both the roots and flowers of Britishness might thus be ascribed to the energy needed to construct a national identity for the first time.

Augustanism: Translating the Ancients: Dryden, Pope, Bentley

Oh Happy Age! Oh times like these alone
By Fate reserv'd for Great *Augustus* Throne!
When the joint growth of Armes and Arts forshew
The World a Monarch, and that Monarch *You.*

John Dryden, Astraea Redux (1660) (ll. 320–3)

The period spanning the late seventeenth and early eighteenth century is often referred to as the Augustan Age. While this designation is primarily a retrospective construction of later critics, writers and politicians of the time did often allude to the association between England in their own time and the glory of the Roman Empire under the rule of Augustus Caesar. As Dryden's lines demonstrate, there were both political and cultural elements to this comparison. Like Rome under Augustus, England saw itself as re-establishing political stability under Charles II in 1660. Indeed, the restored monarch's entrance into London in 1661 was celebrated with the erection of a number of triumphal arches in the Roman fashion, to underline the comparison.[15] Furthermore, like the Roman Empire, English imperial and mercantile sway was expanding during this period, an achievement fortuitously joined to political stability at home. For writers, this comparison between England and Rome became part of the definition of their cultural role. Like Horace and Virgil, authors thought it appropriate to involve themselves in England's political destiny, either celebrating imperial expansion and domestic peace, or satirizing social ills. In fulfilling this function, English poets began at times to imagine themselves as equal to the great Latin writers. In poetic practice, the lyric forms and ornamental language popular among the Cavalier poets of the Interregnum were discarded in favor of (mock) epics, odes, and longer discursive compositions. The balanced regularity of the heroic couplet came to be seen as the most dignified meter of which English verse was capable. Of course, the comparison between Britain and Augustan Rome had a dark underside. It was hard to avoid acknowledging that, just as the Roman Empire had risen, so had it fallen, destroyed by corruption within and powerful enemies without. Furthermore, even though poets like Horace and Virgil had flourished under Augustus, others, like Ovid, had faced punishment for their conflicts with the Emperor. The exact nature of Augustan political stability, the question of whether it had merely been the successful suppression of dissent, and its necessary correlation to artistic achievement were often interrogated during the period. Thus, the relationship of many "Augustan" poets to their classical antecedents was more complicated than simple identification. This is perhaps most obvious in the "mock epics" of the period but is apparent in many translations and imitations as well.

One manifestation of the ongoing comparisons between the British and Roman Empires was a drive to bring classical texts into contemporary literary discourse. Although major translations of Homer and others into English had been completed during the Renaissance, the art of translation flourished throughout the later seventeenth and eighteenth centuries. Particularly during the Restoration, poets tried to forge a connection of literary greatness between themselves and the writers of antiquity. Thus, late seventeenth-century ideas about translation tended to presume an identity between the contemporary writer and the ancient one. In *An Essay on Translated Verse* (1684), for example, the Earl of Roscommon advises translators to pick texts on the basis of psychological similarity:

> Examine how your *Humour* is inclin'd.
> And which the *Ruling Passion* of your Mind;
> Then, seek a *Poet* who *your* way do's bend,
> And chuse an *Author* as you chuse a *Friend.*
> United by this *Sympathetick Bond,*

You grow *Familiar, Intimate* and *Fond*;
Your *Thoughts*, your *Words*, your *Stiles*, your *Souls* agree,
No Longer his *Interpreter*, but *He*. (ll. 94–101)

And John Dryden, in his preface to *Sylvae*, describes the relationship between his translation of Virgil and the original in this way: "my own is of a piece with his, and that if he were living, and an Englishman, they are such, as he woul'd probably have written" (III, 4). At the same time, however, as translation elevates the translator to the level of his or her illustrious ancestor, it also subordinates the lyric imagination of the translator to that of the poet translated as he recapitulates his ancestor's content and form: a complex and unstable relationship.

As well as being a prolific and celebrated poet and dramatist, John Dryden was perhaps the best and certainly the most prolific translator of the late seventeenth and early eighteenth centuries. This, combined with other aspects of his poetry, has led the poet to be closely associated with the idea of an Augustan Age. As Samuel Johnson wrote in his *Life of Dryden*:

> Perhaps no nation ever produced a writer that enriched his language with such a variety of models. To him we owe the improvement, perhaps the completion of our metre, the refinement of our language, and much of the correctness of our sentiments...What was said of Rome adorned by Augustus may be applied by an easy metaphor to English poetry embellished by Dryden...he found it brick, and he left it marble.[16]

After he lost his poet laureateship in 1688, Dryden turned increasingly to translation as a way of supporting himself. He codified his thoughts about translation in his preface to *Ovid's Epistles* (1680). There are three kinds of translation, he argues: metaphrase, an exact, word-for-word rendering of the original; paraphrase, translation with latitude, in order to make the original elegant in English; and imitation, in which "the translator assumes the liberty not only to vary from the words and sense, but to forsake them both as he sees occasion," in other words, "to run division on the groundwork" – to improvise as one would in musical performance. The translator is in the difficult position of determining the best approach to his source material. Ovid, for example, "sometimes cloys his Readers instead of satisfying them: and gives occasion to his Translators, who dare not cover him, to blush at the nakedness of their Father" (I, 112). Dryden here alludes to the story of Noah and his sons (Genesis 9: 18–29), and sets up a filial relationship between ancient and modern.[17] The translator may not always be comfortable with the material he translates, even as he bows to the genius of ancient writers.

Dryden most admired the middle ground, "paraphrase," and suggested that the imitator will lose the name of the translator altogether. Nevertheless, imitation was an important genre during the period. Poets not only translated the language of the originals, but also transposed their setting from the classical world to the contemporary. These imitations set up an uneasy relationship between antiquity and modernity. They offer both comparison and critique, as does the mock epic. Paul Hammond writes:

> Translation demanded of its practitioners and readers a comparative movement between past and present which enabled a sharper understanding of their difference. Through poetry's recurring marks of separation from its supposed origins – its many signs that the translation was not the original, that England is not Rome, and Pope's Homer is not Homer's Homer – the culture of the present is made legible.[18]

One light-hearted example of imitation is Swift's "imitation" of one of the stories from Ovid's *Metamorphoses*, "Baucis and Philamon," in which the elderly couple are imaged as a pair of English rustics.

Translations also helped bring what had been a canon of literature reserved for the elite to a broader reading public. Once exclusively the domain of the aristocratic or wealthy men to whom a classical education was available, much of the literature of antiquity could now be read by all the merchants, women, and others who could read only English. Although Pope later wrote many imitations of classical texts, such as his Horatian epistles, he first staked his poetic reputation on his translation of the *Iliad*, and there is much in that translation for women and other eighteenth-century readers to appreciate. As Claudia Thomas points out, "Pope made his Iliad appealing to contemporaries by adjusting certain scenes and characters to resemble the patterns of refinement suggested by genteel culture, such as plays and periodical essays."[19] Reworking Greek hexameter into elegant, dignified heroic couplets, Pope presented Homer as a moral writer, even a sentimental one, who emphasized the emotional impact of the Trojan War, exemplifying human nature in a transhistorical way. This appeal to a more heterogeneous audience was not always celebrated. Samuel Johnson, for example, criticized Pope's translation of *The Iliad* for targeting female readers too explicitly. "It has . . . been objected with sufficient reason, that there is in the commentary too much of unseasonable levity, and affected gaiety," Johnson writes in his *Life of Pope*, "that too many appeals are made to the ladies, and the ease which is so carefully preserved is sometimes the ease of the trifler."[20] Yet, this very ease made Pope's *Iliad* extremely popular in its day.

The translation's appeal to a broad audience, however, was linked in the minds of Pope's critics to his lack of traditional scholarly credentials. In "Remarks upon Mr Pope's Translation of Homer" (1717), his old enemy, John Dennis, sneers that Pope had "undertaken to translate *Homer* from *Greek*, of which he does not know one word, into *English*, which he understands almost as little."[21] A contrasting approach to the texts of classical antiquity, typified by Richard Bentley and his followers, emphasized the recovery of knowledge of the details of the ancient world. This endeavor, known as grammatical criticism at the time, but similar to what we would call philology, worked against the Augustan desire to identify with and imitate the past poets. For Bentley, Pope's *Iliad* was "a pretty poem, but it is not Homer" (Samuel Johnson, *Life of Pope*). As Joseph Levine has demonstrated:

> [T]he very advances in philological and archeological learning, the real addition to the understanding of the classical authors that resulted, began to threaten the confidence in imitation and in the ancient wisdom on which the whole [Augustan] revival [of classical texts] was based. To know Homer or Pythagoras too well was to open a gulf that divided them from modern life, rather than identifying them with it. It was in the end to make them useless in any immediate practical fashion. Of what value was the teaching of a poet who sang his songs aloud to a group of tribal warriors whose manners and customs seemed closer to the American Indian than the eighteenth-century gentleman?[22]

In this ongoing cultural debate over the practical uses of classical texts for the present, Pope was associated with those who celebrated the inimitable triumphs of the "ancients," a group which also included most of the other wits and satirists of the day, while Bentley sided with those who believed that the "moderns" might learn from the achievements of antiquity, and someday better them.

Translations of classical texts, then, were an important aspect of the Augustan Age because they allowed a vantage point for comparisons between the British Empire and its Roman predecessor. By exploring this relationship between the present and the illustrious past of another empire, writers were able to offer a vision of national identity based on political and literary achievements. The comparison between Britain and Rome, however, as even these few examples evidence, was complex and unstable. Writers of the early eighteenth century debated the correlation between political stability and artistic achievement, and the degree to which political stability under the last Stuart monarchs, William and Mary, and Anne, was enlightened rule rather than quiet repression. They also practiced their own claims as British writers against the accomplishments of antiquity.

Patriotism: Alexander Pope, *Windsor-Forest*

Patriotism is usually defined as the love of one's country, and is associated with seeing one's country as superior to all others. Artistic production was one important expression of patriotism during the eighteenth century, and the production of patriotic texts was a significant function of poets and artists during the Augustan era. Such panegyrical art was often written on the occasion of some national triumph, as an offering to, or commissioned by, the monarch or an important statesman. George Frederick Handel's oratorio, *Judas Maccabaeus*, written in celebration of the Duke of Cumberland's victory over the Jacobites at Culloden, is one example, as is his *Music for the Royal Fireworks*, which George II commissioned for the commemoration of the Peace of Aix-la-Chapelle in 1749. Benjamin West's 1771 painting of the death of General Wolfe at the battle of Quebec is another instance of this kind of commemorative work.

Alexander Pope's poem *Windsor-Forest* also falls into this category of patriotic literature. Like his *Iliad* translation, this poem was composed early in Pope's career while he was still trying to establish a reputation as cultural spokesman. It was written on the occasion of the Peace of Utrecht, which ended the War of Spanish Succession in 1713, and is dedicated to George Granville, Lord Lansdowne, Secretary for War under Queen Anne. The Treaty of Utrecht stabilized the balance of power in Europe and brought England new colonial holdings in Canada and Africa. England also took possession of the Assiento grant, a monopoly contract to supply 4,800 slaves a year to the Spanish colonies in the Americas. The treaty was an important step in the global growth of the British Empire. As Howard Weinbrot has documented, the event inspired a number of poems, including Pope's, celebrating the peace as further evidence of Augustan glory as a new version of the "Pax Romana."[23]

Pope uses Windsor Forest as an iconic national spot, capable of embodying England's political and artistic achievements, as well as its natural beauty. Its opening lines firmly link together poetry, landscape, and the state: "Thy Forests, Windsor! And thy green Retreats,/At once the Monarch's and the Muse's Seats,/Invite my Lays" (ll. 1–3). Indeed, the opening paragraphs of the poem seem to be purely loco-descriptive, as in this famous example of the rhetorical trope of *concordia discors*:

> Here Hills and Vales, the Woodland and the Plain,
> Here Earth and Water seem to strive again,
> Not *Chaos*-like together crush'd and bruis'd.
> But as the World, harmoniously confus'd:
> Where Order in Variety we see,
> And where, tho' all things differ, all agree. (ll. 11–16)

In its use of this trope, and in its setting near the Thames, *Windsor-Forest* self-consciously draws on earlier models, such as John Denham's *Cooper's Hill* (1642) (see also ll. 264–6).[24] The poem's representation of the forest's heterogeneous elements also conveys a kind of stability and peace, in which opposites are reconciled in an image of tranquility. It then quickly moves to associate these natural attributes with England's national greatness. Comparing England's flora to that of other countries, *Windsor-Forest* reveals both its international context and its argument for England's superiority:

> Let *India* boast her Plants, nor envy we
> The weeping Amber or the balmy Tree,
> While by our Oaks the precious Loads are born,
> And Realms commanded which those Trees adorn. (ll. 29–32)

The oak, thus, becomes a symbol of England's trading power. Representing British mercantile and military fleets in terms of the wood out of which the ships are constructed, Pope reminds his reader that all the world's goods are available to Britons at home. The harmony and fecundity of the landscape turn out to be not natural after all, but rather a function of the proper political order: "Peace and Plenty tell, a *Stuart* reigns" (l. 42).

The poem then traces the way English history has embedded itself in Windsor Forest by describing both actual historical events and invented mythological ones. It celebrates the gradual transition from the tyranny of the Norman Conquest to a more benevolent form of monarchy. As this transformation unfolds, good government once again is linked explicitly to natural abundance:

> The Forests wonder'd at th'unusual Grain,
> And secret Transport touch'd the conscious Swain.
> Fair Liberty, Britannia's Goddess, rears
> Her cheerful Head, and leads the Golden Years. (ll. 89–92)

The transformation of "the Land" from "A dreary Desart and a gloomy Waste" to a fecund and beautiful place closes with a triumphant comparison of Queen Anne to Diana, "Th'Immortal Huntress" (l. 44, l. 160).

This semi-historical rendering of the past is complemented by a mythological account of the origin of the river Loddon, one of the tributaries of the Thames. Pope imagines a nymph, Lodona, with whom the god Pan is infatuated. "Burning with Desire," Pan pursues the reluctant Lodona through the forest with considerable violence:

> Now fainting, sinking, pale, the Nymph appears;
> Now close behind his sounding Step she hears;
> And now his Shadow reach'd her as she run,
> (His shadow lengthen'd by the setting Sun)
> And now his shorter breath with sultry Air
> Pants on her Neck, and fans her parting Hair" (ll. 191–6).

Finally, like a character in Ovid's *Metamorphoses*, Lodona escapes rape by being transformed into the stream Lodona, which "forever murmurs, and for ever weeps" (l. 206). The immediacy and physicality of Pope's description of the nymph's flight from the god emphasizes the tranquility and beauty of her later life as a river, reflecting the beauty of the forest to "musing" Shepherds: "Thro' the fair Scene rowl slow the lingring Streams / Then foaming pour along, and rush into the *Thames*" (ll. 217–18). This mythological pastiche functions to give Windsor Forest the stature and complexity of a classical landscape (Pope alludes to the *Mosella* of Ausonius). Some critics, like Howard Weinbrot, also see Lodona's past suffering as further emphasizing England's present peace. Pan's rapacious hunting, Weinbrot argues, associates him with the earlier outrages of the Norman Conquest, and the present transgressions of the French king Louis XIV.[25] At the same time, however, this unsuccessful sexual assault strikes an odd note of violence in a poem primarily concerned with pastoral peace.

Critics have assigned various meanings to the traces of violence in *Windsor-Forest*, seen in the attempted rape of Lodona and in the poem's earlier description of the death of a pheasant during a hunt.

> Thus (if small things we may with great compare)
> When Albion sends her eager Sons to War,
> Some thoughtless Town, with Ease and Plenty blest,
> Near, and more near, the closing Lines invest;
> Sudden they seize th'amazed, defenceless Prize,
> And high in Air Britannia's Standard flies.
> See! From the Brake the whirring Pheasant springs,
> And mounts exulting on triumphant Wings;
> Short is his Joy! He feels the fiery Wound,
> Flutters in Blood, and panting beats the Ground.

Ah! What avail his glossie, varying Dyes,
His Purple Crest, and Scarlet-circled Eyes,
The vivid Green, his shining Plumes unfold;
His painted Wings, and Breast that flames with Gold? (ll. 105–18)

The closely observed beauty of the pheasant and the pathos of its death have led many readers to view this passage as one of the poem's interpretive cruxes. Some critics see in these lines evidence of Pope's knowledge of and sympathy for the natural world of Windsor Forest, and the pastoral rituals carried out within it, gathered when he lived in Binfield, Hampshire as a young man; others have read the passage as an adumbration of the way the English countryside would come to be more valued for its aesthetic beauty than for its productivity or wilderness.[26] E. P. Thompson has argued that these scenes of forest sports demonstrate Pope's sympathy with traditional uses of the land soon to be abolished by the harsh anti-poaching laws of the Walpole regime.[27] Another line of argument sees this rural bloodshed as having less specific and more allegorical resonance. Laura Brown, for instance, reads the simile comparing hunting to imperial war that precedes the description of the pheasant's death as revealing "the complicated evocation and displacement of violence typical of 'Windsor-Forest.'": "in this passage, characteristically, Pope makes the real issue – imperial war – into the vehicle and uses it as an illustration of the event at hand in the poem, the hunter netting the feeding partridges."[28] For all camps, however, the sympathy and admiration the poet lavishes on the game bird, connected through metaphor with the victims of Britain's imperial expansion, seem to disrupt the poem's celebration of the bucolic sports of rural life.

The poem closes with a prophetic address by the personified Thames, long a symbol of English patriotism and power.[29] The river welcomes a new age of peace and prosperity, in which hunting will replace foreign wars: "The shady Empire shall retain no Trace / Of War or Blood, but in the Sylvan Chace" (ll. 371–2). Significantly, however, this new era of peace will not slow the growth of England's trading empire. Instead, in a repeated substitution of trees for human beings, England's oaks will go out to collect the world's riches, while England's swains stay home.[30]

Thy Trees, fair *Windsor*! Now shall leave their Woods,
And half thy Forests rush into my Floods.
Bear *Britain's* Thunder, and her Cross display,
To the bright Regions of the rising Day [.]
[...]

For me the Balm shall bleed, and Amber flow,
The Coral redden, and the ruby glow,
The Pearly Shell its lucid Globe infold,
And *Phoebus* warm the ripening Ore to Gold. (ll. 385–8, 393–6)

Using personification and synecdoche, the poem is able to preserve a double and contradictory vision of national identity. On the one hand, England is a peaceful, primarily agricultural, place, whose identity is centered on the traditional rituals of rural life. On the other hand, however, England is a powerful nation on the global stage, characterized by the variety of foreign luxury goods its inhabitants can purchase, its identity predicated on the strength of its cosmopolitan display: "Earth's distant Ends our Glory shall behold,/and the new World launch forth to seek the Old" (ll. 401–2). Rhetorically, this paradox is made possible by the poem's figuration of Windsor's trees acting independently of human direction.

Windsor-Forest gives us a good idea of some of the elements of national identity upon which patriotism was based during the Augustan period: a belief in national prosperity closely connected with international trade; pride in the beauty and fecundity of the countryside, and the chronological depth of English history and art embedded in it; and a celebration of good monarchy and English liberty. In writing the poem, Pope took up one of the most important roles of the poet during the Augustan era: praising the achievements of the monarchy and celebrating the good elements of the world in which he lives. If Pope later turned to caustic satire of eighteenth-century culture, *Windsor-Forest* stands as one of the greatest panegyrics to it.

Historicism: Gibbon, Hume, Macaulay

In the second half of the eighteenth century, Augustanism underwent two transformations: first, it reconsidered its similarity to Augustan Rome; second, it re-evaluated the nature of the English revolution and the Restoration. The monumental achievement of the first line of inquiry was Edward Gibbon's *Decline and Fall of the Roman Empire* (1776–88), of the latter, David Hume's *History of Great Britain from the Invasion of Julius Caesar to the Revolution in 1688* (1754). Numerous other popular historical works also appeared during the century, including William Robertson's *History of Scotland* (1759). One such history with a distinctive approach was Catharine Macaulay's *History of England* (1763–83), which celebrated the republican figures of the Interregnum. These histories have an important place in an understanding of national identity because they implicitly celebrated British progress, both in knowledge and in other cultural achievements. Echoing the narrative of *Windsor-Forest*, Gibbon wrote, "we compare the boats of osier and hides that floated along our coasts with the formidable natives which visit and command remotest shores of the ocean. Without indulging the fond prejudices of patriotic vanity, we may assume a conspicuous place among the inhabitants of earth."[31] Indeed, an interest in history seemed to be one of the national characteristics of eighteenth-century Britain. Hume wrote, "I believe this is the historical Age and this the historical Nation."[32] To think about history writing's relationship to national identity, we need to consider three aspects of these texts: the subject matter of the history; the political principles expressed in conjunction with it; and the method by which both content and principles are represented.

As we have already seen, there was, throughout the period, a good deal at stake in how Britain's own past, and that of its cultural antecedents, would be represented. In response to this intense interest, the method and purposes of writing history changed significantly during the course of the century. In some ways, different strategies for writing history continued earlier battles between the "ancients" and the "moderns." Ancients advocated narrative history, modeled on the practice of classical historians like Livy and Tacitus, which would provide moral and practical lessons for the present. Moderns, in contrast, proposed "a way of penetrating into the whole life of the past and recovering things otherwise unknown, a topical and analytical alternative to narrative."[33] Like those earlier debates, as well, eighteenth-century history was concerned with the uses of documentary sources. Historical writing during the period thus explores both the didactic and the mimetic cultural functions of narratives of the past.

The topics of historical writing began to shift as well. While most earlier accounts of Britain's past had focused on the actions and characters of prominent men, eighteenth-century histories began to provide a broader, more economically varied, description of social and cultural life.

> The eighteenth century was a critical moment in the adaptation of classical understandings of literature to the needs of a modern, commercial, and increasingly middle-class society. Eighteenth-century social analysis no longer permitted a definition of history that restricted itself to the conventional narrative of politics – the story of the public actions of public men...History did not abandon its traditional concern with public life, but it significantly widened its scope as it created a new social narrative that could stand beside and even subsume the conventional account of political action. For the first time, evocation became an important goal of historical narrative, and sympathetic identification came to be seen as one of the pleasures of historical reading.[34]

As this description shows, the lines between history and literature were less sharply drawn during this period than they have subsequently become: both were considered *belles lettres*. If history offered more intellectual content, readers still could expect much the same kind of emotional pleasure from each. Furthermore, historians were expected to write with an elegance equal, if not superior, to that of fiction writers.

Eighteenth-century historians were also keenly aware that historical writing could be politically interested, could carry its own political agenda. One such interested history which served as a negative example for many later historians was Clarendon's royalist *History of the Rebellion* (1702–4). Throughout the early part of the century, unsettled public opinion about the traumatic events of the seventeenth-century – the Civil Wars, the Restoration, and the Act of Settlement of 1701 – made agreement about what constituted an objective view of the past difficult. "Early eighteenth-century . . . historians of Britain, in particular, felt that they were responding to a cultural demand for an explanatory and legitimating emplotment of British history after a period of dynastic and constitutional discontinuity."[35] Writing after the middle of the century, both Hume and Macaulay claimed to be rescuing British history from the distortions of party politics. For Hume, "two generations from the decisive events of 1688, it evidently seemed possible at last to write an impartial and reflective history of this earlier and more turbulent time."[36] He declared in the last volume of his history that "no man has yet arisen who has paid entire regard to truth, and has dared expose her, without covering or disguise to the eyes of the prejudiced public."[37] Presumably, Hume imagined himself to be that man. Macaulay also claims that her republicanism (and thus lack of party affiliation) will provide a clearer view of English history.

> Party prejudice, and the more detestable principle of private interest, have painted the memoirs of past times in so false a light, that it is with difficulty we can trace features, which, if justly described, would exalt the worthies of this country beyond the fame of any set of men, which the annals of other nations can at any one period produce. . . . I have ever looked upon a supposed knowledge of facts seen in the false mirror of misrepresentation as one of the great banes of this country. Individuals may err, but the public judgment is infallible. They only want a just information of facts to make a proper comment. Labour, to attain truth, integrity to set it in its full lights, are indispensable duties to an historian.[38]

Macaulay thus combines a call for objectivity with a nationalist claim for the greatness of British past. She characterizes the historian's task as duty to the nation. Yet, while her "labor" and "integrity" lead her to celebrate the triumphant republicans of the Civil Wars, Hume's lead him to dare a sympathetic portrayal of the death of Charles I. Impartiality was, as always, in the eye of the beholder.

Although Gibbon's subject matter had no obvious pertinence to the battles over the meaning of Britain's recent past, Roman history still seemed to many to have implications for Britain's present. Gibbon's account of the fall of Rome cast a disturbing light on the progress of the British Empire, since it pointed out that Rome had been destroyed by its own success. He wrote, "The decline of Rome was the natural and inevitable effect of immoderate greatness. Prosperity ripened the principle of decay; the causes of destruction multiplied with the extent of conquest; and as soon as time or accident had removed the artificial supports, the stupendous fabric yielded to the pressure of its own weight."[39] Since the first volume of Gibbon's *Decline and Fall of the Roman Empire* was published during same year that saw the beginning of the American War of Independence, its more pessimistic implications seemed all too clear: the fabric of the British Empire might be beginning to be stretched too tight. Yet Gibbon maintained that the British Empire would not be susceptible to the same pressures as the Roman. For one thing, he believed in the protection offered by technological progress: "Cannon and fortifications now form an impregnable barrier against the Tartar horse; and Europe is secure from any future irruption of barbarians, since before they can conquer, they must cease to be barbarians" (p. 628). For another, he hypothesized that in the face of a barbarian threat, "the remains of civilized society" might flee westward to "the American world, which is already filled with her colonies and institutions" (p. 627).

The Decline and Fall of the Roman Empire covers not only the early days of the Roman Republic and Empire, but also the history of the Eastern Empire, the Holy Roman Empire and the Crusades. Its range stretches from AD 100 to AD 1500. Gibbon claimed to have been taken with the idea of writing a history of Rome at one precise moment: "It was at Rome, on the 15th of October 1764, as I sat musing amid the ruins of the Capitol, while the barefooted friars were singing vespers in the Temple of Jupiter, that the idea of writing the decline and fall of the city first started to my mind." "Whatever idea books may have given us of the greatness of that people, their accounts of the most flourishing state of Rome fall infinitely short of the picture of its ruins." The history was tremendously popular; 3,500 copies of the book sold in just over a year.

Gibbon sharply recast the reign of Augustus as that of a "subtle tyrant," helping to undermine the correlation between Britain and Rome that had enabled the literary glories of the earlier Augustan era. Other traditional assumptions fell as well in *The Decline and Fall of the Roman Empire*. Like many historians of the time, Gibbon "approached the rise of Christianity itself from a naturalistic standpoint, adopting a detached and often ironic stance."[40] Indeed, some readers thought him too sympathetic to paganism, since he assigns Christianity a significant role in the fall of Rome. Gibbon's ironic and detached attitude towards the emergent religion is evident, for example, in his account of the glorification of chastity in the early church:

> The chaste severity of the fathers in whatever related to the commerce of the two sexes flowed from … their abhorrence of every enjoyment which might gratify the sensual and degrade the spiritual nature of man. It was their favorite opinion that if Adam had preserved his obedience to the Creator, he would have lived forever in a state of virgin purity, and that some harmless mode of vegetation might have peopled paradise with a race of innocent and immortal beings. (p. 288)

Yet Gibbon also believed that such asceticism had had important consequences for the Roman Empire, since "the Christians were not less adverse to the business than to the pleasures of this world."

> [T]hey refuse to take any active part in the civil administration or the military defence of the empire … it was impossible that the Christians, without renouncing a more sacred duty, could assume the character of soldiers, or magistrates, or of princes … This indolent or even criminal disregard of the public welfare exposed them to the contempt and reproaches of the pagans, who very frequently asked, What must be the fate of the empire, attacked on every side by barbarians, if all mankind should adopt the pusillanimous sentiments of the new sect? (pp. 290–1)

Thus, among the many reasons that Christianity helped undermine the Roman Empire was the way it encouraged its adherents to turn towards spiritual duties, and away from civic ones.

Hume's *History of England* was famous for bringing this irony and detachment to bear on England's own history. Although he had already gained fame as a philosopher, Hume reaped great profits and an expanded readership from his history. He sold the copyright to each volume, and made at least 3,200 pounds for the whole. Yet, money was not his only object in writing the history. In his essay, "Of the Study of History," for example, Hume wrote, "The advantages found in history seem to be of three kinds, as it amuses the fancy, as it improves the understanding, and as it strengthens virtue." Hume's representation of the way national identity manifested itself in and through history had several elements that would have been particularly appealing to eighteenth-century readers.

First, he stressed the importance of economic growth to political stability and happiness, and "insist[ed] that commerce, in England, at least, had caused the appearance and expansion of liberty."[41] Secondly, he celebrated the ideal of a mixed constitution, the theory that the will of the people, or parliament, would be balanced by the power of the monarchy, and vice versa. Thus, rather than lamenting the excesses of the Stuart kings, he merely opined that Charles I, for example, was born at a time when the limits of monarchical power seemed unfixed.

What is distinctive about Hume's method of presenting these ideas is his movement between representing the past as differing significantly from the present, in the belief that "it seems unreasonable to judge of the measures, embraced during one period, by the maxims, which prevail in another," and his sharply evocative scenes of individual historical characters, which seemed designed to strengthen the reader's connection to the past through powerful emotions. Hume's description of Charles I's trial and execution is one example of the way "History, the great mistress of wisdom, furnishes examples of all kinds; and every prudential, as well as moral precept, may be authorized by those events which her enlarged mirror is able to present to us":

> It is confessed, that the king's behavior during this last scene of his life does honor to his memory; and that, in all appearances before his judges, he never forgot his part, either as a prince or as a man. Firm and intrepid, he maintained in each reply, the utmost perspicuity and justness both of thought and expression; mild and equable, he rose into no passion at that unusual authority which was assumed over him. His soul, without effort or affectation, seemed only to remain in the situation familiar to it, and to look down with contempt on all the efforts of human malice and iniquity.[42]

This sympathetic description does seem to have provided a helpful example for at least one individual: France's Louis XVI is said to have prepared for his own execution by rereading Hume's account of a doomed monarch. Despite such sentimental interludes, however, Hume's *History* has been remembered primarily in the twentieth century for his thoroughgoing skepticism. In *Metahistory*, for example, Hayden White writes:

> When Hume turned from philosophy to history, because he felt that philosophy had been rendered uninteresting by the skeptical conclusions to which he had been driven, he brought to his study of history the same skeptical sensibility. He found it increasingly difficult, however, to sustain his interest in a process which displayed to him only the eternal return of the same folly in many different forms.[43]

No one could have accused Catharine Macaulay of skepticism; for this writer, the heroes and victims of English history were clear. Indeed, Natalie Zemon Davis usefully contrasts Hume's skepticism to the way Macaulay "approached history with belief, religious and especially political."[44] Macaulay's *History of England* was published between 1763 and 1783. She used a variety of manuscript sources, including memoirs and political pamphlets, as well as early histories to document her claims. Her position as a female writer of erudite histories made her unusual, and yet Macaulay commanded a good deal of respect through most of her career.[45] The first volumes of the history were extremely popular, although the latter volumes, which appeared in the more conservative 1780s, were criticized for their radical republicanism. Macaulay, for example, cast aspersion on the sacred memory of the Glorious Revolution of 1688 as missed opportunity for significant political change, claiming the old Stuart policies were simply carried forth by the new Whig parliament.[46] In a collegial spirit, Macaulay sent a copy of her history to Hume, who received it gracefully, replying, "I flatter myself that we differ less in facts, than in our interpretation and construction of them." She expressed her esteem and respect for him in her reply, but noted that his "position that all governments established by custom and authority carry with them obligations to submission and allegiance does, I'm afraid, involve all reformers in unavoidable guilt, since opposition to established error must needs be opposition to authority."[47]

Macaulay might be numbered among the last Augustans, as she drew upon classical models for her history of the English Revolution, using analogies to Republican Rome to celebrate the seemingly lost cause of English republicanism. In contrast to Hume's sympathy for figures like Charles I, Macaulay celebrated republican figures like Rachel Russell, the widow of William Russell, executed for participating in the Rye House plot. She argues that the evidence shows that

> It was the sense of religion, the duties of a mother, and promise she had made Lord Russell in the hour of parting, that she would preserve her life for the sake of his children, which alone prevented her from following the example of the Roman Arria, in the act of conjugal heroism for which this illustrious woman is so justly celebrated.[48]

As Susan Wiseman points out, however, Macaulay's strategies for illustrating the greatness of the past would soon become archaic; her "use of classical models was to be replaced by a search for the 'origins' of identity in the land, through Indo-Germanic roots, favouring the 'illusion of organic community.' Macaulay's *History*, though innovative in building a carefully researched historical method, is also situated at the end of a particular tradition of republican history."[49] As we will see, the poets discussed in the next section exemplify this new direction in the articulation of British national identity.

The magisterial histories of the eighteenth century thus present us with a variety of ideas about British national identity. Although Gibbon never addressed recent British history directly, he provided readers with both a disturbing delineation of an empire destroyed by its own success (and excess), and assurances that the progress of technology and commerce would defend Britain from such a fate. Hume also traces the path of British progress, celebrating the stability of a mixed constitution, upheld by a prosperous economy. Macaulay differs from both, arguing that an important element of British identity has been lost with the defeat of Republicanism, and an accompanying complacency towards the biased "traditions" of British politics. Yet, in their commitment to an accurate representation of the past, and their conviction that seeing the past more clearly would enable the present to understand itself, all three writers contributed to the self-image of eighteenth-century Britons.

Recovering Celtic and Anglo-Saxon Britain: Chatterton, Percy, Burns, Gray, and Macpherson

By mid-century, English literary culture had shifted its energies from a drive to find the origins, or models, for British literature in Greek and Roman literature to an attempt to locate them in earlier English writers, and to then find an origin for British national identity in Britain itself. Like the Augustan revival, the literature generated by this shift, broadly construed, found a source for national identity in the past, albeit a very different past than classical antiquity. This past was primitive, tribal, full of powerful emotions and archaic bonds of loyalty and hierarchy. Yet, like the debate over how best to appreciate classical texts, this literature encompassed two different ways of exhuming British history: imagining a continuity between personages of the primitive past and eighteenth-century society, arguing that the past had moral lessons to teach us; and a kind of philological interest in the difference and obscurity of that past.

Furthermore, such literature looked beyond the metropolitan culture that had occupied center stage during the Augustan era to the seemingly still wild peripheral spaces of Britain – Scotland, Wales, and Ireland – as places where an authentic, original culture might still persist. This literary movement manifested itself in the collection of artistic productions of earlier, preliterate cultures, as in the ballad collections put together by Thomas Percy and later by Robert Burns, and in the work of individual poets, such as Gray, Macpherson, and Chatterton, who experimented with reproducing the voices of those earlier times. This interest in England's primitive past is often associated with the Gothic revival, which generated an interest in the medieval period, but writers like Gray and Macpherson looked farther back, to a pre-Christian era. In reviving ancient British culture, the poet took on a new voice, unlike that of the cultured advocate of civil culture of the Augustan era. He – for this was almost exclusively a masculine position – became a bard. In this role, the poet became a conduit for the primitive, but authentic, sentiments of ancient days.

These sentiments were expressed in a very different kind of language than that privileged by the Augustan poets. This new form of poetic language was often rough, obscure, and repetitive; it celebrated the emotional impact of sound over the economical and elegant constructions of grammar. Whereas Pope's *Essay on Criticism* urged readers to "Praise the easy vigour of a line / Where Denham's strength and Waller's sweetness join" (ll. 360–1), Thomas Percy explained the value of the poetic artifacts he recovered in *Reliques of Ancient English Poetry* (1765) thus: "The old minstrel-ballads are in the northern dialect, abound with antique words and phrases, are extremely incorrect, and run with the utmost license of metre; they also have a romantic wildness, and are in the true spirit of chivalry."[50] Although they each went about it differently, these poets all worked to defamiliarize the common language of late eighteenth-century Britain in order to increase the emotional and cultural impact of their poetry. "Nobody understands me & I am perfectly satisfied," Thomas Gray wrote to William Mason in 1757 with regard to his poems "The Bard" and "The Progress of Poesy." Poets who wrote in this style might be said to be evoking in print culture the forms and power of an oral culture that had already disappeared.

When Thomas Gray published *Odes by Mr Gray* in 1757, he was already famous as the author of the tremendously popular *Elegy Written in a Country Churchyard* (1751). The long poems in this volume, however, *The Progress of Poesy* and *The Bard*, represent a departure from the everyday world and sententious virtue of his more famous poem. Rather than the regular, "elegiac" stanzas of the earlier piece, these poems use the irregular, rapid, and allusive form of the Pindaric ode. *The Bard*, in particular, employs a repetitive, almost ecstatic style as it imagines the prophecy made by the last bard of Wales about England's future to the invader, Edward I, before he leaps to his death over the side of a cliff. The bard speaks in the collective voice of all the other lost bards: "Avengers of their native land/With me in dreadful harmony they join/and weave with bloody hands the tissue of thy line" (ll. 46–8).

> "Edward, lo! To sudden fate
> (Weave we the woof. The thread is spun)
> Half of thy heart we consecrate.
> (The web is wove. The work is done.)"
> Stay, oh stay! Nor thus forlorn
> Leave me unbless'd, unpitied here to mourn!
> In yon bright track, that fires the western skies!
> They [the other bards] melt, they vanish from my eyes.
> But oh! What solemn scenes on Snowdon's height
> Descending slow their glitt'ring skirts unroll?
> Visions of glory, spare my aching sight,
> Ye unborn Ages, crowd not on my soul!
> No more our long-lost Arthur we bewail.
> All hail, ye genuine kings, Britannia's issue, hail! (ll. 97–110)

In its incantatory force, the scene forges a historical continuity between ancient Britain and eighteenth-century Britain. Like *Windsor-Forest*, it prophesies the troubles of the past being replaced by the triumphs of the present. In this case, however, the imagined past is not a classical pastiche, but rather the lost grandeur of an oral, tribal culture on British soil.

Despite the power of the scene, however, many readers were not immediately pleased with Gray's *Odes*. Such "puerilities of obsolete mythology" seemed to signal a departure from the accepted morally and socially instructive function of poetry, as Johnson states in his *Life of Gray*: "We are affected only as we believe; we are improved only as we find something to be imitated or declined. I do not see that 'The Bard' promotes any truth, moral or political" (p. 641).[51] Johnson further objects to the language of these poems:

> These odes are marked by glittering accumulations of ungraceful ornaments; they strike, rather than please; the images are magnified by affectation; the language is labored into harshness. The mind of the writer seems to work with unnatural violence....He has a kind of strutting dignity, and is tall by walking on tiptoe. His art and his struggle are too visible, and there is too little appearance of ease and nature. (p. 642)

Gray's odes, then, mark a move away from the neoclassical ideals of language and typical poetic persona of the Augustan era: poem and poet are both characterized by "ease and nature." In place of these ideals, they offer poetry willing to use harsh language in its pursuit of authenticity and emotional impact. In the figure of the bard, they substitute a homegrown British literary presence for the Greek and Roman sages.

When James Macpherson published *Fragments of Ancient Poetry, Collected in the Highlands of Scotland, and Translated from the Gaelic or Erse Language* in 1759, and its companion pieces *Fingal* (1762) and *Temora* (1763), he went one better than Gray. Rather than merely imagining the words of an ancient British bard, Macpherson claimed to have discovered such a bard – the Scottish Ossian – and to be presenting his translated works. These works caused an immediate literary sensation, and were some of the most internationally popular texts of the later eighteenth century. Both Gray and Blake were enthusiastic about them, as was Goethe in Germany; Napoleon is said to have carried a copy of the poems into exile on St Helena with him. Yet, from the first, the Ossian poems also aroused suspicion as to their authenticity. Macpherson was accused of completely fabricating Ossian and his poetry. When Samuel Johnson was asked whether any modern man could have written the poems, he replied "yes, Sir, many men, many women, and many children." The legitimacy of the poems was not decided until 1805, after Macpherson's death, when a special investigative committee of the Highlands Society decided that, although he had used some Gaelic originals, he had liberally edited them and inserted poetry of his own composition.[52]

Part of both the suspicion of, and the attraction to, the Ossian poems derived from their claim to be written records of a lost oral culture – that of ancient Scotland. As if to emphasize the importance of the human voice, the Ossian poems, like Gray's "Bard," rely more heavily on sound images for their effect than did the more visually oriented poetry of the Augustan era. The blind bard Ossian, for example, asks:

> Who comes with songs from the mountain, like the bow of the showery Lena? It is the maid of the voice of love. The white-armed daughter of Toscar. Often hast thou heard my song, and given the tear of beauty. Dost thou come to the wars of thy people, to hear the actions of Oscar? When shall I cease to mourn by the streams of echoing Cona? My years have passed away in battle, and my age is darkened with sorrow.[53]

Katie Trumpener argues that "the rustling, sighing, burbling and echoing of wind, grass, and water punctuate many Ossianic poems, serving the blind bard as a natural mnemonic to remember the voices of the dead." This use of sound imagery reveals that the poems' "true subject is not epic heroism but the vicissitudes of oral tradition: acts of heroism are overshadowed by the act of narration, anticipated, recounted, celebrated, commemorated, and mourned, at Fingal's court, through rituals of bardic song."[54]

The Ossian poems' elegiac account of a glorious, lost Scottish past appeared just as anti-Scottish sentiment was peaking against Lord Bute in London, and gave Highlanders and Lowland Scots alike a reason to celebrate their heritage. Of course, enthusiasm for the poetry of Gray and Macpherson was not limited to the Scots and Welsh. Throughout Britain, interest in authentic, if now peripheral, indigenous British cultures was intense, if marked by nostalgia. In all the rural parts of the kingdom, these older societies, along with their languages, seemed to be disappearing under the onslaught of modernity. Yet this nostalgia was paradoxical; in many cases, those cultures had been destroyed by the very groups that now sought to commemorate and celebrate them. In the Scottish Highlands, for instance, many traditional social and cultural practices had been suppressed by the draconian laws enforced by the English government after the Jacobite defeat at Culloden in 1745. In the face of economic and social misfortune, enormous numbers of Highlanders emigrated in the second half of the eighteenth century, leaving the landscape imagined by the Ossian poems physically vacant. It was as if the culture of the Scottish Highlands could become an object of literary interest only after it had ceased to be a military threat. Yet even though they celebrate a lost, unique, Celtic culture, some critics have argued that these poems served to obscure and unify the differences between the various parts of Britain, and those between the present and the past. Leith Davis, for instance, argues that "what is most striking about Macpherson's 'forgeries' is that they present the people of the British Isles as homogeneous... The Ossianic poems portray a Britain that both the English and Scots can identify with... The poems of Ossian gloss over the distinction between the Scots, both Highlanders and Lowlanders, and the English."[55] Adam Potkay has demonstrated that the poems perform the same unifying function with regard to time; as Ossian's heroes act with the manners of eighteenth-century gentlemen, they "reconcile the age's nostalgia for the ancient polis with a modern taste for civility."[56] Thus, Macpherson's poetry both emphasized Celtic difference, and subsumed it into a native and continuous British identity.

Even if he invented more than he discovered, Macpherson sought to recover and revivify an ancient culture he perceived as vital to British national identity – that of Gaelic Scotland. Other writers, like Thomas

Chatterton, carried out similar projects in England itself. A native of Bristol, Chatterton was a precocious and ambitious poet. Like Macpherson, however, his best-known poetic production was written in the voice of an imagined persona, in this case, a medieval monk named Thomas Rowley. Chatterton created the corpus of Rowley, a fictitious Bristol monk, by making a glossary of medieval terms he had found in Chaucer and in etymological dictionaries, writing poems using these words, and then, for an added boost of authenticity, copying them onto old pieces of parchments. Building on the interest in antiquities stimulated by Percy's *Reliques*, Chatterton was able to represent some of the Rowley poems as genuine medieval discoveries.[57] Soon enough, however, he was accused of forgery. Horace Walpole, whose own faux-gothic *The Castle of Otranto* was originally presented as a medieval "discovery," led the charge against the Rowley poems:

> I think poor Chatterton was an astonishing genius – but I cannot think that Rowley foresaw metres that were invented long after he was dead, or that our language was more refined in Bristol in the reign of Henry V than it was at court under Henry VIII...there is not a symptom in the poems but the old words that savours of Rowley's age. Change the old words for modern, and the whole construction is of yesterday.[58]

Such attacks drove Chatterton to despair, and, either intentionally or accidentally, he died from an arsenic overdose in 1770 when he was only eighteen. His *Poems, Supposed to have been Written at Bristol, By Thomas Rowley, and Others, in the Fifteenth Century* were published posthumously in 1777. Chatterton's early death, seemingly precipitated by misunderstood genius, endeared him to the Romantic poets; Wordsworth calls him "the marvelous boy" in *Resolution and Independence*, and enshrines him in romantic myth by generalizing from his example; "We poets in our youth begin in gladness / But thereof come in the end despondency and madness" (ll. 41–2).

Yet Walpole put his finger on a crucial aspect of Chatterton's poetry: what difference does the substitution of old words for new make? Why could Chatterton write more freely and happily in voice of a medieval monk than in his own voice, just as Macpherson also seemed to write more freely in the voice of Ossian? A retreat from the common language of the present, the desire to make words, and not just the sentiments they expressed, seem new to the reader, apparently drove the poetic practice of both writers. Furthermore, in the works of both Macpherson and Chatterton, the authority of the poet and the authority of the "modern" archivist are combined, as they annotated the obscure vocabulary of their poems themselves.

At stake in all this work by Gray, Macpherson, and Chatterton is how the British past, and thus the nature of an indigenous British identity, could be documented and recognized as "true." One can think of all these poets as practicing the kind of translation of earlier works Dryden called paraphrase. Rather than working with the texts of Greek and Roman antiquity, however, these poets claimed to have produced new, printed versions of the oral compositions of the British past. Yet these are translations for which no original document existed – they were formulated within the author's imagination. For this reason, some of the authors in this section were accused of being fakes, while others were celebrated for their ability to tap into the affective life of the British past. This poetry explores the nature of literary authenticity, leading us to ask what makes something an original work of art, and what makes it a forgery. Reactions to all three poets reveal the importance that printed artifacts had assumed as legitimate evidence by the later eighteenth century. Macpherson was condemned not for reconfiguring ancient Gaelic poetry, but for claiming that he had discovered written artifacts of the oral past. Chatterton, too, paid the price for fabricating printed evidence. Percy, in contrast, was careful to publicly display the written versions of his ancient ballads; the "Percy folio" of seventeenth-century manuscripts was exhibited at the British museum. These controversies illustrate the importance of print culture to British national identity during this period, as literary culture searched for art forms that predated such inventions, yet sometimes refused to believe in their legitimacy until shown written proof.

Forging a National Literary Tradition: Editing Shakespeare

Aristotle himself . . . would fall prostrate at his feet and acknowledge [Shakespeare's] supremacy. . . . When the hand of time shall have brushed off his present Editors and Commentators, and when the very name of *Voltaire*, and even the language in which he has written, shall be no more, the *Apalachian* [sic] mountains, the banks of the *Ohio*, and the plains of *Scioto* shall resound with the accents of this Barbarian: In his native tongue, he shall roll the genuine passions of nature; nor shall the griefs of *Lear* be alleviated, or the charms and wit of *Rosalind* be abated by time, there is indeed nothing perishable about him.

Maurice Morgann, *Shakespearian Criticism* [59]

If one literary figure can be said to have played the greatest role in consolidating national identity during the eighteenth century, that figure would be William Shakespeare. As Maurice Morgann declares above, Shakespeare's works capture the essence of humanity, recording "the genuine passions of nature." Yet they also represented the triumph of the English language, not only in England, but also throughout the world. Michael Hudson identifies this contradiction as a central element of Shakespeare's position as a national figure: "directly inspired by Nature to voice the universal truths of humanity ... the timeless and transcendent Bard must none the less be claimed as specifically and uniquely English."[60] This idea of Shakespeare's importance, however, took much of the century to develop. Indeed, given that the eighteenth century invented the image of Shakespeare and the practice of his plays with which we are still familiar today, the period saw a surprising variety of conceptions of Shakespeare. Even before the Interregnum, very few of Shakespeare's plays remained in the repertory, and even after the Restoration there was no edition of the plays newer than the Second Folio from 1632. By the end of the century, however, a variety of authoritative editions had appeared, women performed the female parts in the plays, and Shakespeare's characters, especially the John Bull-like Falstaff, were considered exemplars of psychological depth and complexity.[61]

During the Restoration and early eighteenth century, Shakespeare did not hold quite the place of adulation he was later accorded. Many of Shakespeare's plays were produced, but actors and writers felt they deserved the liberty of changing the plays to suit contemporary taste and ideas of theatrical decorum. Examples of such practice included Dryden's version of *The Tempest*, called *The Enchanted Island*, and Nahum Tate's *King Lear*, in which the king survives and is restored to power, while Edgar and Cordelia marry. Such authors did not think of their plays as adaptations; rather, like Augustan poets, they called their reworkings of earlier material "imitations" or "alterations."[62] This freedom with Shakespeare's plays illustrates how differently literary property was understood in the early eighteenth century than in our own time. As Laura Rosenthal explains with regard to Tate's *Lear*: "At the same time that Tate represents Shakespeare as the original owner of the story, Shakespeare does not become, as in our own age, the *perpetual* owner of the text."[63] That is, these "imitators" believed that, while Shakespeare might have provided impressive raw material, his status as creator did not preclude others refining and improving his language and his plots.

As the eighteenth century progressed, attempts were made to edit Shakespeare so as to preserve his works in a pristine condition. As these editions became more elaborate and definitive, the practice of altering the plays for the stage declined. The philosophy behind, and hence the nature of, these editions varied greatly, however. Alexander Pope published an edition in 1725 that praised Shakespeare's art while attempting to make his language and grammar conform to eighteenth-century norms. Lewis Theobald criticized Pope's scholarship in *Shakespeare Restored* (1726), an attack that earned him the role of "hero" in the first version of *The Dunciad*. The preface to this work reveals the connection between the establishment of Shakespeare as a national poet and earlier efforts to reclaim the authors of antiquity: "As SHAKESPEARE stands, or at least ought to stand, in the nature of a Classic Writer, and indeed, he is corrupt enough to pass for one of the oldest Stamp, every one, who has a Talent and Ability this Way, is at liberty to make his Comments and Emendations upon him."[64] Theobald published his own edition of Shakespeare's work in 1734, in which he removed many of the changes made to the text after Shakespeare's death and tried to correct corrupt passages. This edition was also innovative in "Theobald's refusal to judge early seventeenth-century grammar by early eighteenth-century rules"; unlike Pope's edition, it allows Shakespeare's "incorrect" usages to stand.[65]

Samuel Johnson published his own edition in 1765, which did not greatly advance textual scholarship but defended Shakespeare's dramatic practice against charges of irregularity. Johnson also appended a preface that helped define Shakespeare's genius for future generations. He not only claims that Shakespeare offers "a faithful mirror of manners and of life" but also defends the playwright's frequent excursions into the fantastic:

> Shakespeare approximates the remote and familiarizes the wonderful: the event which he represents will not happen but, if it were possible, its effects would probably be such as he has assigned; and it may be said that he has not only shown human nature as it acts in real exigencies, but as it would be found in trials to which it cannot be exposed. (*The Lives of the English Poets*, p. 303)

In other words, Shakespeare's grasp of human nature is such that he can depict "realistic" responses to impossible events. Finally, Edmond Malone published an edition in 1799. In 1778 he had made the first serious attempt to establish the chronological order of the plays. As Margreta de Grazia has demonstrated,

> Malone's [editorial] apparatus establishes Shakespeare's qualifications as proprietor of his own works; his edition variously encodes a relation of

ownership into editorial practices that insist on the exclusivity of both Shakespeare's words and their meaning.... The text needs to be interpreted by inferring what Shakespeare had in mind rather than explained and evaluated by appealing to assumed standards of intelligibility and correctness.[66]

These editions, therefore, illustrate both the way Shakespeare's status increased over the course of the century, and the development of the modern understanding of genius and authorship.

Shakespeare's emergence as a true national poet, however, occurred courtesy of the actor-manager David Garrick. A close friend of Johnson's (they arrived in London together from Lichfield in 1737), Garrick was the foremost interpreter of Shakespeare during the middle of the century, and restored Shakespeare to a central place not only in dramatic history, but also in dramatic practice. Garrick was renowned for his performance of Hamlet in particular, and the playwright and actor gradually fused in the public's mind. A poem in the *London Magazine*, for instance, imagined Shakespeare's appreciation of Garrick thus:

> Unnotic'd long thy Shakespear lay,
> To dullness and to time a prey;
> But lo! I rise, I breathe, I live
> In you, my representative![67]

In 1769, Garrick organized the Shakespeare jubilee in Stratford-upon-Avon. None of Shakespeare's plays were actually performed, and the highly anticipated parade of Shakespeare's characters was rained out, yet the festival succeeded in consecrating the spot as the poet's birthplace and an important tourist attraction. The jubilee also fostered the marketing of Shakespeare's image with which we are still familiar today: busts, medals, and porcelain and pewter mementos bearing the dramatist's image were popular commodities. Shakespeare became a "national saint – chips of his chair were on sale as relics."[68] The detachment of Shakespeare, as a creative figure, from his plays can also be seen in the proliferation of books excerpting Shakespeare's "beauties" (quotable selections), changing the plays into other forms, such as Charlotte Lennox's *Shakespeare Illustrated: or the Novels and Histories, On Which the Plays of Shakespeare are Founded, Collected and Translated from the Original Authors* (1753–4), and Charles and Mary Lamb's *Tales from Shakespeare. Designed for the Use of Young Persons* (1807), and extrapolating on the psychological features of his characters, such as Anna Jameson's *Characteristics of the Women* (1832), which analyzed the personalities of his heroines.

In the Shakespeare revival, then, Britons found a site in which artistic achievement and national pride could be cemented together – a suturing that has remained firm ever since. In *Mansfield Park* (1818), for instance, Jane Austen has Fanny Price's suitor Henry Crawford declare:

> Shakespeare one gets acquainted with without knowing how. It is part of an Englishman's constitution. His thoughts and beauties are so spread abroad that one touches them every where, one is intimate with him by instinct. – No man of any brain can open at a good part of one of his plays, without falling into the flow of his meaning immediately.

And even his rival, Edmund Bertram, is forced to agree: "No doubt one is familiar with Shakespeare in a degree...from one's earliest years. His celebrated passages are quoted by every body; they are in half the books we open, and we all talk Shakespeare, use his similes, and describe with his descriptions."[69] By the beginning of the nineteenth century, then, Shakespeare had come to embody all the most desirable traits of British national identity: liberty, sincerity, virtue, and civility. Furthermore, his language had ceased to seem uncouth or primitive, and become an exemplar of British literary eloquence.

Print Culture and the Public Sphere

The knowledge of letters is one of the greatest blessings that ever God bestowed on the Children of Men. By this means we preserve for our own use, through all our lives, what our memory would have lost in a few days, and lay up a rich store of knowledge for those that shall come after us.

Isaac Watts[1]

Reading and Meditation is that to our souls, which food and nourishment is to our bodies, and become part of us in the same manners, so that we cannot do ourselves either a little good, or a little harm by the books we read.

William Law[2]

The term "print culture" designates a society in which the most important medium of communication (across both space and time) is print. "Print" can take the form of newspapers, broadsheets, novels, scientific treatises, conduct books, or any text replicable in a relatively small, purchasable form. In the middle of the seventeenth century, or just after, this kind of society began to emerge in Great Britain. The English Civil Wars of the 1640s and 1650s brought about the end of most kinds of censorship, and simultaneously more people learned to read the political propaganda, ballads, and sermons that resulted. This development, of which we may now be reaching the end, changed both the way Britain structured itself as a community, and the ways in which British people imagined themselves as individuals.

Evidence suggests that the largest jump in literacy rates occurred during the later part of the seventeenth century. The increase in people learning to read was influenced by two factors. Perhaps the more important of these was religious. Members of many of the dissenting Protestant sects that emerged during this period, such as the Quakers and Baptists, were encouraged to read and interpret the Bible, now available in English, for themselves in order to establish an intimate and individual relationship with God. Literacy became, in these circles, a sign of piety and devotion.[3] At the same time, the expansion of trading networks and colonial production forced merchants to rely more heavily on news transmitted from afar. The literate businessman living in this first information economy could make higher profits by keeping abreast of his own ships and foreign wars through public papers and private letters. Thus, in 1800, 60–70% of adult males could read, whereas in 1600 only 25% could. Female literacy increased as well, to about two-thirds that of men: so, in the 1750s, when 60% of men could read, about 40% of women could. Interestingly, the areas with the highest literacy were in Scotland and the North American colonies, followed closely by metropolitan London.

Despite the freedom of the Interregnum, however, control over publishing increased again after the Restoration; the passage of the Licensing Act of 1662 allowed the government to regulate publications and the Stationer's Company to monopolize commercial publishing. Yet this situation improved quickly: the Licensing Act lapsed in 1695, making the print trade almost unregulated, although laws against libel and sedition were still very much in effect. An author usually sold his or her copyright to a work to a bookseller, who paid a flat fee for the right to all further profits from its publication. In 1709, a Copyright Act granting authors the copyright to their works for 14–21 years came into effect. Only in the last quarter of the eighteenth century was the booksellers' control over publication undermined. What is revealed most clearly by all this legislative wrangling is that print became a profitable commodity during this period – why else argue over it? An amazing variety of works, in both old and new genres, entered this marketplace: criminal as well as spiritual autobiographies; political propaganda; all kinds of fiction, including the novel; poetry, plays and essays; travel narratives from around the globe.

This flood of texts revealed certain representational features unique to print. Print had the capacity to render the person who wrote the work anonymous since the reader did not need to have any physical contract with the author. Thus, men could write in the voices of women – like Daniel Defoe's *Moll Flanders* – and vice versa. Multiple authors could adopt a single persona, such as Mr Spectator or Martin Scriblerus, discussed below. Furthermore, the fact that authority was held by the words on the page, rather than the body of the writer, allowed authors from all walks of life, and both genders, to enter the field. For this reason, someone like Alexander Pope, physically unprepossessing, and, as a Catholic, legally and socially marginalized, could become one of the cultural authorities of the age. The detachment of a durable and portable text from the fallible and limited body of the author at times seemed to give print an aura of permanence and objectivity. At others, mere paper seemed disturbingly ephemeral and untrustworthy. The debatable capacity of print to tell the truth, thus, became one of the persistent concerns of the day – manifesting itself, for instance, in the Ossian controversy described in chapter 1.

The loosening of restrictions on the press also changed the way politics were conducted during the period. Opposition between Whigs and Tories had originated in the Exclusion Crisis of 1679, when the Whigs had attempted to exclude James II from the throne on the grounds of his Catholicism, but the reign of Queen Anne (1702–1714) was an era of particular partisanship. Party allegiances were complicated things, but, generally speaking, the Whigs were made up of members of the aristocracy and the new class of merchants, while Tories came primarily from the landed gentry. Tories were conservative, in the sense that they wanted to see as few changes as possible in the church and crown, while Whigs supported new developments in the cultural and economic marketplace, and were associated, at least by their enemies, with political expediency, self-interestedness, and greed. Yet, these struggles were no longer the private domain of an elite group surrounding the monarch and ministry; political opinion and scandal were now accessible to anyone who could read the newspapers and party propaganda that circulated widely.

At the same time, an extra-political realm of print culture began to emerge, one associated with the social structure that has been called the public sphere. Matters previously considered the exclusive domain of governmental or royal authority were entered into public debate, along with issues considered to be of private economic interest only. Such questions became available for discussion among an expanding number of thinking persons.[4] Ideally, these interlocutors, despite their differences, cohered as a community. Much of the growth of the public sphere was facilitated by the development of print technology and printed materials. The growing number of newspapers was particularly important in this regard, as readers learned to link their own apprehension of cultural and national life to those of other readers. As Benedict Anderson has argued, newspaper reading "is performed in silent privacy, in the lair of the skull. Yet each communicant is well aware that the ceremony he performs is being replicated simultaneously by thousands (or millions) of others of whose existence he is confident, yet of whose identity he has not the slightest notion."[5] This sense of shared experience and consensus fostered by the individual experience of reading was produced by the periodical essay and the novel as well. The public sphere also contained counter- or alternative public spheres within it and alongside it.[6] For example, some periodicals at the time, such as the *Female Tatler* (in the voice of a Mrs. Crackenthorpe, though probably written by a man) and the *Female Spectator* (edited and written by Eliza Haywood) were explicitly addressed to women. Later in the century, radical groups sought to create working-class publics through print.

Some of the other interactions that characterized the public sphere, however, took place in the new sites for sociability that sprang up throughout London during the eighteenth century, particularly the 551 coffee houses that had opened by 1739. Coffee houses provided a place for people to meet, exchange news and gossip, and conduct business. The historian John Brewer describes them as "the precursor of the modern office, but once you were there, you were as likely to talk about matters of general interest – the latest play, sexual scandal, or political quarrel – as carry on business."[7] Although they served alcohol as well as coffee and chocolate, "the coffee house ... combined democratic aspirations with a space of discourse less contaminated by the demands of the body for pleasure and release than that of the tavern."[8] Women were rarely welcome in the coffee houses, but they participated in other forms of public sociability, such as the salon, the pleasure gardens of Ranelagh or Vauxhall, and the more intimate setting of the tea party.[9] These settings emphasized the art of polite conversation as much as the benefits of literacy. Thus, an oral, face-to-face culture was not completely replaced by print culture at this time, if it ever was.

Nevertheless, in the later seventeenth century and the early eighteenth century, it seemed that everyone was sure that British society was changing through the growth of literacy and print, and not necessarily for the better. Almost all the works introduced below self-consciously highlight their own modernity, their own effort to grapple with a new and changing world. Although this novelty excited many, and prompted praise such as that recorded in the epigraphs to this section, others were concerned with the damage that print culture might do to the existing social structure. This was particularly true at the beginning and at the end of the period. John Dryden, for example, decried the way the lack of censorship during the Interregnum had taken texts literally out of the hands of the elite; during the Civil Wars, "the tender page with horny fists was galled,/and he was gifted most that loudest bawled." And one peer advised Charles II to clamp down on public discussion of politics, arguing "controversy is a Civill War with the Pen, which Pulls out the Sorde soone afterwards." In the later eighteenth century, an interest in teaching members of the laboring classes to read created a certain amount of anxiety about what they would be reading. As Olivia Smith has demonstrated, "The problem that worried contemporaries of the 1790s and the post-Napoleonic War period was not so much that the lower and middle classes were reading, but that they were reading unconventional material. A significant difference exists between reading chap-books, ballads, and almanacs and reading pamphlets and newspapers that challenge one's social status or criticize the government."[10] One might say, then, that as much as the emergence of print culture fostered an ideal of consensus, or at least of rational argument, in the public sphere it also created anxieties about the splintering of that space by the unruly elements of society.

Other eighteenth-century concerns about the effect of texts on the psyches of those who read them still resonate with us today. Even as strong a proponent of the benevolent effects of print culture as Richard Steele also feared its destructive excesses. One could become "addicted to news," he warned his readers, describing a political upholsterer who neglects his business and family in his pursuit of the latest information: an example "for the particular Benefit of those worthy Citizens who live more in a Coffee-house than in their Shops, and whose Thoughts are so taken up with the Affairs of the Allies that they forget their Customers" (*Tatler* No. 155, April 6, 1710). Others worried about the susceptibility of young girls reading novels. The Bluestocking Hester Chapone, for example, warns female readers away from emotionally engaging narratives in 1773:

> Both the writing and sentiments of novels and romances are such as are only proper to vitiate your stile [sic], and to mislead your heart and understanding. – the expectation of extraordinary adventures – which seldom ever happen to the sober and prudent part of mankind – and the admiration of extravagant passion and absurd conduct, are some of the usual fruits of this kind of reading.[11]

Like contemporary arguments about the effects of sexuality or violence in the media, then, eighteenth-century debates about print often focused on the power of representations to alter the behavior of their consumers. Thus, the proper nature of print culture and the public sphere was a contested domain, and defined as much by what it excluded as by what it included. The texts discussed in this section make visible the struggle in eighteenth-century culture to define or control the effects of print and the nature of the public sphere. Thus, Addison and Steele deride Delarivier Manley's politically motivated publishing, figuring her as a malevolent teacher, who "by the help of some artificial poisons conveyed by smells, [has] within these few weeks brought many persons of both sexes to an untimely fate" (*Tatler* No. 63, 1709). By comparing her texts to criminal tools that affect the body, they imply that Manley is a witch-like figure who does not belong in the decorous, intellectual space of the public sphere. Manley, in turn, retaliates against Steele, making public accusations about his private vices by depicting him as Mr Ingrat in *The New Atalantis*. In *The Dunciad*, Pope takes up satirical arms against a host of intruders into print, the dunces. One dunce, for instance, wins a race through the offices of Cloacina, goddess of the sewers: "Renew'd by ordure's sympathetic force, / As oil'd with magic juices for the course. / Vig'rous he rises; from th'effluvia strong / Imbibes new life, and scours and stinks along" (II, 103–106). Again, the descent into bodily functions and fluids disqualifies these writers from the public sphere. Samuel Johnson, too, worries about the encroachments of popular culture, specialists, and French into the realm of standard English usage. As much as they celebrated the new developments of print culture and the public sphere, then, many eighteenth-century texts on the subject also worry about whether print has the power to unite and elevate British culture, or whether print will degrade that culture, and rip it apart.

Joseph Addison and Richard Steele, the *Tatler* and the *Spectator*

Had the Philosophers and great Men of Antiquity, who took so much Pains in order to instruct Mankind, and leave the World wiser and better than they found it; had they, I say, been possessed of the Art of Printing, there is no Question but they would have made such an Advantage of it, in dealing out their Lectures to the Publick. Our common Prints would be of great Use were they thus calculated to diffuse good sense through the Bulk of a People, to clear up their Understandings, animate their Minds with Virtue, dissipate the Sorrows of a heavy Heart, or unbend the Mind from its more severe Employments with innocent Amusements.

Joseph Addison, *Spectator* No. 124, Monday, July 23, 1711

In the *Tatler*, the *Spectator*, and the *Guardian* the public held up a mirror to itself; it did not yet come to a self-understanding through the detour of reflection on works of philosophy and literature, art and science, but through entering itself into "literature" as an object ... The public that read and debated this sort of thing read and debated about itself.

Jürgen Habermas, *The Structural Transformation of the Public Sphere*[12]

The periodical essay was one of the important innovations of early eighteenth-century print culture. Popular, pleasurable, and influential in both their content and form, these texts staked out an intermediate ground between the topical information about war and finance supplied by the newspapers, and the more specialized demands of philosophy and neoclassical poetry. They eschewed the fingerpointing of contemporary satire and scandal (as practiced by Pope, at times, and by Manley) in favor of an urbane and amusing general critique of the foibles of society. In this way, they helped generate a public sphere by articulating a field of "general concerns" – issues in which any literate and virtuous reader might be interested and might express an opinion about. Although they have no perfect contemporary equivalent, these essays combined elements of what we find today in newspaper editorials and discussions of lifestyle in monthly magazines. Ideally, then, these essays gave their readers' private concerns back to them in a material, public form, and thus helped legitimate the importance of both readers and issues. As Addison states above, the essays also self-consciously make use of print to create new spaces of social, yet intellectual, interaction. Famously, Mr Spectator declared: "It was said of Socrates, that he brought Philosophy down from Heaven, to inhabit among Men; and I shall be ambitious to have it said of me, that I have brought philosophy out of Closets and Libraries, Schools and Colleges, to dwell in Clubs and Assemblies, at Tea-Tables, and in Coffee Houses" (*Spectator* No. 10, Monday, March 12, 1711).

Richard Steele edited the *Tatler*, which appeared three times a week between April 1709 and January 1711, and wrote most of its essays. The first few issues were distributed free, and subsequent ones cost one penny. In March 1711, the *Tatler* was replaced by the *Spectator*, which Steele co-edited with Joseph Addison, who had also contributed a number of essays to the *Tatler*. The *Spectator* came out six times a week, and the first series, numbering 555 issues, continued until December 1712. Addison edited a second series with Eustace Budgell and Thomas Tickell in 1714. Along with Addison and Steele, a number of other contributors wrote for the periodicals, including Jonathan Swift, and the publication sometimes printed letters from readers. Occasionally, the essays also offer the speeches and behavior of fictional yet representative persons, such as Sir Roger de Coverly, an aristocrat, Sir Andrew Freeport, a merchant, or Ned Softly, a poet. The essays, however, were primarily written in the voices of fictional personae: Isaac Bickerstaff in the *Tatler*, and Mr Spectator in the *Spectator*.

The persona of Isaac Bickerstaff is something of a joke. Invented by Swift to mock the quack astrologer John Partridge, Bickerstaff was supposed to have authored the satirical pamphlet, "Predictions for the Year 1708." Steele borrowed the persona, thus acquiring a voice in keeping with the conversational, self-mocking tone of the *Tatler*. Mr Spectator is a different kind of creation. In the first issue, he declares:

> I live in the world, rather as a Spectator of Mankind, than as one of
> the Species...I am very well versed in the Theory of an Husband, or a
> Father, and can discern the Errors in the Oeconomy, Business, and Diversion
> of others, better than those who are engaged in them; as Standers-by dis-
> cover Blots, which are apt to escape those who are in the Game.... In short,
> I have acted in all the parts of my Life as a Looker-on, which is the
> Character I intend to preserve in this Paper. (*Spectator* No. 1, Thursday,
> March 1, 1711)

This image of a person who knows everything, and yet does not have a
personal stake in anything, has led some to see Mr Spectator as a forerun-
ner of the emergent figure of the "critic": a disinterested "expert" on the
manifestations of contemporary life whom Terry Eagleton describes as
"less the castigator of his fellows than their clubbable, co-discoursing
equal, spokesman rather than scourge." Both Bickerstaff and Mr Spectator,
then, take up an important role in the public sphere: they are imaginary
figures who speak for nobody in particular, but rather for what "every-
body" thinks. They produce "the casual polymorphous expertise of one to
whom no sector of cultural life is alien – who passes from writer to reader,
moralist to mercantilist, Tory to Whig and back, offering himself as little
more than the vacant space within which these diverse elements may con-
gregate and interbreed."[13]

Yet who exactly participated in this fertile congregating and interbreed-
ing of ideas? The audience for the *Tatler* and the *Spectator* was predomi-
nantly the "middle classes," the growing group of urban readers who were
neither aristocrats nor laborers, although readership certainly extended
beyond this group. Indeed, by articulating areas of general value and
concern, the periodicals worked to consolidate a middle-class reading
public that was defined and given an identity through its tastes and interests
as much as by its economic standing. They performed the cultural work
of shaping this disparate group into a recognizable class. Women were an
important part of this audience, although their status within it was problematic. While Addison and Steele often included female readers as part
of their public, they also argued that women's place was strictly in the
private sphere; they were overtly nostalgic for the era when "the most
conspicuous woman...was only the best housewife" (*Spectator* No. 57,
May 5, 1711). As Kathryn Shevelow has demonstrated, "it is in the periodical that one particular formation of femininity most persistently manifested itself on the popular level: the notion of women as different in kind
rather than degree from men, possessing in the household a 'separate but
equal' area of activity and authority."[14] The public sphere of print gener-

ated by the periodicals, then, was heterogeneous in terms of the status of its participants.

The *Tatler* and the *Spectator* hoped to reform eighteenth-century life, not simply to reflect it. Yet, they planned to do so through ironic, subtle chiding, rather than forceful chastisement. Again, this effort took place not in the realm of politics but in the more generalized arena of manners and morality. Although both Addison and Steele were explicitly connected with the Whig government, the periodicals excluded any topical political news, except for the first few issues of the *Tatler*. Nonetheless, the essays have a generally Whiggish bent. They look askance at the new institutions of the stock exchange, and the markets in goods and print, but they do not condemn them outright, more typically suggesting that they could be regulated and improved by properly moral behavior. This vein of advice extends into the areas of fashion and taste. Addison, for example, mocks the extravagance of women's modish clothing like the hoop-skirt (*Tatler* No. 116). Yet, as Erin Mackie points out, the interrogation of fashion and taste in these essays is paradoxical, since the authors depend on the novelty of the market they also critique; thus, they "register a deep ambivalence about fashion, especially their own fashionability as modish lifestyle magazines. In them we find the logic of antifashion fashion: what is really stylistically desirable is defined against what is merely 'fashionable.' "[15] Yet, perhaps the most important area in which improvement was modeled by the *Spectator* and adopted by others was its rhetorical style. As Samuel Johnson says in his *Life of Addison*:

> His prose is the model of the middle style; on grave subjects not formal, on light occasions not groveling; pure without scrupulosity, and exact without apparent elaboration; always equable, and always easy, without glowing words or pointed sentences...Whoever wishes to attain an English style, familiar but not coarse, and elegant but not ostentatious, must give his days and nights to the volumes of Addison.[16]

In this, as in many other ways, the *Tatler* and the *Spectator* offered their readers an example of how to make an authoritative entrance into the public sphere of print.

Delarivier Manley, *The New Atalantis*

This day (the year I dare not tell)
Apollo played the midwife's part;
Into the world Corinna fell.
And he endued her with his art.

But Cupid with a satyr comes:
Both softly to the cradle creep:
Both stroke her hands and rub her gums,
While the poor child lay fast asleep.

Then Cupid thus: "This little maid
Of love shall always speak and write":
"And I pronounce," the satyr said,
"The world shall feel her scratch and bite."

Swift, Corinna, A Ballad, ll. 1–12

Jonathan Swift's poem, *Corinna* (1711–12), is often taken to be a description of Delarivier Manley, with whom, despite his mocking tone in these lines, Swift shared a collegial working relationship. Even if it does not refer to Manley specifically, however, the verses raise several important questions relevant to Manley's career, and to her best-known work, *Secret Memoirs and Manners of Several Persons of Quality of Both Sexes, From the New Atalantis, an Island in the Mediterranean*, better known simply as the *The New Atalantis* (1709). What does it mean to have Apollo, Cupid, *and* a satyr bestow their gifts on a female writer? Presumably, the result will be an author who deals with the timeless, lawless, private realms of erotic passion, alongside the topical, public concerns of satire. And Manley, in *The New Atalantis*, in which an often sympathetic account of love's transgressions against social law coexists with the scratching and biting of political intervention, fulfills these expectations. This combination has divided critics of the work, who typically treat the text either as a stage in the development of the novel, or as part of the emergence of politics into the public sphere. Swift's lines also raise a further question: are these gifts used differently by a female writer than they would be by a male writer? Probably they are, since, although the work shares some generic features with political satire written by men during the period, Manley also inserts her own autobiography into the text as the story of Delia.

Delarivier Manley lived during the first blossoming of political parties in England, and dedicated most of her literary career to that conflict. She was a party writer for the Tories during the reign of Queen Anne, turning scandal and gossip into thinly veiled allegory and "fiction." Manley once received fifty pounds from Robert Harley, the Tory prime minister, but she claimed that was "all I ever received from the public for what some esteem good service to the cause."[17] Yet, her partisanship is certainly what brought her success. Manley turned to writing party propaganda after being duped, at an early age, into a bigamous marriage with her cousin, John Manley. This relationship left her a fallen woman with an illegitimate child, as scandalous a figure as most of those about whom she wrote. She was later the mistress of John Tilly, the warden of Fleet Prison, and of John Barber, the printer. In addition to *The New Atalantis*, Manley wrote several other scandalous allegories, including one on the career of Sarah Churchill, Anne's favorite and a Whig, called *The History of Queen Zarah and the Zarazians* (1705), several plays, and an autobiographical narrative, *Rivella*, as well as taking over the editorship of the *Examiner* from Swift in 1711. These profitable ventures into print culture earned her the epithet, "Scandalosissima Scoundrelia."[18]

The New Atalantis recounts the journey of Astrea, the goddess of justice, to the island of Atalantis and its capital city of Angela (England and London, respectively) to gather information to help her in tutoring the island's next ruler.[19] Once there, she meets her "mother," Virtue, and the two are given a tour of the principal people and places of the kingdom by Lady Intelligence, "first lady of the bedchamber to the Princess Fame," whose "garments are all hieroglyphics."[20] The three travel invisibly, and Lady Intelligence conveys the elaborate, scandalous histories of the people they encounter. Occasionally, another character will speak directly to the three women: perhaps most importantly Mrs. Nightwork, a midwife who knows particularly intimate details about the shocking sexual exploits of the Atalantians, and whose presence links the birth of (illegitimate) babies to the "birth" of scandal. Despite their collegial relationship, the main narrators have different reactions to the stories they hear. While the goddesses, Astrea and Virtue, tend to draw moral lessons from the anecdotes they hear, Lady Intelligence seems interested in covering as much scandalous ground as possible. Intelligence, indeed, seems at times to lose patience with her more celestial charges. She also competitively defends her role, telling Mrs. Nightwork, "I'm afraid you are taking my province from me, and engrossing all the scandal to yourself" (p. 138). This may be because both Lady Intelligence and Mrs. Nightwork know that their livelihood, unlike that of the goddesses, depends on the retail of gossip. As Nightwork says: "we should be but ill company to most of our ladies, who love to be amused by the failings of others, and would not always give us so favourable and warm a reception, if we had nothing of scandal to entertain them with" (p. 139). Giving the reader multiple perspectives on the action allows Manley to oscillate between two configurations of femininity: an ancient preconception of female interlocutors as gossips, and an emerging idea that women should serve as the moral censors of social interaction (as promulgated by Addison and Steele[21]). Although most critics believe that Manley has a closer allegiance to Lady Intelligence than the goddesses, her inclusion of both allows the reader to avoid choosing between moral judgment and the pleasure of scandal.

The New Atalantis was so successful that the first volume had gone into three editions by the time the second was published. The piece as a whole went into six editions in ten years, making it the "best-selling novelistic fiction of the decade".[22] The extent to which its numerous readers recognized the characters of *The New Atalantis* as real people is open to dispute. Keys which "identified" characters were published separately, but they do not definitively link each character to an actual person.[23] To work as scandal, then, the reader must already know at least part of the story being told allegorically, and enjoy hearing it told again. Some in power certainly did read it that way – though without much enjoyment: Manley, the publishers, and the printers of the text were indicted for seditious libel in October 1709, but she was discharged without sentence after her trial in February 1710. In a more general sense, however, the work was certainly political, as it participated in, and helped shape, the transition between politics imagined as the private doings of royalty, military, and ministers, and politics imagined as public knowledge discussed by the general reader. Thus, even if the average reader does not know that Count Fortunatus is supposed to be the Duke of Marlborough, he or she can consider and discuss that character's method of doing political business. Ironically, this transmission from the private to the public sphere is enabled by the traditionally debased mode of women's gossip.

Much of *The New Atalantis*, however, seems to work on two levels: as scandal, and as autonomous novelistic anecdotes, or "amatory fictions," and it is this quality which has earned the text its place in the history of the novel. Several sections have been singled out by critics as particularly interesting for their exploration of the vagaries of erotic passion (and the pleasures of reading about it). One is an episode recounting the Duchess *de l'inconstant* (the Duchess of Cleveland) being tricked into sleeping with Germanicus (Henry, Baron Dover) by her lover Count Fortunatus (the Duke of Marlborough), who has grown tired of her. This anecdote explores the questions of female sexual aggression and voyeurism, as the Duchess, finding Germanicus asleep where she expected the Duke, gives "her...time to wander over beauties so inviting," which "increase[s] her flame," so "with an amorous sigh she gently threw her self on the bed, close to the desiring youth" (p. 21). Another is the seduction of Charlot by her guardian (identified by the keys as the Earl of Portland and his ward, Stuarta Werbuge Howard), which deals with the question of incest and the role of texts in sexual transgression.[24] The description of the "new cabal," a group of aristocratic women who dress as men and conduct affairs with other women, has also raised the question of whether Manley envisages a feminine utopia in the midst of the corruption and scandal of Atalantis. A number of other episodes also deal with incest, polygamy, and infanticide, and raise the more abstract and "novelistic" question of whether an individual has the right to break society's moral laws. Those that do so usually are punished in the text, and yet the narrators consistently express sympathy for characters who feel driven to commit these crimes. On one level, then, Manley suggests that the sexual transgressions of the Whigs are symptoms of their political corruption, linking public and private through the retail of scandal. On another level, however, she pushes prose narrative into a new role in public life by making private sexual choices the material for public discussion.

Alexander Pope, *The Dunciad*

It is to *The Dunciad* that we must turn for the epic of the printed word and its benefits to mankind. For here is the explicit study of plunging the human mind into the sludge of an unconscious engendered by the book: Pope is telling the English world what Cervantes had told the Spanish world and Rabelais the French world concerning print. It is a delirium. It is a transforming and metamorphosing drug that has the power of imposing its assumptions upon every level of consciousness.[25]

If *The Dunciad* is "the epic of the printed word" it is also an anti-epic, a self-canceling epic of destruction. The poem's intense deconstructive energy makes it one of the most difficult works in the eighteenth-century canon, but also one of the most wildly inventive and rewarding. While the authors of the *Spectator* hoped that the expansion of print culture would lead to greater general order and knowledge, Pope predicted that only a kind of "sludge" of disorder and disharmony would result from opening the floodgates of print. As Martin Scriblerus says of the author, "He lived in those days, when (after Providence had permitted the invention of Printing as a scourge for the sins of the learned) Paper also became so cheap, and Printers so numerous, that a deluge of Authors covered the land."[26] Yet, even as the poem rails against the mess of print culture, that muck is also a powerful creative catalyst for the satiric voice – the poet seems to gain enormous pleasure from the grotesqueries of the dunces. *The Dunciad* encompasses both Pope's personal response to his critics, and his apocalyptic sense that a literary era, one that had made him a cultural superstar, was ending.

Pope produced four versions of *The Dunciad* between 1728 and 1743; the poem grew as the varieties of his outrage against eighteenth-century culture multiplied. The first version, published on May 18, 1728, was made up of three books and featured the scholar Lewis Theobald (pronounced Tibbald) as its antihero. Theobald earned this unenviable place by publishing a book called *Shakespeare Restored: Or, a Specimen of the Many Errors, as well Committed, as Unamended, by Mr Pope in his Late Edition of this Poet*. The title itself reveals how he earned Pope's enmity. Making Theobald alone the public focus of his satire did not satisfy Pope, however, and, in 1729, *The Dunciad Variorum* appeared which replaced the poem's asterisks with the real names of all the dunces. On the advice of Swift and the other Scriblerians,[27] and with their help, this *Dunciad* also sported the elaborate fake prefaces, footnotes, and commentaries that would adorn all future versions of the poem. In 1742, however, finding emerging varieties of dullness to rail against, Pope published *The New Dunciad*, a separate fourth book in a more serious tone. That year, too, a new character entered the picture. George II's poet laureate, the actor and playwright Colley Cibber, published a lampoon of Pope, based on a popular rumor of his impotent adventures with a prostitute, claiming to have "found this little hasty Hero, like a terrible Tom-Tit, pertly perching upon the Mount of Love."[28] Cibber paid dearly for this foray into satire, replacing Theobald as the "hero" of the final version of *The Dunciad*: *The Dunciad, in Four Books*, published in 1743. This *Dunciad* extends its satiric reach into all aspects of popular culture, and, arguably, makes more political jabs at the recently fallen government of Robert Walpole.

The existence of so many versions of the poem, and of so many pieces (footnotes, prefaces, etc.), begs the question of which one is the "real" *Dunciad*, and of how much of its surrounding material is necessary to the poem. This has proved a difficult editorial problem, but the very multiplicity of its parts reveals something important about the text. Even as *The Dunciad* rails against the effects of print culture, it itself is a poem that could only have been produced within a culture centered on print. As Emrys Jones says of the work's physical materiality:

> *The Dunciad* on the page is a formidable object, dense, opaque, intransigently and uncompromisingly itself. Its apparatus of prefatory material, voluminous annotation, and after-pieces helps to create something like a spatial sense of the area occupied by the central object, the poetic text. One can indeed contemplate it as something with real physical dimensions. Just as the Lilliputians one day found the sleeping man-giant Gulliver

within their kingdom, so Pope's contemporaries can be imagined as discovering this strange offensive object, lying in a public place like an enemy weapon or ponderous missile: essentially not a set of abstract verbal statements but a thing, to be walked around and examined, interpreted and possibly dealt with.[29]

Thus the poem embodies the paraphernalia and possibilities of print culture even as it parodies them. Take the poem's may varieties of footnotes, for example. In all the versions that appeared after 1729, the poem includes false footnotes supposedly authored by Richard Bentley and by the fictional Martin Scriblerus. These notes make fun of the newly popular practice of footnoting, providing dubious classical references and a good deal of pretentious speculation. Another set of footnotes is written in Pope's own voice; these tend to defend the poet against personal attacks. And two more sets of explanatory footnotes were added later: by Pope's literary executor Warburton, and by contemporary editors. Thus, paradoxically, as much as the poem satirizes the footnotes, it cannot be understood without reference to the footnotes. This can be a thorny issue for the modern reader: does *The Dunciad* exist as a poem separate from all its "extras"? This thicket of references reveals another tension in satire as a genre: the poem's success depends on its familiarity and facility with the elements of the world it satirizes – yet that familiarly undermines the moral distance upon which its satiric force depends. Pope's satire is enmeshed in the print culture it satirizes.

The appearance first of Lewis Theobald, then of the numerous named dunces, and finally, the replacement of Theobald by Cibber, raises another crucial question for *The Dunciad*, and for many of Pope's major satires: the satiric efficacy of naming names. Psychologically, of course, it makes a good deal of sense: if Pope's own name was going to be so brutally attacked, why shouldn't he make his counterattack equally direct? And yet the effect of including so many eighteenth-century names is to increase the topicality of the poem, while decreasing its accessibility to modern readers. Ironically, most of the dunces are only remembered today as the objects of Pope's scorn – by deriding their insignificance, he preserved them for posterity. And yet this paradox highlights some central issues in the genre of serious satire: does the poet write to reform the world in which he lives, or to produce a timeless work of art? Is the poet's duty to chastise general vice, or to expose particular offenders against society? Pope himself justified his practice to his friend Dr Arbuthnot in these terms:

I would...do it with more restrictions and less personally; it is more agreeable to my nature...but General Satire in times of General Vice has no
force, & is no Punishment: People have ceas'd to be ashamed of it when
so many are joined with them; and 'tis only by hunting one or two from
the Herd that any Examples can be made. If a man writ all his life against
the collective body of the Banditti, or against Lawyers, would it do the
least good, or lessen the body? But if some are hung up, or pillory'd, it may
prevent others. And in my low station, with no other power than this, I
hope to deter, if not reform.[30]

The combination of a sense of public duty with a wolfish aggressivity in
this passage tells us a good deal about how Pope saw the place of the satirist
in the eighteenth-century world.

The Dunciad in Four Books is a poem with a profusion of characters and
an efflorescence of details, but, underneath this elaboration, it adheres to
a classical epic plotline. It follows the selection of Cibber as the favorite of
Dulness, the "Mighty Mother." Book I describes Cibber's elevation to this
post. Book II relates the public games and contests in honor of Cibber's
election – in the manner of Virgil's *Aeneid* – in which all the dunces of
Grub Street participate. In Book III, Cibber is transported to the Temple
of Dulness, and shown a vision (again mimicking epic conventions) of the
reign of Dulness, past and future. Finally, in Book IV, the prophecies of
Book III come to pass, and the "Restoration of Night and Chaos" concludes
the poem. Before that happens, however, Dulness receives a parade of
scholars, collectors, and other representatives of the corruptions of modern
learning. As this summary makes clear, the poem encompasses two newly
significant areas of eighteenth-century culture: Grub Street, and what we
now call academia. Grub Street was an actual street in London, but also
the symbolic site of the rise of professional writing. Here Dulness finds
"The Cave of Poverty and Poetry," which pours forth new forms of print
culture as if they were sentient beings:

> Hence Miscellanies spring, the weekly boast
> Of Curl's chaste press, and Lintot's rubric post;
> Hence hymning Tyburn's elegiac lines,
> Hence Journals, Medley's, Merc'ries, Magazines:
> Sepulchral Lyes, our holy walls to grace,
> And New-year Odes, and all the Grub-street race. (I, ll. 37–44)

At the same time, the poem enters into the "Ancients and Moderns" debate
on the side of the "Ancients," satirizing the new "instruments of classical
scholarship, the commentary, the dictionary, index, and above all the foot-

note…[which] appeared to impede the desire for elegance and eloquence."[31] Thus Pope has Richard Bentley[32] proudly proclaim in Book IV:

> "Ah, think not, Mistress! More true Dulness lies
> In Folly's Cap, than Wisdom's grave disguise.
> Like buoys, that never sink into the flood,
> On Learning's surface we but lie and nod.
> […]
> For thee we dim the eyes, and stuff the head
> With all such reading as was never read
> For thee explain a thing till all men doubt it,
> And write about it, Goddess, and about it[.] (IV, ll. 239–42, 249–52)

The redundant rhyme in the last couplet of the passage (it/it) and the extra
syllable in line 252 help convey Pope's belief in the awkwardness and
superfluity of much eighteenth-century scholarship. Grub Street and
academia might seem separate, then, but are joined by their novelty in
eighteenth-century culture, their role in remaking authorship as a professional occupation, and their parasitical relationship to what Pope considers
true learning.

The poem's mock-epic structure also places it in relation to the Augustan
project of recovering classical learning. *The Dunciad*, says Scriblerus, was
in fact Homer's first poem, preceding *The Odyssey* and *The Iliad*. Thus,
"forasmuch as our poet had translated those two famous works of Homer
which are yet left, he did conceive it in some sort his duty to imitate that
also which was lost" (p. 303). As much as this assertion participates in
poem's satire of modern learning, it also foregrounds a central anxiety in
The Dunciad and elsewhere in print culture: One nightmare of print culture
is that it makes all learning material, manifest on paper; and paper itself
has a finite lifespan, is as ephemeral as man's own body. This anxiety manifests itself in the extreme physicality accorded to printed objects in the
poem. Dulness, for example,

> …beholds the Chaos dark and deep,
> Where nameless Somethings in their causes sleep,
> 'Till genial Jacob, or a warm Third day,
> Call forth each mass, a Poem or a Play:
> How hints, like spawn, scarce quick in embryo lie,
> How new-born nonsense first is taught to cry[.](I, ll. 55–60)

The generation of print out of nothingness underlines the question
of what exactly produces literature. Inspiration? Profit? Furthermore,
their involvement in the creation of such "embryos" and "new-borns"

sometimes compromises the masculinity of the Dunces. Cibber lies infan-
talized on the lap of Dulness at the beginning of Book III, while Book IV
offers the grotesque story of Annius, who swallows the gold coins he collects, and Mummius, who declares he "bought them, shrouded in that
living shrine/And at their second birth, they issue mine" (IV, ll. 385–6).
And, of course, the monstrously powerful maternity of Dulness herself,
a (pro)creativity used for horrifying ends, unsettles conventional eighteenth-century gender roles.

And yet the Dunces have their own wild exuberance, especially in Book
II – pissing, sliding through excrement, diving headfirst into the polluted
Thames. The poem ridicules them, and yet it can't seem to get enough of
them. They thrive in numbers; even though all versions of the poem have
a singular epic hero, there is also a way in which the poem's satire works
by displaying the corporate body of Dunces: the shoal, the throng, the
hive. Their multiplicity represents the horror of the marketplace – its dis-
solution of individual personalities into a cultural stew – but it gives the
Dunces their own manic energy, which attracts as much as it repels. Thus
the poet's relationship to the Dunces is more complicated than simple
disapproval or disgust; much of the satiric energy Pope invests in skewer-
ing the dunces derives from an effort to differentiate himself from them.
Although he wasn't associated with Grub Street or Oxbridge, Pope supported himself through the sale of his works – and thus participated, very
skillfully, in the literary marketplace. Could one do that without descending into Dulness? Pope's formidable, even brutal, display of poetic skill in
The Dunciad can be seen as an attempt to carve out such a place for himself,
and forcefully to expel other writers, in an effort to patrol the borders of
that space.

The poem "imitates that which is lost" on another level as well. As much
as the reign of Dulness is a new event, the result of the present disastrous
flood of print, it is also the reassertion of a primordial state of affairs, of
"*Night* Primaeval, and of *Chaos* old" (IV, l. 630). Dulness is introduced in
Book I trying "still her old Empire to restore" (I, l. 17), and at the end of
Book IV she accomplishes just that. The structure of Book IV, of the
unfolding of a long-predicted apocalypse, places the poet in an awkward
position. Speaking on the brink of the destruction of all he knows, he is
forced to beg Dulness to "Suspend a while your Force inertly strong/Then
take at once the Poet and the Song" (IV, ll. 7–8). The poem, then, records
a cultural instant the poet knows to be as perishable as his own body, both
doomed to disappear "at once." The ambitions of the poem thus oscillate

between an epic permanence and an abrasive, if fragile, ephemerality. And yet the end of the poem finally holds out the possibility that Dulness is just a drama queen, staging a vast and scary pantomime, until she finally "lets the curtain fall" on her shaken audience (IV, 1. 656).

Samuel Johnson, "Preface to *A Dictionary of the English Language*"

Although it may seem to be merely a reference book, or aid for writing, a dictionary has a distinct cultural role. It codifies a standard version of a language, arbitrating which words, and which definitions of those words, will be recognized as "standard usage." A dictionary helps define a culture or a nation through a printed artifact, holding out the promise that access to that community can be achieved by mastering its language. Yet, the strictures of inclusion and exclusion involved in compiling a dictionary reveal both the democratic and the antidemocratic possibilities of print culture. On the one hand, inscribing a standard version of a language makes that language available to any literate person by virtue of his or her literacy, rather than his or her birthright or wealth. On the other hand, a standard version of a language lowers the status of, or even excludes, those persons who use language differently, through regional dialects or lack of education. The act of establishing such a standard is a culturally powerful one, and it is usually done by committee or under the aegis of a national academy of some kind. Samuel Johnson, however, compiled his dictionary on his own, with the help of a few secretaries, in private rooms in London. In the dictionary he compiled, and in his "Preface" to that undertaking, there's a good deal of evidence that he intended the dictionary to have a broader social function than simply defining words. Geared to learners, it offered moral lessons in addition to definitions.[33]

The English came late to the project of compiling a dictionary of their national language. Both France and Italy had preceded England in producing dictionaries to correct and improve their tongues. Yet, despite proposals from Swift and Dryden, England still had no national dictionary when, in 1746, a group of booksellers asked Samuel Johnson to write one for a commission of 1,575 pounds. The task took Johnson nine years, and it marked a turning point in his career, from being a Grub Street writer, to being a respected cultural arbiter. The publication of the dictionary coincided with Mr Johnson becoming Dr Johnson, by virtue of an honorary degree from Oxford University, the institution he'd been forced to leave many years earlier because he'd been unable to pay the fees. It is for these reasons, perhaps, that the preface Johnson wrote for his *Dictionary of the English Language* is one of his most personal pieces.

Johnson put together his definitions using illustrations from earlier English poets, scientists, and prose writers. His favorites included Shakespeare, Spenser, Waller, and Dryden, whom he regarded as "the pure sources of genuine diction" (p. 289).[34] Using these writers had a double effect: even as they enabled him to define standard English usage, he helped them become part of the standard canon of English writers. Moreover, in using these examples, Johnson designated the Renaissance as the golden age of English, between the barbarity of the medieval period and the corruption of the present. He also set out to demarcate a middle ground of English usage, between the specialized language of professionals, and the "fugitive cant" of "the laborious and mercantile part of the people," which "cannot be regarded as any part of the durable materials of a language, and therefore must perish with other things unworthy of preservation" (p. 293). Here, as in other places in the "Preface," we can see the way a "middle" class comes to represent the national standard.

One of the central questions of Johnson's "Preface" revolves around whether the primary purpose of the dictionary is to "fix" the English language, to correct and refine it, or simply to reflect the language as it is spoken and written. Johnson articulates both goals in the course of his preface. He finds English to be "copious without order, and energetic without rules," and dreams of "fix[ing] the language and put[ting] a stop to those alterations which time and chance have hitherto been suffered to make in it without opposition" (pp. 277, 293). Yet, at the same time, he acknowledges that he must sometimes submit to the historical, irregular shape of a language, for "every language has its anomalies which, though inconvenient and in themselves once unnecessary, must be tolerated among the imperfections of human beings" (p. 278). "It must be remembered, that, while our language is yet living, and variable by the caprice of every tongue that speaks it, these words are hourly shifting their relations, and can no more be ascertained in a dictionary than a grove, in the agitation of a storm, can be accurately delineated from its picture in the water" (p. 286).

Making use of the trope of *concordia discors* (order in chaos), here, Johnson admits that, insofar as a language is both spoken through living bodies, and itself can be compared to a living body, it cannot be fixed in print. And yet, as this implicit allusion to the language of artistic composition reveals, language also exceeds the comparison to the body or other forms of nature. It is a human artifact, like a set of laws or a constitution, and this, in Johnson's view, is what gives it permanence and value: "there is in constancy and stability a general and lasting advantage, which will always overbalance the slow improvements of gradual correction" (p. 280).[35] The "Preface" moves back and forth, then, between the desire to "fix our language" and the recognition that "to enchain syllables and to lash the wind are equally the undertakings of pride" (pp. 293–4).

Some of this ambivalence is produced by the historical conditions that make a dictionary both desirable and difficult to compose. The only community in which a language might remain stable, Johnson proposes, is an isolated community, "raised a little, and but a little above barbarity" (p. 294): "men thus busied and unlearned, having only such words as common use requires, would perhaps long continue to express the same notions by the same signs" (p. 295). Ironically enough, such a community, without history or the possibility of future change, would not need a dictionary. A culture like England, however, with a far-flung trading network abroad and a complicated division of labor at home, is bound to have a language constantly in flux: "commerce, however necessary, however lucrative, as it depraves the manners, corrupts the language" (p. 294). Yet, the very forces that make the language more mutable also enable a large project like a dictionary to be imagined, since "those who have much leisure to think will always be enlarging the stock of ideas" (p. 295). The very conditions which make it possible to the nation to envisage producing a dictionary – having intellectuals at leisure to think up such an idea – make it impossible for such a project to be wholly successful. Thus, compiling a dictionary emerges as a distinctly modern project, dictated by the demands of an expanding commercial and print culture.

Johnson presents himself as a kind of antihero of that culture. Most famously, he admits his ambitions for the dictionary "were the dreams of a poet doomed at last to wake a lexicographer" (p. 291). Writing a dictionary is a laborious, diffuse, and ill-defined task, and some of the energy of Johnson's preface comes from his search for metaphorical equivalents for such a project. Typically, he draws the metaphors describing his ambitious plans from archaic modes of heroism. Setting out to write the dictionary, he tells us, "I pleased myself with the prospect of the hours I should revel away in feasts of literature, with the obscure recesses of northern learning I should enter and ransack; the treasures with which I expected every search into those neglected mines to reward my labor" (p. 291). The rapaciousness of these images, combined with the anxiety over foreign influences on the English language in the "Preface," has led some readers to link the composition of the dictionary with the concerns surrounding England's contemporaneous colonial expansion.[36] If so, Johnson's own ambivalence about British imperialism shows through, as he continually punctures his own fantasies of power. As his ambitions are stymied, the metaphors deflate into images of hard, repetitive work. A lexicographer is "considered not as the pupil, but the slave of science, the pioneer of literature, doomed only to remove rubbish and clear obstructions from the paths through which learning and genius press forward to conquest and glory, without bestowing a smile on the humble drudge who facilitates their progress" (p. 277). This metaphorical pattern is revealing. It tells us that Johnson was concerned to emphasize the pathos of his undertaking. Yet it also tells us that Johnson imagined his labor in the dictionary as an element of the literary marketplace: "the *English Dictionary* was written with little assistance of the learned, and without any patronage of the great; not in the soft obscurities of retirement or under the shelter of academic bowers, but amidst inconvenience and distraction, in sickness and in sorrow" (p. 297). Johnson takes the role of the professional writer, then, and humanizes it; it is as if he has taken the position of one of Pope's Dunces and argued that its frenzied activity is the noble suffering of hard work.

Johnson's dictionary and the "Preface" that accompanies it are projects of their specific historical moment, but it was not a moment that was to last long. The dictionary, along with Johnson's other great editing projects – the edition of Shakespeare, and the *Lives of the English Poets* – turn out to have been written at a pivotal point in the history of print culture. After the "Age of Johnson" it became nearly impossible for one man to hold the knowledge of his age in his head alone – to draw it out of his personal memory, as Johnson did, more or less, in writing the definitions in his dictionary. After Johnson, knowledge of a rapidly expanding world of books exceeded any single mind.

3

The City

Introduction

For the people of eighteenth-century England, and of the world beyond, London was an awe-inspiring, and sometimes terrifying, phenomenon. Growing at an incredible pace, it held 400,000 people in 1650, and almost a million by 1801. It was ten times larger than any other English city. Throughout the century, its inhabitants pushed out from the old walls of the medieval City of London, building new neighborhoods to the west, east, and on the south side of the Thames. Due to the growth of England's trading empire, almost any kind of commodity, from any part of the world, could be purchased in the city. Complicated new financial structures – stock markets, insurance companies, joint-stock companies – flourished there. To many, it seemed that if anything important of a cultural, economic, or political nature were to happen during their lifetimes, it would happen in London. Of course, eighteenth-century London was also filthy and dangerous, crisscrossed by open sewers and traversed by the polluted Thames, afflicted by both disease and crime. Yet, it was truly a metropolis, the largest city in Europe, drawing innovative practitioners of every field from all over Great Britain and the world.

London as the Renaissance had known it disappeared in 1665 and 1666 in the wake of an epidemic of bubonic plague, closely followed by the Great Fire of London. The plague year of 1665 killed almost one in six Londoners, about 80,000 people. The subsequent fire, in September 1666, destroyed nearly four-fifths of the medieval city, razing more than 373 acres in the city itself, and leaving 100,000 persons homeless. After these calamities, however, the city rebounded with tremendous vigor. Streets were rebuilt and renamed. A new Royal Exchange and Customs House were built. London continued its expansion beyond the walls of the old medieval city, particularly towards the west. Luxurious new environments, such as Cavendish Square, Grosvenor Square, Hanover Square, and New Bond Street, were built, while older areas to the east continued to fill up.[1]

Innovative public places for socializing, such as the pleasure gardens of Ranelagh and Vauxhall, were constructed. Neighborhoods were sharply divided between rich and poor, but the density of the city made it possible for its inhabitants to be familiar with all walks of life.

Yet despite this burst of building, much of the physical landscape of London still differed vastly from what we would consider a modern city. For one thing, open sewers ran through the middle of many streets. All of London's refuse washed down into the Thames, as Swift vividly depicts in *A Description of a City Shower*. For another, the commercial streets of the capital were crowded overhead by signboards advertising the purpose of shops and public houses to the primarily illiterate population. These signs were a visceral part of the city, creating a kind of canopy over the streets. Addison observes in *Spectator* No. 28: "Our streets are filled with blue boars, black swans and red lions; not to mention flying Pigs, and Hogs in Armour, with many other creatures more extraordinary than any in the Desarts of Africk." By the third quarter of the century, however, these distinctive features of London began to disappear. A series of measures, beginning with the Westminster Paving Act of 1762, decreed that the sewers should replaced by gutters running along the sides of the roads, as well as underground drains. Signboards hanging out over the streets were to be replaced by signs on the sides of buildings, presumably as a fire safety measure. These improvements transformed the streets for greater pedestrian use and enjoyment.

The inhabitants of this new city were remarkably diverse. Emigrants from other parts of Great Britain – Scotland, Ireland and Wales – were drawn by the economic and social opportunities offered by the city – particularly, and perhaps most profitably, the Scots after the Act of Union in 1707. Emigrants from Europe made up an important part of the city's population as well. Close to 200,000 Jews lived in the East End, specializing chiefly in the fabric trade and tailoring. A large number of Huguenots, Protestant immigrants from France, made up the core of the East End silk-weaving community. Not all of London's emigrants were white, or voluntary, however; 5,000–10,000 people of African descent, many slaves or former slaves, also lived in the city. Yet most of London's new inhabitants came from the provincial regions of England itself. By 1770, one in eight Englishmen lived in the metropolis. This volatile cultural mixture was an important part of London's allure. Indeed, two of the writers discussed in this section came from elsewhere to establish cosmopolitan, intellectual identities in London: Swift from Ireland, and Boswell from Scotland. Yet, the heterogeneity and fluidity of the city raised important questions about its identity. With so many "foreign" residents, could London really be considered an English city? Or was it a new kind of social phenomenon – a cosmopolitan metropolis detached from the nation as a whole? Conversely, could the social mobility of the city guarantee success based on individual merit and character? Or was success still dependent on national or class allegiances?

The astonishing growth of the city also provoked both celebration and anxiety among those who tried to measure and map the value of its population and its use of resources. One of the first to attempt to chart the increase in the city's population was John Graunt, whose *Natural and Political Observations made upon the Bills of Mortality* (1662) used the death tables (Bills of Mortality) to deduce the causes of the growth and character of London during the seventeenth century. Graunt finds much to champion about the city in the statistics he collects. He observes, for instance:

> That but few are *Murthered*, vz. Not above 86 of the 22950 [sic] which have died of other diseases, and casualties; whereas in Paris few nights scape without their *Tragedie*.
>
> The reasons of this we conceive to be *Two*: One is the *Government*, and *Guard* of the City by *Citizens* themselves, and that alternately. No man settling into a trade for that employment. And the other is, The natural and customary abhorrence of that inhumane *Crime*, and all Bloodshed by most Englishmen: for all that are *Executed* few are for *Murther*.[2]

For Graunt, this set of numbers reveals a moral distinction between Londoners and European city dwellers (even if the English abhorrence of bloodshed does not extend to capital punishment). Yet, while Graunt sees Londoners as the epitome of English virtue, Gregory King, in his *Two Tracts: Natural and Political Observations and Conclusions upon the State and Condition of England* (1696), finds reason to distinguish the urban population from the rural one. He concludes:

> That the reason why each marriage in London produces fewer children than in the country seems to be,
>
> 1 From the more frequent fornications and adulteries.
> 2 From a greater luxury and intemperance.
> 3 From a great intenseness to business.
> 4 From the unhealthfulness of the coal smoke.
> 5 From a great inequality of age between husbands and wives.[3]

Thus the immoral city was pitted against the salubrious countryside, a tendency that was to increase as the century progressed. Often, this distinction was articulated through theories of the rate of growth of the city in relation to the countryside.

Indeed, the city consumed an amazing amount of the nation's resources. Georgian London imported 2,957,000 bushels of flour, 100,000 oxen, 700,000 sheep and lambs, 238,000 pigs, 115,000 bushels of oysters, 14,000,000 mackerel, 160,000 pounds of butter, and 21,000 pounds of cheese a year.[4] The city's size and avidity frightened some observers, who saw in it a kind of immoral and debilitating luxury which would eventually slow population growth. One writes:

> The discouragement to matrimony in London is a grand operating cause of the diminution of the christenings, and consequently of the excess of burials. The unmarried ladies and gentlemen of the city, of moderate fortunes, which are the great bulk, are unable to support the expense of a family with any magnificence; and thereby cannot intermarry together, without retiring from high life, and submitting to relinquish those pleasures of the town, to which their appetites have long been raised; they therefore acquiesce in celibacy; each sex compensating itself, as it can, by other diversions. – Persons also of inferior situation in London, have their taste for pleasure inflamed; and avoid, with caution, the marriage state with their equals.[5]

The unfortunate children who resulted from this luxurious immorality were a source of great concern, and their misery led to the establishment of the Foundling Hospital in 1745, and the Magdalen Hospital for reformed prostitutes in 1758. Yet, despite the apparent debauchery, the city continued to grow. The statistical theorist Richard Price wrote:

> I have observed that London is now...increasing. But it appears that in truth, this is an event more to be dreaded than desired. The more London increases, the more the rest of the kingdom must be deserted; the fewer hands must be left for agriculture; and consequently the loss must be plenty, and the higher the price of all means of subsistence.[6]

Although alarmist, there is some substance to Price's account of population movement. Today, England remains the most urban country in Europe.

London's remarkable growth was sustained by its vigorous economic expansion. Some of Charles II's most important acts after the Restoration were to establish a number of Royal Charters for joint-stock companies (companies with many stock-holding "owners") including the Royal African Company (1672) and the Hudson Bay Company (1670) (the East India Company had been granted a royal charter by Elizabeth I in 1600). After the Glorious Revolution, financial development continued. The Bank of England was founded in 1694. An institution designed to lend money to the government at a favorable interest rate, it created the possibility of national debt. The Stock Exchange was founded during William's reign as well. Other familiar companies, such as the insurance brokers Lloyd's of London, Christie's auction house, Chippendale furniture and Twinings Tea also were founded after 1688. This kind of financial expansion triggered England's first modern financial disaster, the South Sea Bubble of 1720. Another joint-stock company, the South Sea Company had been established in 1711, its business consisting primarily of trading slaves between Africa and the Spanish West Indies. Although the Company was not very profitable, the price of its shares rose continuously, until the "bubble" of speculation collapsed in 1720; an enormous number of people, both ordinary and elite, lost money. The specter of irresponsible investment haunted London for the rest of the decade.

Yet, because of this expansion of foreign trade, the city became a vast and exotic marketplace, where everything could be purchased. With great pride, Addison famously declares in *Spectator* No. 69:

> Our ships are laden with the Harvest of every Climate: Our tables are stored with Spice and Oils, and Wines: Our rooms are filled with Pyramids of *China*, and adorned with the workmanship of *Japan*: Our Morning's-Draught comes to us from the remotest Corners of the Earth: We repair our Bodies by the Drugs of *America*, and repose ourselves under *Indian* Canopies. (1711)

Addison's palpable excitement at having so many of the world's goods at his fingertips was widely shared and has led historians to dub this the era of the first consumer revolution.[7] Women seemed to stand at the center of this revolution since among the novel leisure activities open to them was visiting the multitude of new specialty shops opening in the city. Indeed, the verb "to shop" was only coined in the eighteenth century. Thought to be the most prodigious consumers of luxury items, they were imagined to be both the inspiration and the benefactors of international trade.[8] As Addison says in the same number of the *Spectator*, "The single dress of a Woman of Quality is often the Product of a hundred Climates."

Yet, this new wealth and prosperity went hand-in-hand with great criminality and corruption. If anything could be purchased, anything could be stolen, and petty crime, of the type at which Moll Flanders excels, flourished in London. In Samuel Johnson's dyspeptic poem about the city, *London* (1738), he warns:

Prepare for death, if here at night you roam,
And sign your will before you sup from home.
Some fiery fop, with new commission vain,
Who sleeps on brambles till he kills his man;
Some frolic drunkard, reeling from a feast,
Provokes a broil, and stabs you for a jest.
[...]
In vain, these dangers past, your doors you close,
And hope the balmy blessings of repose:
Cruel with guilt, and daring with despair,
The midnight murderer bursts the faithless bar;
Invades the sacred hour of silent rest,
And leaves, unseen, a dagger in your breast. (ll. 224–9, 236–41)

Along with these violent crimes, prostitution flourished in eighteenth-century London, as amply evidenced by Boswell's *London Journal*. In 1758, one writer observed that at least a hundred women could be found between Temple Bar and Charing Cross, advertising themselves in open windows or doors, and openly accosting men in the street.[9] But, if criminality was rife, the law was draconian. In particular, the punishments for crimes against property became especially severe during the century. One historian notes, "There had been fifty capital offenses in 1689; by 1800 there were four times that number. Many specified death for small-scale theft such as pick-pocketing goods valued more that 1s., or shoplifting items worth more than 5s."[10] The infamous Waltham Black Act of 1724 was responsible for creating fifty of these new capital crimes, mostly involving minor poaching and going in disguise (thought to signal organized criminal activity). If convicted of these crimes, the only way to escape death was, after the Transportation Act of 1719, a period of indentured labor in the West Indies or the North American plantations. Transportation allowed authorities a more flexible approach to crime, but it was perceived by many as both detrimental to the law-abiding citizens of the colonies, who would be forced to cohabit with law-breakers, and beneficial to criminals themselves, who were given the chance to remake themselves, as evidenced again by Defoe's Moll Flanders.

The public was enormously interested in the criminal underworld, devouring criminal biographies, ballads, and broadsides, as well as flocking to Tyburn Hill to witness executions and hear the dying criminal's last words. "A convict reprieved from the gallows at the last minute was likely to return to Newgate to find his own dying speech already being hawked about the streets."[11] As we can see in *The Beggar's Opera*, the place of execution, the gallows at Tyburn, was a site of great excitement. Here, the balance of power between the law and the crowd constantly shifted. In his study of the rise of crimes against property, *Whigs and Hunters*, E. P. Thompson relates the story of one Thomas Reynolds, who was executed for being armed with a pick-axe and for going disguised with "a woman's gown and a woman's straw hat" in 1736: "He was cut down by the executioner… but as the coffin was fastening, he thrust back the lid, upon which the executioner would have tied him up again, but the mob prevented it, and carried him to a house where he vomited three pints of blood, but on giving him a glass of wine, he died."[12]

Thus, the sparkling prosperity of London and a thriving criminal underworld existed side by side, working not in parallel, but in a complicated dynamic of attraction and repulsion. To many it seemed as if the two worlds depended on each other for sustenance. As Bernard Mandeville wrote in his allegorical poem of London, *The Fable of the Bees*: "Vast numbers throng'd the fruitful Hive;/Yet those vast numbers made 'em thrive;/Millions endeavouring to supply/Each other's Lust and Vanity;/While other Millions were employ'd/To see their Handy-works destroy'd[.]" (ll. 31–5).

The writers discussed in this section all took on the challenging project of describing the emerging cultural, social, and economic practices of eighteenth-century London to an audience eager to learn about the new world in which they lived. To represent the novel features of the metropolis, they had to transform existing literary conventions, and to invent new ones. Swift, for example, parodies the poetic forms of georgic and pastoral in his city poems, as Gay does in the generic context of drama and opera. Defoe and Haywood, in contrast, turn to the emerging forms of prose fiction in their accounts of individual adventure in London. Finally, Boswell expands the private dimensions of journal writing to encompass the new elements of metropolitan life. Although it is often unclear whether authors thought of London as an adversary or a muse, the city's expansion certainly changed the way literature was written in the eighteenth century.

Jonathan Swift: *A Description of the Morning* and *A Description of a City Shower*

In his two vibrant poems of everyday London life in the early eighteenth century, Jonathan Swift takes great delight in rewriting the conventions of classical literature so as to emphasize the new conditions of the urban world. *A Description of the Morning* describes the interlocking activities of all classes of city-dwellers as the day begins, while *A Description of a City Shower* gives instructions for "proper" behavior, again for all types of Londoners, under the onslaught of a rainstorm. Both poems were published in the *Tatler*, *Morning* in No. 9, *Shower* in No. 238, a circumstance that points to the casual, yet topical, tone of the two works, as well as to the broad audience Swift expected them to reach. These are not poems that reach for epic or lyrical heights. Rather, they are sharply perceptive, witty accounts of an intensely energetic urban world poised on the brink of chaos and anarchy, one which many of their readers would have recognized immediately. Introducing the author of *A Description of the Morning*, the editor of the *Tatler*, Richard Steele, wrote that the poet had "run into a way perfectly new, and described things as they happen: he never forms fields, or groves where they are not, but makes incidents just as they really appear" (The *Tatler*, No. 9, April 30, 1709).

The opening of *A Description of the Morning* (1709) can be usefully compared to more classical descriptions of dawn breaking over a beautiful landscape, such as this one from Milton's *L'Allegro* (1645):

> Right against the eastern gate,
> Where the great sun begins his state,
> Robed in flames and amber light,
> The clouds in thousand liveries dight;
> While the plowman near at hand
> Whistles over the furrowed land,
> And the milkmaid singeth blithe
> And the mower whets his scythe,
> And every shepherd tells his tale
> Under the hawthorn in the dale. (ll. 59–68)

Swift's poem, in contrast, begins: "Now hardly here and there an hackney-coach/Appearing, show'd the ruddy morn's approach./Now Betty from her master's bed had flown,/and softly stole to discompose her own." The sun here, rather than being clothed in flame and attended by elaborately costumed clouds, is simply ruddy, an adjective with working-class, and even drunken, connotations. And, instead of the industrious openness of the singing milkmaid, and the story-telling shepherd, Betty's first task of the new day is to disguise the fact that she has been sleeping with her employer; like many of the poem's characters, she spends the morning concealing the activities of the night before. In this, and in the discordant urban, sounds of the poem ("The small-coal man was heard with cadence deep,/Till drown'd in shriller notes of chimney sweep," ll. 11–12), the poem reminds us how much morning in London differs from the rural mornings enshrined in pastoral poetry.

A Description of a City Shower (1710) takes on a different set of poetic conventions. Written "In Imitation of Virgil's Georgics," the poem begins as an urban version of those poetic books of advice to farmers and other agricultural workers: "Careful observers may fortell the hour/(By sure prognostics) when to dread a show'r[.]" It gives its readers signs to look out for ("the pensive cat gives o'er/Her frolics" "your shooting corns"), and tells them what to do ("go not far to dine"). Later, the poem uses an extended mock-heroic simile to delineate the not particularly heroic behavior of a particular type of Londoner.

> Box'd in a chair the beau impatient sits,
> While spouts run clatt'ring o'er the roof by fits;
> And ever and anon with frightful din
> The leather sounds, he trembles from within.
> So when Troy chair-men bore the wooden steed,
> Pregnant with Greeks impatient to be freed,
> (Those bully Greeks, who, as the moderns do,
> Instead of paying chair-men, run them thro.)
> Laocoon struck the outside with his spear,
> And each imprison'd hero quaked for fear. (ll. 43–52)

The comparison does not seem very flattering. Whereas the Greek soldiers inside the Trojan horse are scared of the great warrior Laocoon, the eighteenth-century beau is frightened by a common natural phenomenon. Yet, simply by juxtaposing the two scenes, Swift imbues the rain-drenched city with a combative energy similar to the epics of the Trojan War, if not their accompanying heroism. Swift conveys this energy using a full sensory spectrum. The city provides not only visual and aural sensations, but also olfactory and even physical ones: "Returning home at night, you'll find the sink/Strike your offended sense with double stink/[...]/Old aches throb, your hollow tooth will rage" (ll. 5–6, 9–10), he advises.

Both poems are remarkable, almost anthropological, in their depiction of a wide swathe of London's inhabitants. *A Description of the Morning* concentrates on urban laborers of various sorts: maids, apprentices, chimney-sweeps, and prisoners put to work stealing for the turnkey. *A Description of a City Shower* includes characters from all walks of life: laundresses, politicians, ladies of leisure, even a "needy poet." Both poems are structured deceptively like lists, straightforward accounts of all the things going on in the city. Yet the poems also work to reveal the connections between a diversity of Londoners, the structures that join them together as an urban polity or, at least, a collectivity. In both instances, this binding is accomplished most obviously through natural phenomena: morning, rainfall. The shower ensures, for instance, that "various kinds by various fortunes led" will "commence acquaintance underneath a shed" (ll. 39–40). One might also argue that the people of London are brought together by particular patterns of (mis)behavior: dissembling about the night before in *Morning*; dissembling to avoid the rain in *City Shower*.

At the end of the latter poem, however, Swift sketches a more elaborate, if not entirely positive, vision of the infrastructure holding London together. The powerful rainstorm sweeps the city's debris into the sewers that flowed down the middle of many of London's streets (the open sewers that were to be abolished by the Paving Act of 1762).

> Filth of all hues and odors seem to tell
> What street they sail'd from, by their sight and smell.
> They, as each torrent drives, with rapid force
> From Smithfield, or St Pulchre's shape their course.
> And in huge confluent join at Snow-hill ridge,
> Fall from the conduit prone to Holborn-bridge. (ll. 55–60)

The garbage, then, channeled through the infrastructure of the sewer system (the "swelling kennels"), provides a map of the city to those who read its "hues and odours" – from Smithfield east of the old City, to its final destination in the Thames. Of course, the civic value of such a map is equivocal. What the sewer brings together are the bodies of dead animals and the "sweepings from the butchers' stalls, dung, guts and blood." Yet the force of this image, as its "torrent drives" through the center of urban life, provides a potent metaphor for the crowded, jostling, diversity of human bodies in London itself: distasteful, perhaps, but undeniably powerful.

Daniel Defoe, *Moll Flanders*

In *Moll Flanders* (1722), the demands of representing the new world of early eighteenth-century London are intimately enmeshed with the innovations in prose narrative that produced the novel as a genre. Indeed, this narrative of a female orphan (her mother is a transported criminal) who marries five times, sinks to a life of (quite successful) crime and prostitution, is transported herself to North America, returns, undergoes a religious conversion, and ends her life in middle-class comfort provides a near-perfect illustration of the representational mode Ian Watt famously dubbed "formal realism." The elements of formal realism, according to Watt, constitute "a set of narrative procedures which are so commonly found together in the novel, and so rarely in other literary genres, that they may be regarded as typical of the form itself." These procedures support:

> The premise, or primary convention, that the novel is a full and authentic report of human experience, and is therefore under an obligation to satisfy its reader with such details of the story as the individuality of the actors concerned, the particulars of the times and places of their actions, details which are presented through a more largely referential use of language than is common in other literary forms.[13]

In other words, novels are written according to a set of conventions that together make up a literary form – a form that we read as representing "real life." For much of *Moll Flanders*, Defoe gives substance to those forms by mining the particularities of the early eighteenth-century city.

For example, Defoe renders Moll's mid-life career as a thief "realistic" by directing our attention to the "particulars of time and place" involved in picking pockets in London. After robbing a little girl of her gold necklace, Moll describes her escape route: "I went thro' into *Bartholomew Close*, then turn'd round to another passage that goes into *Long-lane*, so away into *Charterhouse-Yard* and out into *St John's Street*, then crossing into *Smithfield*, went down *Chick-lane* and into *Field-lane* to *Holbourn-bridge*, when mixing with the Crowd of People usually passing there, it was not possible to have been found out" (p. 151).[14] Like Swift, Defoe is fascinated by the network of streets linking London together as a polity, making knowledge of those streets part of Moll's talent for survival. The juxtaposition of the specific place names with the anonymity of the crowd that Moll joins creates a distinctly urban setting.

Although it is certainly not devoid of metaphors and other figurative devices, *Moll Flanders* does adhere to the early novel's norm of unadorned, idiomatic language through most of the narrative. Indeed, the framing preface emphasizes this quality by claiming that Moll's language was even more colloquial and crude before the editor revised it. What we read is "her own tale in modester Words than she told it at first; the Copy that first came to Hand, having been written in Language more like one still in Newgate, than one grown Penitent and Humble, as she afterwards pretends to be" (p. 3). This disclaimer alerts the reader to the tension between ordinary speech and demands of literary representation.

The question of how the novel proves to us that Moll is an individual is particularly interesting. In many early novels, characterization begins by giving a protagonist an ordinary, rather than a typological or allegorical, name, Robinson Crusoe, say, or Pamela Andrews. Yet, Moll Flanders is not Moll's real name, but rather the "street name" of a successful criminal (who may or may not be our Moll), which she adopts for the course of the narrative. She explains her motives for hiding her given name from the reader in the first paragraph of the novel:

> My True Name is so well known in the Records, or Registers at Newgate, and in the Old-Baily [sic], and there are some things of such Consequence still depending there, relating to my particular Conduct, that it is not to be expected I should set my Name, or the Account of my Family to this Work; perhaps, after my Death it may be better known; at present it would not be proper, no, not tho' a general Pardon should be issued, even without Exceptions and reserve of Persons or Crimes. (p. 7)

The individual who is *not* named Moll Flanders, then, flourishes in the space between her official existence in the legal and bureaucratic records of the prisons and courts, and her unrecorded, extra-legal activities, whose consequences may still be pending. Indeed, Moll several times exploits the difference between herself and "Moll Flanders" to maintain her innocence, as when she tries to explain her presence in Newgate to her "Lancashire" (and favorite) husband; "I told him I far'd the worse for being taken in the Prison for one *Moll Flanders*, who was a famous successful Thief, that all of them had heard of, but none of them had ever seen, but that *as he knew well* was none of my Name" (p. 233). Thus Moll, as an individual, is defined only by her actions; names serve only as temporary and strategic masks. In this, the novel explores the creative possibilities of anonymity and self-fashioning. Despite her inability (or refusal) to claim a name, to draw support and self-definition from a family or community, Moll is able to make her way in the world through her wits and self-composure. The self-interested, socially fluid world of London helps make this possible.

At the same time, however, Moll's caginess about naming herself, even to her favorite husband, also demonstrates her resemblance to actual eighteenth-century thieves. As one popular criminal biography says of the pick-pocket Anne Holland:

> This was her right name, tho' she went by the Names of *Andrews, Charlton, Edwards, Goddard,* and *Jackson*, which is very usual for Thieves to change them, because falling often-times into the Hands of Justice, and as often convicted of some Crimes, yet thereby it appears sometimes that when

they are arraign'd at the Bar again, that is the first Time they have been taken, and the first Crime whereof they have ever been accus'd.[15]

Thus, although Moll Flanders does not appear to have been modeled on any particular "real-life" criminal, Defoe clearly drew on this popular, and profuse, genre of nonfiction narratives for his novel. Part of the attraction of such accounts derived from their alleged authenticity. Although they may have been no more accurate than the fictional *Moll Flanders*, they gave off the allure that "true-crime" books or "reality TV" still exert today. It is this fascination with the "truth" that Defoe is trying to appropriate for his novel when he asserts in the preface that "The Author is here suppos'd to be writing her own History" (p. 3).

And yet *Moll Flanders* is designed to be not only truthful but also morally instructive. This is a difficult task, as the writer of the preface acknowledges, in a narrative primarily concerned with the excitement and rewards of a life of crime and deception.

> It is suggested there cannot be the same Life, the same Brightness and Beauty, in relating the penitent Part as in the criminal Part: If there is any Truth in that Suggestion, I must be allow'd to say, 'tis because there is not the same taste and relish in the Reading, and indeed it is too true that the difference lyes not in the real worth of the Subject so much as in the Gust and Palate of the Reader. (p. 4)

Here, Defoe lays the problem explicitly on the reader's plate: only an immoral reader would enjoy Moll's immoral activities more than her moral ones. Over the years, readers have wrestled with the issues raised by the moral oscillation of the narrative.[16] Is Moll's brief description of her religious conversion, coming as it does after such a lengthy description of her successful criminality, convincing, even to the morally inclined reader? Whatever the reader decides, however, the few pages describing Moll's prison conversion are important in that they represent the novel's most sustained attempt to describe the interior process of psychological change.

In one of her few uses of metaphorical language, Moll describes the deadening effect of life in prison. "Like the Waters in the Caveties, and Hollows of Mountains, which petrifies and turns into Stone whatever they are suffered to drop upon, so the continual conversing with such a Crew of Hell-Hounds as I was, ... had the same common Operation upon me as upon other People. I degenerated into Stone" (p. 217). Drawing from the natural world, Moll finds a way of describing the impact of social environment upon character.[17] Using same oppositions of hardness and fluidity, and again emphasizing the duration of the process, she then articulates her developing ability to reflect on her own actions.

> Guilt begain to flow in upon my Mind: In short, I began to think, and to think is one real Advance from Hell to Heaven; all that Hellish harden'd state and temper of Soul, which I have said so much of before, is but a deprivation of Thought; he that is restor'd to his Power of thinking, is restor'd to himself. (p. 220)

Here, with the help of religious inspiration, Defoe asserts that the intellectual capacity of the individual reasserts itself against the formative powers of the surrounding culture. And, given the evidence of her intelligence in the rest of the novel, we might well believe that, in being restored to thought, Moll is being restored to herself, albeit in a more virtuous form. These passages emphasize a gradual, interior process over any sudden exterior event in promoting psychological development – a narrative mode that was to become vital to the later eighteenth-century novel.

In the rest of *Moll Flanders*, the majority of the moral issues that might trouble the modern reader about the novel have to do not with Moll's life as a criminal, but rather with her life as a woman – her movements not as an economic agent, but as a sexual one. The first part of the narrative concerns Moll's misadventures in the marriage market, and her growing realization of the importance of money, rather than love, to conjugal unions. These sections may serve, Moll hopes, as "a Storehouse of useful warning to those that read" (p. 210). Another puzzling aspect of the novel is Moll's attitude to her many children, whom she loves and leaves and loves again seemingly at random. While at one level, these incidents illustrate the slightly less intimate relationship early modern mothers may have had with their children, many of whom were destined to die in infancy, it also manifests Moll's strategic sense of morality. As Virginia Woolf put it, "From the outset the burden of proving her right to exist is laid upon her. She has to depend entirely upon her own wits and judgment, and to deal with each emergency as it arises by a rule-of-thumb morality which she has forged in her own head."[18] One episode, however, illustrates that, even for Moll, a self-forged morality cannot negotiate all situations. She finds herself incapable of continuing her otherwise comfortable marriage to her own brother once she discovers their relationship. The novel's interdiction of incest (like the interdiction of cannibalism in *Robinson Crusoe*) manifests itself as a physical imperative; Moll says, "everything added to make Cohabiting with him the most nauseous thing to me in the world...I could almost as willingly have embraced a Dog, as have let him offer anything of that kind to me" (p. 78). Aside from its sheer shock value, then, the incest episode makes the limits of individualized morality clear, particularly in the realm of sexual relations.[19] Significantly, this episode takes place in England's North American colonies. It might be said to illustrate that those seemingly untrammeled and anarchic spaces present Moll with greater dangers than the autonomy and freedom of early eighteenth-century London.

Eliza Haywood, *Fantomina: Or, Love in a Maze*

Like *Moll Flanders* (1725), Eliza Haywood's novella describes the way London allows a young woman to escape the strictures of the social position into which she is born. As in Defoe's novel, we never learn the heroine's true name; she moves through the narrative under her self-chosen, and appropriate, alias: Fantomina. A "Young Lady of distinguished Birth, Beauty, Wit and Spirit," she carries out an elaborate sexual adventure, taking on four separate identities, in pursuit of a single man, Beauplaisir, who never realizes that he has slept with the same woman on every occasion. Although it ends on a much more pessimistic note than *Moll Flanders*, *Fantomina* first explores the joys of self-invention in the diverse, anonymous, spaces of the eighteenth-century city.

Eliza Haywood reinvented her own life by leaving her husband of ten years in Norfolk, and moving to London to become a professional writer. There, she produced plays, translations, political propaganda, and a widely read periodical, the *Female Spectator*, in a career that extended into the 1750s. She achieved her greatest success, however, in the emerging genres of the novel and short prose fiction. For example, Haywood's first novel, *Love in Excess* (1719), went through four editions before 1724. This narrative, like Haywood's other works of the 1720s, is a complicated story of multiple seductions, focusing on the allure and danger of sexual pleasure for young women. Indeed, most of Haywood's early novels record the suffering of women who have been seduced and betrayed. Fantomina differs from those works in that it is the heroine who sets out to seduce a male object of desire. The popularity of her works, and their lack of elevated content, earned Haywood the honor of appearing among the hack writers of *The Dunciad* (she is a prize in a scatological competition between two booksellers). In a note to the poem, Pope describes her as one of "those shameless scriblers . . . who reveal the faults and misfortunes of both sexes, to the ruin or disturbance of publick fame, or private happiness." Despite these characteristics, or perhaps because of them, Haywood's novels were extremely popular.[20]

These narratives do not adhere to the conventions of "formal realism" in the same way as *Moll Flanders* does. Their heroines have names out of romances rather than real life, such as "Idalia" or "Cleomelia"; although *Fantomina* takes place specifically in London, other Haywood narratives often take place in exotic, but ill-defined, locales. They use extravagant and hyperbolic language, rather than a measured and quotidian tone. For these reasons, prose fiction by Haywood and by her near contemporaries Delarivier Manley and Aphra Behn, has long been left out of standard histories of the novel. Recently, however, revisionist accounts have argued for the importance of these less "realistic" forms of "amatory fiction" to the genre throughout the eighteenth century.[21] Despite their differences, however, Haywood's narratives, including *Fantomina*, share one formal characteristic with novels like *Moll Flanders*. Because they both admit the pleasures of sexuality and other forms of transgression, and delineate the dangers of such behavior, they make it difficult to decide whether they function primarily as cautionary tales, or as titillating, even subversive, explorations of socially unacceptable behavior.

The heterogeneity and anonymity of the public spaces of London, particularly its sites of entertainment, are central to Fantomina's project, and to her success. Her adventures begin when she arrives in London after a childhood spent in the country. During a night at the theater, the relative social freedom of the setting allows her to sit near enough to observe one of "those Women who make sale of their Favours,"[22] and the men who flirt with her. The sight of men behaving so differently with this woman than they do with her fosters Fantomina's curiosity about what it would be like to be such a woman. Free from parental supervision, she acts on this curiosity, and goes to the theater the next night dressed as a prostitute, mimicking the behavior she has witnessed.

In this attire, she is able to attain her desired result: she becomes Beauplaisir's mistress, under the name Fantomina, while also continuing her ordinary life as a well-born young woman. But this is only the beginning of Haywood's narrative of seduction and disguise. Beauplaisir soon tires of Fantomina's charms – as the novella implies all men will do when they have made a sexual conquest. She then assumes three subsequent identities to keep his attentions: that of a Bristol maid, of a widow, and finally that of another woman of the town, Incognita. Beauplaisir enjoys each in turn, seemingly unaware that they are all the same woman, whom he also knows in her "true" identity. His ignorance is puzzling, and Haywood offers two complementary explanations for it. She makes clear the limitations that class position places on individual identity. Beauplaisir "looked in [Fantomina's] Face, and fancied, as many others had done, that she very much resembled that Lady whom she really was; but the vast Disparity there appeared between their Characters, prevented him from entertaining even the most distant Thought that they could be the same." Just as importantly, Haywood reveals Fantomina's genius in the art of disguise:

> Besides the Alteration which the Change of Dress made in her, she was so admirably skilled in the Art of feigning, that she had the Power of putting on almost what Face she pleased, and knew so exactly how to form her Behavior to the Character she represented, that all the Comedians at both Playhouses are infinitely short of her Performances: She could vary her very Glances, tune her Voice to Accents the most different imaginable from those in which she spoke when she appeared herself. (p. 795)

Here, Fantomina is aligned with the figure of the actress, and the space of the theater, her self-transformations dubbed both an art and a power. Yet, throughout the narrative, her intelligence and skill are linked troublingly to her abject pursuit of Beauplaisir: her art is directed to a single goal, in which she can never achieve final success. Much of the tension in the narrative thus results from the unstable balance of power between the lovers.

Fantomina is subtitled, "A Masquerade Novel," and the social conventions of the masquerade play an important role in the narrative. Like the theater, public masquerades, admission into which was guaranteed with a ticket and a costume, offered a site for greater social mixing than ordinary life. Masquerades were tremendously popular throughout the period, as Terry Castle points out:

> During the second and third decades of the century, Count Heidegger's elaborate masquerades at the Haymarket drew up to a thousand antic "masks" weekly. Later, public masquerades at Vauxhall and Ranelagh, the Dog and Duck Gardens, Almack's, and the Pantheon, Mrs. Cornelys's extravaganzas at Carlisle House, and those prodigious constumed assemblies held in celebration of special events – the Jubilee of 1749, the King of Denmark's visit in 1768, the Shakespeare Jubilee of 1769 – attracted crowds numbering in the thousands. . . . Up to a point, like the protean City itself (with which it was metaphorically connected) [the masquerade] was indeed a "strange Medley" of persons – a rough mix of high and low.[23]

Due to this seemingly unregulated mixture of persons, masquerades were also figured as sites of promiscuity and sexual danger. Indeed, Haywood wrote a narrative for the *Female Spectator* about a young woman raped at a masquerade after going home with a stranger dressed in the same costume as the chaperone with whom she'd arrived.

Fantomina, too, ultimately finds that her female body makes her vulnerable. While she moves with great freedom when she employs the rules of the masquerade in the unregulated social spaces of London, there is one thing she cannot disguise. Her discovery that she has been impregnated by Beauplaisir coincides with her mother's return to London to oversee her behavior. She tries to conceal her condition from her mother "by eating little, lacing prodigious straight, and the advantages of a great Hoop-Petticoat." But when she attends one last ball at Court, this time in her real identity, she succumbs to labor pains. Her uncontrollable physical pain rips away the layers of disguise that have won her freedom and pleasure. Fantomina's mother finds out the name of her lover, Beauplaisir takes the child, but refuses to marry Fantomina, and she is exiled to a French monastery as punishment for her transgression. An ambiguous tale, *Fantomina* both illustrates the freedom offered by the mixed social spaces of London, and delineates the limits of those freedoms for even the most artful young woman.

John Gay, *The Beggar's Opera*

The Beggar's Opera (1728) was one of the great success stories of the eighteenth century. Durably popular, it ran for a remarkable 62 performances in its first season. There were only two theaters with royal licenses for legitimate operation in London in the 1720s: Drury Lane, run by Colley Cibber; and Lincoln's Inn Fields, run by John Rich. When Gay's play was produced at Lincoln's Inn Fields, it was such a hit that people said "it made Rich gay, and Gay rich." The play's fame and influence were so great that images from it were reproduced on other objects, such as fans, playing cards, and decorative screens (one of the first instances of the "spin off" products now so common for movies or television shows). In the several scenes William Hogarth painted from the play, the viewer can see more of its effects on offstage life. In one, the Duke of Bolton, who fell in love with Lavinia Fenton, the actress playing Polly, can be seen gazing adoringly at her from the audience. The play's popularity continued throughout the eighteenth century and into the nineteenth, although by the later eighteenth century Macheath is neither hung nor reprieved: his sentence is commuted to three years on the prison hulks and he eventually reforms. The play is perhaps most famous these days as the source for the Brecht/Weill musical, *The Threepenny Opera*, and its well-known song "Mack the Knife," later memorably sung by Frank Sinatra.

The play belongs to the hybrid genre known as the "ballad opera." That is, it sets new words to familiar ballad tunes. On one level, this works to poke fun at Italian opera, which was very popular in London during this period. On another, it expresses a kind of oral nationalism, asserting that English songs are as good as Italian arias. Assuming that his audience knew the traditional words to the tunes, Gay often uses this technique to communicate the brutality and immorality of the city through the ironic juxtaposition of cynical words and light-hearted or sentimental tunes. Thus, at the end of the play, the imprisoned Macheath sings a bitter song about class hierarchies to the tune of the Renaissance love song, "Greensleeves."[24]

Like *Moll Flanders*, the play draws on the eighteenth-century fascination with criminals and the intricacies of a life of crime. Peachum is often seen as a version of the famous criminal, Jonathan Wild, hanged in 1720, who both fenced stolen goods, and "peached" thieves to the authorities when he was dissatisfied with them; Macheath can be read as a version of the criminal Jack Sheppard, who made several notorious escapes from Newgate. The play compellingly represents the details of a historically specific criminal milieu, particularly the workings of the great prison, Newgate. Through most of the eighteenth century, the prison system in England was very different than the one today. Rather than being places where wrongdoers were reformed, prisons were holding areas, where the accused waited for judgment and punishment. Prisons were thus chaotic spaces; there was no separation of the sexes, or standards for cleanliness. They were ruled over by governors and their underlings, who expected to profit from their position by selling liquor and other goods to prisoners, and by facilitating the extortion and prostitution that went on inside prison walls. In *The Beggar's Opera*, the corrupt Lockit occupies this position. By setting so much of its action within Newgate's walls, and revealing the similarities and close allegiance between the seemingly law-abiding Lockit and the criminal Peachum, the play begs the question of the difference between the prison and the city outside it: both appear to run by the same rules.

Often, the play has been read as a political satire, specifically attacking the Prime Minister Robert Walpole and his system of government. Walpole has been called the first prime minister because he was the first to make that office the principal seat of governmental power. He pioneered the cabinet system of government, consulting his ministers in private and insisting that they follow his policies or resign. Walpole held power for a very long time, 1721–42, in part because he was a consummate politician, using patronage and bribery to maintain his position, and in part because the kings he served under, George I and George II, were weak and unintelligent. He was sometimes called the "screenmaster general," because he screened or protected his friends and allies from harm and prosecution, particularly during the South Sea Bubble. Walpole had no interest in, or even respect for, artistic production. He made sure that the poet laureateship was awarded on the basis of a poet's willingness to write propaganda in the government's favor, rather than artistic merit: thus Colley Cibber became Laureate, while Alexander Pope never did. For this reason, Walpole was hated by the major satirists of the day, all Tories, and versions of him appear as villains in many of their important texts: *Gulliver's Travels, The Dunciad,* and *The Beggar's Opera.*[25]

In *The Beggar's Opera*, the specter of Walpole appears in several characters. Most obviously, Peachum can be seen as a version of the prime minister. From a safe spot "behind the scenes" of criminal activity, he orchestrates who will profit from it, and who will not. His only loyalty, it seems, is to the accumulation of money and to maintaining his own position of power. He draws the comparison explicitly himself, advising Lockit: "In one respect indeed, our employment may be reckoned dishonest, because, like great statesmen, we encourage those who betray their friends" (II, x). Yet, Macheath, too, takes on aspects of Walpole's perfidiousness. Captain of a gang of highwaymen, all his charm and gallantry cannot hide the fact that he is a thief. Thus, the two opposing forces in the play, Peachum and Macheath, while compelling in their own right, are allegorical in a multiple sense; they reminded the eighteenth-century audience of actual notorious criminals, and also of the ruling government. Indeed, the correspondence between the criminal underworld and politics is one of the central insights and pleasures of the play. As Lockit sings, in a moment of defeat: "Ourselves, like the great, to secure a retreat,/When matters require it, must give up our gang" (III, xi). At times, the different consequences of criminal activity for rich and poor become a point of sharp critique, most explicitly in Macheath's Newgate lament:

> Since laws were made for every degree,
> To curb vice in others, as well as me,
> I wonder we han't better company
> Upon Tyburn tree!
> But gold from law can take out the sting;
> And if rich men, like us, were to swing,
> 'Twould thin the land, such numbers to string
> Upon Tyburn tree! (III, xiii)

More often, however, the comparison is made without a sustained critique of class inequity.

There is another manner, however, in which the two opposing camps of the play, Peachum's and Macheath's, play out a conflict between two socioeconomic systems: between an emergent system of commercial alliances and information, as practiced by Peachum, and an older system of charisma and generosity, as practiced by Macheath.[26] Although we might expect the underworld to be an anarchic place, it is actually tightly controlled by Peachum's information and profit gathering systems. On his first entrance, Peachum is carrying "a large book of accounts." He then proceeds to tally up the criminals in his domain, reckoning whether they are worth more money to him freely practicing their trades, or turned in for a reward.

> I hate a lazy rogue, by whom one can get nothing till he is hanged. A register of the gang. (Reading.) "Crook-fingered Jack." A year and a half in the service. Let me see how much the stock owes to his industry: one, two, three, four, five gold watches, and seven silver ones. A mighty clean-handed fellow!... "Wat Dreary, alias Brown Will," an irregular dog, who hath an underhand way of disposing of his goods. I'll try him only for a session or two longer upon his good behavior. (I, iii)

Rarely leaving his own house, Peachum never has to exert brute force to turn a profit; rather, his power comes from intelligence, good account keeping, and careful surveillance: an early version of an information economy. Treating his criminal organization as a company, in which the stock is increased by industrious workers, Peachum's "honor," to which he alludes on many occasions, derives from what might be called a bourgeois, or "middle-class," code of privacy, safe investments, the accumulation of profits, and alliances made on the basis of mutual interest.

Macheath, by contrast, rules his gang by virtue of his strength, personal charisma, and generosity. The gang believes, as Jemmy Twitcher says, that "what we win...is our own by the law of arms and the right of conquest" (II, i). Unlike Peachum, they act on the principle that the purpose of money and goods is their expenditure. Matt of the Mint proclaims: "The world is avaricious, and I hate avarice. A covetous fellow, like a jackdaw, steals what he was never made to enjoy, for the sake of hiding it. These are the robbers of mankind, for money was made for the freehearted and generous" (II. i). Macheath's honor resembles an older, aristocratic code, in that it derives from his sexual and financial liberty and his loyalty to members of his gang. The play implies, however, that this mode of life is ultimately dependent on Peachum's good will. In order to turn a profit, the highwaymen need a good fence for their stolen goods, and this puts them in Peachum's power.

Furthermore, the loyalty of the gang cannot hold against the allure of gold, and Jemmy Twitcher finally turns Macheath in. Gay thus suggests that, despite the appeal of an aristocratic way of life, capitalist values will triumph. As Macheath says of the outcome of the play: "*T*'Tis a plain proof that the world is all alike, and that even our gang can no more trust one another than other people" (III, xiv).

The only things Macheath both accumulates, and spends freely, of course, are women. While he seduces Polly, Lucy, Jenny Diver, and any number of others, and moves on, they cling to him, ultimately helping to determine his fate. The representation of women in the play is somewhat contradictory. On the one hand, women are imaged as coins, units of value to be exchanged or accumulated. As Mrs. Peachum sings:

> A maid is like the golden ore,
> Which hath guineas intrinsical in't
> Whose worth is never known before
> It is tried and impressed at the mint.
> A wife's like a guinea in gold,
> Stamped with the name of her spouse,
> Now here, now there, is bought or sold,
> And is current in every house. (I, vi)

On the other hand, women are presented as powerful, unstable forces, the cause of men's accumulation of other goods, and likely to betray them. As Lockit sings: "What gudgeons are we men!/Ev'ry woman's easy prey./ Though we have felt the hook, again/ We bite, and they betray" (III, i). Since Macheath consistently seduces and betrays women, rather than they him, the latter depiction seems questionable. Nonetheless, the two representations jostle for primacy in the play. Polly Peachum seems to transcend both characterizations, however; her love for Macheath is pure and unwavering. The play's eighteenth-century success seems to have depended a great deal on the poignant appeal of its heroine.

The Beggar's Opera takes it name from the fact that it is supposed to have been devised by a beggar, who proposes the play to an actor in the first scene, and appears with him at the end to assess the results. In the penultimate scene of the play, the beggar and the player debate the virtues of morality and generic form. The beggar argues that Macheath should be hanged, providing the play "a most excellent moral": "that the lower sort of people have their vices in a degree as well as the rich, and that they are punished for them" (III, xvi). The player insists that operas must have happy endings, and that "the taste of the town" demands that Macheath be reprieved at the last minute. The player's views prevail, and this self-conscious ending raises a number of interesting questions about *The Beggar's Opera*'s status as satire or social critique. At several points in the play, characters insist that "all the world is alike," and that "it is difficult to determine whether (in the fashionable vices) the fine gentlemen imitate the gentlemen of the road, or the gentlemen of the road the fine gentlemen" (III, xvi). In this oddly homogeneous society, where can the beggar, or the playwright, find a position from which to criticize these urban vices? When the beggar capitulates to the player's wishes, he seems to give up the possibility of the play reforming "the town." By blaming the ending on the audience's sympathy for an immoral hero, the play casts doubt on our own capacity for being educated by satire. Indeed, the play has often been categorized as a comedy rather than a satire, and the ending demonstrates that it is quite self-conscious about its own genre and social function. Thus, *The Beggar's Opera* is a reflection of the city in a double sense: it records versions of contemporary heroes and practices, and it also addresses the tastes of contemporary audiences.

James Boswell, *London Journal*, 1762–3

I then sallied forth to the Piazzas in rich flow of animal spirits and burning with fierce desire. I met two very pretty little girls who asked me to take them with me. "My dear girls," said I, "I am a poor fellow. I can give you no money. But if you choose to have a glass of wine and my company and let us be gay and obliging to each other without money, I am your man." They agreed with great good humour. So back to [The Shakespeare's Head] I went…We were shown into a good room and had a bottle of sherry before us in a minute. I surveyed my seraglio and found them both good subjects for amorous play. I toyed with them and drank about and sung *Youth's the Season* and thought myself Captain Macheath; and then I solaced my existence with them, one after another, according to their seniority.

London Journal, May 19, 1763

In the journal James Boswell kept during 1762 and 1763, he records his confrontation with both the physical realities of London, and its pull on the imagination through literary and dramatic representation. In this instance, and in many like it, his pleasure in enjoying the "women of the town" is clearly matched by the pleasure of comparing himself to Gay's dashing urban anti-hero (in a pub aptly named after a literary giant), and using the flowery language of romance ("I solaced my existence"). By the second half of the eighteenth century, at least for Boswell, the two sorts of engagement with the metropolis are so intertwined as to be inseparable.

In another instance, he compares his own encounter with a prostitute to the character Sir John Brute's similar adventure in Vanbrugh's *The Provok'd Wife* (Friday, March 25). Boswell seems to believe that the city will transform him into a version of these literary heroes. After only a few days in London, he declares: "Since I came up, I have begun to acquire a composed genteel character very different from the rattling uncultivated one which for some time past I have been fond of. I have discovered that we may be in some degree whatever character we choose. Besides, practice forms a man to anything" (November 21, 1762).

Boswell's belief in the power of the city to radically remake his identity is particularly well revealed by the journal form.[27] Introducing the journal, he says: "It will give me a habit of application and improve me in expression; and knowing that I am to record my transactions will make me more careful to do well. Or if I should go wrong, it will assist me in resolutions of doing better." Boswell feels himself particularly in need of transformation due to his family situation and his regional identity. Born the heir of Alexander Boswell, the eighth Laird of Auchinleck, a prosperous and respectable Scottish judge, he rejected both the law as a profession and the comfortable life of the Scottish gentry. He came to London looking for excitement through a commission in the Footguards and association with literary and theatrical personages. The journal provides him with a means of articulating this split with his father. As he writes in December 1762: "To get away from home, where I lived as a boy, was my great object. It was irksome beyond measure to be a young laird in the house of a father much different from me, of a mind perfectly sound, and who thought that if I was not a man of business, I was good for nothing."

Once in London, however, Boswell finds that his Scottish identity is not particularly easy to shed. The city was in the grip of widespread anti-Scottish feeling. The Jacobite rising of 1745, in which supporters of the Stuart pretender to the throne, Charles Edward, many of them Scottish Highlanders, had fought their way almost to London, had taken place in recent memory. The controversial prime minister, John Stuart, Earl of Bute, was Scottish, and often attacked for favoring other Scots. Boswell maintains an ambivalent attitude towards his own Scottish identity. At times, he experiences fiercely nationalist feelings, as when he observes two Highland officers being hissed at and pelted with apples in the theater (December 8, 1762): "My heart warmed to my countrymen," he records, "my Scotch blood boiled with indignation." At other moments, as in his famous disclaimer on meeting Johnson – "indeed I come from Scotland, but I cannot help it" – Boswell appears much less comfortable with his cultural heritage (May 16, 1763). In this ambivalence, the journal captures the perspective of a member of a marginal ethnicity struggling to find a place in the dominant society of his era. It reveals that London culture oscillated between being a truly metropolitan community, in which all intelligent and energetic members would be welcome, and a more circumscribed English world, which continued to exclude members of traditionally subordinate groups.

Boswell's journal of these years was believed lost until 1930, when it was discovered in Fettercairn House in Scotland. It was never intended to be a purely private document. It was written for his friend John Johnston and sent to him in more or less weekly bundles. Thus, Boswell could fall days behind, and then catch up at his leisure; this extra time perhaps accounts for the journal's many highly wrought set pieces of dialogue and adventure. The journal was complemented by daily memoranda, these clearly intended to be private, which primarily consist of Boswell's instructions to himself. The memorandum for December 31, 1762, for example, reads in part: "At six, Sheridan's. Be like Sir Richard Steele. Think on Prologue [he wanted to write the prologue for a play by Mrs. Sheridan], and of being in the Blues, and so pushing your fortune fine. Write to Somerville about Kirk. Study calm and deliberate." Throughout his time in London, Boswell devotes almost as much attention to the form of his journal as he does to its content. For example, he writes:

> I am really surprised at the coolness and moderation with which I am proceeding. God grant that I may continue to do well, which will make me happy, and all my friends satisfied. (I have all along been speaking in the perfect tense, as if I was writing the history of some distant period. I shall after this use the present often, as most proper. Indeed, I will not confine myself, but take whichever is most agreeable at the time.) (December 2, 1762)

Here, Boswell connects his composition to the sense of transformation he feels in London. His confidence about which tense to use seems to spring directly from the "coolness and moderation" he sees as part of his metropolitan identity. Of course, Boswell's self-belief and ambition alternated regularly with moments of anxiety and self-doubt; the journal also proves the perfect medium for the self-castigation these times inspire.

Like Fantomina's, an important aspect of Boswell's enjoyment of London is the arena the city allows for sexual freedom, and the journal supplies a good deal of information on eighteenth-century practices of prostitution. Yet, one of the great set pieces of the journal, Boswell's love affair with the actress he calls Louisa, does not involve prostitution in the explicit sense. Here, again, we can see the way reality and imagination combine in the writer's apprehension of the city – except that in this case the two eventually collide. Thrilled to be the lover of a seemingly glamorous actress, Boswell makes every effort to represent their relationship as conforming to the codes of amorous intrigue. After an embarrassing, and unliterary, episode of impotence, for example, he describes the following events thus:

> The time of church was almost elapsed when I began to feel that I was still a man. I fanned the flame by pressing her alabaster breasts and kissing her delicious lips. I then barred the door of her dining-room, led her all fluttering into her bedchamber, and was just making a triumphal entry when we heard her landlady coming up. "O Fortune why did it happen thus?" would have been the exclamation of a Roman bard. We were stopped most suddenly and cruelly from the fruition of each other. (January 2, 1763)

We might speculate that Boswell fans his flame as much by using the tropes of romance ("alabaster breasts") as much as he does by caressing Louisa. Yet his relationship with her does not live up to this ethereal standard. Only weeks later, Boswell finds himself forced to write one of the immortal lines of eighteenth-century literature: "Too, too plain was Signor Gonorrhea" (January 19, 1763). Louisa, it turns out, was no chaste or genteel woman, and their relationship had stronger roots in financial convenience than he had imagined.

Boswell also enjoys participating in the intellectual life of London, meeting the Sheridans, Garrick, and James McPherson, the reputed discoverer of Ossian, among others, and participating in the lively conversations of the coffee shops. Indeed, Boswell's journal of this visit to London contains what might be called the defining moment of his life: his meeting with Samuel Johnson. His description of first meeting the great man provides a more raw and intriguing view of his contradictions than the more heavily mythologized version offered by *The Life of Johnson*.

> Mr Johnson is a man of a most dreadful appearance. He is a very big man, is troubled with sore eyes, the palsy, and the king's evil. He is very slovenly in his dress and speaks with a most uncouth voice. Yet his great knowledge and strength of expression command vast respect and render him very excellent company. He has great humour and is a worthy man. But his dogmatical roughness of manners is disagreeable. (May 16, 1763)

Despite their awkward meeting, however, the two quickly become affectionate, if unlikely, friends. Johnson presumably enjoyed the attention and admiration of the younger man, while Boswell found a possible father figure who also embodied all his intellectual fantasies about the metropolis. Indeed, in the last parts of the journal, in the company of Johnson, Boswell seems to find his true vocation as a listener and recorder of others' conversations. As he writes on one occasion: "I sat with much secret pride, thinking of my having such company with me. I behaved with ease and propriety, and did not attempt to show away; but gently assisted conversation by those little arts which serve to make people throw out their sentiments with ease and freedom" (July 6, 1763).

At moments like this, of which the journal contains many, the cultural mix of London is as much the hero of the journal as is Johnson, or even Boswell himself. A paean written to the city shortly after he arrives might serve as an epigraph not simply to Boswell's journal, but to all the texts treated in this section.

> In reality, a person of small fortune who has only the common views of life and would just be as well as anybody else, cannot like London. But a person of imagination and feeling, such as the Spectator finely describes, can have the most lively enjoyment from the sight of external objects without regard to property at all. London is undoubtedly a place where men and manners may be seen to the greatest advantage. The liberty and the whim that reigns there occasions a variety of perfect and curious characters. Then the immense crowd and hurry and bustle of business and diversion, the great number of public places of entertainment, the noble churches and the superb buildings of different kinds, agitate, amuse, and elevate the mind. Besides, the satisfaction of pursuing whatever plan is most agreeable, without being known or looked at, is very great. Here a young man of curiosity and observation may have a sufficient fund of present entertainment, and may lay up ideas to employ his mind in age. (December 5, 1762)

The Countryside

Introduction

My eye descending from the Hill, surveys
Where Thames amongst the wanton vallies strays.
Thames, the most lov'd of all the Ocean's sons,
By his old Sire to his embraces runs,
Hasting to pay his tribute to the Sea,
Like mortal life to meet Eternity.

John Denham, Cooper's Hill, 1642, ll.159–64

In *Cooper's Hill*, John Denham works to make the landscape iconic: when the poet surveys the Thames, he finds not only physical beauty, but also moral comparisons between foreign countries and Britain's "genuine, and less guilty wealth" (l.167). Denham was one of many seventeenth and eighteenth-century writers who developed ways of seeing the countryside that emphasized both its material and symbolic richness. The prospect poem, or survey poem, like *Cooper's Hill*, is one such generic innovation. In such poems, the poet looks down at the landscape from a great height, symbolically uniting and possessing the terrain below with his eye. As John Dyer writes in *Grongar Hill* (1726): "Now I gain the mountain's brow/What a landscape lies below!/No clouds, no vapours intervene,/But the gay, the open scene/Does the face of nature show/in all the hues of heaven's bow!" (ll. 41–6). Perhaps no area of English literature has been seen as so *emblematic* of Englishness as descriptions of rural communities and the surrounding natural world.

During this era, representations of the countryside crystallize English ethics, aesthetics, and political beliefs. Raymond Williams begins his powerful and influential book, *The Country and the City*, by noting the deep resonance of the word "country": "In English, 'country' is both a nation and a part of a 'land': 'the country' can be the whole society or its rural area. In the long history of human settlements, this connection between the land from which directly or indirectly we all get our living and the achievements of human society has been deeply known."[1] This correspondence seems to have gathered even greater strength during the eighteenth century. The very idea of the English countryside as a place "open" to the pleasure of the observer – who enjoys looking *at* it rather than laboring *in* it – may have been an eighteenth-century invention. Donna Landry argues that during this period "'countryside' ceased to refer to a specific side – east, west, north, or south – of a piece of country, or a river, valley or a range of hills, and became 'the countryside,' an imaginary, generalized space."[2] Such images came to seem not only ideal but also more authentic than scenes of urban life, revealing a truth about Englishness not otherwise available. Some particularly resonant examples have been in the heroic mode of Pope's Father Thames in *Windsor-Forest*, who, "with joyful pride survey'st our lofty woods" and knows that there are "No seas so rich, so gay no banks appear,/No lake so gentle, and no spring so clear" (ll. 220, 225–6) as England's; others have been elegiac, like Gray's "mute inglorious Milton," buried in a crudely marked grave, or Goldsmith's yearning for a lost rural self-sufficiency, "a time...ere England's grief's began,/when every rood of ground maintained its man" (Oliver Goldsmith, *The Deserted Village*, 1774, ll. 57–8).

As the nostalgic tenor of the later eighteenth century examples intimates, and as critics long have noted, the desire to find an essential Englishness in a landscape uncorrupted by commerce and industry only increased as such a landscape became more and more unattainable. The correspondence between nation and countryside was, by the eighteenth century, more a myth than a reality. It is possible to say, then, that the poignant intensity we associate with literature of the countryside emerged during the eighteenth century. Throughout the century, observers were fascinated by the countryside as a place of retreat, peace and authenticity. Yet they were, perhaps, enthralled by it to the extent that the place they imagined was disappearing for ever. This new way of seeing and thinking about rural places arose in concert with a transformation of the countryside that paralleled the massive changes we have already seen in urban life. Some of these reforms genuinely made life easier for many; the "agricultural revolution" enabled more food to be produced, while improvements in road maintenance made travel from one part of England to another faster and more reliable. Others changed rural life for the worse, undermining and uprooting traditional rural communities. The enclosure movement that accompanied the agricultural revolution displaced many people from land they had inhabited for centuries, changing subsistence farming to wage labor.

Perhaps the greatest change in eighteenth-century rural life was the spread of an ideology of private property to areas and activities that had been seen as common rights. This shift in ways of thinking about the land manifested itself in many ways. In 1723, for example, a large number of activities that had been tolerated as common usage were transformed into capital crimes by the passage of what came to be known as the Black Act (9 George I c. 22). This law newly enabled capital punishment for at least 50 offenses, including hunting deer on private lands, poaching rabbits or fish, and cutting down trees; the most severe punishments were reserved for perpetrators who were armed, disguised, or "blacked" (i.e., those who had painted their faces). While the death penalty may not have been carried out in every indictment, the legal strategy of invoking it for relatively minor crimes has led one influential historian to describe the shapers of the Black Act as "men, for whom property and the privileged status of the propertied were assuming, every year, a greater weight in the scales of justice, until justice itself was seen as no more than the outworks and defences of property and of its attendant status."[3] The new tension around these traditional, if marginal, activities swirls around literary characters that make their living by both maintaining and crossing the boundaries of private property, such as the gamekeeper Black George in Fielding's *Tom Jones*.[4]

We can see the effects of the new priority accorded private property in small-scale activities like gleaning – the practice of allowing the landless poor to remove the remaining wheat or barley from a harvested field – which became more and more strictly forbidden over the course of the eighteenth century. In 1730, the "Autumn" portion of James Thomson's long poem, *The Seasons*, urged the reciprocal relationships between land-owners and the landless poor.

> The gleaners spread around; and here and there,
> Spike after spike, their sparing harvest pick
> Be not too narrow, husbandmen! But fling
> From the full sheaf, with charitable stealth,
> The liberal handful. Think, oh grateful think!
> How good the God of Harvest is to you;
> Who pours abundance o'er your flowing fields;
> While these unhappy partners of your kind
> Wide-hover round you, like the fowls of heaven,
> And ask their humble dole. The various turns
> Of fortune ponder; that your sons may want
> What now, with hard reluctance, faint, ye give. (ll. 165–76)

But when these lines were used as part of the protest against the prosecution of gleaners in the 1780s, they fell upon deaf ears. Even the remains of the crop were now treated as the private property of landed farmers.[5]

But the clearest evidence of the new importance of private property rights was the enclosure movement. Landowners could ask for an Act of Parliament to make common lands their private property, or they could agree to it among themselves. Between 1760 and 1799, between 2 and 3 million acres of waste came into cultivation, mostly as fields and pasturage were enclosed in these ways.[6] Many of these acts enabled greater agricultural productivity. Changes in the way the land was managed produced fatter livestock, as well as heavier crops, and allowed England to feed a growing population: the nation could sustain 50 percent more people in 1800 than it could in 1750. Corn yields went up by 43 percent. Reforms also worked to stop the spread of disease among livestock, and between livestock and people. These reforms were motivated by an ideology of private property – the idea that a single owner, rather than a group holding land in common for differentiated use, could control access to and use of the land. Arthur Young quoted one landless worker tersely saying, "Parliament may be tender of property; all I know is, I had a cow, and an Act of Parliament has taken it from me"[7] Some enclosures, furthermore, were carried out for aesthetic reasons; whole villages were sometimes moved to create picturesque vistas.

Enclosure primarily hurt those who were dependent on the common lands to sustain themselves, relying on occasional grazing rights for their livestock, gleaning or poaching. As one historian notes, "When . . . enclosure acts extinguished common right from most of lowland England in the late eighteenth and early nineteenth centuries, its loss played a large part in turning the last of the English peasantry into a rural working class."[8] As one anonymous nineteenth-century poet declared:

> The fault is great in man or woman
> Who steals a goose from off a common;
> But what can plead that man's excuse
> Who steals a common from a goose?[9]

Enclosures made such people wholly dependent on wage labor to sustain themselves, producing in the countryside a proletariat of rural laborers in much the same way that the industrial revolution generated a population of urban wage laborers. Some scholars have speculated that these were the same group of people who had migrated from the country to newly urban areas in search of work, but that probably isn't entirely true. The laws for supporting the poor only made it possible to get help within your own parish, so many people were effectively trapped.

Improvements in roads and other forms of transportation also changed life in the countryside, just as improvements in sea travel changed England's relationship to its empire. At the beginning of the century, rutted, muddy roads made travel slow and difficult for both goods and people for most of the year: it took 256 hours to get from London to Edinburgh in 1700. But this gradually changed: the same journey took only 150 hours in 1750 and 60 in 1800. These improvements were facilitated by Turnpike Acts. Like Enclosure Acts, Turnpike Acts, which made local landowners responsible for the roads in their vicinities (and allowed them to charge tolls), prolifer-ated during the eighteenth century. Road quality improved at the end of the century due to the new expertise of engineers like Thomas Telford and John MacAdam. This "transportation revolution," like the agricultural revolution, allowed people to regard the landscape as malleable to private control and technological betterment. As Greg Laugero puts it,

> improvement becomes a way of articulating a conception of society as unfolding within a landscape: that is, the organization of the landscape to facilitate the circulation of people, objects, and information became the basis for "society"...Like Parliamentary sanctioned enclosures, turnpike trusts became one of the ways in which the law physically entered and arranged the landscape to facilitate the accumulation of capital.[10]

Better roads bolstered the capitalist economy by enabling the circulation of goods and services to and from London and between different prov-inces. Farmers with new, steadier markets for their goods prospered. At the same time, good roads brought urban ideas to the country, and rural people to urban spaces. As Roy Porter has written, "improvements in roads sped turnover and the pace of life, and sucked the dark corners of the land into the hectic economy of exchange and consumption."[11] Given the changes they brought to British life in the provinces, it is unsurprising that, to many, England's newly wide clear roads symbolized a kind of safety and modernity dear to national identity. As Austen's Henry Tilney famously says to Catherine Morland when she imagines that his father is a murderer, "Does our education prepare us for such atrocities? Do our laws connive at them? Could they be perpetrated without being known, in a country like this, where social and literary intercourse is on such a footing; where every man is surrounded by a neighborhood of voluntary spies, and where roads and newspapers lay everything open?"[12] Of course, General Tilney shortly kicks Catherine out onto those same "open" roads, and the ironic resonance of Henry's statement reverberates throughout the novel. Nevertheless, the idea that all of England had been "laid open" was a tantalizing ideal and heartening to many.

These developments meant that the countryside could now be packaged for urban audiences, and for those moving even farther away, into Britain's colonies. As Elizabeth Helsinger notes, "rural imagery becomes a signifying practice that constructs a national public. Reading or viewing brings the nation into being by creating conscious national identifications around representations of English rurality."[13] One function of the literature of rural life, then, was to be compensatory or consoling: it helped a newly urban and mobile people remember what was no longer there (or, indeed, what had never been). The literature oscillates between attempting to depict the countryside accurately and using it as a malleable space in which to conduct experiments in imagination.

The Poetry of Retreat: Philips, Cowley, Finch, Pope, Thomson, and Collins

For poets from classical times onward, the rural world could be an idyllic place that provided refuge from the economic, political, and even sexual norms of the greater world. In trying to describe this idyll, English poets adapted images of retirement from Horace's second epode, the *Beatus Ille*, for their own uses. The resulting collection of tropes that made up "retirement literature" was, according to Maynard Mack, "as 'available' . . . and as fully charged with imaginative meanings, as the traditions of satire or epic."[14] In adapting, however, eighteenth-century poets excised Horace's irony (Horace's speaker is a usurer, thinking of turning farmer, who later changes his mind). Instead, as Raymond Williams points out, they converted "the conventional pastoral into a localized dream and then, increasingly in the late seventeenth and early eighteenth centuries, into what can be offered as a description and thence an idealization of actual English country life and its social and economic relations."[15]

Such "localized dreams" may have first functioned in Restoration and eighteenth-century English poetry as a retreat from the violent politics of the civil wars. In such poems, the countryside is presented as a haven from the vanities of commercial culture, and the hierarchical striving of court life. The genre developed in English poetry, then, in a political context: the seclusion of the country allowed a new way to imagine being English, in contrast to the faction and strife of the civil wars. Visions of the pleasures of retreat could thus provide a positive perspective on political exile. We can distinguish such poems from pastoral poetry because, while the poet writing pastoral conventionally takes on the persona of a rural swain, the poet celebrating retreat writes as him or herself (more or less), or, more accurately, as someone imagining a newer, more authentic self that could come into being in a safer, simpler world. Despite its location in the countryside, then, the space of retreat can be the interior space of "the mind," which, in Marvell's vivid words, "withdraws into its happiness," and "creates...far other worlds and other seas,/annihilating all that's made/ To a green thought in a green shade."[16] Thus, although the poetry of retreat explicitly calls for simplicity and quiet, it can also be wildly, even ecstatically, imaginative.

In *The Wish*, for example, the Royalist lyric poet Abraham Cowley explicitly contrasts his rural retreat with the tensions of the "great hive, the city" (l. 8): "Pride and ambition here/Only in farfetched metaphors appear;/ Here naught but winds can hurtful murmurs scatter,/and naught but Echo flatter" (ll. 25–8). While Marvell longs for solitude in his *Garden* – ("two paradises 'twere in one/To live in paradise alone", ll. 63–4), Cowley desires "one dear she...who is all the world, and can exclude/In deserts, solitude" (ll. 34–6), his wish for a small, idyllic community resonated with other Royalist writers who had lived in self-imposed isolation during the Interregnum, and found its best expression in the poetry of Katherine Philips, the "Matchless Orinda." Circulating her poems in manuscript within a small coterie of primarily female friends, Philips imagines a world of passionate female friendship, or, rather, a world in which, because it is removed from political strife and the conventions of traditional marriage, the passion of female friendship can be fully expressed. Thus, in *A retir'd Friendship. To Ardelia*, Philips declares,

> In such a scorching Age as this,
> Who would not ever seek a shade,
> Deserve their Happiness to miss,
> As having their own peace betray'd
>
> But we (of one another's mind
> Assur'd) the boisterous world disdain;
> With quiet Souls and unconfin'd
> Enjoy what Princes wish in vain. (ll. 29–36)

The poetry of retreat may have been particularly attractive to women poets because it makes a virtue of necessity. The domestic seclusion about which many women had no choice could be reimagined as the opportunity for a rich, emotional life. Philips's poems celebrate the intensity of emotions women can feel for each other in such secluded situations – an almost physical intensity that has led some readers to see the poems as expressions of lesbian desire. Retreat from the social and political norms of the urban world makes such a challenge to heteronormativity possible.[17]

Poetic retreat, then, is often as much psychological as it is physical, and does not mean that the poet intends to rough it in the wilderness. Anne Finch's luxurious description of idyllic retirement in *The Petition for Absolute Retreat*, written after she and her husband had left London for political reasons after the Glorious Revolution, is a case in point. As close to Marvell's *Upon Appleton House* as it is to *The Garden*, the poem celebrates not only the quiet but also the plenty of life in a secluded country house. "Courteous Fate!" the poet implores, "Afford me there/A table spread, without my care,/With what the neighboring fields impart,/Whose cleanliness be all its art" (ll. 22–5).

The psychic and imaginative opportunities offered by retreat and retirement continued to be alluring as the century progressed, but the landscape inhabited by those pursuing such idylls became progressively more wild and more solitary. James Thomson's wildly popular poem, *The Seasons*, for instance, abandons the well-manicured estate of Finch's *Petition* for a rougher habitation, and exchanges Finch's pithy couplets for stately Miltonic blank verse:

> Now, all amid the rigors of the year,
> In the wild depths of winter, while without
> The ceaseless winds blow keen, be my retreat
> A rural, sheltered, solitary scene;
> Where ruddy fire and beaming tapers join
> To chase the cheerless gloom. There let me sit,
> And hold high converse with the mighty dead – ("Winter")

The poet's only companions in his retreat are books, although in other portions of the much-revised poem he leaves even those behind in his search for poetic vision. He asks his muse to "bear me then to high embowering shades;/To twilight groves and visionary vales;/To weeping grottos and to hoary caves;/Where angel forms are seen, and voices heard,/Sighed in low whispers that abstract the soul/From outward sense far into worlds remote."[18] Echoing Marvell's image of interiority as a "green shade," the more the poet withdraws into the natural world, the more he leaves the natural world behind, as the soul is "abstracted" from "outward sense."

Similar images of a nature fading before the even more powerful forces of imagination occur in Collins's *Ode to Evening*, in which the speaker implores a personified Evening,

> ...lead, calm vot'ress, where some sheety lake
> Cheers the lone heath, or some time-hallowed pile,
> Or uplands fallows gray
> Reflect its last cool gleam.
> But when chill blustering winds, or driving rain.
> Forbid my willing feet, be mine the hut,
> That from the mountain's side,
> Views wilds, and swelling floods,
> And hamlets brown, and dim-discovered spires,
> And hears their simple bell, and marks o'er all
> Thy dewy fingers draw
> The gradual dusky veil. (ll. 29–40)

Here, Collins seems to use the ideal of retreat to revise the generic topoi of the prospect poem. The speaker asks Evening to lead him farther into a landscape which is gradually being deserted by both color and people. But he also imagines himself "viewing" the world below from a mountainside. Unlike the speakers in *Cooper's Hill* or *Grongar Hill*, however, this speaker does not celebrate what he can gather into his gaze. Instead, he imagines human habitation gradually being obscured by nightfall, leaving him alone with his imagination. *The Seasons* and Collins's *Odes*, with their images of a sublime nature that both dwarfs man and inspires his imagination, have been read as mid-century precursors to the tempestuous landscapes of the Romantic poets. If the topoi of retreat were born out of the political struggles of seventeenth-century civil wars, it may have eventually paved the way for the psychological and aesthetic revolutions of the Romantic era.

Pastoral and georgic

If the literature of retirement presents an ideal of solitude (or shared solitude), the pastoral genre, in contrast, depicts the joys of social interaction amongst rural dwellers. Pastoral poetry celebrates the peace and tranquility of an idealized natural setting. It uses familiar conventions, such as shepherds sitting under trees and singing. The genre originated in ancient Greece, in the poetry of Theocritus, and in Rome, in Virgil's *Eclogues*. A classical genre, "imported" into English settings, the form and function of pastoral was the subject of a good deal of debate during the eighteenth century. Although Dryden translated Virgil's *Eclogues*, and Milton reinvigorated the genre with *L'Allegro*, even at the beginning of the eighteenth century, there was a sense that the pastoral genre needed to be rewritten to reflect the times. Was the purpose of pastoral poetry to describe the countryside as it really was or to offer readers a picture of a beautiful, if partly imaginary, way of life? Should the pastoral be made specific to the *English* countryside? If the pastoral did portray a "golden age" without labor, did it claim that such an era had actually occurred, or did it posit the pastoral scene as a mythic ideal, outside of historical time? But if pastoral poetry was simply generated out of a literary tradition, with no regard to real world referents, what was to stop it degenerating into a series of repeated tropes? By mid-century, for example, Samuel Johnson lamented that writers of "pastoral performances"

> have generally succeeded after the manner of other imitators, transmitting the same images in the same combinations from one to another, till he that reads the title of a poem, may guess at the whole series of the composition; nor will a man, after the perusal of thousands of these performances, find his knowledge enlarged with a single view of nature not produced before. (*Rambler*, No. 36, July 1750)

During the eighteenth century, the decision not to represent the countryside as it presently existed was taken as a political decision. Thus, eighteenth-century pastorals can be enjoyed as lyrical effusions or comic diversions. But their representations of pretty milkmaids and lovelorn swains are also engagements with a very serious debate about literature's relationship to the history of the English countryside.

This problem percolated throughout the century, and was the subject of a public quarrel in its first decades. Both Alexander Pope and Ambrose Philips had published sequences of pastoral eclogues in Tonson's *Miscellany* of 1709. Pope's poems reflected his belief that the beauty and peace of country life were pastoral poetry's chief concern: "we must...use some illusion to render a pastoral delightful; and this consists in exposing the best side only of a shepherd's life, and in concealing its miseries," he proclaimed. Philips, however, felt that the pastoral should be expanded to include more of the details of actual life in the countryside. He experimented with writing pastorals that used local place names, and English (as opposed to idealized Mediterranean) fauna, and included some of the more gritty details of rural life. In this spirit, Lobbin, in Philips's first pastoral, for example, asks his love, Lucy, "O! come, my love; nor think th' employment mean, / The dams to milk, and little lambkins wean, / To drive a-field, by morn, the fattening ewes,/Ere the warm Sun drink up the coolly dews [.]" (ll. 83–6). A series of essays in the *Guardian* in 1713 praised the realism of Philips's poems, and all but ignored Pope's. Piqued, Pope himself wrote an essay for the *Guardian*, adopting the same voice as the previous pieces, and arguing, ironically, that the pastoral should be made even more earthy and realistic.

An unexpected result of this quarrel occurred when John Gay took up Pope's satiric suggestion, and criticized the project of making pastoral poetry "realistic" by pushing the project to an absurd extreme, burlesquing the gritty details of country life in *The Shepherd's Week*. But if Gay's intention was to demonstrate that poetic beauty and the actual details of rural life did not mix, in practice his poems had a slightly different effect. Shrinking the rural seasons of Spenser's *Shepherd's Calendar* into six arduous days, for instance, Gay's poem undermines pastoral poetry's claim to bring to life a "golden age." Like Philips, Gay imagines the outlines of rural love amid the flocks, in this case Bumkinet's love for the dead Blouzelinda:

> Whilome I've seen her skim the clouted Cream
> And press from spongy Curds the milky stream.
> But now, alas! These Ears shall hear no more
> The whining Swine surround the Dairy Door,
> No more her Care shall fill the hollow Tray,
> To fat the guzzling hogs with Floods of Whey.
> Lament, ye Swine, in Gruntings spend your Grief,
> For you, like me, have lost your sole Relief. (*Friday*, or *The Dirge*, ll. 61–9)

Generations of readers and critics have taken the poems not as parodies, but as "just representations of rural manners and occupations."[19] Unfamiliar with the quarrel that inspired these pastoral experiments, they have found that the crude, if realistic, images of grunting pigs do not entirely overwhelm the pathos of a rural worker who has lost his "sole relief." John Barrell notes that when Grubbinol quotes Blouzelinda's dying words ("see mother, yonder shelf,/There secretly I've hid my worldly pelf,/Twenty good Shillings in a Rag I laid,/Be ten the Parson's for my Sermon paid./The rest is yours –", ll. 119–22), we

> read the passage not in terms of a bathetic contrast with the elevated and lyrical effusions of dying Arcadians, but as a token of Blouzelinda's innocent charity, and housewifely concern with the details of farm life – a concern that does her credit, and the more so in contrast with the thoughtless ease and luxury which those who would merely laugh at this passage must claim to enjoy.[20]

Thus, despite it origins in an academic quarrel about genre, Gay's poem was immensely popular through most of the eighteenth century, and its alternately comic and sentimental characters seem to have expanded the possibilities of representing rural life with a kind of realistic affection.

Yet, in the face of the changes taking place in rural England, representations of pastoral life could acquire a political edge, as they do in Goldsmith's long poem, *The Deserted Village* (1770). Goldsmith begins his poem by drawing on the conventions of English pastoral to express the happiness of rural life:

> The never failing brook, the busy mill,
> The decent church that topt the neighbouring hill,
> The hawthorn bush, with seats beneath the shade,
> For talking age and whispering lovers made.
> How often have I blest the coming day,
> When toil remitting lent its turn to play,
> And all the village train from labour free
> Led up their sports beneath the spreading tree,
> While many a pastime circled in the shade,
> The young contending as the old surveyed. (ll. 11–20)

The kind of happiness Goldsmith portrays here led the later poet, George Crabbe, to accuse him of depicting an ideal drawn from literature rather than life: "Yes, thus the muses sing of happy swains,/ Because the Muses never knew their pains," Crabbe writes in the first book of *The Village* (1783), before going on to describe a much grimmer picture of rural life (ll. 21–2).[21]

Yet Goldsmith's idyll plays a distinctly political role. Rather than placing the villagers' happiness in a distant golden age, or in a mythical present, Goldsmith insists that their happy life has only recently been destroyed by an improving landlord. He uses this nostalgic image as a poignant counterpoint to images of the village's present-day ruin. The fields that made the village self-sufficient have been enclosed as part of the estate owner's landscaping scheme: "... The man of wealth and pride/ Takes up a space that many poor supplied;/ Space for his lake, his park's extended bounds,/ Space for his horses, equipage and hounds/.../ His seat, where solitary sports are seen,/ Indignant spurns the cottage from the green" (ll. 275–8, 281–2). Goldsmith blames the "sickly greatness" of "luxury" for these innovations, a way of life that privileges pleasure over virtue and conspicuous consumption over self-sufficient thrift.[22] The village's inhabitants are forced to leave, sadly emigrating to the city and to North America.

Playing on the pastoral conventions that imagined the countryside to be full of virtuous, if comic, rustic maidens like Blouzelinda, Goldsmith turns the land itself into a woman, seduced and abandoned by the innovations of the wealthy: "Thus fares the land, by luxury betrayed,/In nature's simplest charms at first arrayed,/But verging to decline, its splendours rise,/Its vistas strike, its palaces surprise" (ll. 295–8). By imagining the countryside as something that changes (indeed ages) over time, and by representing both its present and its past, Goldsmith implicitly comments on the genre of the pastoral, obviating the possibility of an unchanging "golden age." As Alfred Lutz has argued, "by introducing historical time into the pastoral, Goldsmith has stripped it of its representational pretensions, and nullified its ideological power to naturalize the status quo."[23] In other words, Goldsmith uses the generic conventions of pastoral to make a political point: the pleasures and values of rural life are not timeless attributes, but instead contingent on sociocultural conditions – fragile enough to be destroyed by the advances of capitalism. By representing the past not as a mythical, literary ideal, but as something painfully lost, Goldsmith, Barrell argues, offers a "pastoral vision that has been radicalized."[24] By foregrounding the way village life had once centered on leisure activities, Goldsmith questions an emergent doctrine that located human value in industrious labor, and suggests that the English "bumpkin" "could be as free to dispose of his time as other poetry agreed only the rich man or the shepherd was free to do."[25]

In contrast to pastoral poetry, georgic poems are traditionally poems that teach readers how to do a certain kind of work, usually rural. Virgil's *Georgics* are poems that instruct readers how to do things like plant fruit trees and how to keep bees. Dryden's translations of these poems were very popular throughout the century. The genre can inspire heroic or mock-heroic profusions, celebrating the land that can be home to such productivity. Scholars have long noted that production of georgics overtook that of pastorals over the course of the eighteenth century, only to subside again as the century ended. John Barrell says that "the tradition of English georgic" is "a poetry concerned as much to soften as to recommend the hard moral lessons of Virgil's original *Georgics* to a polite English readership."[26] The genre also offered eighteenth-century poets a flexible literary form; rather than staying within the lyric mode of pastoral, "georgic presented poets with an adaptable middle style that could rise to national prophecy and rapture, or descend to technical detail without breaching generic decorum."[27] The industrializing eighteenth century seemed to gradually favor the georgic – as Donna Landry says, "eighteenth-century pastoral verse becomes increasingly preoccupied with and finally crowded out by a georgic discourse of labor and industry.[28] Karen O'Brien notes that one function georgic performed during the eighteenth century was to connect the industriousness of rural England with the need for colonial expansion: "it was Georgic, more than any other literary mode or genre, which assumed the burden of securing the aesthetic and moral links between country, city and empire."[29] In *The Fleece*, for example, John Dyer writes:

> For it suffices not, in flow'ry vales,
> Only to tend the flock, and shear soft wool:
> Gums must be stor'd of Guinea's acrid coast;
> Mexican woods, and India's bright'ning salts;
> Fruits, herbage, sulphurs, minerals, to stain
> The fleece prepar'd [.] (2: ll. 565–70)

Other eighteenth-century georgics include John Philips's *Cyder* (1708), John Dyer's *The Fleece* (1757), and James Grainger's *The Sugar Cane* (1764). Georgic always had political overtones. Scholars argue that the genre usefully negotiated relationships not only between the country and the city, but also the more complex relationship between city, country, and the broader empire.

An innovative version of the georgic emerges in the laboring-class poet Stephen Duck's *The Thresher's Labour*. A self-educated rural laborer, Duck turned his own experience as a rural laborer into a long consideration of the exhausting effort of agricultural work in this poem. Duck published it as part of *Poems on Several Subjects* in 1730. The volume was very successful, running through ten editions in a single year, and Duck eventually came under the patronage of Queen Caroline. He left rural labor behind, became keeper of the Queen's library, and lived in the Richmond gardens. Unfortunately, Duck did not find permanent happiness in his altered circumstances, and drowned himself in a trout stream in 1756.

Early in *The Thresher's Labour*, Duck documents the opposition between agricultural labor and aesthetic enjoyment of the landscape, envisioning the violence that threshing does to the visual prospect:

> How beauteous all things in the Morn appear,
> There Villages, and pleasing Cots are here;
> So many pleasing Objects meet the Sight,
> The ravished Eye could willing gaze 'till Night:
> But long e'er then, where-e'er their Troops have passed,
> Those pleasant Prospects lie a gloomy Waste. (ll. 234–9)

Duck displays his own mastery of the tropes of prospect poetry – the way the genre points out the "pleasing" sights "here" and "there," the way a beautiful landscape can "ravish" the eye. Yet, by imagining the threshers as an invading army that destroys that "pleasing" image, he makes explicit both the constant flux of the rural landscape and the way that aesthetic tropes can mask the real activities of rural life.

Duck also subordinates the pleasures of pastoral to the rigors of georgic by labeling all moments of relaxation a "cheat." Describing the celebratory feast thrown by the landowner at the end of the harvest, he writes:

> A Table plentifully spread we find,
> And Jugs of humming Beer to cheer the Mind;
> Which he, too generous, pushes on so fast,
> We think no Toils to come, nor mind the past,
> But the next morning soon reveals the Cheat,
> When the same Toils we must again repeat. (ll. 271–6)

Duck juxtaposes two kinds of time here: the momentary enjoyment of the present (we might think of this as the lyric moment of pastoral), here exploited by the landlord, who uses alcohol to make his workers forget the rigors of their job and the endless, repetitive cycle of labor (georgic). It would be a mistake, however, to think of Duck's poem as making a case for "realism"; even as it includes empirical details about many tasks of the rural laborer, it draws on the classical literary tradition to make its points. The brutality of the rural cycle of tasks is driven home with this allusion: "Thus, as the Year's revolving Course goes round,/No respite from our Labour can be found:/Like Sisyphus, our Work is never done" (ll. 279–81). By using such images, Duck both asserts his own literary authority, in an era in which classical learning granted cultural status, and poises the threshers halfway between reality and poetry. Genre, says Raymond Williams, is "both a set of literary conventions and a mode of social under-standing."[30] The tension between pastoral and georgic is thus also a contest between two different ways of understanding not only what kind of life takes place in the countryside, but also the importance of those ways of life for the nation as a whole.

Thomas Gray, *Elegy Written in a Country Churchyard*

Perhaps the most enduring image of rural life bequeathed us by eighteenth-century literature is Thomas Gray's *Elegy Written in a Country Churchyard*. Published in 1751, it was immediately and enduringly popular. It was widely reprinted in many media, and went through eight editions before 1753. This popularity was in part due to the subject matter – there was a vogue for "graveyard poetry" at the time – and in part due to the language of the poem itself. In his *Life of Gray*, Samuel Johnson says,

> In the character of his *Elegy* I rejoice to concur with the common reader; for by the common sense of readers uncorrupted with literary prejudice after all the refinements of subtlety and dogmatism of learning, must be finally decided all claim to poetical honours. The *Church-yard* abounds with images which find a mirror in every mind, and with sentiments to which every bosom returns an echo. The four stanzas beginning "Yet even these bones" are to me original: I have never seen the notions in any other place; yet he that reads them here persuades himself that he has always felt them.[31]

The *Elegy*'s resonant lines have provided titles for numerous books – i.e., Thomas Hardy's *Far From the Madding Crowd* – and movies – such as Stanley Kubrick's World War I epic, *Paths of Glory*. Generations of critics, beginning with Gray himself, have puzzled over why the language of the poem so appeals to "the common reader," especially in contrast to Gray's later poetry. Roger Lonsdale, among others, attributes the quality to the poem's heavy use of allusions, which produce the "echo chamber" effect Johnson describes – it seems as if we have *almost* heard many of its phrases and images before.[32]

The puzzling power of the language is certainly integral to the poem itself. Like the examples of pastoral and georgic we have seen, the *Elegy* engages with the nature of the rural community; it focuses, however, on both the affective ties holding that community together, and the division between that community and the luxurious, urban world of the educated elite; that division, according to the poem, is reinforced by a differentiated relationship to the written word. The poor are illiterate not simply because they may not be able to read, but also the very simplicity of their "annals," the "rudeness" of their texts, their vulnerability to being forgotten if their memorials are lodged only in the hearts of their loved ones, rather than being more concretely enshrined in "storied urn or animated bust" (l. 41).

Since Gray's poem makes illiteracy – and the cultural ephemerality the eighteenth century associated with illiteracy – one of the distinguishing markers of rural life, it is ironic that, as John Guillory has shown, the poem itself became an iconic marker of the cultural literacy associated with the emergent vernacular canon. The poem, Guillory argues, was *linguistic capital*: "the means by which...that literacy was produced in the schools. There is much evidence to suggest that Gray's *Elegy* accrued enormous capital of [this] sort, since it rapidly established itself in the school system as a perfect poem for introducing school children to the study of English literature."[33] It is doubly ironic that Gray's poem came to hold this position, since he himself was supremely uninterested in general schooling and the "common reader." Gray was a shy man throughout his life – he made his best friends during his time at Eton: Richard West and Horace Walpole (son of the prime minister). Although, there is no evidence that these relationships were explicitly sexual, it is clear that Gray's closest emotional attachments were to other men.[34] He was devastated by West's early death, and the event seems to have spurred him into poetry. For most of his life, Gray was Professor of Modern History at Cambridge, though he never delivered a lecture or worked with students.

The *Elegy*'s journey into print reveals Gray's ambivalent relationship to publicity and literary fame. He initially sent the poem privately to Walpole, who allowed a copy to be taken of it some time around 1750. When Gray found out that the *Magazine of Magazines*, a well-known low-brow publication, was about to publish a copy of the poem, he wrote to Walpole:

> [The editors] tell me, that an *ingenious* Poem...has been communicated to them, which they are printing forthwith: that they are inform'd, that the *excellent* Author of it is I by name, & that they beg not only his *Indulgence*, but the *Honor of his Correspondence*, &c: as I am not at all disposed to be either so indulgent or so correspondent, as they desire; I have but one bad Way left to escape the Honour they would inflict upon me, & therefore am obliged to desire you would make Dodsley print it immediately...from your copy, but without my Name...(February 11, 1751)

Gray views any publication at all as a "bad way," but preferable to having his poem appear in a less elevated setting. The poet himself was the first to distrust the popularity of his own poem – and seems to have almost intentionally shied away from pursuing further popularity, both in his career (he was offered the position of Poet Laureate but refused) and in his later poetry, which became more obscure both in language and in subject matter. Paradoxically, then, he was at once the most private of poets and the most celebrated.

Like Goldsmith's later poem, *The Deserted Village*, Gray's *Elegy* is as much about the poet's imaginative recreation of a deserted landscape as it is about the people who may have once inhabited that place. The *Elegy*, however, finds a powerful vocabulary for that process in its representation of the liminal time of twilight. Like Collins's *Ode to Evening*, the poem uses the ebbing away of light to foster the imagination. As the poem begins, the living residents of the countryside disappear, "leav[ing] the world to darkness, and "to [the poet]." The poem's prosody is consistent and relatively simple. Its rhetorical structure, however, is complex; since the poet imagines the lives once lived by the dead buried in the church-yard, rather than simply describing living persons, the emotional lives of the rural poor are all presented in the subjunctive tense – he is imagining *what might have been*. The structure of "what might have been" makes the most poignant points of the poem. If Goldsmith would later see the greatest threats to his villagers as being material ones, Gray instead focuses throughout on oblivion. The poem is about the need for memorials for those whose lives won't be remembered because they are not connected to the structures that make public memory. Like the speaker in Goldsmith's poem, the speaker in Gray's takes on himself the responsibility for memory. Whereas Goldsmith presents this problem as a socioeconomic issue – rural life has been erased by enclosure – Gray presents it as a timeless source of melancholy – the inevitability of death. Gray's church-yard is simply deserted because it's nighttime, and everyone is either asleep or dead.

For these reasons, Gray's poem has often been seen as a conservative version of rural melancholy. For William Empson, for example, the lines:

> Full many a gem of purest ray serene
> The dark, unfathomed caves of ocean bear;
> Full many a flower is born to blush unseen
> And waste its sweetness on the desert air. (ll. 54–7)

simply evidence the fact that:

> eighteenth-century England had no scholarship system or *carrière ouverte aux talents*. This is stated as pathetic, but the reader is put into a mood in which one would not try to alter it....By comparing the social arrange-ments to Nature he makes it seem inevitable, which it was not, and gives it a dignity which was undeserved. Furthermore, a gem does not mind being in a cave, and a flower prefers not to be picked.[35]

For Gray, however, the restrictions of the rural poor also have advantages. For every villager whose creative powers have been stymied by a lack of education, for every "mute, inglorious, Milton," there is one whose destructive passions have also been curtailed, a "Cromwell guiltless of his Country's blood."

The poem eventually circles back around to the more personal aspects of the situation, however, as the poem considers the problem of the forgotten poet. After maintaining a strict unity of perspective through its first 92 lines, as a single authorial voice meditates on the vagaries of class status, the poem fissures into several different voices as it nears its close. The poet first addresses the person who, "mindful of th'unhonour'd dead," has carved their gravestones (although "the lines" that tell this "artless tale" could refer just as easily to the poem itself). And yet, this unnamed person appears to be dead, and the poem introduces a "hoary-headed Swain" to narrate his story. The Swain's story ends with the rural writer's death, however, and he refers the poet to the youth's gravestone. "Approach and read (for thou can'st read)," he says, marking the divide of literacy between the classes once again. The poem ends by quoting this rural "Epitaph" in full.

The beginning of the *Elegy* is remarkably clear, despite its rhetorical complexity, but the ending is almost vertiginous in the ambiguity of its pronouns and profusion of perspectives. Scholars have devoted a good deal of time to trying to sort out who says what to whom – the inter- pretative debate has been labeled the "stonecutter controversy."[36] But Gray's revisions of the ending of the poem imply that there was some- thing disturbing him about the proximity of the plight of the "unhonour'd" rural poor to that of the unhonoured metropolitan poet. Indeed, an alter- native manuscript ending introduces neither the "kindred spirit" of line 96, nor the hoary-headed Swain. In this version, the person relating "artless tales" is more clearly the poet himself, who concludes the poem by chiding:

> No more with Reason & thyself at Strife
> Give anxious Cares & endless Wishes room
> But thro' the cool sequester'd Vale of Life
> Pursue the silent Tenour of thy Doom.

The poem thus makes the "sequestering" of rural people simply a figure for the obscurity shared by most people of all classes. The published version of the poem, interestingly enough, both closes down this more personal vision, and keeps our attention on the divisions between literate urban people, and the illiterate, rural poor. Gray's poem, like Goldsmith's later one, reminds us that eighteenth-century writers used the "seques- tered vales" of the poor to work through the problems of poverty and illiteracy that surely plagued urban spaces as well. The geographical differ- ences between country and town often stand in for the socioeconomic differences of a still entrenched class system, even as the countryside becomes a space for personal contemplation.

Natural Voices: Robert Burns and Ann Yearsley

As the popularity of Duck's poetry indicates, the eighteenth-century interest in finding authentic images of the countryside resulted in the "discovery" and celebration of plebeian poets. Two of the more well-known
representatives of this group are Ann Yearsley and Robert Burns.

For most of her life, Ann Yearsley supported herself and a family that
included six children and her mother by selling milk in Clifton, near Bristol.
Her brother taught her to read, however, and after perusing Milton, Pope
and Young, she started writing poems of her own. In 1785, the poet and
educator Hannah More, who was also from Bristol, learned of Yearsley's
poetry from her cook. More, and to a lesser degree the wealthy bluestocking
Elizabeth Montagu, became Yearsley's patrons – giving her books, and eventually arranging for the subscription publication of a volume of Yearsley's
work: *Poems, on Several Occasions* (1785). More included a letter to Montagu
in the collection that reveals the ambivalence surrounding the "talent" of
the rural writers: she says of Yearsley, for example, that "If her epithets are
now and then bold and vehement, they are striking and original; and I
should be sorry to see the wild rigour of her rustic muse polished into elegance, or laboured into correctness." The uneducated poet is both admired
for something more educated writers lack, and condescended to for just
those qualities. As the tone of this letter intimates, More felt that being
Yearsley's benefactor entitled her to make decisions on the poet's behalf, and
she set herself and Montagu up as the trustees of the profits from *Poems*
(which were a substantial 350 pounds). Yearsley, however, was not as agreeable to this sort of patronage as other impoverished poets, male and female,
had been in the past, and struggled with More and Montagu over the money.
She managed to wrest control of her finances away from them, but broke
bitterly with those who had "discovered" her in the process. Nevertheless,
Yearsley went on to have a relatively successful literary career, primarily
in Bristol, publishing two more volumes of poems, a play, and a novel.

Yearsley is acute in her description of what it is like to be an unlettered
poet. In her poem in praise of one of her bluestocking benefactors, *On
Mrs. Montagu*, she writes:

> Oft as I trod my native wilds alone,
> Strong gusts of thought would rise, but rise to die;
> The portals of the swelling soul, ne'er op'd
> By liberal converse, rude ideas strove
> Awhile for vent, but found it not, and died.
> Thus rust the Mind's best powers. (ll. 51–6)

Here, the poet explains the dilemma of the "mute inglorious Milton" from the inside, complementing (or challenging) Gray's outsider's perspective with the intimate understand that results from having lived in that position. Using imagery drawn from nature, Yearsley imagines thoughts as wind, and education as a door: when the door cannot be opened, thoughts poignantly atrophy, or rust. As her struggle with Moore over control of the profits from her writing indicates, Yearsley was concerned to demonstrate that her talent and her authority as a writer were not contingent on her class or education. Yearsley was not shy about taking on the major genres of her day. In *Clifton Hill*, her long poem about a Bristol landmark, for example, she approaches and revises the genre of the prospect poem. Donna Landry has written of the poem that it

> consists of a remarkable transformation of Lactilla's [Yearsley's name for herself] scene of labor as a milkwoman into a high literary landscape that nevertheless preserves the traces of its working-class origins in its confrontational shifting of perspectives. *Clifton Hill* presents us with a feminized and socialized landscape significantly different from the view from Denham's *Cooper's Hill*, Pope's *Windsor-Forest*, Dyer's *Grongar Hill*, or the more contemporary landscapes of Cowper and Crabbe.[37]

Yearsley also reimagines the elegy, particularly Gray's *Elegy*, as she meditates at the grave of her beloved mother:

> Dead! Can it be? 'twas here we frequent stray'd,
> And these sad records mournfully survey'd.
> I marked the verse, the skulls her eye invite,
> Whilst my young bosom shudder'd with affright!
> My heart recoil'd, and shun'd the loathsome view;
> "Start not, my child, each human thought subdue,"
> She calmly said; "this fate shall once be thine,
> My woes pronounce that it shall first be mine."
> Abash'd, I caught the awful truths she sung,
> And on her firm resolves one moment hung. (ll. 77–92)

As does Gray, Yearsley underlines the difference between literate and illiterate viewers of graves; when they "survey'd" the graves together, the daughter "marked the verse" while the mother looked at images of skulls. And yet rather than taking it upon herself to imagine the lives of those interred within, as Gray does, Yearsley gives her mother's voice pride of place here. That voice offers sentiments very similar to those of Gray's *Elegy* ("The paths of glory lead but to the grave"), but in much less figurative language. The mother's voice here is ghostly, but resolved, and bridges the gap between literate and illiterate: the daughter's memory undimmed by the mother's death. The vehemence and pride in Yearsley's poetry would be striking even if we did not know about her artistic and financial struggles with Hannah More.

Much better known to posterity than Yearsley, Robert Burns published his first book of poems just one year after Yearsley did. Burns was the son of a tenant farmer in the western Scottish Lowlands. He worked in the fields, but also found time to educate himself. He read constantly, even while eating, and read everything, including both English and Scottish poetry. He fathered three illegitimate children, and hoped at one point to go to Jamaica as a way of fleeing from that financial liability. On the brink of enacting this plan, however, Burns sold the book he had been writing, *Poems, Chiefly in the Scottish Dialect*, which was published in 1786. The volume was an instant success; some even date the beginning of the Romantic era to its publication. Reviewers praised Burns's "native genius" and "untutored fancy," dubbing him the "Heaven-taught plowman." Wordsworth wrote admiringly that Burns "showed my youth/How verse may build a princely throne/on humble truth."[38] Burns went to Edinburgh, which was a key literary community at that point, and was celebrated there. In 1788, he began contributing to a collection of Scottish folksongs, refusing payment for the task; he wrote or rewrote over 250 songs, finding the music first and then contriving words to it: Burns is the actual author of some familiar songs we take to be folk songs, such as "Auld Lang Syne." He lived the rest of his life, till he died at age 37 of heart disease, as a tax collector in Dumfries.

Like Yearsley, Burns self-consciously presented himself as an untaught poet. As an epigraph to the 1786 volume, he wrote:

> The Simple Bard, unbroken by rules of Art,
> He pours the wild effusions of the heart:
> And if inspir'd, 'tis Nature's pow'rs inspire:
> Her's all the melting thrill, and her's the kindling fire.

Unlike other laboring-class poets we've discussed – Duck and Collier – and Mary Leapor, whom we will later consider, Burns does not invoke classical learning. Indeed, he goes out of his way to disown it, stating that all his poetic skill comes from nature, from himself. He stakes out a claim to be Gray's "mute inglorious Milton," suddenly given voice.

Burns's frequent use of Scottish dialect – his deviation from standard English is often what associates him with the idea of being untaught – but we need to think of him not as a poet who wrote that way because he could not write in a different manner, or even as one who wrote that way because it was more authentic. Rather, we should think of his language as arising from a profound canniness and artistry about how he wanted his poetry to sound. Burns uses dialect words very inconsistently; they are almost always words the non-Scottish reader can understand because they sound like English words, or at least have an English equivalent. And he switches in and out of that diction seemingly at will. In his famous poem, *To a Mouse*, for instance, the phrase "bickering brattle" means "haste" in Scottish, but the English connotation of "argumentative" also lies behind Burns's use of it. The juxtaposition of that phrase with the phrases "man's dominion" and "Nature's social union" – which are very polished, very much in keeping with late eighteenth-century learned diction – evidence the extent to which Burns was in control of his poetic diction.

To a Mouse presents us with an interesting conjunction of the world of the rural laborer and the natural world of animals. Unlike poems like *The Seasons*, or Collins's *Odes*, *To a Mouse* does not explore the sublimity of wild nature, its inhuman capacity to dwarf and engulf those who venture into it. Like *The Thresher's Labour*, Burns's poem is inspired by an occasion of real labor – he notes the month and year that he wrecked the mouse's nest in an epigraph. Also, like Duck, Burns reveals the violent potential in the georgic, imagining the destruction wrought on the landscape by human work. As is characteristic of late eighteenth-century poetry, however, rather than maintain the difference between man and nature, *To a Mouse* uses this mundane incident to tease out a complicated relationship of similarity and difference, of sympathy and alienation, between man and animal. As if testing the limits of empathy, the poet tries to imagine what the mouse must feel seeing her home destroyed as winter approaches. He at first concludes that such an event would affect man and mouse in much the same way – "But Mousie, thou art no thy-lane, / In proving *foresight* may be vain[.]" (ll. 37–8) – and coins the famous lines: "The best laid schemes of o' *Mice* and *Men*, / Gang aft agley" (ll. 39–40) – claiming a kind of sympathetic community between man and the rest of the natural world. Yet the last verse of the poem breaks that sympathetic, if imaginary, bond:

> Still, thou art blest, compar'd wi' *me*!
> The *present* only toucheth thee:
> But Och! I *backward* cast my e'e,
> On prospects drear!
> An' *forward*, tho' I cannot *see*,
> I *guess* an' *fear*!

Burns thus uses the ordinariness of the mouse, her nonthreatening and pathetic cuteness, to spin out a philosophical consideration of man's relationship to the countryside. It is a consideration of the failure of reciprocal bonds, of how "Man's dominion/Has broken Nature's social union" (ll. 7–8). Thus, although man and mouse are "earth-born companion[s]" and "fellow-mortal[s]," the poet/ploughman finds himself destroying the mouse's shelter. Moreover, man's capacity for imagination makes his fate worse than the animals.

While they share some characteristics with laboring-class poets from earlier in the century, like Mary Leapor or Stephen Duck, we should also note how different the poetry of Burns and Yearsley is from those precursors. They foreground their own lack of learning and they use language that highlights that difference. Yet they don't foreground their own labor as does the georgic poetry of Duck or Mary Collier. Rather, they write more lyrical, meditative poetry; spinning tales, in the case of Burns; digressing on issues, as does Yearsley. They make the proto-Romantic case that talent is independent of class or education.

5

Individuality and Imagination

Introduction

Momus, the ancient god of finding fault, once proposed that a glass be installed in the human breast, to reveal each individual's secret thoughts. Near the beginning of *Tristram Shandy*, its protagonist meditates on this suggestion:

> [H]ad the said glass been there set up, nothing more would have been wanting, in order to have taken a man's character, but to have taken a chair and gone softly, as one would to a dioptrical bee-hive, and looked in, – viewed the soul stark naked; – observed all her motions, – her machinations; traced all her maggots from their first engendering to their crawling forth; – watched her loose in her frisks, her gambols, her capricios; and after some notice of her more solemn deportment, consequent upon such frisks, &c. – then taken your pen and ink and set down nothing but what you have seen, and could have sworn to: – But this is an advantage not to be had by the biographer in this planet;...our minds shine not through the body, but are wrapt up here in a dark covering of uncrystallized flesh and blood; so that, if we would come to the specific characters of them, we must go some other way to work. (pp. 96–7)[1]

The passage exemplifies both the eighteenth-century fascination with interior life and individual psychology, and the difficulties literature faced in making those dynamics visible and comprehensible to readers. "In this planet," one cannot simply watch the mind as if it were a dancer on a stage and determine the nature of a man's character by sight alone. Instead, eighteenth-century writers had to "go some other way to work" and find new theories and new languages to represent the inner working of individual character.

By the beginning of the eighteenth century, the nature of character and the workings of the human mind had become important objects of philosophical investigation. John Locke had argued that the mind held no innate ideas, but rather formed itself through experience and self-reflection: "So much as we our selves consider and comprehend of Truth and Reason, so much we possess of real and true Knowledge. The floating of other Men's Opinions in our brains makes us not one jot the more knowing, though they happen to be true. What in them was Science, is in us but Opinatrety" (John Locke, *Essay on Human Understanding*, 1.4.24). In Lockean theory, examination of one's own consciousness became paramount, and identity was rooted in consciousness of that self:

> For as far as any intelligent being can repeat the idea of any past action with the same consciousness it had of it at first, and with the same consciousness it has of any present action; so far it is the same personal self. For it is by the consciousness it has of its present thoughts and actions, that it is self to itself now, and so will be the same self, as far as the same consciousness can extend to actions past and to come; and would be by distance of time, or change of substance, no more two persons, than a man be two men by wearing other clothes today than he did yesterday, with a long or short sleep between. (*Essay on Human Understanding*, 2.27.10)

Thus, the concrete experience of an individual body in time became at once primary, and subordinated to a noncorporeal consciousness. As Charles Taylor points out, "it is assumed that something we call consciousness or self-consciousness could be clearly distinguished from its embodiment, and the two allowed to separate and combine in various thought experiments, that our self-awareness is somehow detachable from its embodiment."[2] This idea of a self that interrogated its own experiences tied Lockean thought to the kind of spiritual self-examination that was already a vital part of English Protestantism.

The concept of a self constituted by self-awareness, however, also led to some interesting paradoxes about the continuity of identity. How could we account for a self when the body is unconscious, for instance?

> If a Man charges me with a Murder done by some body last Night, of which I am not conscious; I deny that I did the Actions, and cannot possibly attribute it to my Self, because I am not conscious that I did it. Again, suppose me to be seized with a short Frenzy of an Hour, and during that time to kill a Man, and then to return to my Self without the least Consciousness of what I have done; I can no more attribute that Action to my Self, than I could the former, which I supposed done by another. The mad Man and the sober Man are really two as distinct Persons as any two Other Men in the World.[3]

And if the self is merely the awareness of an accumulation of sense impressions, how can we distinguish it from a machine? As the satirical "Mechanical Essay on the Operations of the Mind" put it,

> we have in common with other Animals a certain Machine of a curious and exquisite Workmanship, the principal Springs whereof are Imagination and Memory. If we carefully examine this Machine, we shall find it exactly the same in Men and Beasts, every thing being done in both in a manner merely passive and necessary. To be convinced of this, let us but consider that all outward Objects do, by the exterior Organs of Sensation, send into the Brain certain Images, which meeting with the animal Spirits aptly disposed, excite in the Machine some determined Motion or other. The Machine itself is incapable of any Choice, but is always actuated by the strongest Impression, which generally depends on the Disposition it is in at the very Instant it receives it...[4]

When the consciousness is thus dependent on the contingency of sense impressions, there is a suspicion that "thinking has become an automatic response to the physical stimuli of mental images"[5] and identity can only be imagined as necessarily embedded in the physical world.

Small wonder, then, that eighteenth-century ideas of individuality were rarely abstract, but were rather concerned with how one's identity played out in, and was even shaped by, the material conditions in which one found oneself. Eighteenth-century literature is rich with such investigations. Bunyan's story of salvation explores the details of rural Bedfordshire, Rochester's erotic poetry examines the conflict between pure desire and the body's inevitable failures, and Sterne considers the material conditions of conception on the development of character. Despite, or perhaps because of, this sense that identity was contingent on social and material surroundings, however, eighteenth-century literature shared with philosophy an interest in distinguishing the "natural" attributes of humanity from the "artificial." *Robinson Crusoe* narrates just such an experiment, as do the numerous anecdotes of young women raised in seclusion from the vagaries of the fashionable world.[6]

To be an individual, then, involved understanding the ways in which one's own experience was unique. However, it also meant distinguishing one's own will and agency from that of others – it meant self-determination. In other words, to be an individual was defined as controlling one's own person and capacities. In C. B. McPherson's influential formulation, such "possessive individualism" is defined as proprietorship of the self:

> [Individualism's] possessive quality is found in its conception of the individual as essentially the proprietor of his own person or capacities, owing

nothing to society for them. The individual was seen neither as a moral whole, nor as part of a larger social whole, but as owner of himself ... The individual, it was thought, is free inasmuch as he is proprietor of his person and capacities. The human essence is freedom from dependence on the wills of others, and freedom is a function of possession. Society becomes a lot of free equal individuals related to each other as proprietors of their own capacities and of what they have acquired by their exercise. Society consists of relations of exchange between proprietors. Political society becomes a calculated device for the protection of this property and for the maintenance of an orderly relation of exchange.[7]

These socioeconomic ideas about freedom and selfhood surface in literary representations of identity as well. Walter Chernaik argues that libertine ideology reflects this new emphasis on competition and possession in its understanding of sexual conquest.[8] And, while Clarissa's letters allow us to follow the minute workings of her consciousness as it reflects upon experience, her insistence on self-determination and control of her own body (and funds) suggest that this emergent idea of freedom and identity is at work in that text as well.

Both of these ideas – that identity is shaped by experience, and that the self is constructed through the properties it possesses – came together in the profound eighteenth-century belief that the self can be remade through education and discipline. This remaking, many believed, could be accomplished through reading, or writing, or indeed, reading what one had written about oneself. Richardson's early work, *Familiar Letters* (1741), for example, taught its readers new methods of self-presentation by offering a series of letters that could be adapted to readers' own circumstances. The new interest in journal-keeping also attested to the use of reading and writing to both understand and remake the self. As John Brewer puts it, "to read one's own journal was to be a spectator of oneself. Such self-consciousness, a form of self-examination that looked at appearances as well as the inner self, helped shape a polite person."[9]

All the texts discussed in this section demonstrate that eighteenth-century theories of identity and individuality were not only articulated in print, but also entangled in the new resources of print culture. The proliferation of printed material gave people new ways of understanding themselves. This process may have begun in the seventeenth century, as the greater distribution of the English Bible introduced a new and powerful language for describing interiority. But more secular models were used as well: people described their experiences in relation to those of characters they had read about in books – they *identified* with Clarissa, or Tristram Shandy. They came to a greater understanding of themselves through reading. Thus, paradoxically, these experiments with the exploration and representation of inwardness were tied up with the ever-increasing publicity of print culture, and with the novel in particular. As Ian Watt noted half a century ago: "It is paradoxical that the most powerful vicarious identification of readers with the feelings of fictional characters that literature had seen should have been produced by exploiting the qualities of print, the most impersonal, objective and public of the media of communication."[10]

Bunyan, *Grace Abounding to the Chief of Sinners*

The spiritual autobiography, powerfully exemplified by Bunyan's *Grace Abounding*, had an extensive influence on eighteenth-century religious and literary practices, as well as on conceptions of the individual. The spiritual autobiography records an individual's personal revelation of God's grace. It is both a record of experience and a way of providing evidence of one's spirituality for others. Some Protestant sects, including Bunyan's, demanded them of every member of the congregation. When these groups were forbidden from congregating publicly during the last decades of the seventeenth century, they became dependent on written texts – autobiographies, sermons, or pious letters – which could be passed from hand to hand. Groups like Bunyan's could not have survived without a high rate of literacy and the proliferation of print technology.

> To the written word, above all else, was due the preservation of nonconformity. By this means the letter of the law could be observed. Ministers might not only preach over a sermon several times to ensure their people could meet safely in small groups, but might also, like Obadiah Grew, have it transcribed "to be read to four or more writers in short-hand, every Saturday night or Lord's day morning; and every one of these read it to four new men who transcribed it also; and so it was afterwards read at twenty several meetings."[11]

Thus, as much as *Grace Abounding* is a record of Bunyan's "secret thoughts" and interior life, it is also a public text, produced by Bunyan to hold his congregation together as a community of readers.

John Bunyan was born in Bedfordshire in 1628, the son of a tinker, although the family had seen better times. His parents were able to provide him with some schooling, but his early life was spent in his father's profession, and no one could have predicted that he would become a spiritual leader – he was much more interested in chapbook tales of chivalry and newspapers than the Bible during this part of his life. In 1644, however, he joined Cromwell's New Model Army, and there his religious education began. Bunyan left the Army in 1647, married in 1648, and by 1655, after the years of spiritual searching described in *Grace Abounding*, he had joined a congregational church and begun to preach. Under the strict laws against religious congregation outside the established church that were passed immediately after the Restoration, he was imprisoned in 1660. Bunyan was one of the first nonconformist preachers to be taken, a fact he seemed to regard happily as a sign of being chosen for religious martyrdom. He remained in prison, aside from the occasional furlough, for the following eleven or twelve years. While imprisoned, Bunyan wrote: first, *Grace Abounding*, published in 1668; then, during a later period of imprisonment, *Pilgrim's Progress*, published in 1678. Both books were extremely popular: *Grace Abounding* went through six editions before Bunyan's death in 1688; *Pilgrim's Progress*, perhaps one of the most widely read pieces of English literature throughout the world, went through twelve editions in the first ten years after it was published.

The spiritual autobiography is an odd genre because it depends on two different axes of interpretation. The personal revelation it describes must match the model of revelation described in the Bible; there must be a "sweet correspondence," as Bunyan later was to put it, between experience and scripture. Thus, the individual's apprehension of grace must fit into a strict form in order to be considered legitimate. Usually, this form recounts a three-step process: first, preconversion, during which the individual indulges in all manner of sins; then, the process and event of conversion; and finally, the saved soul's postconversion trials. Bunyan, notoriously, spends most of his time on the strenuous process of conversion. Even as it adheres to the paradigms set forth in the Bible, however, the spiritual autobiography must also contain enough individualized evidence to demonstrate that the events described really happened to the person relating them. In this sense, the genre is oddly empirical; it adumbrates the novel in that it depends on particular details about the protagonist's life to validate the narrative's truth. A striking example of this is the miracle Bunyan is tempted to perform on the bad roads of Bedfordshire: "one day as I was betwixt Elstow and Bedford, the temptation was hot upon me to try if I had faith by doing some miracle; which miracle at that time was this, I must say to the puddles that were in the horsepads, Be dry; and to the dry places, Be you the puddles" (paragraph 51). In both its specific location, and its careful attention to the less picturesque aspects of rural England, this episode aligns a universal temptation with local details and everyday plebeian life. In other words, the spiritual autobiography demands that the individual be mapped onto a universal paradigm, and, conversely, that a universal paradigm be worked out in the details of an individual's life. Needless to say, the two axes sometimes pull against each other.

The spiritual autobiography is a retrospective narration; the reader discovers how the person being described got to be the person doing the telling. Thus, this genre, like the novel, suggests that the individual is shaped and remade by experience. The underlying supposition of the conversion narrative is change; it implies that a person is not condemned to the station and personality he or she is born into. To prove this point, it offers the author as example; Bunyan seeks to reform his readers by telling them about his own reformation in the hope that they will emulate his actions. More importantly, perhaps, the individual's introspection, his or her attention to the minute occurrences of inner life, becomes uniquely valuable because of the evidence it provides of intimacy with the divine.

The need to tie the universal to the particular also generates the odd mix of biblical language and concrete, mundane detail about rural Bedfordshire in *Grace Abounding*. Addressing his congregation, Bunyan says "Have you never a hill Mizar to remember? Have you forgot the Close, the Milk house, the Stable, the Barn, and the like, where God did visit your soul?"[12] Bunyan's text is also noteworthy for its claims for a new mode of discourse. His way of speaking is not adorned, he explains (a claim he shared with later novelists like Defoe), because of the importance of his message.

> I could also have stepped into a style much higher than this in which I have here discoursed, and could have adorned all things more than here I have seemed to do: but I dare not: God did not play in convincing of me; the devil did not play in tempting of me; neither did I play when I sunk as into a bottomless pit, when the pangs of hell caught hold upon me: wherefore I may not play in my relating of them, but be plain and simple, and lay down the thing as it was. (p. 3)

Nevertheless, his writing is heavily invested with metaphor, especially when it comes to describing the effects of revelation. Often, as with the horse pads on the road to Bedfordshire, quotidian events are invested with powerful spiritual symbolism. This is the case with Bunyan's encounter with "three or four poor women" of Bedford, "sitting at a door in the sun, and talking about the things of God" (paragraph 37). An everyday sight: there is nothing distinguished or unusual about these women, except their understated, happy piety. Yet Bunyan's imagination transforms them into a powerful symbol of salvation:

> The state and happiness of these poor people at Bedford was thus in a kind of vision represented to me: I saw as if they were set on the sunny side of some high mountain, there refreshing themselves with the pleasant beams of the sun, while I was shivering and shrinking in the cold, afflicted with frost, snow and dark clouds; methought also betwixt me and them I saw a wall that did compass about this mountain; now, through this wall, my soul did greatly desire to pass, concluding that if I could, I would go even into the very midst of them, and there also comfort myself with the heat of their sun. (paragraph 53)

In imagination, he eventually finds "a narrow gap, like a little doorway in the wall" and, like a child entering the world, he "at first did get my head, and after that by a sideling striving, my shoulders, and my whole body" and thus enters into the "sun" of religious belief (paragraph 54). The physicality of this language regarding interior life, and its capacity to render Bunyan's spiritual struggles compelling, makes *Grace Abounding* an exciting text to read, despite the lack of any fully developed characters other than Bunyan, the Devil, God, and the Scriptures themselves. Furthermore, it lays the groundwork for later forms of representation which were to articulate individuality in terms of the particularity and drama of inner life.

John Wilmot, Earl of Rochester: Libertine poetry

Rochester lived fast, died young, and, more or less, stayed pretty; or, as Samuel Johnson said of him, "he blazed out his youth and health in lavish voluptuousness." He was a protégé of Charles II and associated with a gang of wits at court. He held a series of appointments from the crown, such as Keeper of the King's Game, and Master of the King's Hawks, which supported him financially. A libertine in deed as well as word, Rochester courted a noblewoman named Elizabeth Malet and, when she and her family rejected him, he abducted her. He was caught, and put in the Tower, but quickly forgiven; two years later, she married him. By all accounts they were happy together, although Rochester also had a notorious affair with the well-known actress Elizabeth Barry. After punishing his body with the libertine life so vibrantly described in his poetry, Rochester died of syphilis at age 33. An account of his deathbed conversion, recorded by Gilbert Burnet, circulated for at least a century as pious literature.

Rochester loved taking on different identities, and he occasionally disguised himself as a beggar, among other characters. He carried on a long charade as a doctor named Alexander Benbo, "a physician skilled in treating barrenness." One can also see this interest in exploring various personae in his poetry; despite their vivid first-person accounts, not all the speakers in Rochester's poems are Rochester. In *The Platonic Lady*, for example, it is hard to tell whether the poem is written in the voice of the Platonic Lady, or to her. And, in *A Letter Fancied from Artemisia in the Town to Chloe in the Country*, he adopts the voice of a female libertine. In *The Disabled Debauchee*, the poet projects a future persona, when he will be "Driven from the pleasing billows of debauch,/On the dull shore of lazy temperance[.]" (ll. 15–16). In this new guise, he will take up the role of storyteller and instigator of others' adventures; he will, "Sheltered in impotence, urge you to blows,/and being good for nothing else, be wise" (ll. 47–8). Despite their overt concern with bawdy adventures, then, Rochester often constructs his poems around the problems of self-examination and self-reflection.

The term "libertine" had a number of meanings during the period, but it usually meant someone who thought earthly or sexual pleasures were the central good of life, and who did not believe in the authority or legitimacy of the conventional structures of society. A brief lyric sometimes attributed to Rochester, *Against Marriage*, makes this position brutally clear:

> Out of mere love and arrant devotion,
> Of marriage I'll give you this galloping notion:
> It's the bane of all business, the end of all pleasure,
> The consumption of youth, wit, courage, and treasure.
> It's the rack of our thoughts, and the nightmare of sleep,
> That sets us to work before the day peep.
> It makes us make brick without stubble or straw,
> And a cunt has no sense of conscience or law.

As this poem reveals, libertine thought generated conflicting views about women, who were both reduced to mere body parts and granted an anarchic desire for pleasure equal to men's. The question of whether a woman could be a libertine herself remains unresolved. The male libertine's goal seemed clear, however: to escape the restrictions symbolized by marriage and to live a life in which pleasure, youth, wit, courage, and money remained in good supply. Yet, the perpetual search for new love objects and new conquests made "restlessness, dissatisfaction, or a sense of incompleteness" the "defining characteristic" of libertine ideology.[13] Thus, although its emphasis on possession seems to align libertinism with the emergence of capitalism, the libertine is always more interested in expenditure – whether it be of money, wine, or love – than accumulation. The libertine moves through a sequence of women, rather than accumulating a waiting harem. In this way, libertinism can be seen as a form of resistance to the rise of capitalist ideology.

Most of Rochester's poems were circulated in manuscript, though some were published after his death.[14] For modern readers, the most striking thing about them may be their sexually explicit content and language, as in the poem quoted above. There are at least three ways of thinking about the purpose or function of that language, ways that may not be mutually exclusive. At times, the language seems to function in much the same way as graffiti, revealing a kind of violence or anger against the structures of society: not explicit protest, perhaps, but nonetheless a way of striking back. Such language can also be seen as a gesture of aristocratic privilege, the kind of self-debasement in which only someone at the top of society could indulge. One critic has said of Rochester that "the reason he could talk in this absolutely plain way was that he was a great lord and a favorite of the king: a person of lower class, such as a university professor or a Puritan preacher, would obviously have to talk in a more affected manner" to uphold their social status.[15] Yet, it is also possible to see in Rochester's explicit language a strange kinship with Bunyan, who also participated in the era's drive to make language clear, plain, concrete, and rooted in the ordinary world. Although that goal took them in different directions, both Bunyan and Rochester shared something with the aims of the Royal Society of Scientists, who "exacted from all their members a close, naked, natural way of speaking; positive expressions, clear senses; a native easiness; bringing all things as near the Mathematical plainness, as they can: and preferring the language of Artizans, Countrymen, and Merchants, before that of Wits or Scholars"[16]

Furthermore, Rochester's poetry, as much as Bunyan's prose, raises crucial questions about conceptions of selfhood and personal identity during the late seventeenth century. Most centrally, by focusing on the desiring subject, it raises the question of whether desire is a physical or psychological drive. Libertine poetry seems to posit that the most important thing in the world is the body and its pleasures, and that to pretend otherwise is hypocrisy. Yet it often ends up presenting a world in which the mind cannot control the body's desires, and thus the mind and the body end up radically divorced. One of Rochester's best-known bawdy poems, *The Imperfect Enjoyment*, takes up this problem in circumstances that initially seem comic. The poet and his lover, "Both equally inspired with eager fire,/melting through kindness, flaming in desire" (ll. 3–4), are ready for passionate intercourse; but the speaker prematurely ejaculates – "melt[s] into sperm, and spend[s] at every pore" (l. 16).[17] His partner is disappointed, the more so because she cannot get him to continue; he says, "Trembling, confused, despairing, limber, dry,/A wishing, weak, unmoving lump I lie" (ll. 35–6). The speaker does not blame his lover for this misfortune, however, but turns his anger on his own body. The entire second half of the poem consists of the poet's tirade against his own penis, which, "Now languid lies, in this unhappy hour,/Shrunk up, and sapless, like a withered flower./ Thou treacherous, base deserter of my flame,/. . ./Worst part of me, and henceforth hated most" (ll. 44–6, 62). In calling down punishments on his own body, however, the speaker's comic exasperation raises some interesting questions about the location of libertine identity. Is he that lump? When the body cannot obey the "wishing" of desire, is the self that desires negated, isolated in the prison of the mind? Does corporeal desire then convert to a hatred of the body?

It should not surprise us that in Rochester's vision of Eden, body and "wish" are perfectly aligned: "Naked beneath cool shades they lay,/ Enjoyment waited on desire;/Each member did their wills obey:/Nor could a wish set pleasure hire" (*The Fall*, ll. 5–8). In the post-Edenic world, however, this union of body and soul has been broken: "But we, poor slaves to hope and fear,/Are never of our joys secure:/They lessen still, as they draw near,/And none but dull delights endure" (ll. 9–12). The body seems to mark the limit of identity, the point at which human will is thwarted, and concepts of identity based on interiority are undermined.

In the libertine's commitment to the material world, then, there is always the possibility that the writing subject will disappear into simple matter. In a loose translation from Seneca's *Troades*, Rochester writes: "After death nothing is, and nothing, death;/The utmost limit of a gasp of breath" (ll. 1–2):

> Dead we become the lumber of the world,
> And to that mass of matter shall be swept,
> Where things destroyed with things unborn are kept.
> Devouring time swallows us whole;
> Impartial death confounds body and soul. (ll. 8–12)

"Confound" here seems to mean both "confuse" and "conflate." The poem suggests that, while we may believe in our own unique identity, that self will in the end be reduced to "lumber" – pure matter that makes all humans indistinguishable from each other.

Furthermore, in positing no world beyond this one, this poetry formulates a disquieting image of the ephemeral nature of personal identity. In the short lyric, *Love and Life*, for example, the speaker's focus on living for the moment paints a disturbing picture of time's power to destroy coherent identity:

> All my past life is mine no more,
> The flying hours are gone,
> Like transitory dreams given o'er,
> Whose images are kept in store
> By memory alone.

> The time that is to come is not,
> How can it then be mine?
> The present moment's all my lot,
> And that, as fast as it is got,
> Phyllis, is only thine.

> Then talk not of inconstancy,
> False hearts and broken vows,
> If I by miracle can be,
> This live-long minute true to thee,
> 'Tis all that heaven allows.

If Marvell used the threat of "Time's winged chariot" to urge his partner on to consummation, Rochester suggests that the poet, the poem, and identity itself have only a minute to live and love. As Carole Fabricant points out, many of Rochester's lyrics in fact seem to work against the *carpe diem* tradition, and celebrate waiting and contemplating more that the act of love itself, at times revealing a "profound revulsion of sexuality itself."[18]

Thus, libertine poetry, while it celebrates the pleasures of this world, often also rails against the degradations of human life. Indeed, the most lasting impression left by Rochester's poetry may be of contempt for the follies and indignities of the material world. In his best-known nonbawdy poem, *A Satyr Against Mankind*, for example, the speaker begins by bemoaning his inability to shed his human identity:

> Were I (who to my cost already am
> One of those strange, prodigious creatures, man)
> A spirit free to choose for my own share
> What case of flesh and blood I pleased to wear,
> I'd be a dog, a monkey, or a bear,
> Or anything but that vain animal,
> Who is so proud of being rational.

Rochester here, as in so much of his libertine verse, articulates the central paradox of the satirist: he is already, despite his wishes, one of the group he criticizes, bound to a failing body and ephemeral convictions of a unique identity. Contemplation of the self and its pleasures works to delineate the limits of identity in the material and temporal world.

Samuel Richardson, *Clarissa*

When Pamela's demands for respect lead her aristocratic suitor (and employer) to propose an honorable marriage, Richardson's first novel, *Pamela* (1747–8), seemed to prove that, as its subtitle states, virtue could be rewarded. The novel's happy ending, however, begged the question of instrumentalism: was the purpose of virtue the material comfort of acquiring a comfortable house, nice clothes, and a prominent husband? Was it possible, instead, for women to pursue virtue for its own sake, even if they were never materially rewarded for it? In his second novel, Richardson seems to have set out to answer that question – though in the process the problem of what constitutes feminine virtue became infinitely more complicated. *Clarissa* tells the story of a beautiful, intelligent young girl, born into a gentry family that hopes to increase its own standing by marrying her off to a rich man whom she despises. Intrigued by Lovelace, a handsome aristocrat who promises to save her from this marriage, Clarissa is duped into running away from her family home. Lovelace's protestations of good will prove false, however, and he imprisons Clarissa in a house of ill repute in London, where he more and more brutally tries to bring her under his control. Finally, he rapes her. Clarissa flees, and, disowned now by her family, spends almost the entire second half of the novel gradually declining into death. Lovelace, who has realized the error of his ways, also dies, in a duel in Europe. The novel asks us how Clarissa's virtue can survive her reputation, her physical violation, and her exile from the society into which she was born.

The epic battle of wills between Clarissa and Lovelace plays out through an epistolary narrative. In *Pamela*, almost all the letters are written by the heroine herself, and the unitary perspective both focuses and narrows readers' interpretations of the plot. In *Clarissa*, however, both protagonists give their version of events – Clarissa writing to her friend Anna Howe, Lovelace to his friend Belford (even as Belford gradually becomes Clarissa's ally). This structure multiplies both perspective and words – at over a million words, *Clarissa* is the longest novel in the English language. It also generates many different interpretations of the characters – especially since Richardson endows Lovelace with charm, wit, and intelligence as he plans his calumnies. Both characters articulate their identities through writing, and readers have seen the contest between them as a contest between Lovelace's interest in the play and indeterminacy of language, and Clarissa's commitment to straightforward referentiality.[19] Thus Richardson found himself in a protracted battle with his most valued readers, who wanted Lovelace to convert (as Mr. B. had done) and Clarissa to get the happy marriage she deserved. Anxious to corral such readers, Richardson continued to revise and expand his novel as it went through three editions; he added 22 footnotes, for instance, instructing the reader on the evils of Lovelace's character. He also excerpted the important bits of his novels in *A Collection of the Moral and Instructive Sentiments, Maxims, Cautions, and Reflexions, Contained in the Histories of Pamela, Clarissa, and Sir Charles Grandison* (1755), just in case his readers failed to realize which those were.

Samuel Johnson once famously said: "If you would read Richardson for the story, your impatience would be so much fretted that you would hang yourself. But you must read him for the sentiment."[20] He meant this as a compliment. And indeed, many eighteenth-century readers seemed to have enjoyed *Clarissa* not simply for the states of high feeling it represents but also for the intense reactions it provoked in them. Lady Braidshaugh, one of Richardson's most valued correspondents, sent him a dramatic record of her reading experience: "When alone, in agonies would I lay down the book, take it up again, walk about the room, let fall a flood of tears, wipe my eyes, read again, perhaps not three lines, throw away the book, crying out, excuse me Mr. Richardson, I cannot go on."[21] Though Lady Braidshaugh proved to be recalcitrant in hoping that Clarissa and Lovelace would marry, this is exactly how Richardson hoped his novel would work: the emotions felt by the characters would be echoed by the reader, who would reform accordingly.

Even within the novel, Clarissa's captivity narrative, like the autobiographical narrative Bunyan wrote for his congregation while imprisoned in Bedford jail, reforms a community of readers who vow to preserve her memory – most prominently, Lovelace's friend Belford.[22] Yet, is Clarissa's life as exemplary as Bunyan's? Although Richardson urges us to read her as virtuous almost to the point of saintliness, many of her actions are questionable by eighteenth-century standards. She defies her parents in refusing to marry Solmes, her parents' choice; she finds Lovelace attractive, and says she might have been able to love him. She may even be said to will her own death. In constructing a heroine whose virtue transcends all material or social punishments or rewards, Richardson also found himself with a character who challenged the mores of eighteenth-century femininity.[23]

As characters, both Lovelace and Clarissa are interesting commentaries on the ideas of selfhood developed by libertine culture. Lovelace is a development of the rake – but imagined in a very different way than Rochester. Rochester was able to abduct his wife and later marry her – Lovelace loses everything for just such an attempt. The novel emphasizes his capacity for cruelty and sadism, and he dies bereft of all his beliefs. Clarissa herself seems the ultimate challenge to a system that locates identity in the body and in earthly pleasure. Transcending the violation and subsequent wreck of her body, she asserts the value of her spirit, even as she dies (as do those around her). The plot of the novel puts these views onto a collision course. As Frances Ferguson has written, "Rape . . . dramatizes a problematic about the relationship between the body and the mind; although a rake like Lovelace may imagine that carnal 'knowing' includes knowing someone else's mind, a character like Clarissa – virtuous even in her violation – suggests that one knows about mental experience as much in despite of the body as through it."[24] Yet, the paradoxes inherent in both Lovelace's absorption by the body and Clarissa's contempt for it are played out in the representation of the rape – or, more precisely, the lack thereof. Lovelace, famously, writes the briefest letter of the novel to record the event: "And now, Belford, I can go no farther. The affair is over. Clarissa lives"[25] (883). The act that is supposed to give him dominion over both her body and soul leaves him instead with a sinking sense that the body is merely a meaningless shell. A few days later, Lovelace brutally records his disappointment in finding that raping Clarissa has not brought him any closer to the control he craves:

> At times I cannot help regretting that I ever attempted her; since not one power of either body or soul could be moved in my favour; and since, to use the expression of the philosopher, on a much graver occasion, There is no difference to be found between the skull of king Philip and that of another man. (L 259, p. 885)

Yet, if Lovelace realizes (as does Rochester) that all bodies are mere matter, and that all matter is interchangeable, Clarissa, paradoxically, finds that she is tied to her own particular body, and the marks of its violation; she cannot escape the position in which it places her. Meticulously planning her own funeral and burial, she admits, "this vile body ought not so much to engage my cares. It is a weakness – but let it be called a *natural* weakness, and I shall be excused" (L 465). But Clarissa is right to take such care with the presentation of her "remains," for in some ways her virtue is as tied to the evidence of her dying body as Pamela's is to her virginity. This spectacle engrosses her admirers almost as much as her words. One part of Belford's long description of her death reads:

> One faded cheek rested upon [Mrs. Lovick's] bosom, the kindly warmth of which had overspread it with a faint, but charming flush; the other paler, and hollow, as if already iced over by death. Her hands, white as the lily, with her meandering veins more transparently blue than ever I had seen even hers (veins so soon, alas! To be choked up by the congealment of that purple stream which already so languidly creeps rather than flows through them!) (L 474)

In attempting to locate identity not in the body but in the soul, Richardson finds himself still entangled in the problems of ocular proof. In trying to divorce feminine virtue from corporeality, he finds himself offering up the manifestations of that virtue on the body as evidence, be it Clarissa's mesmerizing fragility or Lady Braidshaugh's tears.

Laurence Sterne, *Tristram Shandy*

The century's other great narrative experiment in the representation of the self is *Tristram Shandy*, which appeared in five installments between 1759 and 1767. Although Sterne's novel is as digressive as Richardson's is narrowly focused, and as bawdy as Richardson's is self-consciously chaste, the two share a drive to interrogate exhaustively the workings of an individual mind. Both, furthermore, equate the capacity to write with life itself – and thus the end of narrative with a literal death. Sterne's hero sets out to tell the story of his life, but notoriously gets caught up in the circumstances of his conception, and the difficulties surrounding his birth. The baby Tristram does not enter the world – or the book – until volume four. Instead, most of the novel relates the learned disquisitions and rants of Tristram's father, Walter, the adventures and eccentricities of his Uncle Toby, and various interpolated sermons and tales. The novel presents us with layer upon layer of storytellers – Walter, Toby, and Toby's servant, Corporal Trip, to name a few – whose efforts complement Tristram's own struggle to explain his curious circumstances. The digressive and associative elements of the novel, however, defy summary: as one enthusiastic but baffled eighteenth-century reviewer wrote, "This is a humorous performance, of which we are unable to convey any distinct idea to our readers."[26]

Sterne, like Richardson, became a celebrity late in life. He was born in Ireland, though his father, an army ensign, was the penniless son of a distinguished Yorkshire family. These Yorkshire relatives paid for Sterne's Cambridge education and his training as an Anglican priest. After this inauspicious beginning, Sterne spent the greater part of his life as an obscure clergyman, notorious only for his sexual indiscretions, and that only locally. He published *Tristram Shandy*, his first novel, in his mid-forties, but it was an immediate success. Sterne embraced the fame that the publication of *Tristram Shandy* brought him, encouraging the confusion between himself and the title character, traveling to London and befriending the rich and famous. The "Shandean" manner he perfected was much imitated. James Boswell, an admirer, described him thus:

> By fashion's hands completely drest,
> He's everywhere a welcome Guest:
> He runs about from place to place
> Now with my Lord, then With his Grace
> And mixing with the brilliant throng,
> He strait commences Beau Garcon.
> In Ranelagh's delightful round
> Squire Tristram oft is flaunting found.
> A buzzing whisper flys about,
> Where'er he comes they point him out;
> Each Waiter with an eager eye
> Observes him as he passes by:
> That there he is, do, Thomas! Look
> Who's wrote such a damn'd clever Book.[27]

Sterne did not live to enjoy his fame for long, however. He died in 1768, three weeks after the publication of his second novel, *A Sentimental Journey through France and Italy*.

Its full title, *The Life and Opinions of Tristram Shandy*, marks Sterne's text as a fictional autobiography, and thus as a novel. Yet its lack of lack of narrative, and its interest in displaying, digesting, and satirizing the whole of Western learning, from Rabelais to Locke, and through the by-ways of eighteenth-century medicine – seem to differentiate *Tristram Shandy* from the novel, and bring it closer to the traditions of learned wit, and to satirical texts like Swift's *Tale of a Tub*. Sterne certainly saw himself as a literary descendant of Swift's, if not as bawdy: "I deny I have gone as farr as Swift," he said, "He keeps a due distance from Rabelais – & I keep a due distance from him – Swift has said a hundred things I durst Not Say – Unless I was Dean of St. Patricks –."[28] Other readers have argued that Sterne's departures from what had already emerged as the conventions of novel writing – his nonlinear narrative, his use of graphic symbols, and Tristram's meta-commentary on his own process of writing – make him the first postmodern writer, an eighteenth-precursor of twentieth-century authors like Thomas Pynchon. Recently, however, Thomas Keymer has argued that many of the seeming innovations of *Tristram Shandy* also appeared in other novels of the 1750s. After the spectacular success of novels by Richardson and Fielding in the 1740s, this decade doubted the continued viability of the genre, as no new literary giants appeared on the scene. The novels produced in these years seemed to feel the need to be as experimental and self-conscious as possible to draw attention to themselves.[29]

One thing *Tristram Shandy* shares with novels of the preceding decade is an interest in the status of the book as a material object. Even Richardson had experimented with making the lines on the page visually reflect the inner workings of the mind; the "fragments" that Clarissa writes in her madness after the rape are set askew and sideways on the page. Sterne goes farther, however, in exploiting the visual possibilities of the book as printed object to comic, and sometime poignant, effect. A black page, functioning as a kind of memento mori, follows the announcement of Parson Yorick's death, itself inscribed in an outlined tag in the middle of the page: "Alas, poor YORICK!" Like Swift, Sterne signals his awareness of the reader's imaginative input into a text by filling spaces with dashes or asterisks. Tristram even leaves a blank page on which the reader can paint his own image of Uncle Toby's erstwhile love interest, the widow Wadman: "Sit down, Sir, paint her to your own mind – as like your mistress as you can – as unlike your wife as your conscience will let you – 'tis all one to me – please but your own fancy in it" (vol. VI, chapter 38, p. 450). Such appeals to the reader's sexual imagination led at least one reviewer to label Sterne a libertine: "Why you might as well write broad Rochester as set down all these obscene asterisms! – setting the reader's imagination to work, and officiating as pimp to every lewd idea excited by your own creative and abominable ambiguity."[30] But as interested as he is in innuendo, Sterne also uses graphic inventiveness to tweak the sentimental convention of language's inability to convey true feelings. When Corporal Trim flourishes his stick to demonstrate the joys of bachelorhood, Tristram notes: "A thousand of my father's most subtle syllogisms could not have said more for celibacy" (vol. IX, chapter 4, p. 576).

Tristram devotes himself to finding the causes of the self's formation, and famously begins with the unfortunate circumstances of his own conception.

> I wish either my father or my mother, or indeed both of them, as they were in duty both equally bound to it, had minded what they were about when they begot me; had they duly considered how much depended upon what they were then doing; – that not only the production of a rational Being was concerned in it, but that possibly the happy formation and temperature of his body, perhaps his genius and the very cast of his mind; – and, for aught they knew to the contrary, even the fortunes of his whole house might take their turn from the humours and dispositions which were then uppermost: – had they duly weighed and considered all this, and proceeded accordingly, – I am verily persuaded I should have made a quite different figure in the world, from that, in which the reader is likely to see me. (p. 36)

Tristram's mother interrupts his father with a question about the other activity he performs one Sunday a month – winding the clock – and thus dissipates his vital powers. Sterne draws here on an early modern belief that the parents' thoughts at the moment of fertilization influence a child's mental and physical makeup, a variation on the contemporary belief that a woman who looked at a picture of a monster while pregnant could give birth to a monstrous child. As Dennis Todd points out, this belief had the queasy effect of fusing the workings of the mind and the workings of the body; it posits that "imagination deformed a fetus by incorporating mind in body."[31] This small incident sets up the series of provocative questions that power the novel; Sterne uses this originating moment to trouble assumptions about cause and effect; a chance arrangement of "humours and dispositions" effects the whole house of Shandy into perpetuity. Where, he asks, can we find the beginning of a seemingly arbitrary chain of events? The far-reaching consequences of minute actions ask us to interrogate the nature of duty and "responsibility" – a volatile topic in the later eighteenth century: the "homunculus," the embryo, Sterne asserts in the next chapter, is a "BEING guarded and circumscribed with rights" (p. 36). How much, the novel's opening sentences ask, does identity depend on events that happened before we were born, and thus wholly out of our control?

Sterne explores the effect of external events on the construction of identity through another character as well: Tristram's Uncle Toby. Toby spends four years bedridden after being wounded in the groin at the siege of Namur, during the War of the Spanish Succession. Visitors to his sick bed ask him for his story, believing that "the history of a soldier's wound beguiles the pain of it" (p. 100). Toby, however, finds these inquiries torturous, "and the many perplexities he was in, arose out of the almost insurmountable difficulties he found in telling his story intelligibly" (p. 103).

Driven close to madness by his inability to give an exact description of the events at Namur, he devotes himself to building a scale model of the battle (and eventually many more battles) on his bowling green. This preoccupation with military technology consumes his time and sentiments – to the great disappointment of the voluptuous Widow Wadman. Nonetheless, Toby is depicted as a generous, gentle, sentimental man – one who literally cannot hurt a fly. Walter Scott, in his *Lives of the Novelists*, calls Toby "a lively picture of kindness and benevolence . . . with whose pleasures we are so much disposed to sympathize." William Hazlitt praised the characterization of Toby as "one of the finest compliments ever paid to human nature." The novel challenges us to reconcile Toby's assertion that war is the natural duty of man (made in his apologetical oration decrying the Treaty of Utrecht) with his ready sympathy and generosity (as to Le Fever). Melvyn New finds authorial irony in Sterne's characterization of "a person who, while sympathetic towards a fly, re-enacts with pleasure battles in which tens of thousands are killed or wounded" (pp. 76–7). Yet, Keymer argues that Toby's "obsessional re-enactments" of battles reveal a very modern pathology: "the victim of an originating trauma that he is endlessly doomed to act out, Toby is a fictional precursor of the shell-shocked veterans of more recent trench warfare, helplessly fixated on an unspeakable past."[32]

Along with detailing the debt owed by individual identity in the present to the blows of an uncontrollable past, *Tristram Shandy* is concerned with delineating the minute movements of the mind in the present. Jonathan Lamb argues that the novel presents a model of the mind similar to that of the associationist, David Hartley, positing a "direct mechanical linkage of matter and mind via Newtonian vibrations."[33] In his *Observations on Man, His Frame, His Duty and His Expectations* (1749), Hartley had written: "Every Action, or bodily Motion, arises from previous Circumstances, or bodily Motions, already existing in the Brain, i.e. from Vibrations, which are either the immediate Effect of Impressions then made, or the remote compound Effect of former Impressions, or both."[34] At its most concrete, the contingent association of ideas describes Tristram's parents' unfortunate focus on clock maintenance, rather than the marriage bed, simply because both take place on the first Sunday of the month. At its most abstract, the narrator finds that words remind him of other words, regardless of their relevance to the story at hand:

> In mentioning the word gay (as in the close of the last chapter) it puts
> one (i.e. an author) in mind of the word spleen – especially if he has any-
> thing to say upon it: not that by any analysis – or that from any table of
> interest of genealogy, there appears much more ground of alliance betwixt
> them, than betwixt light and darkness, or any two of the most unfriendly

> opposites in nature – only 'tis an undercraft of authors to keep up a good
> understanding amongst words, as politicians do amongst men – not
> knowing how near they may be under a necessity of placing them next
> to each other[.] (p. 479)

Here, words take on a life of their own, promiscuously mixing and fighting,
as men do unless governed by politicians. The associative quality of the
novel's language produces some interesting effects, including its notorious
proliferation of double entendres.

We are always conscious, however, of the person writing, who equates
the pages he produces with the continuation of his own life. Tristram's life
has always been haunted by the shadow or suspicion of impotence and
castration, after the "man midwife" Dr Slop crushes his nose (or "nose")
with his forceps, and after an injury by a sash window. Thus betrayed by
his body, Tristram is unusually aware of how much of his identity is caught
up in print. Ever conscious of how his narrative is being perceived, even
as he continues to write it (remember that *Tristram Shandy* appeared in
serial form), he forgives the "Monthly Reviewers" for the injuries they have
done him:

> being determined as long as I live or write (which in my case means the
> same thing) never to give the honest gentleman a worse word or a worse
> wish, than my uncle Toby gave the fly which buzzed about his nose all
> dinner-time. – "Go, – go poor devil," quoth he, "– get thee gone, – why
> should I hurt thee? This world is surely wide enough to hold both thee and
> me." (vol. III, chapter 4, p. 175).

Thus, Sterne explores the limits of the structure of retrospective narration
pioneered in spiritual autobiographies like Bunyan's. In a text like *Grace
Abounding*, the retrospective narrator is a remote presence organizing the
experiences of his younger self; in *Tristram Shandy*, that narrator takes over
much of the text, his self-examination obscuring the autobiographical
story he purports to tell. Finally arriving at the moment of his own birth
in volume III, for instance, Tristram focuses on his present feelings, rather
than on the progress of his infant self:

> I enter upon this part of my story in the most pensive and melancholy
> frame of mind, that ever sympathetic breast was touched with. – My
> nerves relax as I tell it. – Every line I write, I feel an abatement of the
> quickness of my pulse, and of that careless alacrity with it, which every
> day of my life prompts me to say and write a thousand things I should not.
> – And this moment that I last dipped my pen into my ink, I could not help
> taking notice what a cautious air of sad composure and solemnity there
> appeared in my manner of doing it. (vol. III, chapter 28, p. 222).

Keymer calls this dynamic a "prolonged drama of digressive writing and progressive disease ... in which Tristram fails to record his life in the past while watching it waste in the present."[35] Tristram Shandy's investment in writing as a means of both prolonging his life and giving it meaning reveals how closely ideas of selfhood were caught up with innovations in print culture during the eighteenth century.

6

Religious Experience

Introduction

The Augustan period was inaugurated by religious conflict. The decades that preceded it, the years of the of the Civil War and Interregnum, had been characterized by religious freedom and a burgeoning number of dissenting sects – groups dissenting from doctrine of the Anglican Church – including Quakers, Baptists, Ranters, and Anabaptists. Many of these sects relied on or encouraged literacy in their members to facilitate a personal reading and understanding of the Bible. At the same time, censorship laws relaxed, allowing more religious works to be written and published and English translations of the Bible to become widely available. Many of these writings were personal testimonies or expressions of belief.

After the Restoration of Charles II, this religious freedom was linked to the political fervor that had led to the turmoil of the Interregnum, and the state attempted to impose a number of restrictions on religious expression outside the state church. More generally, dissenting religious zeal, known as "enthusiasm," came to seem untrustworthy, risible, and/or potentially treasonable. In *Religio Laici* (1682), for example, Dryden characterizes the religious freedom of the Interregnum as the parasitical growth of decay.

> *Study* and *Pains* were now no more their Care;
> *Texts* were explain'd by *Fasting*, and by *Prayer*:
> This was the Fruit the *private Spirit* Brought;
> Occasion'd by *great Zeal* and *little Thought*.
> While Crouds unlearn'd with rude Devotion warm,
> Around the Sacred Viands buzz and swarm,
> The *Fly-blown Text* creates a *crawling Brood*;
> And turns to *Maggots* what was meant for *Food*.
> A *Thousand daily Sects rise up and dye*;
> A *Thousand more the perish'd Race supply*[.] (ll. 413–22)

Indeed, much eighteenth-century religious thought was characterized by the struggle to differentiate between dangerous enthusiasm and serious, responsible religious practice.

Although the Anglican Church never regained the political and social power it had held before the Interregnum, various acts were imposed to keep a tight rein on religious expression. Collectively, they were known as the Clarendon Code, and they forbade sectarian meetings, and imposed prison sentences for refusing to pay tithes or take oaths in court. The Conventicle Act, increasing the severity of punishments, was passed in 1664. The Test Acts of 1673 and 1678 restricted public office-holders to those willing to take communion in the Church of England, and prevented Catholics from sitting in the English parliament. The reign of Charles II was also marked by conflict over the religious identity of the British crown. An alleged "Popish Plot" to unseat Charles in favor of his Catholic brother James was concocted in 1678 by Titus Oates and sent a number of Catholics to their deaths. Between 1679 and 1681, Parliament tried unsuccessfully three times to pass bills excluding James from succeeding to the throne. James's indulgences of Catholic friends contributed to the Glorious Revolution of 1688, and to acts forbidding other Catholics from the British monarchy. The Toleration Act of 1689, however, was an acknowledgment that the Church of England could never hold the monopoly it once had: "Even a High Tory Anglican like Sir John Reresby recognized in May 1688 that 'most men were now convinced that liberty of conscience was a thing of advantage to the nation.'"[1]

One important, though unintended, consequence of the Toleration Act, however, was the establishment of Dissenting Academies. These institutions created an alternative educational possibility to Oxford or Cambridge (from which dissenters were barred through the Test Acts). While the universities delivered an education in the classics, the Dissenting Academies emphasized the practical elements of life, teaching science, accounting, and literature written in English. Throughout the eighteenth century, prominent writers appeared from academies like that in Newington Green in London, including Defoe and, later, Anna Barbauld and William Godwin.

Religion during the Restoration and early eighteenth century became more concerned with accommodating human reason to religious belief, as in the work of John Locke. The work of Isaac Newton suggested that the universe had been made by a "divine clockmaker" who then stepped aside to let his creation run on its own (the "argument from design" seemed to most a further proof of God's existence). Scholars today continue to debate whether eighteenth-century England was still a country dominated by the

Church and Christian modes of thinking, or whether the Enlightenment was the beginning of a pervasive secularization of everyday life. Yet, "the greatest volume of print production continued to consist of religious and didactic works."[2] A particularly influential theologian was William Law, who wrote *A Serious Call to a Devout and Holy Life* (1729), among many other works. Law's emphasis on the expression of piety through everyday activities, and the importance of interior conversion, influenced the Wesleys, and many others. Despite the increased emphasis on secular achievements, serious religion did not disappear from eighteenth-century life, as evidenced by Methodism in the middle part of the century, and Evangelicals both inside and outside the Anglican Church in the last decades of the century.

There has been a good deal of debate about the meaning of the success of the Methodist movement in mid-eighteenth century Britain. To many, Methodism seemed to mark a return to enthusiasm. John Wesley and George Whitefield preached outside to the poor and inspired responses of great emotion. It was said that Whitefield's first sermon drove fifteen people mad. Some think that Methodism fulfilled a need for community among an increasingly rootless and isolated urban nation, others that adherents were dupes of hypocritical ministers. Making fun of Methodists was a great mid-century pastime, in which Hogarth, Smollett, and a host of others participated. Yet, like the sectarians of the seventeenth century, Methodists produced a good deal of personal writing. Perhaps inspired by, or in reaction to, the success of Methodism, there was a great revival in serious Christianity in the last decades of the eighteenth century. Like Methodists, serious Christians both inside and outside the Anglican Church emphasized the moment of individual conversion. Unlike Methodists, however, Evangelicals turned to politics. Hannah More and William Wilberforce, founders of the Clapham sect, turned their attention to the antislavery movement, among other causes. In their hands, writing would be a tool for social reform.

Literature in the eighteenth century defined itself both through and against religion – a dynamic often overlooked in recent years. As Paula McDowell notes,

> while revisionist historians increasingly argue for the continued centrality of religion as a social and cultural force, literary studies and cultural criticism remain strikingly unaffected by these developments. Despite a few promising signs, religious writing remains marginalized in our literary histories and cultural studies models, its place in our field of vision directly inverse to its actual importance in the period we study.[3]

We should recognize, however, that religious reading had a direct impact on secular reading. The great rise in literacy associated with Protestant sectarianism and the spread of vernacular religious literature, including the Bible, made possible the success of emerging popular literary forms, pre-eminently the novel. Furthermore, the spiritual autobiographies demanded by many groups provided an important paradigm for the novel's stories of individuals. The spiritual awakenings of Robinson Crusoe and Moll Flanders depend on that model, as does the careful self-scrutiny of Pamela Andrews. For poets, the sentiments and forms of scripture provided impor-tant resources. Implicitly, as well, Christianity furnished a moral code by which to distinguish good characters from villains throughout the period. Yet, the novel also drew some of its popularity from its rejection of certain kinds of "inappropriate" religion. J. Paul Hunter, for instance, argues that, "early on, the novel repeatedly attacked Methodism and in fact achieved some of its acceptance in the broader social community by its intemperate tirades against Methodist faith"[4]

Poetry, too, was often defined against the "nonliterary" quality of reli-gious poetry.

> The development of a distinctly religious poetry in the eighteenth century charts for that poetry a course which diverges radically from the main stream of more "secular" poetry...For the poets of religion in the eigh-teenth century...become more concerned with clarity, with the perceived need to address a general and heterogeneous audience, at the same time as poets less directly concerned with religious issues acknowledge that their poetry has become "vocal" only to a small and select group.[5]

Yet, as John Sitter intriguingly argues, theological ideas may also have affected the aesthetics of eighteenth-century poetry. He claims that Law's "emphasis on God's words as acts, rather than as descriptions of acts, has its secular counterpart in a conspicuous fascination with verbal power on the part of the authors of sublime odes," including "the self-completed *Song* of Smart ('DETERMINED, DARED, and DONE!')."[6]

The texts treated in this section, then, deal with two important aspects of religion in eighteenth-century culture. At stake throughout the period was the problem of proper religious expression: the propriety of women speaking in church; the impropriety of enthusiasm; and the propriety of hymn singing. This concern with propriety is related to the question of translation that animated neoclassical poets. Religious writers asked how the word of God, which they believed was clearly transcribed in the Scriptures, could be made to live in the modern world; could the modern writer, or reader, they asked, approach the condition of spiritual inspiration evident in the psalmist and the apostles. Also at stake, in a way it had not been in earlier periods, was the compatibility of religion with dominant modes of literary expressions.

Margaret Fell Fox, "Women's Speaking Justified"

The Society of Friends, called Quakers by those who derided their expressions of emotion during meetings, originated during the Interregnum under the leadership of George Fox. Their belief system was founded on the idea of an "inner light," which came directly from God. This connection with God was supposed to place Friends in the same spiritual condition as Jesus' original apostles. Thus, they were not dependent on scripture for transmission of God's word because they understood that word directly for themselves. The inner light did not differentiate with regard to either gender or class. George Fox said in 1646: "The Lord Opened unto me that being bred at Oxford or Cambridge was not enough to fit and qualify men to be ministers of Christ; and I stranged at it because it was the common belief of the people."[7] This rejection of traditional hierarchies initially opened many opportunities for women inside the movement. Female Friends preached, prophesied, and wrote a great deal. Katherine Evans, who traveled as a missionary to Malta, said, "whatsoever I have written, it's not because it is written in the Scripture, but in obedience to the Lord I have written the things which I did hear, see, tasted, and handled of the good word of God"[8]

After the Restoration, Quakers also suffered from the "backlash" against sectarian religions – they were prosecuted for meeting and imprisoned for their beliefs. Since Friends were restricted from meeting publicly, letter writing, and other forms of writing became more important during this period. Women, who had enjoyed increased prominence within many dissenting sects, suffered a proportional curtailment of their freedoms. Yet, while many other seventeenth-century sects, like Muggletonians or Ranters, disappeared in the face of such restrictions, the Society of Friends managed to survive and prosper by instituting a number of self-regulating measures. Quakers instituted an organizational structure, including modes of self-censorship, which allowed their movement to survive the restrictions of the Restoration and the eighteenth century. Phyllis Mack writes: "the history of late seventeenth-century Quakerism presents the observer with a virtually ideal type of radical religious movement: a loose egalitarian group under charismatic leadership evolving into a tightly knit, bureaucratized, hierarchical church."[9] The Quaker doctrine of nonviolence originated at this time, as did separate women's meetings. The movement decided that women should only preach and speak inside these separate meetings, although they were still given an important role in supervising family life and charity.

Margaret Askew was born into a landowning family in the north of England, married a prominent judge named Fell, and raised a family there. She later converted to Quakerism and became a leader of the religion. She was active in the Quaker movement from its beginnings, lending her house, polemical pen, and bargaining power to its efforts. On many occasions she helped to get imprisoned Friends released. When her husband the judge died, she married the Quaker leader George Fox in 1669, although she was, at 55, older than her husband. Margaret Fell's publications exemplify the way certain aspects of the religious freedom of the Interregnum, in conjunction with increased access to print, survived into the Restoration.

"Women's Speaking Justified" is not an argument that women should be allowed to speak in church for the first time, but that they should be allowed to continue to do so within the Quaker movement. The tract itself exemplifies Fell's confidence in her talent for Scriptural exegesis. She takes on the troubling assertion in Paul's *First Letter to the Corinthians* that women should remain silent in church. She begins with the simple assertion that "God put no such difference between the Male and Female as men would make."[10] Yet the tract continues by establishing the special significance of women in the Christian tradition. Her opening salvo in this effort is to put a new twist on the story of Adam and Eve, by emphasizing Eve's determination to "speak truth unto the Lord," and God's institution of enmity between the woman and the serpent.

> Let this Word of the Lord, which was from the beginning, stop the mouths of all that oppose Women's Speaking in the Power of the Lord; for he hath put enmity between the Woman and the Serpent; and if the Seed of the Woman speak not, the Seed of the Serpent speaks; for God hath put enmity between the two Seeds, and it is manifest, that those that speak against the Woman and her Seed's Speaking, speak out of the enmity of the old Serpent's Seed. (p. 4)

Fell goes on to argue that the Church itself is imaged as a woman, and thus "those that speak against this woman's speaking, speak against the Church of Christ" (p. 5). Then, in a strategy shared by many women writing for female equality in the early eighteenth century, she elaborates on the significance of women in the Bible, particularly those intimate with

Jesus himself: the Woman of Samaria, Martha, Mary Magdalene and others. It was women, she points out, who received the message of Christ's having risen.

> Mark you this, you that despise and oppose the Message of the Lord God that he sends by women, what had become of the Redemption of the whole Body of Mankind, if they had not believed the message that the Lord Jesus sent by these women, of and concerning his Resurrection. And if these women had not thus, out of their tenderness and bowels of love, who had received Mercy and Grace, and forgiveness of sins and Virtue, and Healing from him, which many men had received the like, if their hearts had not been so united and knit unto him in love, that they could not depart as the men did, but sat watching and waiting, and weeping about the Sepulchre until the time of his Resurrection, and so were ready to carry his Message, as is manifested, else how should his Disciples have known, who were not there? (p. 7)

In this emphasis on the unique quality of love women were able to offer Jesus, Fell's tract seems to move from an earlier Quaker position that there was no difference between men and women when it came to revelation to an assertion that women are different than men, and have a special way of being holy.[11]

In order to counter *I Corinthians* 14: 34–5, Fell argues that this has been misinterpreted. She posits that Paul's influential words – "Let your women keep silence in the churches: for it is not permitted unto them to speak; but they are commanded to be under obedience, as also saith the law. And if they will learn anything, let them ask their husbands at home: for it is a shame for women to speak in the church" – refer to a specific situation among the Corinthians, who had not yet accepted revelation. For this reason, the Corinthians were still under the law, whereas Quaker women who had found the Light within were not constrained by this rule. "And what is all this to Women's speaking? That have the Everlasting Gospel to preach, and upon whom the Promise of the Lord is fulfilled, and his Spirit poured upon them according to his word," she asserts (p. 9).

Despite the fact that it was published from the radical fringes of belief in the late seventeenth century, Fell's pamphlet inaugurates two important aspects of the developments of the religious self in the eighteenth century: the idea, unthinkable before the upheavals of the Civil War but commonplace afterwards, that a personal, readerly involvement with the Scripture was central to belief; and, that women had special qualities of love, patience, and belief that might make them more perfectly religious than men.

Swift, *A Tale of a Tub*

Swift's satirical allegory, *A Tale of a Tub* (1704), needs to be seen in the context of the early eighteenth-century distrust of and anxiety about any religious practice that differed from the Church of England, particularly those that seemed to spring from "enthusiasm." By this point, the dominant Anglican culture had contrived two ways to deal with the perceived threat of dissent from the state religion: through political restrictions like the Clarendon Code and the Test Acts; and through elegant derision, as exemplified in the Earl of Shaftesbury's "Letter Concerning Enthusiasm" (1707). The latter text suggests: "It was heretofore the Wisdom of some wise Nations, to let People be Fools as much as they pleas'd, and never punish seriously what deserv'd only to be laughed at, and was, after all, best cur'd by that innocent Remedy."[12] Swift's *Tale* seems to straddle the two approaches: it laughs at religious excess, and yet it is hard to deem its laughter gentle or "innocent."

The text takes its title from a contemporary term for a whimsical riff, the tub seamen throw out to distract a threatening whale. The narrative is an elaborate allegory of the fissures in Christianity after the Reformation, interspersed with five "digressions" on nonreligious questions of learning and interpretation. The main narrative of the *Tale* concerns the adventures of three brothers – Peter (standing for the Catholic Church), Martin (standing for the Anglican Church), and Jack (standing for radical dissent) – whose father wills them each a coat (the Scriptures). Although their father leaves them "plain, easy directions about the management and wearing of their coats, with legacies and penalties, in case of obedience or neglect," the brothers soon fall out about the proper way to maintain and display their garments.[13]

Peter, the eldest, teaches the other brothers how to interpret their father's will in such a way as to allow them to alter the coats to conform with current fashions and ostentation, including shoulder-knots, red satin, fringe, and painted figures. Peter soon styles himself "Lord Peter" or "Emperor Peter," and prostitutes himself for money and grandeur. Through him, Swift satirizes many of the practices of the Catholic Church, including its belief in the sacred properties of holy water:

> Another discovery for which [Peter] was much renowned was his famous universal pickle. For having remarked how your common pickle, in use among housewives, was of no farther benefit than to preserve dead flesh and certain kinds of vegetables, Peter, with great cost as well as art, had

contrived a pickle proper for houses, gardens, towns, men, women, children and cattle; wherein he could preserve them as sound as insects in amber.[14]

Finally, the two younger brothers revolt against Peter's authoritarian ways, steal a copy of the will (i.e., make a vernacular translation of the Bible), and are kicked out by Peter for their transgression.

The younger brothers – Jack and Martin – then set about returning their coats to some resemblance of their former condition. Martin simply does the repairs necessary to make his coat seemly, but Jack, overtaken by zeal, rips his coat to tatters, "So that he looked like a drunken beau, half rifled by bullies; or like a fresh tenant of Newgate, when he has refused the payment of garnish; or like a discovered shoplifter left to the mercy of Exchange women; or like a bawd in her old velvet petticoat, resigned into the secular hands of the mobile" (p. 316) – in short, he renders himself both unseemly and unmanly. Paradoxically, Jack's zealous rejection of all finery makes him looks strangely like Peter; "For, as it is the nature of rags to bear a kind of mock resemblance to finery, there being a sort of fluttering appearance in both, which is not to be distinguished at a distance, in the dark, or by short-sighted eyes" (p. 348). The elaborate metaphor of the coats and their permutations and vicissitudes brings up the satirical conflations of inside and outside and visible and invisible that animate many of Swift's works, including *A Tale of a Tub*. To what degree can religious belief be imagined as a material object? And does the destruction of that material object, in an attempt to denigrate its importance, as Jack does, simply give that object more power? Indeed, Jack, in a satirical version of dissenting interpretative practices, uses his father's will as a kind of raw material, "so that it served him for a nightcap when he went to bed, and for an umbrella in rainy weather" (p. 342). Imagining religion as a concrete object enables many of Swift's satirical points, but to allegorize Christianity as a coat is a dangerous move. "The coat itself is artificially fabricated (in contrast to the natural growth of the body it covers) and is external, a covering that both protects and conceals"; can we say the same about Christianity?[15]

Swift's satire of the confusion between the invisible nature of spirit and the visible qualities of the body reaches one of its peaks in his description of Jack's founding of a sect called the Aeolists. The Aeolists "maintain the original cause of all things to be wind" (p. 321). They take this notion so literally that they "affirm the gift of BELCHING to be the noblest act of a rational creature" (p. 322). This image of immaterial things confused with material substances enables Swift to present "all pretenders to inspiration whatsoever" as vulgar beings. It also allows him to satirize particular aspects of dissenting practice, such as the kind of female religious speech defended by Margaret Fell Fox. The "prophecies" of the Aeolists "were frequently managed and directed by female officers, whose organs were understood to be better disposed for the admission of those oracular gusts, as entering and passing up through a receptacle of greater capacity, and causing also a pruriency by the way, such as with due management hath been refined from a carnal to a spiritual ecstasy" (p. 324). Here, Swift plays on the association between vulgar feminine sexuality and disruptive religious practice.

Through the inclusion of five digressions, however, the satire of *A Tale of a Tub* extends its religious allegory to comprehend other problems of interpretation, particularly the pretensions to learning of modern scholars. In this arena, too, men are led away from the contemplation of the immaterial qualities of spirit and mind through pragmatic and materialistic shortcuts. "We of this age," the speaker proclaims,

> [h]ave discovered a shorter and more prudent method of becoming scholars and wits, without the fatigue of reading or thinking. The most accomplished way of using books at present is two-fold: either first, to serve them as some men do lords, learn their titles exactly, and then brag of their acquaintance. Or secondly, which is indeed the choicer, the profounder, and politer method, to get a thorough insight into the index, by which the book is governed and turned, like fishes, by the tail. For, to enter the palace of learning at the great gate, requires an expense of time and forms; therefore men of great haste and little ceremony are content to get in by the back door... Thus physicians discover the state of the whole body, by consulting only what comes from behind. (p. 318)

Here, as the speaker waxes eloquent on such shortcuts, it becomes apparent that he himself is an object of satire, a persona whose foibles Swift exploits through his comparison of poor learning and excrement.

The ways in which the speaker is himself caught up in the confusion between material and immaterial substances is most apparent in what has become the most famous part of the *Tale*, "A Digression Concerning the Original, the Use and Improvement of Madness in a Commonwealth." In this section, the speaker presents his own theory about the causes of madness ("vapors from below") and how those we deem mad might be put to work for the improvement of the commonwealth. The speaker here aligns himself with those, like the coat worshippers and the Aeolists, who believe that outward forms supersede, indeed preclude the existence of, an invisible "inner" spirit. He declares that "the outside hath been infinitely preferable to the in," and proves it through "some late experiments." "Last week I saw a woman flayed, and could hardly believe how much it altered her appearance for the worse. Last week I ordered the carcass of a beau to be stripped in my presence, when we were all amazed to find so many unsuspected faults under one suit of clothes" (p. 333). In this description, we can see the brutality and violence of those who believe there is no immaterial part of humanity. At the same time, however, the body's own inevitable "faults" are the object of disgust. While the speaker does indeed "digress" from the problem of religion strictly considered, here too the question of inspiration comes up, possibly in a more disturbing form. The speaker concludes that

> [i]f the moderns mean by madness, only a disturbance or transposition of the brain, by force of certain vapours issuing up from the lower faculties, then has this madness been the parent of all those mighty revolutions that have happened in empire, in philosophy, and in religion. For the brain, in its natural position and state of serenity, disposeth its owner to pass his life in the common forms, without any thought of subduing multitudes to his own power, his reasons or his visions. (p. 331)

The satirical point here is notoriously unstable. Are we to read the speaker, in his defense of madness, as expressing the exact opposite to what Swift would have us conclude? This is tempting, especially since the speaker eventually reveals himself as "a person, whose imaginations are hardmouthed, and exceedingly disposed to run away with his reason," i.e., mad (p. 336). Yet, if so, what are we to make of his seemingly true assertion that so many great changes in our world have come about through ideas that have been considered "mad"? Without madness, without inspiration, we would live in a static society, unchanged since the Stone Age.

A Tale of a Tub demonstrates that the question of religious practice during the eighteenth century was bound up with the problems of interpretation and authority considered more broadly. Even the mad narrator takes his readers to task, castigating the "superficial vein among many readers of the present age, who will by no means be persuaded to inspect beyond the surface and the rind of things":

> Whereas wisdom is a fox, who after long hunting will at last cost you pains to dig out. 'Tis a cheese, which by how much the richer, has the thicker, the homelier, and the coarser coat; and whereof to a judicious palate, the maggots are the best. 'Tis a sack-posset, wherein the deeper you go, you will find it the sweeter. Wisdom is a hen, whose cackling we must value and consider, because it is attended with an egg. But then, lastly, 'tis a nut, which unless you choose with judgement, may cost you a tooth, and pay you with nothing but a worm. (p. 277)

What is wisdom, spiritual or otherwise? Can we trust the speaker's analogies? Or do these comparisons reveal a mind already driven mad by the vagaries of interpretation?

The Eighteenth-Century Hymn

Let mortals ne'er refuse to take
Th'Hosanna on their tongues;
Lest rocks and stones should rise, and break
Their silence into song.

Isaac Watts, "Hosanna to the Royal Son," 1707

It is hard to remember that something now taken for granted – singing hymns in church – was the subject of much controversy throughout the eighteenth century. At issue were the questions of whether singing should be permitted in church services at all and, if so, whether only psalms set to music should be sung, or whether new compositions on religious themes – known as hymns – could be sung as well. The Church of England, throughout the eighteenth century, subscribed to the position that only "metrical psalms" – psalms set to music – could be sung in church, and that only after services were over. Born out of this controversy, hymns themselves form a paradoxical genre. Authors of hymns were reluctant to take credit for the creative force behind their compositions, preferring to assign the inspiration to God. And yet the best hymns give voice to a yearning that is both personal and collective. The question of whether poetry was compatible with religious expression in any way was also a live one during the period. Writing of Isaac Watts, a poet he admired enough to insist upon including in his magisterial *Lives of the English Poets*, Samuel Johnson writes: "His ear was well-tuned, and his diction was elegant and copious. But his devotional poetry is, like that of others, unsatisfactory. The paucity of its topicks enforces perpetual repetition, and the sanctity of the matter rejects the ornaments of figurative diction. It is sufficient for Watts to have done better than others what no man has done well" (p. 310). Donald Davie has argued that, "for Christian poets like Dryden and Watts, poetry is distinctly not worship, though it may be an adjunct to worship or a component of it."[16] By the end of the eighteenth century, however, hymn singing in churches of all denominations was taken for granted, and some of the most enduring hymns in English had been written, including "Our God, Our Help in Ages Past" (Isaac Watts), "Rock of Ages," "Cleft for Me" (Augustus Toplady), "Amazing Grace" (John Newton) and "Oh for a Closer Walk with God" (William Cowper). Women also turned their hand to hymn writing, especially among the dissenting churches, including Watts's disciple Elizabeth Rowe and the Baptist Anne Steele.

The most famous hymn writer of the eighteenth century, and one of the most prolific and best-loved writers of all genres during the period, was Isaac Watts. Born into a prominent dissenting family, he published *Hymns and Spiritual Songs* in 1707. This work speaks strongly for the importance of human composition as an element of worship as opposed to metrical psalms. Watts states in the Preface that singing in church is "that part of Worship which of all others is the nearest akin to Heaven; and it is a pity that this, of all others, should be performed the worst upon Earth." The book was a great success, going through eighteen editions before Watts's death in 1748. Johnson praises him as "one of the first authors that taught the Dissenters to court attention by the graces of language...He showed them that zeal and purity might be expressed and enforced by polished diction."[17] In one of his most famous hymns, *Man Frail, and God Eternal* ("Our God, our help in Ages Past"), Watts "imitates" Psalm 90, ll.1–6, in the same sense that Johnson or Pope "imitated" the satires of Juvenal. He explains God's transcendence of time in simple, "metrical" language suitable to an eighteenth-century congregation: "Before the hills in order stood,/or earth received her frame,/from everlasting thou art God,/To endless years the same" (ll. 9–12). Watts also published in a number of other fields, including philosophy and, importantly, education, particularly his *Improvement of the Mind*. In one of his *Divine Songs Attempted in Easy Language, for the Use of Children*, he famously wrote "Against Idleness and Mischief": "How doth the little busy bee/Improve each shining hour,/And gather honey all the day/ From every opening flower."

The most influential hymn writers of the mid-century were John and Charles Wesley, the founders of Methodism. Their movement began in the religious club formed by the Wesleys and George Whitefield at Oxford. Inspired by William Law, they began paying careful attention to the ways – the methods – by which Christian belief should be manifested. Later, after John Wesley came into contact with Moravian missionaries in North America, the "Methodists" began to emphasize the miracle of Christ's salvation of the individual believer, and the moment of conversion. Methodism scandalized much of eighteenth-century society by its extremely rapid growth in popularity, by the seeming informality of its vast open-air meetings, and by the importance it attached to hymn singing. Its popularity and seeming disregard for the forms of Anglican worship (though the Wesleys always maintained their allegiance to the established Church) brought many to associate it with the rebellions of the seventeenth century. An article in the *Gentlemen's Magazine* in May 1739 states: "Those who are acquainted with ye History of former Times... know what monstrous Absurdities in Opinion, and what vile Practices Enthusiasm will produce; from what small Beginnings... the greatest Disturbances in Church and State have arisen. The last Century furnishes us with a melancholy proof."[18] The Wesleys thought of their hymns as both religious and poetic expression. Their thousands of compositions were eventually gathered in *A Collection of Hymns for the Use of the People Called Methodists* in 1780. Many of these hymns emphasize the overpowering emotion evoked by conversion and salvation. For example, in *Wrestling Jacob*, Charles Wesley writes:

> 'Tis Love, 'tis Love! Thou died'st for me,
> I hear thy whisper in my heart.
> The morning breaks, the shadows flee:
> Pure Universal Love thou art;
> To me, to all, thy bowels move,
> Thy nature and thy name is Love.
>
> My prayer hath power with God; the grace
> Unspeakable I now receive,
> Through faith I see thee face to face,
> I see thee face to face, and live:
> In vain I have not wept and strove,
> Thy nature and thy name is Love. (ll. 37–48)

It was the fervent singing of hymns like this that caused Methodist meetings to be known as love fests. The cultural and political significance of all this emotion has puzzled scholars. Some historians have argued that the powerful emotion turned to self-scrutiny by Wesley's mostly plebeian followers diverted their energy from the material realities of political oppression, assuring that an event like the French Revolution never occurred in eighteenth-century England. Others have argued that such belief in the equality of all before God contributed to the reforms of the early nineteenth century.[19]

Christopher Smart

While Smart, like Watts, wrote hymns, his were never sung in congregations. Indeed, although Smart's genius is recognized today, his poetry begs the question of the degree to which personal religious belief can be made accessible to a reading public. For Smart is often considered the first of the "mad" poets of the later eighteenth century, to be followed by Collins, Cowper, and Chatterton. Although he earned an early reputation for literary talent at Cambridge, and began a successful career as a journalist in London, Smart eventually fell prey to a "religious monomania." He was sent to St Luke's Hospital for the insane in 1757 and released a year later uncured. He was also confined for madness between 1759 and 1763, during which time he wrote two of his most important poems, *Jubilate Agno* (begun in 1759, not published until 1939) and *A Song to David* (1763). The symptoms that led him to be confined, however, remind us that what the later eighteenth century considered pathological – public prophesying – was common practice during much of the seventeenth century. Johnson, an admirer of Smart, said: "I do not think he should be locked up. His infirmities were not noxious to society. He insisted on people praying with him, and I'd as life pray with Kit Smart as with anyone else. Another charge was he did not love clean linen; and I have no passion for it."[20] Smart himself never doubted that he was saved. His reputation for madness, however, affected his ability to make a living as a poet, and he died in 1771 in the debtors' prison.

Like the earlier Augustan poets, Smart's poetry was influenced by translations from ancient texts, particularly the ideas about Hebrew poetry set forth by Bishop Lowth in "De Sacra Poesia Hebraeorum" (1753). *Jubilate Agno*, for example, is based on Lowth's theories of the antiphonal or responsive structure of Hebrew poetry. Lowth also argued that poetry is the product of powerful emotion:

> The origin and first use of poetic language are undoubtedly to be traced into the vehement affections of the mind...for what is meant by that singular frenzy of poets, which the Greeks, ascribing to divine inspiration, distinguished by the appellation of enthusiasm, but a style and expression directly prompted by nature itself, and exhibiting the true and express image of a mind violently agitated.[21]

Here, then, we can see the rehabilitation of an idea of enthusiasm, reimagined as poetic inspiration. Smart also saw some of the same ideas in classical sources. He said of Horace that his "beauty, force and vehemence of Impression" was a "talent or gift of Almighty God by which genius is empowered to throw an emphasis upon a word or sentence in such wise as it cannot escape any reader of good sense or true critical sagacity."[22]

We can see in Smart the ideal of being taken over by another voice, or rather, of letting an authentic voice from elsewhere speak through the poet. Northrop Frye has identified this as one of the characteristics of the late eighteenth-century poetry of sensibility. In poems like *Jubilate Agno*, Frye writes, "God, the poet's soul and nature are brought into a white-hot fusion of identity, and imaginative fiery furnace in which the reader may, if he chooses, make a fourth."[23] In Smart's case it means letting something like David's voice speak through him. "A Song to David," for instance, has this epigraph from the Second Book of Samuel: "David the son of Jesse said, and the man who was raised up on high, the anointed of the God of Jacob, and Sweet psalmist of Israel, said, 'The Spirit of the Lord spake by me, and his word was in my tongue'" (*2 Samuel* xxiii: 1, 2). In Smart's poetry, the ecstatic quality of the voice itself carries much of the meaning of the poem.

Written in fragments during Smart's confinement, *Jubilate Agno* was not published until 1939. There is some evidence that Smart intended the poem as an addition to the Anglican liturgy, a long poem to be recited or sung by two choirs as part of the service. That idea was never put into practice, but elements of it remain in the poem's sequences of lines beginning "Let," seemingly supposed to work in concert with another series beginning "For" (the scheme seems to eventually break down). Throughout the poem, as elsewhere in Smart's poetry, the sound of words carries an impact irreducible to their referential meaning. He loved puns and the multiple meanings of words.

> Let Libni rejoice with the Redshank, who migrates not but is translated to the upper regions.
>
> *For I have translated in the charity, which makes things better, and I shall be translated myself at the last.* (*Jubilate Agno*, Fragment B, ll. 12–13).

Throughout the poem, as in these lines, the world of the gospels is precisely, if idiosyncratically, aligned with the natural world, and with the inner world of the poet. All creatures are become symbols of God's grace. Nowhere is this more evident than in Smart's sustained meditation on his cat in Fragment B.

> For I will consider my Cat Jeoffry.
> For he is the servant of the Living God duly and daily serving him.
> For at the first glance of the glory of God in the East he worships in his way.
> For this is done by wreathing his body seven times round with elegant quickness.
> For then he leaps up to catch the musk, which is the blessing of God upon his prayer.
> For he rolls upon prank to work it in.

> For having done duty and received blessing he begins to consider himself.
> For this he performs in ten degrees.
> For first he looks upon his forepaws to see if they are clean.
> For secondly he kicks up behind to clear away there.
> For thirdly he works upon stretch with the fore-paws extened.
> For fourthly he sharpens his paws by wood.
> For fifthly he washes himself.
> For sixthly he rolls upon wash.
> For seventhly he fleas himself, that he may not be interrupted upon the beat.
> For eighthly he rubs himself against a post.
> For ninthly he looks up for his instructions.
> For tenthly he goes in quest of food. (ll. 695–712)

The precision of the cat's activities is related to his precise placement in the natural world: "For the Cherub Cat is a term of the Angel Tiger" (l. 723). Furthermore, the precision of the description not only celebrates the cat, but also educates the observer: "For by stroking of him I have found out electricity" (l. 760). And it brings the writer closer to God: "For I perceived God's light about him in both wax and fire" (l. 761). Writing and observation reveal the unity and joy of God's creation.

These themes are also present in *A Song to David*. Some eighteenth-century readers took the elaborate structure of *A Song to David* as further evidence of Smart's insanity. Upon reading it, the poet William Mason wrote to Thomas Gray that Smart was "as mad as ever." Yet, if it is mad, it is the madness of system. David as the architect of Solomon's temple, an important idea to Freemasons like Smart, is important to both the content and form of the poem.

> The pillars of the Lord are seven,
> Which stands from earth to topmost heav'n;
> His wisdom drew the plan;
> His WORD accomplish'd the design,
> From brightest gem to deepest mine,
> From CHRIST enthron'd to man. (st. xxx).

Here, in a way that seems central to Smart's thinking, "the design" is simultaneously artistic (David's plan for Solomon's temple), linguistic (the poem goes on to assign a Greek letter to each pillar), natural ("from brightest gem to deepest mine"), and spiritual ("from CHRIST...to man"). Crucially, language does not simply describe the structure of the world, but itself is part of the making and being of the world. The word

"Adoration," for instance, moves up and down the stanzas, beginning around l. 300, a pattern that has been identified with the act of bowing.

Yet, the words are not the only things that move in *A Song to David*; the world also is animated in its celebration of God's grace.

> Of beasts – the beaver plods his task;
> While the sleek tigers roll and bask,
> Nor yet the shades arouse:
> Her cave the mining coney scoops;
> Where o'er the mead the mountain stoops,
> The kids exult and brouse. (st. xxv)

Patricia Meyer Spacks has noted in this stanza "the reiterative insistence that all forms of activity participate in the universal praise of God."[24] Yet the poem's emphasis on the continual, interlocking activity of the world leads to a peculiar sense of a suspended present, in which all actions are simultaneous, instead of being linked through cause and effect.

> But stronger still, in earth and air,
> And in the sea, the man of pray'r;
> And far beneath the tide;
> And in the seat to faith assign'd,
> Where ask is have, where seek is find,
> Where knock is open wide. (st. lxxvii)

In this ecstatic vision of a world in which prayer has absorbed all questioning and searching into the present tense of the verb "to be," Smart has reached the apex of the eighteenth century's fascination and identification with David, poet, king, and God's beloved. The poet seems "translated at the last."

Methodists and evangelicals

Along with the Methodists, the later eighteenth century saw a revival of serious Christianity within the Anglican Church. Such believers put a good deal of emphasis on prayer, but also on philanthropy, and in that context they had a decided effect on the literary culture of Britain. Evangelicals believed sincerely in the didactic power of literary texts. Two important contexts in which they put that belief to the test were the nascent antislavery movement, and the education of the poor.

A representative figure of this evangelical use of literature is Hannah More. Educated by her father, More ran a school in Bristol with her sisters. In the earlier part of her life, she moved in both the bluestocking circle and in that of Samuel Johnson and Hester Thrale. She was particularly friendly with the famous actor and producer David Garrick, who helped her produce her successful tragedy, *Percy* (1777). In the 1780s, More became increasingly religious, withdrew from London society, and ceased writing for the stage (she would not even attend a revival of *Percy* in 1784). She did, however, continue writing poetry and prose on serious subjects until her death in 1833. One of the most popular and successful writers of the late eighteenth and early nineteenth centuries, More was also one of the most conservative.

Slavery, A Poem, was written specifically to help with a political cause: to aid William Wilberforce open his parliamentary campaign against the slave trade in 1788. More wrote her sister: "if it does not come out at the particular moment when the discussion comes on in Parliament, it will not be worth a straw."[25] The poem firmly declares for racial equality, asking, "does then th'immortal principle within / Change with the casual colour of a skin?" Its claim for equality, however, is based on an idea of equality in the eyes of God. The poem ends with this threat:

> And THOU! Great source of Nature and of Grace,
> Who of one blood didst form the human race,
> Look down in mercy in thy chosen time,
> With equal eye on Afric's suff'ring clime:
> Disperse her shades of intellectual night,
> Repeat thy high behest – LET THERE BE LIGHT!
> Bring each benighted soul, great GOD, to Thee,
> And with thy wide Salvation make them free! (ll. 349–56)

The passage reveals the evangelical aspect of the antislavery campaigns. Campaigners like More hope for an end to slavery; yet, one of the chief goods of that event will be the embrace of Christianity by Africans. Or rather, since the Africans are mostly passive in this poem, that God's light will be allowed to shine on Africa. Here, the opposition between black and white skins is replaced by a distinction between the darkness of "intellectual night" and the light of Christianity.

More first became involved in the Sunday school movement when she visited the town of Cheddar with Wilberforce and her sisters and was shocked by the illiteracy and poverty of the inhabitants. They started a school there, and then many others in the surrounding towns. The aims of these schools were both intellectual and moral; they taught laboring class children to read, but also tried to inculcate religious values and decorous behavior. More's schools were among the many opened throughout Britain at the end of the eighteenth century. Thomas Laqueur notes that

200,000 children attended them in 1800, 2,100,000 in 1851. These schools were one of the important ways that print culture spread to the working classes: "The Sunday School Union alone sold some 10,000,000 reading and spelling books in the first half of the century.... Tracts, books, testaments and Bibles were distributed in tens of millions."[26] While some Anglicans argued against teaching the poor to read, Evangelicals, convinced of the importance of the Bible to religious salvation, saw it as their duty: "The Bible is the gift of God to men in general, for general advantage ... It must be admitted that the poor and un-learned are as much entitled to the Book as the rich and the learned. Christ came to save all men."[27]

It is debatable what proponents of Sunday schools expected their poor students to learn from the Bible: simply to know God, or also to obey their betters and submit to the status quo. Hannah More certainly wanted to use the printed word to influence the behavior of working-class readers. In poems like *Patient Joe, or The Newcastle Collier* (1795), she outlines a model of submission to social and economic oppression.

> If the land was afflicted with war, he declared
> 'Twas a needful correction for sins which he shared;
> And when merciful Heaven bid slaughter to cease,
> How thankful was Joe for the blessing of peace!
>
> When taxes ran high, and provisions were dear,
> Still Joseph declared he had nothing to fear;
> It was but a trial he well understood
> From Him who made all work together for good. (ll. 17–24)

Here, explicitly, the problems of the poor are sent as a trial from God, and submission is the evidence of virtue and belief. More's grandest experiment in communicating this lesson to the newly literate was the Cheap Repository Tracts. Modeled on the chapbooks that had hitherto been the chief reading material of the poor, these tracts offered moral lessons in simple, clear language. More wrote fifty of them between 1795 and 1797; two million tracts had been distributed by 1796. More hoped the tracts would "allure these thoughtless creatures on to higher things."[28] Yet, for all More's efforts, the basic fact of literacy may have trumped her desire to control the social and political behavior of the poor. After all, once they could read, a new world of political pamphlets was open to them. Evangelicals, then, contributed to the literary culture of eighteenth-century England first and foremost by promoting the spread of literacy. Furthermore, their fervent belief in the capacity of reading and texts to change minds and lives carried the didactic tradition of eighteenth-century fiction into the nineteenth century.

Female Sexuality and Domesticity

Introduction

In 1821, one of Walter Scott's aunts, remembering a youthful pleasure, asked her nephew to send her some of Aphra Behn's work. When she received the requested item, however, the aunt was so horrified at what she read that she sent the package back, noting that it was "a very odd thing that I, an old woman of eighty and upwards, sitting alone, feel myself ashamed to read a book, which, sixty years ago, I had heard read aloud for the amusement of a large circle, consisting of the first and most creditable society in London."[1] The shift felt by Scott's aunt can also be seen in Frances Burney's *Evelina* (1778), when the heroine expresses her discomfort in watching one of Congreve's Restoration-era plays.

Evelina

Congreve

> The play was *Love for Love* and though it is fraught with wit and entertainment, I hope I shall never see it represented again, for it is so extremely indelicate, – to use the softest word I can, – that Miss Mirvan and I were perpetually out of countenance, and could neither make any observations ourselves, nor venture to listen to those of others.[2]

Here, too, material deemed appropriate for a broad audience in 1695 proves indelicate for the "gentler sex" by the last quarter of the eighteenth century. These moments remind us that we should include a revolution in ideas about sexuality, particularly female sexuality, when considering the major changes of the era.

While modesty has always been an important component of feminine virtue in British culture, the late seventeenth and early eighteenth centuries still invested a good deal of power in the display of female beauty. When the Empress in Margaret Cavendish's *The Blazing World* wants to subdue her enemies, for instance, she simply dresses up:

> The Emperess [sic] appeared upon the face of the Water in her Imperial Robes; in some part of her hair she had placed some of the Star-Stone, near her face, which added such a luster and glory to it, that it caused a

great admiration in all that were present, who believed her to be some Celestial Creature, or rather an uncreated Goddess, and they all had a desire to worship her; for surely, said they, no mortal creature can have such a splendid and transcendent beauty, nor can any have so great a power as she has, to walk upon the Waters, and to destroy whatever she pleases, not only whole Nations, but a whole World.[3]

Despite Cavendish's characteristic hyperbole, we can see here the cultural force attributed to feminine (and aristocratic) display. By the mid-eighteenth century, however, such display had become scandalous, and women were celebrated instead for their restraint. As one conduct book writer puts it, "One of the chief beauties in a female character is that modest reserve, that retiring delicacy, which avoids the public eye, and is disconcerted even at the gaze of admiration."[4]

Scholars have explained this great shift in perceptions of femininity in different ways. Mary Poovey, for example, argues that the sublimation and denial of female desire produced a transition from woman as a seductive "Mother of our Miseries" to the Victorian "Angel in the House": "In the seventeenth century even champions of women felt it necessary to admit that most women 'live as if they were all body,' but by the last decades of the eighteenth century, even to refer to the body was considered 'unladylike.'"[5] Thomas Laqueur has explained the same historical shift through the prism of biological theory. Whereas during the Renaissance and earlier, the female body had been imagined as a lesser version of the male (a version that held its sexual organs on the inside), during this period scientists began to understand the female body as fundamentally different from the male: "An anatomy and physiology of incommensurability replaced a metaphysics of hierarchy in the representation of women in relation to men."[6] Poovey and Laqueur both connect these transformations in thinking about female bodies to broader political shifts during the era. For Laqueur, "reinterpretations of the body were more than simply ways of reestablishing hierarchy in an age when its metaphysical foundations were being rapidly effaced...feminism too...depends upon and generates a biology of incommensurability in place of the teleological male interpretation of bodies[.]"[7] In an age of revolutions (not least the bourgeois revolution), new justifications for a sexual hierarchy were produced. At the same time, new arguments for female equality, based on the uniqueness of feminine identity/biology, were also generated.

Whatever the reason, however, by the middle of the eighteenth century, British culture had begun to idealize a kind of femininity based on moral virtue rather than sexual display and power. Nancy Armstrong has influentially designated this new way of understanding female value "domesticity." The rise of the domestic woman, Armstrong argues, was associated with a new form of political power which "established its hold over British culture through her dominance over all those objects and practices we associate with private life. To her went authority over the household, leisure time, courtship procedures, and kinship relations, and under her jurisdiction the most basic qualities of human identity were supposed to develop."[8] Under the regime of domesticity, the power women might once have deployed through bodily display was transmuted into a power exerted through moral influence. As one conduct book writer claims, "The power of a fine woman over the hearts of men, of men of the finest parts, is even beyond what she conceives."[9] Yet the process by which women came to have this power was mysterious: was it something they were born with? Or, was it something that had to be inculcated into their otherwise willful, lustful natures by parental guidance and conduct books? Much eighteenth-century literature presents us with that paradoxical figure: an inherently good woman (in most cases a young girl) who needs to be taught how to behave.

An important aspect of domesticity is its alliance with the "private." The distinction between public and private has preoccupied many scholars of the eighteenth century (see chapter 2). And the definition of the "private" evolved as well. Privacy expanded outward from the close-held recesses of the mind to include the physical areas of the household, the domestic space Habermas calls the "intimate sphere."[10] Later still, the newly constituted nuclear family was considered the true locus of domesticity – more distant relatives and servants considered the extraneous inhabitants of the same space. In *Epistle to a Lady*, Pope decreed:

> ...in Public Men sometimes are shown,
> A Woman's seen in Private life alone:
> Our bolder Talents in full light display'd,
> Your Virtues open fairest in the shade. (ll. 199–202)

Yet, while it was long received wisdom that the eighteenth century marked the beginning of women's relegation – even confinement – to the private sphere, more recently scholars have questioned how much eighteenth-century women were really tied to the private, pointing out their involvement in overtly public exercises, such as political campaigns.[11] The ideal of domesticity was strongly affiliated with the new middle-class identity.[12] It defined itself on the one hand against aristocratic women, who, as Pope put it, could not distinguish between a husband or a lapdog's death, and used their leisure for cards, gossip, eating, and flirting; and, on the other, against a laboring class identity, women whose lives were so degraded they were denied the privilege of virtue. It was also defined against the commercialism of prostitution, "a kind of female public visibility that," as Laura Rosenthal notes, "tends to be omitted from discussions of the gendered tensions between the public and the private spheres."[13] My concern in this section is to show the emergence of domestic ideology in eighteenth-century literature, but at the same time to demonstrate the kinds of femininity that fell outside this rubric.

There has been an explosion of interest in this topic in eighteenth-century studies during the past twenty years, a development which has truly changed the face of the field. Other sections of this book demonstrate the vital role that women played in the production of culture during this era (as writers, actresses, and patrons); this section shows that they were also the object of intense cultural scrutiny, expected to conform to new roles that were shaped, but also challenged, by the new media of literature.

Alexander Pope, *The Rape of the Lock*

What dire Offense from am'rous Causes springs,
What mighty Contests rise from trivial things,

Alexander Pope, The Rape of the Lock, 1712

The opening lines of *The Rape of the Lock* have long been used to define the "mock-epic," or "mock-heroic," mode of early eighteenth-century literature. They also focus the reader's attention squarely on sexuality as the preoccupation of the day. In this first couplet, Pope succinctly aligns "am'rous causes" with "trivial things," and announces his intention of spinning a "mighty" saga out of them. "Slight is the subject, but not so the Praise," he announces, suggesting that the poem is as much about the representation of desire as its actions. And thus the first verse paragraph leaves us balancing between the "slight" and the "trivial" and the "dire" and the "mighty" – a tightrope act that continues through five cantos, recording not only Belinda's passion, but also the satirist's complex involvement in the celebration and mockery of femininity.

Long a standard work of eighteenth-century literature, *The Rape of the Lock* arose out of a particular milieu and a specific event. In 1711, a young peer, Robert Lord Petre, really did take a lock of hair from his distant relation, Arabella Fermor. Both Petre and Fermor were from prominent English Catholic families which were plunged into argument by the incident. Pope's friend, John Caryll, asked him to write a poem that would reconcile the two sides. Pope responded with a version in two cantos in 1712. In 1714, he added the "machinery" of the sylphs, the mock battle of the game of Ombre in Canto III, and the Cave of Spleen in Canto IV. As a final touch, Clarissa's speech was added to Canto V in 1717. Pope corresponded with Arabella Fermor, though there is no indication that they ever met. Nevertheless, he certainly knew women like her. Within the very enclosed world of Anglo-Catholic culture, such women lived an exaggerated version of the contradictions that structured the experience of all eighteenth-century women.

> As Catholics, they were offered conflicting accounts of what they were in the world to do. On the one hand routines supervised by nuns at school and by chaplains at home emphasized spiritual priorities, but on the other hand their duty of disposing themselves for their families' best interest was made more urgent by the special needs of a religious minority which now felt its persecution most keenly in financial terms. Thus dressing well, deploying their charms to advantage in the world of "Courtly balls and midnight masquerades" and learning a due respect for the wealth of prospective suitors could ironically be seen as necessary virtues in girls whose confessors urged...a separation as much as possible from amusements, divertissements, and vain entertainments of creatures.[14]

These women were thus caught between the spiritual value of retirement and the socioeconomic value of sexual display.

The Rape of the Lock, among other things, is an amazing record of the material dimensions of feminine sexuality, which is both celebrated and attacked as a source of social power. Samuel Johnson wrote of the poem, "the whole detail of a female day is brought before us invested with so much of decoration that, though nothing is disguised, everything is striking." Two great set pieces on this subject begin the poem. In Canto I, Belinda, with the help of the sylphs, applies her makeup. The mock-heroic apparatus is nowhere more apparent, as she is compared to a warrior readying himself for battle:

> And now, unveil'd, the Toilet stands display'd,
> Each Silver Vase in mystic order laid.
> First rob'd in White, the Nymph intent adores
> With head uncover'd the Cosmetic Pow'rs.
> A heav'nly image in the Glass appears,
> To that she bends, to that her Eyes she rears[.] (ll. 121–6)

The poet here hyperbolically inflates the value Belinda gives to her own image. Yet, as Rumbold points out, women like Belinda did have to value their own beauty as the means of sustaining their families' social position in a precarious world. At the same time, there was a lurking cultural fear that cosmetic enhancement would give women an "unnatural" power over men.[15] Given this tension, it is no wonder Pope's language in this passage is notoriously ambivalent – critics are divided as to the degree to which he castigates Belinda for her false vanity, and the degree to which he sympathizes with her entrapment by social mores that demand she worship her own superficial image.[16] The poem itself, albeit ironically, acknowledges the power of feminine beauty when, in Canto II, Belinda, rivaling the sun's beams, "launches" into her day by sailing down the Thames (II, ll. 1–4). Like Cavendish's Empress, she subdues all before her: "Fair Nymphs and well-drest Youths around her shone,/But every eye was fixed on her alone./ On her white Breast a sparkling *Cross* she wore,/Which *Jews* might kiss, and Infidels adore" (II, ll. 5–8). The poet apologizes for her: "If to her share some Female Errors fall,/Look on her Face, and you'll forget 'em all" (II, ll. 17–18). Using the subjunctive, the poet first raises the possibility of female duplicity, and then subordinates it to the power of surface beauty. Femininity here joins an alluring, distracting surface with an unknowable sexual "error" that may lie beneath. The poem deems this combination provocative, as it is the Baron's "admiration" of her locks here that spurs his ambition "by force to ravish or by Fraud betray." The poem is uneasy about the power of Belinda's beauty and its tendency to invite disaster.

The line between Belinda's accoutrements (her cosmetics, her necklace, maybe even her hair) and the "real" Belinda is hard to draw; this kind of metonymical association of person and object runs throughout the poem, and not just in relation to women. Pope imagines a world "Where Wigs with Wigs, with Sword-knots Sword-knots strive,/Beaus banish Beaus, and Coaches Coaches drive" (I, ll. 101–2); objects don't just designate persons, they eclipse or replace them. Yet, the most powerful scenes of enticing adornment belong to women. The world of objects described in such scenes not only encapsulates the emergence of commodity culture but also feminizes it. It is women who most often seem to lose the distinction between the material and the spiritual; as Pope repeatedly underlines through the figure of zeugma, it is "the Nymph" who is equally worried if she "stain her Honour or her new Brocade." Laura Brown takes the association of women with the world of goods further, and reads the appearance of "the various offerings of the world" – the "glittering spoil" of India and Arabia – on Belinda's dressing table, as evidence of the way "Belinda is adorned with the spoils of mercantile expansion," a process ongoing as Pope wrote his poem: "It is not surprising, then, that *The Rape of the Lock* seems, almost despite itself, to be obsessed with imperialism and its consequences for English culture."[17] Thus an anxiety about the presence of imperial objects in the "private" spaces of English domestic life, Brown argues, is neutralized by its association with "Female Error."

As the discussion so far should make clear, the poem itself is rhetorically highly wrought. Some critics even argue that Pope's seemingly excessive investment in elaborating and adorning his own poem approximates female vanity. The poem is certainly as interested in poetic display as it is in feminine display, albeit the latter is the explicit object of satire, while the former is the implicit locus of pleasure. This is perhaps most apparent in the "Cave of Spleen" episode in Canto IV, as the poet lingers in this space of feminine anger and complaint – ostensibly as a way of explaining Belinda's ongoing rage over the loss of her lock – but also because it allows him a space for fantastical, often bawdy, poetic pyrotechnics:

> Unnumber'd Throngs on ev'ry side are seen
> Of bodies chang'd to various Forms by Spleen.
> Here living Teapots stand, one Arm held out,
> One bent; the handle this, and that the Spout:
> A pipkin there, like Homer's Tripod walks;
> Here sighs a Jar, and there a Goose-pye talks;
> Men prove with Child, as pow'rful Fancy works,
> And Maids turn'd bottles, call aloud for Corks. (IV, ll. 47–54)]

Satire has been likened to the defensive posturing of animals – an aggressive display in response to "threats of encroachment and violation" – and Pope seems to be indulging in something of that kind here.[18] Thus, the *Rape of the Lock* is both a complex representation of the emergent world of commodity culture and an exploration of the poet's complicated place in that world – drawing creative energy from it even as he indicts it. All is refracted through an ambivalent depiction of female vanity and power.

How, then, to draw a moral from this satire? After all, part of the problem the poem must confront is whether a violation as momentous as a "rape" has actually occurred. There is no satisfactory answer to this question: if it is a rape, then the Baron is truly villainous and culpable (in eighteenth-century, if not epic, terms); if it is not a rape, then the poet risks belittling Arabella Fermor's anger over the event (and indeed she was offended by her depiction in the first version). The poem tries to have it both ways in the opening, asking the muse, "Say what strange Motive, Goddess! Cou'd compel/A well-bred *Lord* t'assault a gentle Belle?/Oh say what stranger Cause yet unexplor'd'd/could make a gentle *Belle* reject a Lord?" (I, ll. 7–10). But we might imagine the muse replying – "well, which is it?" Has an assault taken place? Or is the inexplicable rejection of "a *Lord*" justification enough for what has occurred? The matter of who has violated whom is especially complicated by the fact that here, as in most of the rest of the poem, passion, that "mighty rage," dwells in Belinda's "soft Bosom," not the Baron's presumably harder one – even at the end, it is Belinda who wields a phallic and "deadly Bodkin" in the final battle scene.

In the first version of the poem, Pope tried to tie everything up in the final mock battle. In later versions, however, he felt compelled to add a moral speech by the "prude" Clarissa, "to open more clearly the MORAL of the poem." Parodying Sarpedon's speech to Glaucus,[19] Clarissa belittles the pursuit of beauty:

> But since, alas! Frail Beauty must decay,
> Curl'd or uncurl'd, since Locks will turn to grey,
> Since painted or not painted all shall fade,
> And she who scorns a Man must die a Maid;
> What then remains, but well our Pow'r to use,
> And keep good Humour still whate'er we lose? (V, ll. 25–30)

And yet no one listens to her – they go right on fighting. And small wonder, since the poem has gone to great lengths to show that the only power women have comes through beauty. Furthermore, if Belinda had "good-humoredly" accepted the loss of her lock and maybe even married the Baron, there would be no poem. And so the poet, too, ignores Clarissa, and stages an elaborate and delightful mock-epic battle of the sexes, and the lock's apotheosis as a constellation. Thus the *Rape of the Lock* evidences the complications of feminine sexual allure – the way it both troubles and organizes the eighteenth-century social scene – and its complicated entanglement (if you will) with eighteenth-century British literature.

Samuel Richardson, *Pamela*

Scholars of eighteenth-century literature are not alone in believing that something important happened when Samuel Richardson published *Pamela* in 1740 – readers at the time thought so too. The story of a servant girl so virtuous that her master must marry her instead of seducing her, the novel was an immediate and enormous literary success. It went through eight editions in Richardson's lifetime, spawned a multitude of imitations and parodies, and was transformed into a play and a ballad opera. *Pamela* (1740) was a literary sensation, generating "tie-in" products the way a Pixar movie does today. Images from the novel were transposed onto paintings and fans, and its characters sculpted in wax. Pope lost a night's sleeping finishing the novel. The basis for this accomplishment was the way Richardson was able to suture a new idea of femininity to a particular form of literary representation, creating a form that Nancy Armstrong has dubbed the "domestic novel," because it uses the genre to celebrate the emergent value of private life. Armstrong argues that "beginning with Richardson's *Pamela*...one can observe the process by which novels rose to a position of respectability among the genres of writing. This process created a private domain of culture that was independent of the political world and overseen by a woman."[20] The novel did not invent this new kind of femininity, one based on restraint rather than display, interiority rather than exteriority, virtue rather than sexuality, but its heroine certainly crystallized it and made it available for consumption to a wide group of readers. As Ian Watt says, "there is...very little doubt that the appearance of *Pamela* marks a very notable epiphany in the history of our culture: the emergence of a new, fully developed and immensely influential stereotype of the feminine role." Its success dictated that in later novels "the model heroine must be very young, very inexperienced, and so delicate in physical and mental constitution that she faints at any sexual advance; essentially passive, she is devoid of any feelings towards her admirer until the marriage knot is tied."[21] Such a heroine does not display the "mighty passions" of Belinda or tortures of sexual desire felt by the protagonists of countless amatory fictions by Aphra Behn, Eliza Haywood, and others. The novel offers her only one emotional (and physical) outlet: letter writing, which structures the novel's epistolary form.

Until he was 50, Samuel Richardson had a respectable and successful career as a printer. At that age, however, he decided to write a volume of *Familiar Letters* – model letters designed to demonstrate to the newly literate lower-middle classes how to transcribe their thoughts in certain situations (communicating to one's parents the fact that one had proposed marriage to a young lady, for example). Richardson became fascinated with one of those situations – a servant girl writing to her parents for advice on how to thwart her master's approaches – and began to expand it into a longer, epistolary narrative (he claimed it was based on a true story he had heard long ago). When the narrative was finished, he published it as *Pamela*. Perhaps because of his long involvement in the print marketplace, however, Richardson turned out to be no naive first-time novelist. He crafted what William Warner has called an eighteenth-century media event, marketing his novel with care, appending testimonial letters that serve to guide the reader as to how to read the novel.[22] As one such testimony proclaims, the novel "carries Conviction in every Part of it; and the Incidents are so natural and interesting, that I have gone hand-in-hand, and sympathiz'd with the pretty Heroine in all her Sufferings, and been extremely anxious for her Safety, under the Apprehensions of the bad Consequences which I expected, every Page, would ensue from the laudable Resistance she made."[23] As such sentiments indicate, Richardson is very careful to distinguish his work from less respectable narratives – it "is intirely divested of all those Images, which, in too many Pieces calculated for the Amusement only, tend to *inflame* the Minds they should *instruct*," Richardson announces on the title page. Thus, *Pamela* is an explicitly didactic work. It sets out, Richardson states in the "Editor's preface", "to Divert and Entertain, and at the same time to Instruct, and Improve the minds of the YOUTH of both Sexes" (3). Richardson is concerned to harness the power of narrative to moral ends.

By making his heroine a servant, however, Richardson engages with the way female sexuality is inflected by both class and gender. Kristina Straub points out that servants posed particularly troubling questions about female (sexual) agency during the eighteenth century:

> The conduct literature shows a consensus that the servant-woman is a walking sexual target. As the seventeenth-century advisor Hannah Woolley warns the prospective female cook, "beware of the solicitations of the flesh, for they will undo you; and though you may have mean thoughts of your self, and think none will meddle with such as you; it is a mistake, *Hungry Dogs will eat dirty Puddings*." For many writers, however, the sexual magnetism of the servant-woman is understood not only as a social and moral problem, a view rooted in misogynist framings of laboring women's sexuality, but also as a byproduct of such women's (sexually saturated) social volition, yet another twist in the problems allegedly created by servants' economic agency and social mobility.[24]

Servants were thus in a socioeconomically ambiguous position during the eighteenth century – no longer simply considered loyal members of a household, they now were seen as (often subversive or rebellious) mobile wage earners. For female servants, this suspicion was compounded by a sense of their available, yet self-interested, sexuality. Pamela must thus confront assumptions about her sexuality generated by her class status. Female servants were not only thought to be readily sexually available to their employers but also likely to use their sexuality to better their economic situation.

And so Richardson is sure to tell the reader that Pamela is no ordinary female servant. She has been taught to read (and generally educated above her station) by a kind mistress. But when the latter dies, Pamela goes into the service of the mistress's son, whom the narrative designates only as

Mr. B. He soon tries to seduce her (a common and generally accepted mode of behavior). Yet rather than succumb to (or manipulate, or even enjoy) his offers – as countless literary servants had done before her – Pamela struggles to keep her "virtue."

> Look-ye, [says Pamela's fellow servant Mrs. Jewkes], he is my Master, and if he bids me do a Thing that I can do, I think I ought to do it, and let him, who has Power, to command me, look to the Lawfulness of it. Why, [says Pamela], suppose he should bid you cut my Throat, would you do it? There's no Danger of that, said she; but to be sure I would not; for then I should be hang'd; for that would be Murder. Well, said I, and suppose he should resolve to insnare a poor young Creature, and ruin her, would you assist him in that? For to rob of person of her Virtue, is worse than cutting her Throat. (p. 104)

The struggle to define feminine "virtue" thus becomes the central problem of the narrative: does a "good" servant sleep with her master because he orders her to? Or does a "good" servant preserve her chastity because it is more important to her than her life? For Pamela, virtue and chastity are almost entirely conflated.

Pamela's initial connection between seduction and unlawful violence is borne out in the novel. Frustrated in his attempt to seduce her in his mother's home, Mr. B. eventually kidnaps Pamela and holds her captive in his estate in Lincolnshire, where he hopes to convince her to become his kept mistress. Thus the novel borrows from the plots of seduction narratives like Haywood's *Love in Excess*, even as it challenges their conclusions. In this case, rather than showing Mr. B.'s seduction attempts as "masterful" in any way, Richardson stages them as a series of elaborate failures. In one scene, he jumps out of a closet while she is sleeping; in another, he disguises himself as her fellow servant to get into her bed. With the aid of Mrs. Jewkes, Mr. B. seems on the brink of raping Pamela: "Now, Pamela, said he, is the dreadful Time of Reckoning come, that I have threaten'd. – I scream'd out in such a manner, as never any body heard the like. But there was nobody to help me: and both my hands were secured, as I said" (p. 176). Yet, as Watt suggests, Pamela's very debility – her physical inability to countenance impropriety – seems to rescue her from this situation:

> With Struggling, Fright, Terror, I fainted away quite, and did not come to myself soon; so that they both, from the cold Sweats that I was in, thought me dying – and I remember no more than that, when, with great Difficulty, they brought me to myself, [Mrs. Jewkes] was sitting on one side of the Bed, with her Cloaths on; and he on the other with his, and in his Gown and Slippers. (p. 176)

Thus, as Nancy Armstrong writes,

> Richardson stages a scene of rape that transforms an erotic and permeable body into a self-enclosed body of words. Mr. B.'s repeated failures suggest that Pamela cannot be raped because she is nothing but words...as it provides occasion for her to resist Mr. B.'s attempts to possess her body, seduction becomes the means to dislocate female identity from the body and to define it as a metaphysical object.[25]

That is, Richardson has transferred the generation of feminine virtue (and value) from a sexualized body to the articulation of moral discourse. Mr. B. cannot rape Pamela because she has somehow convinced him it is the wrong thing to do.

Central to this transference of value is Pamela's capacity to articulate her experience and ethics in writing – in her letters. The novel's epistolary form is thus closely connected to its ideological purpose. The letters add immediacy to the narrative; Pamela writes "to the moment," and breaks off frequently because she hears a noise, or someone enters the room. The letters become a kind of journal as she is held captive in Lincolnshire – she must hide them in her clothes because she has no way to send them to her parents. "I begin to be afraid my Writings may be discover'd," Pamela writes, "for they grow large! I stitch them hitherto in my Under-coat, next my Linen. But if this Brute should search me!" (p. 120). Here, as Armstrong suggests, Pamela quite literally becomes a body of words. The sheer materiality of the letters has other consequences in the narrative, most importantly the fact that they can be intercepted and read by others. Mr. B., needless to say, gets a hold of them, hoping to penetrate Pamela's intentions in this way if no other. Yet, reading her letters forces him to sympathize with Pamela and eventually to convert his efforts at seduction into an offer of marriage. Through his remarkable heroine, then, Richardson is able to construct an alternative structure of morality in which a servant girl's immaterial virtue is more powerful than all the physical coercion an aristocratic man can exert. And yet the novel ends not with Pamela's escape from Mr. B.'s clutches, but with her happy marriage to him. In what may be the novel's most difficult twist of belief, it turns out she truly loves Mr. B. with a "volunteer love."

In one sense the marriage is Pamela's triumph – her elevation to class status and comfort befitting her virtue – but in another, it serves to reassert the sexual hierarchy. In marriage, Michael McKeon points out, Pamela "encounters a species of status inconsistency that is impervious to the reparations of social mobility"[26]: "the progressive empowerment of individual merit leads in the end to the crucial case of women, a condition of social injustice so deeply rooted that its very disclosure only marks the limits of progressive ideology, the point beyond which it will not venture" (p. 380). In other words, the challenge to class hierarchy posed by progressive writers like Richardson is not an assertion of radical individual equality regardless of gender; the moral authority that Pamela exerts over Mr. B. cannot be confused with other forms of socioeconomic agency. Thus, after marriage, Mr. B. presents Pamela with a list of 48 rules she must follow in her marriage to him. In her work – and it is very much presented as work – to follow them, we can see her engaged in what Helen Thompson dubs the active "practice" of "compliance"[27] "to secure her husband's modernity, she must... exercise the agency of ingenuous subjection that, through her unforced reciprocation of his power, promises transitively to modernize her husband" – "to turn him into a loving husband rather than an arbitrary master" (pp. 8, 96). In other words, to bring Mr. B. into the new order of things, Pamela must proffer a submission to his authority not exacted by force, but willingly given as part of her wifely virtue.

Some critics have argued, however, that despite *Pamela*'s emphasis on its heroine's intangible and ineffable virtue, her body – the materiality of her sexual identity – still plays a central role in the novel. William Warner points out, for instance, that Pamela too admires her image in a scene that mirrors (if you will) Belinda's self-homage at her dressing table. Near the beginning of the novel, Pamela resolves to return to her parents' house. To this end, she divests herself of clothes that have put her above her station and dresses herself to return to own class status.

> up Stairs I went, and lock'd myself into my little Room. There I trick'd myself up as well as I could in my new Garb, and put on my round-ear'd ordinary Cap; but with a green Knot however, and my homespun Gown and Petticoat, and plain-leather Shoes...A plain Muslin Tucker I put on, and my black Silk Necklace, instead of the *French* Necklace my Lady gave me, and put the Ear-rings out of my Ears; and when I was quite 'quip'd, I took my Straw Hat in my Hand, with its two blue Strings, and look'd about me in the Glass, as proud as anything. – To say Truth, I never lik'd myself so well in my Life. (p. 60)

It illustrates Richardson's quite different thinking about female identity and sexuality that Pamela, unlike Belinda, needs no help from sylphs (or maids): this action is evidence of her considerable agency and self-reliance. Nevertheless, the narrative treats the act of getting dressed as one of adornment and disguise: none of the other servants can recognize her in her "proper" clothes. The change also enhances her sexuality – Mr. B., feigning ignorance that this Pamela *"her own self,"* tries (and is allowed!) to kiss this unknown socially inferior woman (p. 61). Comparing Pamela's self-costuming here to Haywood's *Fantomina* (see chapter 3), Warner notes that "Mr. B. reads it as evidence of her intriguing designs upon him. Pamela's defensive insistence that her new dress is her truest clothing, while her recent dress was a kind of disguise, does not ensure that her clothes can be read as reliable signs."[28] The surface of her body, then, not only proves a potentially unreliable index of her interior worth/value/virtue, it also, despite itself, generates meanings of its own – through seemingly inadvertent and inevitable sexual display.

If this episode illustrates the playful and potentially pleasurable aspects of the bodily "surface" in *Pamela,* another episode, late in the novel, demonstrates the dangers of such pleasures, especially for women. Mr. B.'s repeated attempts at rape are thwarted (the novel asserts) by Pamela's virtue, but the narrative also feels the need to make the dangerous consequence of female sexuality, particularly for the lower classes, clear. In the last twenty pages of the novel, it becomes clear that Pamela has had a predecessor in Mr. B.'s affections – a girl named Sally Godfrey. Since she was not possessed of Pamela's moral fortitude, however, Sally's story ended not in marriage but in seduction. In his student days, Mr. B. and Sally "met at *Godstow* often, at *Woodstock,* and every neighboring Place to *Oxford*; where he was then studying, as it prov'd, guilty Lessons, instead of improving ones; till, at last, the Effect of their frequent Interviews grew too obvious to be concealed" (p. 395). The guilty sexual "lessons" Mr. B. learns from Sally are the material correlative of the immaterial moral lessons he learns from Pamela. But it is Sally who suffers for them. Unmarried and pregnant, she must leave her infant daughter behind (later to be adopted by Pamela) and set sail for Jamaica to begin a new life. The story of Sally Godfrey allows the novel to include not only Pamela's happy ending but also, as a kind of warning, the unhappy ending to which a different plot twist would have led her. It illustrates the way the threat of physical punishment (in Sally's case, a kind of banishment) hems in and enforces the dematerialized "happiness" Pamela finds in marriage.[29] Thus, in both Pamela's pleasurable play before the mirror at the outset of the novel and this sad story near the end, the novel demonstrates the important role of the female body even under the regime of domesticity.

Another final important bodily aspect of the domesticity Pamela achieves is her leisure – her freedom from the physical labor she performed as a servant. Indeed, Pamela in effect ceases to be a servant during her

Lincolnshire captivity – the only labor she does is defending her virtue and writing letters. This condition prepares her for the idealized bourgeois marriage, which "becomes the exclusive work of women, a realm of enforced leisure, passive consumption and unpaid labor. What is utopian about Pamela's experience is that with her domestic incarceration comes 'self-employment' and the creative power of writing. The more confined she is, the greater her productivity."[30] Thus *Pamela* has fascinated generations of both scholars and critics because it is both a revolutionary novel and a conservative one: revolutionary because it endows a servant girl with not simply subjectivity and the ability to communicate her thoughts, but also with moral authority; conservative because it restrains that authority within the sexual hierarchy of marriage, and shows the dangerous consequences of ever straying from that space.

Anti-Pamelas: *Shamela* and *Fanny Hill*

The success of *Pamela*'s provocative depiction of laboring-class feminine virtue spawned a rash of responses. The year after its publication, Fielding's *Shamela*, Haywood's *Anti-Pamela*, as well as a tract called *Pamela Censured*, was published. Another text we might count as a response, since it also tells the story of a young girl's rise from lowly origins to married, middle-class happiness, is Cleland's pornographic novel, *Fanny Hill* (1748–9). Together, these texts bring into relief some of the problems in emergent ideas of femininity articulated in Richardson's novel.

The most famous of these is Fielding's *Shamela*, which confronts the problem broadcast by Richardson's subtitle: "virtue rewarded." The full title reads *An Apology for the Life of Mrs. Shamela Andrews*, and it promises to provide "all the matchless ARTS of that young Politician, set in a true and just Light." Shamela is indeed the consummate "politician" in the art of seduction. The narrative rewrites one of the famous "bad" scenes in *Pamela* as a "stratagem" set up by Shamela and a much more devious and immoral Mrs. Jervis – one in which Shamela aims to seduce "Squire Booby" with particular goals in mind:

> I have heard my Mamma say, (and so you know, Madam, I have) that in her Youth, Fellows have often taken away in the Morning, what they gave over Night. No, Mrs. *Jervis*, nothing under a regular taking into Keeping, a settled Settlement, for me, and all my Heirs, all my whole Lifetime shall do the Business – or else crosslegged, is the Word, faith, with *Sham*, and then I snapt my Fingers.[31]

Shamela plays the innocent, and gains her Booby.

As the quotation above makes clear, the question of the relationship between language and class is central to *Shamela*. Shamela takes Pamela's tendency to use colloquialism (colloquialism Richardson almost eradicated in later editions) to extremes. She writes to her mother, for example (who is not like Pamela's poor but virtuous parent)

> Marry come up, good Madam, the Mother had never looked into the Oven for her daughter, if she had not been there herself. I shall never have done if you upbraid me with having had a small One by *Arthur Williams*, when you yourself – but I will say no more. *O! What fine Times when the Kettle calls the Pot.* (p. 281)

Fielding pokes fun of the way reading can lead to erotic satisfaction as well as education in Parson Tickletext. Parodying the celebratory letters Richardson included in Pamela, *Shamela* includes a letter from Parson Tickletext to Parson Oliver:

> I find I am like to do nothing else [but read the text], for I know not long yet to come: because if I lay the Book down it comes after me. When it has dwelt all Day long upon the Ear, it takes Possession all Night of the Fancy. It hath Witchcraft in every Page of it. Oh! I feel an Emotion even while I am relating this: Methinks I see Pamela in this Instant, with all the Pride of Ornament cast off. (p. 277)

Shamela uses her literacy not for self-improvement the way Pamela does, but for manipulation. Fielding's next heroine, Fanny Goodwill in *Joseph Andrews*, cannot read or write at all. Overall, Fielding seems to point out, and disagree with, Richardson's assumption that reading for the lower (and upper) classes will be improving.[32]

Versions of "the whore's story" abounded in eighteenth-century print culture – from lightly fictionalized autobiographies to visual depictions like Hogarth's *Harlot's Progress*. They provided a different perspective on the ideal of domesticity to the rosy view one finds in novels like *Pamela*. As Laura Rosenthal points out:

> Unlike domestic novels that at least on a superficial level offer wish-fulfilling fantasies of romantic attachments that transcend economic interest, prostitute narratives expose the fallout of the period's prosperity, mobility, modernity, imperial expansion, and increasing consumerism. Even before the heroine "falls" sexually, she often "falls" economically, from membership in a family to isolation, homelessness, and the necessity of making her own way in the world.[33]

The proliferation of these narratives, however, suggests that eighteenth-century readers were more interested in hearing about the fate of "real" Sally Godfreys than we might have thought – and not simply interested in their lascivious qualities either, though that clearly played some role in their popularity.[34]

Of course, the best known fictional "whore's story" of the day managed to combine these different attributes – an idealization of domesticity, a fantasy of being able to fall, then ascend the social ladder, and explicit pornography: John Cleland's *Fanny Hill: or, Memoirs of a Woman of Pleasure*. Published in 1748–9, the novel tells the story of Fanny who, orphaned at a young age, slides into a life of prostitution in order to survive in London. Much of the book consists of episodes in her carnal education, graphically described. In the end, however, Fanny leaves this life and marries a respectable man who loves her despite her past.

The narrative is centrally concerned with Fanny's "natural" appreciation of male sexuality. Watching through a keyhole as the bawd Mrs. Brown entertains a customer, she is mesmerized by

> that wonderful machine, which I had never seen before, and which, for the interest my own seat of pleasure began to take furiously in it, I stared at with all the eyes I had. However, my senses were too much flurried...to observe anything more than in general the make and turn of that instrument, from which the instinct of nature, yet more than all I had heard of it, now strongly informed me I was to expect that supreme pleasure which she has placed in those parts so admirably fitted for each other.[35]

Yet, despite this endorsement of heterosexual intercourse, *Fanny Hill* allows for other kinds of female pleasure as well. When Fanny finds herself in bed with a fellow female servant, for instance, she doesn't scream and faint away – she enjoys herself. This scene is perhaps designed primarily for the titillation of a male readership; nevertheless, as Lisa Moore points out,

> the novel's representations of intimacy between women, of female virtue, and of female community often parodically expose the sexual and social alternative from which the bourgeois norms of [other novels] must be wrenched. At times, however, the power of these representations in relation to one another exceeds even parody, spilling over the text's conscious satirical, pedagogical, and heteropornographic intentions to produce pleasure and sexual agency outside those norms.[36]

Thus, both *Shamela* and *Fanny Hill* provide an account of female agency (primarily sexual) that challenges that of domestic ideology. They remind us that other narratives for women – in fiction and in life – existed in eighteenth-century England.

Domestic Labor: Mary Collier, *The Woman's Labour*; Mary Leapor, *Crumble Hall*

Pamela begins life as a domestic servant, and yet, as many have noted, she acts, from the beginning, as if her destiny will transcend that role: she is always already a lady. But despite the rise of domestic ideology, which celebrated a woman with the leisure to devote herself to the moral well-being of her household (or, to put it another way, used her enforced removal from the site of production for moral rather than vicious purposes), a number of working-class women did represent their experience. They wrote in the nascent tradition of the "anti-pastoral," but they also pushed against that generic tradition, demonstrating that women's labor is never confined to the landscape – they must always labor inside the home as well.

In 1739, a female laborer named Mary Collier wrote a response to Stephen Duck's anti-pastoral, *The Thresher's Labour* (1730). Although very little is known about the poet, *The Woman's Labour* is a thoroughgoing critique of Duck's poem. It takes as its starting point Duck's offhand assumption that female laborers have the leisure to stop and chat amongst themselves while men work: "I find, that you to hear us talk are griev'd:/ In this, I hope, you do not speak your Mind,/For none but Turks, that ever I could find,/Have Mutes to serve them, or hid e'er deny/Their slaves at work to chat it merrily" (ll. 65–8). The justification of female speech seems crucial in a poem that seeks to represent the hitherto unrepresented "drudgery" of women's lives. Yet it also reveals the paradox that generates the poem: Collier is concerned to both explain that the lives of laboring-class women are consumed by work – they have no leisure to speak – and to defend their right to speak, not least by writing a poem in her own voice.

In order to critique present conditions, female poets often need to construct an imaginary or hypothetical state that demonstrates that different class and gender roles could exist. Collier, like others, does this through reference to a "Golden Age," which she describes at the beginning of the poem:

> Till Time and Custom by Degrees destroy'd
> That happy State our Sex at first enjoy'd.
> When Men had us'd their utmost Care and Toil,

> Their Recompence was but a Female Smile;
> When they by Arts or Arms were render'd Great,
> They laid their Trophies at a Woman's Feet;
> They in those Days, unto our Sex did bring
> Their Hearts, their All, a Free-Will Offering:
> And as from us their Being they derive,
> They back again should all due Homage give. (ll. 15–24)

In this "Golden Age," female labor was confined to reproduction. The current sexual hierarchy was reversed, and women were worshiped for that unique power. There seems to be no class structure in Collier's "Golden Age": this is a world structured only by sexual difference. In Collier's own world, however, women's labor exceeds that of men because they must perform what is now known as the "third shift" – uncompensated domestic labor that remains after wage labor has been completed. Or, as Collier puts it:

> ...when we home are come,
> Alas! We find our Work but just begun;
> So many Things for our Attendance call,
> Had we ten Hands, we could employ them all.
> Our Children put to Bed, with greatest Care
> We all things for your coming home prepare:
> You sup, and go to Bed without Delay,
> And rest yourselves till the ensuing Day:
> While we, alas! but little sleep can have,
> Because our froward Children cry and rave;
> Yet, without fail, as soon as Day-light doth spring,
> We in the Field again our work begin. (ll. 106–17)

Male labor, she claims, is punctuated by eating and sleeping, while female labor continues unabated day and night. The sexual division of labor, compounded by class differences, means that women "but little sleep can have."

Through its description of laboring-class life, Collier's poem reminds us that middle-class life depends upon the work of poorer women. Along with the "domestic" labor of her own house, the poet must work outside her own home doing laundry for a wealthier woman. A group of women start this task before dawn, but when the sun rises their "Mistress" comes to supervise: "in her Hand, perhaps, a Mug of Ale / To cheer our Hearts, and also to inform / Herself what Work is done that very Morn" (ll. 174–7). Here we have a middle-class or gentry woman performing the monitory

functions Armstrong reveals to be vital to domestic virtue – being charitable to her servants (if only by "perhaps" giving them something to drink),
while also making sure they are performing their tasks properly and economically ("And these most strictly does of us require,/To save her soap
and sparing be of Fire"). Seen from the female laborer's perspective,
though, this woman seems alien, and if not exactly cruel, part of the
oppressive structure of unequal labor. In this vignette, the divisions
between the classes loom as deep as those between the sexes. If the category of woman was unitary during the "Golden Age," in Collier's own
time it is divided by economic status. This section concludes with the most
gothic image of Collier's poem:

> Now we drive on, resolv'd our Strength to try,
> And what we can, we do most willingly;
> Until with Heat and Work, 'tis often known,
> Not only Sweat, but Blood runs trickling down
> Our Wrists and Fingers; still our work demands
> The constant Action of our lab'ring Hands. (ll. 188–91)

Here, even more explicitly than in *The Rape of the Lock*, we can see the
material connections between the "Cambricks and Muslins which our
Ladies wear" and the cost exacted on other bodies by the production of
such finery.

Furthermore, Collier's emphasis here, as in many parts of the poem, on
the busy, almost independent, action of "lab'ring Hands" reminds us that
the hand also stands in metonymical relationship to writing. In *The Woman's
Labour*, the relationship between the laboring hand and the writing hand
is a negative one – the blood spilled in the laundry bucket seems to literally
take the time and energy of ink that might otherwise be spilled in the
writing of poetry (Collier, throughout the poem, reminds us that she
doesn't have time to dream, much less write). If Pamela uses her leisure
time to write, when do laboring-class women, who have no leisure, write?
Yet despite these obstacles, we still have a poem – a poem, moreover, that
combines the brutal realism/empiricism of the passage above with numerous allusions to the literary tradition, as evidenced in the poem's penultimate paragraph:

> But to rehearse all Labour is in vain,
> Of which we very justly might complain:
> For us, you see, but little Rest is found;
> Our Toil increases as the Year runs round.

> While you to Sisyphus yourselves compare,
> With Danaus' Daughters we may claim a Share;
> For while he labours hard against the Hill,
> Bottomless Tubs of Water they must fill. (ll. 238–45)

The poem, thus, does not collapse into literalism but engages with poetic tradition. Danaus's daughters were given this endless task in punishment for murdering their husbands (interestingly enough, a political rather than a sexual crime in the story); Collier's poem transmutes that domestic violence into literary violence – the entity she is trying to kill off is Duck's (and others') representation of women as lazy. Yet the allusion ingeniously draws out both the mythic proportions of domestic labor and the way it keeps other forms of female energy – including creative energy – in check. Here the poem seems to simultaneously cancel itself out (if "rehearsing," or representing, labor is in vain, and women indeed have no time to write), and to open outward into a more transhistorical critique of the feminine condition.

Mary Leapor, too, worries about when she will write, and the propriety of writing for a working-class woman. In the opening of *Crumble Hall*, for example, she describes the desire, and inability, of her persona "Mira" to stop writing:

> With low'ring Forehead, and with aching Limbs,
> Oppressed with Head-ach, and eternal Whims
> Sad Mira vows to quit the darling crime
> Yet takes her Farewell, and repents, in Rhyme. (ll. 3–6)

Leapor seems less concerned than Collier with the lack of time women have to write, and more concerned with the impropriety of a servant taking up a pen. In *The Epistle of Deborah Dough*, for instance, Leapor mocks the way writing detracts from proper plebeian behavior: "Our neighbor Mary – who, they say,/Sits scribble-scribble all the day, . . . throws away her precious time/In scrawling nothing else but rhyme" (ll. 11–12, 17–18). Also unlike Collier, she turns to satire to make her points about the condition of laboring-class women, often using personae in a Swiftian way.[37] But, like Swift in *Verses on the Death of Doctor Swift*, she uses these personae not only to mock the world she lives in, but also to mock herself. In *Mira's Picture: A Pastoral*, for example, she mocks the way intellectual pursuits detract from female sexual attraction. Here, she imagines two shepherds out of the classical tradition, in dialogue, commenting unfavorably on "the artist":

> *Corydon*: What though some freckles on her face appear?
> That's only owing to the time o' th' year.

Her eyes are dim, you'll say. Why, that is true:
I've heard the reason, and I'll tell it you.
By a rush-candle (as her father says)
She sits whole evenings, reading wicked plays.
Phillario: She read! – She'd better milk her brindled cows:
I wish the candle does not singe her brows,
So like a dry furze-faggot and besides,
Not quite so even as a mouse's hide. (ll. 17–26)

Leapor here critiques the objectification of women in the pastoral tradition – its conventional positioning of women as the object of the male gaze – even as she mocks herself.[38] A foundational assumption of the pastoral is that rural labor will enhance the attractions of the "shepherdess," but in Leapor's poem such labor destroys female beauty as surely as does reading (producing freckles, etc.). An example of the poet's gift for shifting the focus of traditional genres, this poem put the poet herself under the gaze of the pastoral tradition, yet by inhabiting those voices critiques them.

In her long poem *Crumble Hall*, Leapor takes on another set of literary conventions – those of the country house poem exemplified by Ben Johnson's *To Penshurst* and Marvell's *Upon Appleton House*, and continued in the eighteenth century in Pope's *To Burlington*. In such poems, while the glorious details of an aristocratic house are extolled, labor is notoriously excised. In Johnson's poem, for example, no work is required to harvest fruit: "The early cherry with the later plum / Fig, grape, and quince, each in his time doth come; / The blushing apricot and woolly peach / Hang on thy walls that every child may reach." Leapor, again turning the tables, describes such a house from the perspective of one who works to maintain it – though in the aptly named "Crumble Hall" such labor is often in vain. She brings the reader into all the nooks and crannies of the house:

Would you go further? – Stay a little then:
Back through the passage – [up] the Steps again;
Thro' yon dark Room – be careful how you tread
Up these Steep Stairs – or you may break your Head
These rooms are furnish'd amiably, and full:
Old Shoes, and Sheep-ticks bred in Stacks of Wool
Grey Dobbin's gears and Drenching-Horns enow
Wheel-spokes – the Irons of a tatter'd Plough. (ll. 94–101)

In Leapor's poem, all the quotidian junk of an old house is brought to light. We see the back stairs and discarded furniture, unlikely subjects for heroic couplets. Like Collier, she combines a commitment to the empirical realities of female lives with an engagement with the literary tradition. As much as *The Rape of the Lock*, *Crumble Hall* uses the mock-heroic mode to both celebrate and deflate eighteenth-century English life.

Like Belinda, the cook, Ursula (one of Leapor's inset, Pope-inspired portraits) is a devotee, albeit at the altar of her dirty dishes rather than her makeup: "The purging Bath each glowing dish refines,/And once again the polish'd Pewter shines." The mode was extraordinarily useful in redirecting the gaze to the minutiae of domestic life.[39]

Yet *Crumble Hall* also reveals the way the new ideals of feminine virtue impinge on the lives of women beyond the middle classes; the poem asks whether domestic ideology is appropriate to servants. As Donna Landry notes, Ursula only recognizes the way her labor supports her oafish, sleeping husband Roger, rather than acknowledging that it primarily supports the owners of the house who pay her wages.

> "Ah! Roger, Ah!" the mournful Maiden cries:
> "Is wretched Urs'la then your Care no more,
> "That, while I sigh, thus you can sleep and snore?
> "Ingrateful Roger! Wilt thou leave me now?
> "For you these Furrows mark my fading Brow:
> "For you my Pigs resign their Morning Due:
> "My hungry Chickens lose their Meat for you:
> "And, was it not, Ah! Was it not for thee.
> "No goodly Pottage would be dress'd by me." (ll. 137–45)

Landry reads Ursula "as trapped by a domestic ideology that foregrounds romance and marriage to the exclusion of other social relations, including her own servitude, as any middle-class mistress capable of forgetting the labor of the servants who make her domestic idyll possible."[40] And with Landry, we should question whether these poems critique domestic ideology itself or simply protest the exclusion of some women from that ideal. If these are political poems, feminist poems, what are they asking for? Do the poets long for their labor to be recognized and dignified or, rather, for a release from that labor?

Sexuality seems to be excised from this poetry – Collier and Leapor's working women hardly have time for it – but in a later description, in Wollstonecraft's *Maria*, we can see the intersection of class status and sexuality presented in a very different way than *Pamela*'s idealization. Wollstonecraft's Jemima finds herself seduced by her employer:

> At sixteen, I suddenly grew tall, and something like comeliness appeared on a Sunday, when I had time to wash my face and put on clean clothes. My master had once or twice caught hold of me in the passage; but I

instinctively avoided his disgusting caresses. One day however, when the family were at a Methodist meeting, he contrived to be alone in the house with me, and by blows – yes, blows and menaces – compelled me to submit to his ferocious desire; and to avoid my mistress's fury, I was obliged in future to comply, and skulk to my loft at his command, in spite of increasing loathing.[41]

Jemina is impregnated by her master and then turned out of the house by her unsympathetic mistress, who sees her lack of virtue as an inherent component of her class status: "she concluded by saying, that I was born a strumpet; it ran in my blood, and nothing good could come to those who harboured me."[42] Unemployed, and on the streets, Jemima turns to a prostitution not nearly as jolly as Fanny Hill's: "I was accosted from different motives, and yielded to the desire of the brutes I met, with the same detestation that I had felt for my still more brutal master. I have since read in novels of the blandishments of seduction, but I had not even the pleasure of being enticed into vice."[43] Wollstonecraft's image of the brutality of laboring-class life only emphasizes the achievement of poets like Mary Collier and Mary Leapor, who were able to make their experience visible while also actively engaging with a poetic tradition that conventionally placed such women as the mute objects of male desire. They have left us a broader understanding of what "domesticity" meant in eighteenth-century England.

Frances Burney, *Evelina*

Like *Pamela*, *Evelina* is an epistolary novel; like *Pamela*, it follows the path of a young, innocent girl from social uncertainty to a happy and advantageous marriage. But *Evelina* differs from *Pamela* in some significant ways: it delineates not the aristocratic retreats of the country house, but rather the mingling of classes in urban amusements. And it was written not by a middle-aged man, but by a young woman in her twenties. Yet, we should not make the mistake of confusing Frances Burney with her heroine. Burney was no "artless" provincial girl – she was very much at home in the urban culture of the metropolis. Her father was a pioneering musicologist (and Burney herself his primary assistant); if her class status was as liminal as her heroine's, it was because she hovered between the worlds of artists and performers and the middle class, rather than between the middle class and the aristocracy, as does Evelina. Burney socialized with opera singers and dancers, as well as actors like David Garrick and poets like Christopher Smart, in her father's house. Indeed, among its other virtues,

Evelina is an extraordinary guide to the public places of performance and sociability of eighteenth-century London.

Yet, although she came from a literary family, Burney nonetheless worried about the impropriety of a woman appearing in print. Thus the publication of *Evelina* in 1778 was accomplished with much secrecy. Frances's brother Charles disguised himself in "an old great coat and a large old hat" to bring the anonymous manuscript to a bookseller. Burney even disguised her handwriting out of fear that her own would be recognized from her copying of her father's works. The novel was an immediate success. It tells the story of an innocent girl, brought up in the country by a guardian, the Reverend Villars, after being abandoned as illegitimate by her profligate aristocratic father. She has no knowledge of the world and, since she has no acknowledged father, she must call herself by the made-up name of Evelina Anville. Friends bring her to London whose complicated social scene – and her "artless" response to that scene – she describes in a series of letters to Villars.

Evelina thus returns us to the problem of female sexual display, as its heroine traverses the public places of the London marriage market. Because she has no acknowledged family, no name, Evelina can only be "known" or understood through her body. Unlike Pope's Belinda, however, Evelina cannot stun others into submission with her dazzling beauty; rather, she must suffer her body to be a misunderstood object. Ignorant of the practices of London social life, Evelina, to her shame, commits so many unwitting *faux pas* that she "think[s] there ought to be a book, of the laws and customs *a-la-mode*, presented to all young people upon their first introduction into polite company."⁴⁴ Mortified, her distress shows itself on her body, and yet, as the novel's rake reminds her, her blush only reveals a latent sexuality. "How conscious you must be," says Sir Clement Willoughby, "all beautiful that you are, that those charming airs serve only to heighten the bloom of your complexion'" (p. 37). Her blush not only makes her more attractive, it also reveals that she understands enough about sexuality to know what kinds of things will offend her modesty. In it, we can see the way the older erotics of display, and the traces of an older understanding of female sexuality, are embedded in a new understanding of femininity. As Poovey explains, "a modest demeanor served not only to assure the world that a woman's appetites were under control; it also indicated that female sexuality was still assertive enough to require control."⁴⁵ Burney takes this understanding even farther: all the characters of *Evelina*, except the heroine herself, are anxiously conscious that all the visible signs of female virtue are only that, exterior marks that *may* reveal an interior truth, or may be simply artifice.

In most circumstances, Evelina's communication is confined to the signs her body (involuntarily) emits by the conduct book injunction to silence. In such texts, women were commonly urged not to speak assertively under any circumstances. If you are truly well bred, one writer tells young women, "You will not be in danger of putting yourself forward in company, of contradicting bluntly, of asserting positively, of debating obstinately, of affecting a superiority to any present, or engrossing the discourse, of listening to yourselves with apparent satisfaction, of neglecting what is advanced by others, or of interrupting them without necessity."[46] Struggling with this admonition, Evelina finds herself in trouble at every turn: hustled by Willoughby into a carriage, and then unable to tell her family about his inappropriate advances; unable to protect her (albeit unappealing) grandmother Madame Duval from Captain Mirvan's practical jokes; unable to even converse with Lord Orville, a man she finds attractive. Burney's novel thus provides a rich interrogation of conduct book strictures and the "paradoxes of propriety" as her heroine gives them a practical application.[47] She is even unable to respond to Orville's honorable approaches, until he rises to a rakish, Willoughby-like, level of aggression.

> "You are going then," cried he, taking my hand, "and you give me not the smallest hope of your return! – will you not, then, my too lovely friend! – will you not, at least, teach me, with fortitude like your own, to support your absence?"
> "My Lord," cried I, endeavoring to disengage my hand, "pray let me go!"
> "I will;" cried he, to my inexpressible confusion, dropping on one knee, "if you wish to leave me!" (p. 290)

Only with such struggle can he propose a proper marriage. Yet, governed by the strictures of modesty, Evelina cannot even transcribe Orville's protestations of love in her letter to Villars. Adumbrating Jane Austen's similar strategy in such situations, she simply states, "I cannot write the scene that followed, though every word is engraven on my heart: but his protestations, his expressions, were too flattering for repetition" (p. 291). The novel's attitude towards silence is thus ambiguous – it both proves the heroine's virtue, and puts that virtue in jeopardy when it allows men to accost her without protest. The ideal of female silence is further complicated by Evelina's incisive *epistolary* voice, which consistently makes the foolishness and artifice of her world sharply visible. After her first "shopping" trip in London, for example, she notes that the male assistants "seemed to understand every part of a woman's dress better than we do ourselves; and they recommended caps and ribbands with an air of so much importance, that I wished to ask them how long they had left off wearing them" (p. 22).[48]

Evelina, then, interrogates the ideology of propriety as much as it rehearses it. If Evelina is as beautiful and virtuous as Pamela, Burney is more concerned than Richardson to show the social construction and social embeddedness of virtue. In both novels, virtue is an interior quality, but *Evelina* shows that, no matter how virtuous a girl might be, she is vulnerable to being judged not only according to her social situation, but also according to her material circumstances. As we have already seen, Evelina is particularly vulnerable to improper advances because of her social placement – she remains unacknowledged by her aristocratic father for much of the novel. But her virtue also comes under suspicion when she finds herself *physically* misplaced. Persuaded by her cousins the Brangtons to visit the "dark walks" of Vauxhall, unlit alleys often used by prostitutes at this eighteenth-century pleasure garden, Evelina finds herself aggressively accosted by men who think she is an "actress" (often a code for prostitute during the period):

> ...a large party of gentlemen, apparently very riotous, and who were hal-lowing, leaning on one another, and laughing immoderately, seemed to rush suddenly from behind some trees, and meeting us face to face, put their arms at their sides and formed a kind of circle, which first stopped our proceeding, and then our retreating, for we were presently inclosed. The Miss Brangtons screamed aloud, and I was frightened exceedingly: our screams were answered with bursts of laughter, and, for some minutes, we were kept prisoners, till at last, one of them, rudely, seizing hold of me, said I was a pretty little creature. (p. 163)

In Evelina's world, as in Pamela's, the threat of physical violence against women is never far away. In Burney's novel, however, the display of femi-nine virtue is hardly enough to keep that threat in check. Evelina is removed from the group of men by Willoughby, who then himself tries to lead her further along the "dark walks," until she struggles back to the public, well-lit places of the garden.

As an antidote to the world of rudeness and (quite threatening) affron-tery, Burney creates a suitor of "true politeness" for her heroine (p. 244). Lord Orville is distinguished throughout the novel by his capacity to over-look Evelina's awkwardness and "misplacements."

His manners are so elegant, so gentle, so unassuming, that they at once engage, esteem and diffuse complacence. Far from being indolently satisfied with his own accomplishments, as I have already observed many men here are, though without any pretensions to his merit, he is most assiduously attentive to please, and to serve all who are in his company; and though his success is invariable, he never manifests the smallest degree of consciousness. (p. 60)

"Such is the effect of true politeness," Evelina notes, "that it banishes all restraint and embarrassment" (p. 244). Through Orville, the novel is able to use marriage to resolve the instabilities of status it explores. His confidence and status are such that he is willing to marry Evelina despite her illegitimate/orphaned state: his love overcomes the incommensurability of class in favor of virtue. As Nancy Armstrong has noted,

> The good marriage concluding fiction of this kind, where characters achieve prosperity without compromising their domestic virtue, could be used to resolve another order of conflict, the conflict between an agrarian gentry and urban industrialists, for one, or between labor and capital, for another. By enclosing such conflict within a domestic sphere, certain novels demonstrated that despite the vast inequities of the age virtually anyone could find gratification within this private framework.[49]

And yet, since Evelina, unlike Pamela, turns out to have a class status worthy of Orville when her father, Lord Belmont, acknowledges her, the novel seems, in the end, less radical than Richardon's. Kristina Straub, however, reminds us that the novel's overall view of marriage may be less sanguine than the Evelina/Orville marriage implies. Evelina's own mother's story (Caroline Evelyn is seduced and betrayed by her aristocratic lover) and the visible oppression of Mrs. and Miss Mirvan by Captain Mirvan all suggest that "whether the young woman marries or remains single, her well-being, health and sanity are probably more endangered than redeemed by the social institution of love and marriage, the main business of women's lives. This pessimistic vision of marriage's role in the female maturing process remains in unresolved and... significant contradiction to the novel's conventional happy ending."[50] Burney thus maintains a double vision: providing an idealized domestic happiness for her heroine, while also criticizing the world that she inhabits and the rules she lives by.

Yet despite its celebration of Orville's politeness, what differentiates *Evelina* from later novels of love and manners like *Pride and Prejudice* is the breadth and materiality of its humor – its physical satire. Thus, rather than ending with Evelina's marriage, the novel concludes with another of

Captain Mirvan's crude practical jokes – the humiliation of the novel's fop, Lord Lovel. Declaring that he has "met a person just now, so like [Lovel], I could have sworn he had been your twin-brother," the Captain, "to the utter astonishment of every body but himself," "hauled into the room a monkey, full dressed, and extravagantly *a-la-mode!*" (p. 331). Amidst the ensuing hubbub, Evelina extends her sympathy to Lovel "who, though an egregious fop, had committed no offence that merited such chastisement" (p. 333). Her creator, however, seems less sympathetic, and details Lovel's humiliation, and the foolishness of other characters, at length. The scene is as characteristic of the novel as scenes of Evelina's delicacy and intro-spection, and reminds us that Burney's vision of the world is as close to Swift's or Smollett's as it is to Austen's (try to imagine a dressed-up monkey in *Pride and Prejudice*). Burney adds a decidedly urbane and satiric edge to the ideal of domestic virtue, reminding us of the material structures, and violent coercion, which supported it.

Wit and Sensibility

Introduction

What rules governed the social interactions of human communities? What caused such interactions to go smoothly, and what disrupted them? How could they be given a firmer foundation in virtue? These questions preoccupied social thinkers throughout the long eighteenth century. Theories of how the smooth and virtuous interaction of human collectivities could be achieved underwent important shifts. Governmental and legal structures regulate social behavior, of course; but, they are also organized by other, less official, standards of behavior: social conventions or mores. Two dynamics that are usually thought of as being characteristic of eighteenth-century England are an ideal of wit and an ideal of sensibility. Wit is usually thought of as characterizing the first part of the era, while sensibility characterized the second part. Wit establishes a hierarchy, carrying with it a recognition that certain social restraints are made to be transgressed by those at the top of the hierarchy. It comprehends social relationships as inherently competitive and antagonistic. Wit derives from breeding, and cuts others down to size. Wit, in practice, manifests itself as the ability to dissimulate one's true desires, while simultaneously intuiting the hidden desires of others. When the standards of social interaction moved away from hierarchical obedience and towards more egalitarian structures, wit declined as an aesthetic and a social arbiter. Sensibility, in contrast, posits sympathy as the primary mode through which social beings work together. While social hierarchies are still maintained through this dynamic, sensibility contends that people will abide by social rules through mutual respect, even, or perhaps especially, those at the top of the social hierarchy. Benevolence, rather than competition, governs social interaction.

Both formations are part of what the sociologist Norbert Elias called *The History of Manners*, the way ideas about proper physical and verbal behavior change over time. At its most concrete, these changes govern what utensils we use to eat our food; at their most abstract, they concern what kinds of emotions we can allow ourselves to feel for others (and for which others). Scholars have pointed to the eighteenth century as a watershed in thinking about the propriety of the body – elevating a restrained body over one that failed to control its physical processes in public.[1] As the century wore on, however, the culture became fascinated by the outpouring of feelings that could not be contained – by sensibility.

The concepts of wit and sensibility are as much aesthetic as they are sociological, spreading their influence over swathes of eighteenth-century literature. Needless to say, however, a regime of wit and a regime of sentiment generated different literary aesthetics. Broadly speaking, wit lent itself to satire, a genre concerned with reforming society by criticizing the faults of those members who behave foolishly, a kind of hyper- or exaggerated realism that focuses on chastising vice and impropriety. Sentimentality, in contrast, hopes to reshape society by presenting it with exemplary figures who can be emulated. This may lead it away from the realistic portrayal of human faults, but it also allows it to avoid the depiction of too much vice – something that became important as the eighteenth century progressed. This section provides one example of wit as a literary aesthetic, Congreve's *The Way of the World*, and three examples of different varieties of sentimentality: the earnest depiction of exemplary behavior in Steele's "sentimental comedy," *The Conscious Lovers*; the playful exploration of the effects of sensibility on one character's mind, pocketbook, and flirting skills in Sterne's *A Sentimental Journey*; and the interrogation of sensibility as rubric for understanding the self in the "sentimental" poetry of the late eighteenth-century writers Charlotte Smith and William Cowper.

William Congreve, *The Way of the World*

Congreve's play revolves around the complicated courtship of a singularly compelling couple: Millamant and Mirabell. Yet, as the title indicates, the play is not only concerned with its love plot but also more broadly with the way the world – at least the wealthy, urban world of London c. 1700 – operates. This was a world symbolized by the newly reopened theaters, and perhaps more generally characterized by a pervasive interest in disguise, performance, and theatricality. When Charles II was restored to the throne in 1660, one of his first acts was to reopen the public theaters closed during the Interregnum. These theaters, however, differed in some crucial ways from those of the early seventeenth century. Rather than the performances "in the round," on an almost bare stage, that Shakespeare had been used to, Restoration theater was performed both on the forestage and behind a proscenium arch. This allowed for much more elaborate scenery and stage machinery, and underlined the importance of disguise and discovery in the plays of the day as characters emerged from behind scenic flats and disappeared into trap doors.[2] The theaters were centrally located, and aristocrats, members of the court (including the king), and newly wealthy merchants and tradesmen from the city of London mingled freely in this milieu. By all accounts, members of the audience liked to engage in their own versions of disguise and performance during the play: women, both aristocrats and prostitutes, came masked and carried on intrigues with their admirers. The change with the most dramatic and lasting impact, however, was the introduction of actresses to the stage. The female characters that would have been played by boys in Renaissance theater were now played by actual women. These actresses were some of the first celebrities – fans paid attention to everything from their love affairs (such as that between Nell Gywnn and the king) to their fashion choices. The impact of this development can be seen in a play like *The Way of the World*, which features so many complex and central parts for women.

Congreve's play is often described as the final flowering of Restoration theater, but it is also a work that looks ahead to a new era of aesthetics and behavior. Perhaps because it teeters on the brink between one era and the next, however, although the play was part of the repertory by 1718 and considered a masterpiece by posterity, it was not immediately successful when it was first performed in March 1700. Norman Holland notes that the title itself comments on the play's position at once inside and outside the world it describes: " 'Way,' in the sense of habitual manner or style, suggests that discrepancy between appearance and nature which is the ubiquitous 'way' of the Restoration world . . . 'Way,' in the sense of path or direction of motion, suggests that moving force of passions which makes existing forms change in the emancipating action of the play."[3] In other words, its characters trace both habitual ways and ways forward.

Congreve's play has a notoriously complex and difficult plot, even by the standards of Restoration comedy. Its opening scene introduces us to the characters who will, in some senses, act as the opposing forces in the play: Fainall and Mirabell – men who interact with perfect manners, but who are actually bitter enemies. Through their conversation, which takes place as they play cards in a Chocolate House, we learn of the conditions that set the plot in motion. Mirabell is in love with Millamant, but, if he marries her without her aunt Lady Wishfort's consent, he will lose Millamant's inheritance of 6,000 pounds. Furthermore, if Wishfort herself marries, he will also lose Millamant's inheritance. Despite his unquestion-able love for Millamant, Mirabell is determined not to marry her without also getting the money, and we gradually learn of the plan he has set up to ensure that this happens.

With the help of Mrs. Fainall, Mirabell's former lover, now stuck in an unhappy marriage to Fainall (who is also carrying on an affair with Mrs. Marwood), Mirabell has arranged the marriage of two of Wishfort's ser-vants, Foible and Waitwell. He has then disguised Waitwell as his (Mirabell's) uncle, "Sir Rowland." He plans to convince Wishfort to marry Sir Rowland and then reveal the marriage as bigamous, thus blackmailing Wishfort into consenting to his marriage to Millamant and granting him the inheritance. The plan moves along smoothly until Mrs. Marwood overhears Mrs. Fainall discussing it with Foible, and writes a letter to Wishfort exposing the scheme. Fainall has Waitwell arrested, and launches his own attempt to blackmail Lady Wishfort by confronting her with evidence of Mrs. Fainall's previous relationship with Mirabell, along with Millamant's involvement with Mirabell. In the nick of time, however, Mirabell is able to produce a contract, written by Mrs. Fainall *before* her marriage, in which she has signed over all her inheritance to Mirabell. This foils the blackmail plot. Mirabell returns Mrs. Fainall's property to her, Lady Wishfort, in gratitude, agrees to the marriage of Mirabell and Millamant, and the play ends happily for its hero and heroine (Millamant and Mirabell), less happily for the villains (Fainall and Marwood) and ambivalently for some characters who perhaps deserve better (Mrs. Fainall, Lady Wishfort).

In Mirabell and Fainall, then, the play offers us two variations on the rake figure. The rake is a standard character in Restoration drama (and one that continues to appear in drama and fiction throughout the eighteenth century). He is a man whose sense of self and status is defined by his sexual conquest of women. He is not interested in a lasting love but rather in moving through as many love affairs as possible. The rake's goal in this perpetual pursuit of sex varies: for some, the desire for sensuous pleasure is paramount ("rake" is often synonymous with "libertine"), and these characters also often enjoy drinking and other kinds of worldly dissipation, as well as sex; for others, conquest is a pleasure in itself; the repetitious exertion of power over others provides their primary source of satisfaction. Before the play begins, Mirabell seems to have been the kind of rake who pursued sexual pleasure – we learn of his affair with Mrs. Fainall, for example. Yet his role in *The Way of the World* differs from the conventional trajectory of the rake. When we meet him, he is already in love with Millamant, nor is he distracted from her by other women over the course of the play. In the end, the only danger to their relationship seems to be his excessive devotion to Millamant; he tells her, "heaven grant I love you not too well, that's all my fear" (V, last scene). In Mirabell, Congreve thus retains the wit and social aplomb associated with the rake, while disposing of the promiscuity. In Fainall, however, Congreve explores another aspect of the rake figure: the thirst for power. Fainall has his sexual conquests – he's been carrying on an affair with Mrs. Marwood outside of his marriage, after all – but he only seems to truly take pleasure in his gambit to wrest Lady Wishfort's fortune away from her, ensure that Mirabell and Millamant never marry, and solidify his control over his wife's fortune. His demand in his blackmail scheme is that Lady Wishfort will "submit your own estate to my management, and absolutely make over my wife's to my sole use" (V, x). Thus, while both Mirabell and Fainall are rakishly manipulative and acquisitive, the former is motivated by love, while the latter is motivated by greed and the desire to dominate others. One is the hero of the play; one is the villain.

Although Millamant has no part in the scheming that makes up the plot of the play, the nature of her relationship with Mirabell is an important part of its resolution, and not only because, as is conventional with comedies, the key relationship being worked out in the play is marriage. The play is justly famous for its "proviso" scene, in which Mirabell and Millamant work out their future relationship in the form of a contract. Their provisos, while still witty, seem to move away from the disguise and manipulation that governs other aspects of the plot towards something else; their bond is governed by the stability of contract rather than the fluctuating struggle for power. Their marriage, they agree, will be more straightforward than the ones around it; Millamant asks Mirabell never to use pet names when they are married, such as "wife, spouse, my dear, joy, jewel, love, sweetheart, and the rest of the nauseous cant in which men and their wives are so fulsomely familiar" (IV, v). Mirabell, in turn, "article[s]" that Millamant "continue to like [her] own face as long as [he] shall, and while it passes current with [him], that [she] endeavour not to new-coin it," and that she never try to hide her pregnancies by "strait-lacing, squeezing for a shape" (ibid.). These conditions have to do with language and appearances, but they seem to presage the possibility that Millamant and Mirabell are working against "the way of the world" towards something else, a relationship in which they bare their "true selves" to each other. Furthermore, the legalistic manner in which they make this agreement, man and woman both acting as equal parties, counterposes the schemes and disguises that make up the main plot of the play.

Beyond the microcosm of Mirabell and Millamant's relationship, however, Congreve's play depicts a world dominated by, to use the play's own word, dissimulation. Juxtaposed to the hero and heroine's pledge to present themselves straightforwardly to each other, we have a multitude of characters constructing elaborately false versions of themselves. This is a play about people caught up in everyday theatrical performance. Some characters, of course, simply pretend to be someone else, as Waitwell pretends to be Mirabell's uncle, and Foible pretends not to be married. Some characters set up elaborate scenarios in order to establish artificial versions of themselves, as when Petulant hires women of pleasure to call on him to prove his own popularity (sometimes, we are told, he makes the elaborate effort to disguise himself and call upon himself!). One of the most humorous, and yet strangest, instances of this kind of behavior occurs when Lady Wishfort, in an attempt to seduce the man she believes to be Mirabell's uncle, uses makeup to make her aged self look more like a portrait of her younger self. Foible, her deceptive maid, informs her:

> *Foible*: ...Your ladyship has frowned a little too rashly indeed, madam. There are some cracks discernible in the white varnish.
> *Lady Wishfort*: Let me see the glass. Cracks, sayest thou? Why, I am arrantly flayed! I look like an old peeled wall! Thou must repair me Foible, before Sir Rowland comes, or I shall never keep up to my picture.
> *Foible*: I warrant you, madam. A little art once made your picture like you; and now a little of the same art must make you like your picture. Your picture must sit for you madam. (III, i)

Here, the distinction between art and life flip-flops, as the face becomes a painting and the painting a living model. Yet the exchange begs the question of what it means to be disguised as yourself. Such levels of dissimulation ask us to consider whether these characters hide a "true" self behind their disguises, or whether selfhood is endlessly theatrical, endlessly performative in social settings.

Richard Steele, *The Conscious Lovers*

We can see the systems of governing behavior start to change in the first decades of the eighteenth century, as both form and content of drama shift. In the new "sentimental comedy," the plot revolves around learning the truth about the main characters, rather than enjoying their clever masquerades and machinations. In Steele's *The Conscious Lovers* (1722), for example, the hero, Bevil Jr, is pressured to marry Lucinda Sealand, the woman his father has chosen for him, even though he is in love with someone else, and his best friend is in love with Lucinda. The threat to this marriage comes neither from Bevil's filial disobedience, nor from any elaborate plot he concocts to set things right. Bevil is in fact ready to sacrifice his desire to marry the woman he does love, Indiana, in order to comply with his father's wishes. Rather, the marriage is threatened by the appearance of impropriety: it seems as if Bevil is supporting Indiana, thought to be an illegitimate French orphan, as his kept mistress, when in reality his generosity is completely chaste. The hero does not resolve the situation through his skilful manipulation of events, as does Mirabell in *The Way of the World*. Instead, the last-minute, accidental, revelation that Indiana is really Sealand's long-lost daughter, lost when the family's ship was overtaken by pirates, makes it possible for Bevil Jr to follow his father's wishes and his heart's desire simultaneously. As Peter Hynes has written:

> The leading couple have little to do besides express their mutual esteem and talk about philosophy; the resolution of their practical difficulties depends on Sealand's chance discovery that Indiana is his daughter, not on anything that Bevil Jr. has done. The hero is in fact a remarkably passive figure...The point of his adventures is that virtue rather than the streetwise maneuvering of the Restoration wit should attract rewards....The new form [of drama] tends to the monumental, both in plot details and in dialogue. Characters *wait* to see what will happen [.][4]

This dynamic sets up a very different aesthetic of plotting; since the hero cannot compromise his virtue by underhanded dealing, the plot must rely heavily on coincidence. While Mirabell proves his prowess, Bevil proves his virtue. The resolution hinges not on the successful playing of a part but on the revelation of one's true character: Bevil Jr is *really* too virtuous to keep a mistress; Indiana is *really* too virtuous to be a kept mistress, and is also *really* a rich merchant's daughter.

One of the objections most often raised against sentimental comedy was that it disregarded an important function of satire: to criticize human foible and reform through stringent critique. Sentimental comedy offers us examples to be emulated, rather than behavior to be shunned. As Lisa Freeman writes, "satirical comedy shows faults to be avoided and sentimental comedy offers models for imitation."[5] Plays like *The Conscious Lovers* also seemed to shift uncomfortably between comedy and something more serious to create a strained, mixed aesthetic. This is what John Dennis famously complained of, as does the anonymous author of *The Censor Censured*:

[P]assions of all kinds may be represented in comedy as well as in tragedy; but then they must be expressed in a different manner, not in the tragical style and not in the tragical tone; nor must distress be so exquisite as to melt the heart with sympathetic grief and render it incapable of relishing the approaching joy. 'Tis unnatural to suppose the mind can fly so readily from one extreme to the other.[6]

Of course, the play's capacity to combine comedy with touching sentiments is what many people enjoyed about the innovation in form: in *Joseph Andrews*, for example, Parson Adams is very pleased that parts of this comedy are "almost solemn enough for a sermon." Perhaps its supporters were in the majority: the play had an initial run of eighteen nights – quite successful for its day. It took in more money than any previous play had at Drury Lane, the theater in which it was first produced.

As it moralized the plot and downplayed the plotting of Restoration comedy, sentimental comedy also cleaned up its language, making it fit for new standards of propriety for women. We can see the movement to change the definition of wit from something licentious to something moral in the prologue, written by Leonard Welsted, which declares:

No more let Ribaldry, with Licence writ,
Usurp the Name of Eloquence or Wit;
No more let lawless Farce uncensur'd go,
The lewd dull Gleanings of a Smithfield Show.
'Tis yours, with Breeding to refine the Age,
To Chasten Wit, and Moralize the Stage.

Refinement has to do both with nature of the characters themselves and with the language that they speak.

It is clear, then, that one of the important things that sentimental comedy did was to set up a new kind of masculinity, one that stood in contrast to the rake-hero of Restoration comedy. If in those plays the rakish hero tries to outwit all around him, subverting and outmaneuvering the social boundaries of his day, in sentimental comedy the upstanding hero respects the bounds of filial obedience and loyalty, using other means to achieve his goals. In *The Conscious Lovers*, Indiana's friend, Isabella, sums up the idea of masculinity that plays like Congreve's were intent on replacing:

There are, among the destroyers of women, the gentle, the mild, the affable, the humble, who all, soon after their success in their designs, turn to the contrary of those characters. I will own to you, Mr. Bevil carries his hypocrisie the best of any man living, but still he is a man, and therefore

a hypocrite. They have usurp'd an exemption from shame, for any base-
ness, any cruelty towards us. They embrace without love, they make vows
without conscience of obligation; they are partners, nay, seducers to the
crime, wherein they pretend to be less guilty. (II, ii)[7]

And Indiana, the heroine, accurately, observes, "But what's all this to
Bevil?" Bevil Jr is indeed a new kind of hero and a new kind of man. One
symptom of this, which shows the author taking a stand on an important
issue of the day, is in the play's disparagement of dueling. Bevil Jr and his
friend Myrtle almost clash swords when Myrtle insults Indiana, but their
restraint prevails. Bevil Jr, in his relief, "reflect[s] how many friends have
died, at the hands of friends, for want of temper" (IV, i). Bevil's masculinity
here is premised not on his violence or physical prowess, but on his restraint
and his respect for social bonds like friendship. He says, "There is nothing
manly but what is conducted by reason, and agreeable to the practice of
virtue and justice" (IV, i).

This emphasis on restraint, sincerity, and lasting friendship (as opposed
to reckless bravery, clever manipulation, and impulsive desire) can be seen
as the play's support for newly emergent middle-class ideals. This idea is
confirmed by the play's explicit stance on the improved social standing of
the merchant classes. Mr. Sealand might, in another context, emerge as the
villain of the piece: it is he who has "lost" Indiana – condemning her to
live her childhood as a penniless orphan in France – and it is he who hopes
to force his other daughter, Lucinda, to marry Bevil against her wishes.
But Sealand is redeemed, thanks to a tearful reunion scene with Indiana,
and the play ends with no hard feelings between father and daughter.
Sealand also delivers a heartfelt speech about the importance of merchants
to Bevil Sr:

> Sir, as much a cit as you take me for – I know the town, and the world –
> and give me leave to say, that we merchants are a species of gentry, that
> have grown into the world this last century, and are as honorable, and
> almost as useful as you landed folks, that have always thought yourselves
> so much above us; for your trading, forsooth! Is extended no farther, than
> a load of hay, or a fat ox – You are pleasant people, indeed; because you
> are generally bred up to be lazy, therefore, I warrant you, industry is dis-
> honorable. (IV, ii)

Sealand here makes a value of the new emergence of the merchant classes
– they are no less important because they have only recently "grown into"
the world; their honor is made of industry.

Lisa Freeman describes the shift in sentimental comedy as "a move away
from an investment in sexual intercourse and towards an interest in social

intercourse. For if wit, as a symbol of sexual potency, was the currency in Restoration laughing comedies, then good breeding, a symbol of sociability, was the currency in eighteenth-century sentimental comedies."[8] Good breeding, she argues, meant both refined language and refined manners, and a focus on the importance of procreative, not simply recreational, alliances. Setting up the groundwork for such alliances in sincerity, sentiment, and social equality was one of the cultural accomplishments of the sentimental aesthetic.

Laurence Sterne, *Sentimental Journey*

Yet sentimentality was not always focused on the formation of conjugal bonds. In the latter part of the eighteenth century, people became increasingly interested in sentiment as a way of understanding both how the human psyche functioned and how human beings interacted in communities. Sentimentality is a philosophy in which feelings and morality are linked. It presupposes that the emotions you feel in response to others' feelings are not only pleasurable or painful but also instructive. These feelings spring from an innate moral sense. Sentimental literature presupposes that "literary emotions herald active ones; a theatrical or fictional feeling creates greater virtue in the audience or reader, and a contrived tear foreshadows the spontaneous one of human sympathy. Sentimental literature is exemplary of emotion, teaching its consumers to produce a response equivalent to the one presented in its episodes."[9] The term "sensibility" usually refers to a personal characteristic, a susceptibility to the feelings of others, particularly their sorrows. Sensibility spurs the person who possesses it towards benevolence, and thus provides an alternate model of interaction to the one offered by the regime of wit.

Sentimentality is premised on an ideal of psychological commonality: the theory that the feelings of others are comprehensible to us because everyone's affective makeup is basically the same. For this reason, we can put ourselves in the place of another person, imagine what they are feeling: empathize. There are, however, two ways you can understand this commonality, and that duality accounts for the very different versions of sentimentality we see at play in eighteenth-century literature and culture, as well as for the arguments critics and readers have about it now. On the one hand, sentimentality has a radically expansive potential. The idea that all minds, all psyches, are essentially similar allows marginalized persons to become visible, and, in some cases, to demand rights that have been denied to them. Thus, we can see sentimentality at play in some of the protofeminist discourse of the period, particularly that dealing with the possible redemption of fallen or mad women. We also see it in calls for benevolence towards the sufferings of the poor, and perhaps most strongly in the opposition to the various forms of coercion and brutality premised on racial inequality that flourished during the period. Much of the eighteenth-century antislavery appeal, for example, was based on the idea that the suffering undergone by slaves was the same as the suffering Europeans would undergo if they were in the same position – and therefore intolerable and unacceptable. Sentimentality, therefore, had a progressive potential in that it could be used to recognize the personhood of those who had formerly not been thought of as thinking or feeling beings.

On the other hand, however, sentimentality could have a conservative or normative effect. The idea that everyone's feelings are structured in the same way might easily turn into the assumption that "everyone feels the same way about the same things that I do." So, the limit of what can be understood about the sufferings of another being (the object of sympathy, or the sentimental object) is the limit of what the sympathetic person (the subject of sympathy) already feels. Anything that falls outside that experience remains invisible. In other words, sentimentality could lead to a kind of rigid anthropomorphism: what happens when we think that animals have the same feelings as people, rather than radically different animal feelings. This had political consequences in situations like the slavery debates, in which the experiences of slaves that fell outside the experience of their British sympathizers were rendered incomprehensible and unimportant. Sometimes there was not much room for difference in sentimental discourse.

It could also be seen as the dynamic that governed relationships involving class difference, rather than sexual difference. In Sterne's second and last novel, sensibility is a less focused and more playful force than it is in *The Conscious Lovers*. Furthermore, the novel manages to critique as well as celebrate sensibility and to tease out the moral ambiguities of sentimentality as a mode of governing behavior. In *A Sentimental Journey*, Sterne extracts a character, whose death is briefly mentioned in *Tristram Shandy* and sends him on a tour of France and Italy. The novel is relentlessly episodic, each episode bringing Yorick into contact with scenes or persons who evoke his sympathetic response. What action there is occurs in the play of Yorick's emotions.

The novel's episodes are connected only as stops in Yorick's travels through France (he never actually makes it to Italy), and for this reason the novel can be read on one level as a parody of the Grand Tour. Taking a

Grand Tour was an alternate form of education for the wealthy during the eighteenth century. Young men would travel through Europe, particularly through France, Italy, and Holland. Such journeys became more popular than before during the eighteenth century, in part because of the improvement of roads and transportation, and in part because people had more disposable wealth for this kind of expensive endeavor. Coaches, for instance, had springs and were upholstered. The tour was a way of acquiring cultural capital, burnishing one's civility, and fostering learning. It also confirmed the greatness of contemporary English civilization in reference to great past civilizations, such as Augustan Rome.

The episodic, digressive quality of *A Sentimental Journey* recalls *Tristram Shandy*, and Northrop Frye's words about the earlier novel apply to the later one as well: "here we are not being led into a story, but into the process of writing a story: we wonder not what is coming next, but what the author will think of next." This is a rhetorical strategy Frye associates with what he dubs the "Age of Sensibility."[10] The casual, intimate, joking quality of Sterne's narrative reminds us of the ways that sentimental discourse shaped particular kinds of reading practices. Sterne wrote: "a true feeler always brings half the entertainment along with him. His own ideas are only called forth by what he reads, and the vibrations within, so entirely correspond with those excited, 'tis like reading himself and not the book."[11] The book here becomes the medium through which the reader understands him- or herself.

In *A Sentimental Journey*, Sterne explores the ways in which sentimentality is a language of the body. The signs of feeling given by Yorick, the signs which readers are supposed to mimic, such as blushing, sighing, and most importantly, tears, are corporeal. This reliance on visible signs makes sentimentality an odd form of empiricism in which the actions of the body provide us with evidence of its feelings and virtue. In *A Sentimental Journey*, Yorick calls sensibility the "SENSORIUM of the world, which vibrates, if a hair of our heads but falls upon the ground."[12] A sensorium is the part of the brain concerned with the reception of sensory stimuli; here, feelings are described in terms of their physical effects – the vibrations they produce. There is a new emphasis here on sense perception. Often in sentimental fiction, the body over which such signs play is female, its virtue "not so much spoken as displayed ... its vocabulary ... that of gestures and palpitations, sighs and tears. The vocabulary is powerful because it is not spoken (but only spoken of); it is everything that punctures or interrupts speech."[13] Sterne, of course, tweaks this by making the primary body in *A Sentimental Journey* Yorick's male one, and his most frequent feelings arguably sexual.

Thanking a shopwoman in Paris, for example, inexorably leads Yorick to touching her:

> Any one may do a casual act of good nature, but a continuation of them shews it is a part of the temperature; and certainly, added I, if it is the same blood which comes from the heart, which descends to the extremes (touching her wrist) I am sure you must have one of the best pulses of any woman in the world – Feel it, said she, holding out her arm. So laying down my hat, I took hold of her fingers in one hand, and applied the two fore-fingers of my other to the artery. (p. 75)

Here, the empirical phenomena of sensibility allow Yorick to engage in physical freedoms that would otherwise seem improper. "Trust me," Yorick imagines saying to his friend Eugenius, "there are worse occupations in this world than *feeling a woman's pulse.*" For him, sensibility makes bodily contact innocent, and if the reader sees it otherwise, the fault lies in the reader's prurience, rather than in Yorick's own lasciviousness.

This is not to say, however, that Sterne does not enjoy taunting the reader with the sexual double entendres that the collision of Yorick's beliefs, behaviour, and rhetoric constantly bring about. Thanking another girl in Paris, he says:

> She bid me adieu twice – I repeated it as often; and so cordial was the parting between us, that had it happened anywhere else, I'm not sure but I should have signed it with a kiss of charity, as warm and holy as an apostle.
>
> But in Paris, as none kiss each other but the men, I did what amounted to the same thing –
>
> – I bid God bless her. (p. 92)

The dashes both account for Yorick's excesses of feeling – they cover what words cannot express – and leave room for the reader's imagination to conjure up lewder interactions than those the text will acknowledge.

The novel's interest in emotionally charged exchanges extends to relationships between men as well. One scene that has captured the imagination of many readers is Yorick's exchange of snuffboxes with a monk he has earlier insulted.

> He stopped ... as soon as he came up to us, with a word of frankness; and having a horn snuffbox in his hand, he presented it open to me – you shall taste mine – said I, pulling out my box (which is a small tortoise one) and putting it into his hand –'Tis most excellent, said the monk; Then do me the favour, I replied, to accept the box and all, and when you take a pinch out of it, sometime recollect it was the peace-offering of a man who once used you unkindly, but not from his heart. (p. 43)

Here, the emotions are not transmitted skin to skin, as they are in Yorick's contacts with women, but rather through the transmission of what Lynn Festa calls a "sentimental object." The sentimental object, Festa argues, provides a kind of counterpoint to the commodification of all exchanges that intensified during the eighteenth century: "self and possession bleed together in the sentimental object, breaking down the neat divisions between the alienable and the inalienable that facilitate commodity exchange. Since sentimental objects cannot be loved by others in the same way, that is, they create a form of *inalienable* value that cannot be replaced by money or goods of like kind."[14] For Yorick, the monk's snuffbox becomes a way not only of remembering the monk but of savoring the emotions connected with the encounter. "I guard this box," says Yorick, "as I guard the instrumental parts of my religion, to help my mind on to something better" (p. 44).

In *A Sentimental Journey*, however, sentimentality not only provides a way of understanding affective intercourse between equals, but also of negotiating issues of class status and social legitimacy. As the eighteenth century progressed, the newly well-off, the emerging middle classes, needed some way of claiming moral value distinct from the sheer fact of their wealth. Acts of charity, such as those Yorick performs, confirm that middle-class citizens are valuable to society because of their virtue. As one critic puts it, such scenes are "characteristic of a self-confessedly sentimental narrative that implicitly assumes and explicitly asserts the values of a middle-class culture intent on demonstrating the naturalness and benevolence of its moral authority... Like most eighteenth-century sentimental narratives, *A Sentimental Journey* suppresses questions about how one acquires the wealth to be able to afford one charitable act after another."[15] Sentimentality thus orchestrates the exchange of cultural capital, as when Yorick distributes money to a crowd of beggars, portioning out his coins according to the sympathy evoked by the faces he sees:

> My Lord Anglois – the very sound was worth the money – so I gave *my last sous for it*. But in the eagerness of giving, I had overlooked a *pauvre honteux*, who had no one to ask a sou for him, and who, I believed, would have perished, ere he could have asked for one himself: he stood by the chaise a little without the circle, and wiped a tear from a face which I thought had seen better days – Good God! – said I – and I have not one single sous left to give him – so I gave him – no matter what – I am ashamed to say *how much*, now – and was ashamed to think, how little, then: so if the reader can form any conjecture of my disposition, as these two fixed points

are given him, he may judge within a livre or two what was the precise sum. (p. 60)

Here, the ebb and flow of sentiment become a calculus of charity. The reader's own moral sensibility is engaged, as he or she is challenged to put a figure on Yorick's emotional almsgiving. The critic quoted above dubs Yorick's acts of benevolence the "theatrics of bourgeois virtue," as they allow him to both perform and disavow his superior economic status.

If sentimentality centrally concerns sense perception, the sense that it is most concerned with is visual perception. For this reason, most of its pleasures derive from spectacle and tableau, rather than from plot or narrative. We can learn a great deal about the way emotions can be elicited by the careful orchestration of images from a famous passage in *A Sentimental Journey* we now know was influenced by Sterne's correspondence with the Afro-British writer Ignatius Sancho.[16] Yorick is about to be thrown into the Bastille, and is reminded of the suffering caused by captivity by his encounter with a bird. Forced to confront the possibility of his own future suffering, he tries to imagine the dynamics of captivity for himself:

> I sat down close to my table, and leaning my head upon my hand, I began to figure for myself the miseries of confinement. I was in a right frame for it, and so I gave full scope to my imagination.
>
> I was going to begin with the millions of my fellow creatures born to no inheritance but slavery; but finding, however affecting the picture was, that I could not bring it near me, and that the multitude of sad groups in it did but distract me.–
>
> I took a single captive, and having first shut him up in his dungeon, I then look'd through the twilight of his grated door to take his picture. (p. 70)

Here, Yorick attempts to empathize with himself. That is, in order to imagine what it would feel like to be imprisoned himself, he paints a picture of others in captivity, and tries to sympathize with those persons. Finding he can't sympathize with groups, he "takes" a single captive, but the picture he paints for himself – the emotions he has generated in himself – cause him to burst into tears and look away.

The dynamics of sympathy in *A Sentimental Journey* are both playful and serious. Sentiment generates both pleasure and pain (although sometimes even the pain is pleasurable). Sterne uses the structures of sympathetic response to investigate both the forces that draw persons together and govern their interactions, and the construction of the self, the patterns of behavior that register individuality. In his hands, sentimentality becomes a tool for self-interrogation.

Charlotte Smith, *Elegiac Sonnets* and William Cowper, *The Castaway*

When we move from the sentimental fiction of the third quarter of the eighteenth century to the sentimental poetry of its final decades, it is tempting to trace a progression from an expansive sensibility, moving out to encompass more persons and places, to a sentimentality focused on the self, particularly on the lacunae and limitations of self-knowledge or self-analysis. The poetry of the last quarter of the eighteenth century has been called the "poetry of sensibility." Northrop Frye notes that this poetry is characterized by the way poets define their own voices through metaphorical identifications with others. He points out that: "In the age of sensibility some of the identifications involving the poet seem manic, like Blake's with Druidic bards, or Smart's with Hebrew prophets, or depressive, like Cowper's with a scapegoat figure such as a stricken deer or castaway, or merely bizarre, like Macpherson's with Ossian or Chatterton's with Rowley."[17] But for many of these poets the dynamic of sympathetic identification was anything but simple. We need to recognize that a number of these poems work not only by invoking such identifications, but also by repudiating them. With some frequency, the kinds of identifications Frye describes collapse – leaving the poet alienated and isolated from the bonds of sympathy he or she has tried to forge. We might posit, then, that while the "poetry of sensibility" explores the power of sentimental identifications to construct poetic identity, it also tries to imagine what poetry would sound like if the demands of sympathy were somehow thwarted.

In one sense, sentimentality is a way of making the emotions of others accessible. Yet, for these late eighteenth-century poets, the potentially radical difference of individual minds is more daunting than it was for Sterne. If for Sterne, sympathy is always threatening to collapse the walls of the self into an orgasmic merging, for poets like Smith and Cowper, sympathy is always on the verge of revealing the impermeability of the walls around the self, its profound isolation. These texts represent the way sentimentality can prove the impossibility as well as the possibility of human social relations – the inability of the feeler to get beyond his or her own mind.

Charlotte Smith grew up in comfort, but was forced into an unfortunate marriage to Benjamin Smith at age fifteen. The marriage and its consequences were enormously unhappy. By the time she was twenty-five, Smith had been married for nine years and had six children. That number soon grew to ten. Though her husband's family was wealthy, when her father-in-law died, his will was so complicated that Smith's children did not receive their share of their inheritance until 37 years later; Smith herself did not see any of that inheritance during her lifetime. Under these circumstances, Smith attempted to support herself and her children as a professional writer – and by and large succeeded. Her volume of *Elegiac Sonnets and Other Essays* first appeared in 1784, and went through eight gradually expanding editions by 1800. Realizing that prose would be more remunerative than poetry, Smith next set her hand to writing novels, publishing ten in the course of her career, including *The Old Manor House*, and two novels of the French Revolution, *Desmond* and *The Banished Man*. Smith also published translations, longer poems like *The Emigrants* and *Beachy Head* and stories for children. Her work was well received during her lifetime.

Smith is widely credited with sparking the "sonnet revival" of the later eighteenth and early nineteenth century. Her technical mastery of a lyric form that had been denigrated and ignored during the eighteenth century inspired the efforts of Romantic poets like Wordsworth, Keats, and Shelley. Although the sonnet had been used for serious, non-amorous themes before by poets like Milton and Donne, Smith's capacious musings on psychology, art, and nature had a direct influence on the Romantic poets. Although Smith's work was already beginning to be forgotten by the mid-nineteenth century, her immediate successors often praised her. Wordsworth, for example, said that she was a poet "to whom English verse is under greater obligations than are likely to be either acknowledged or remembered."[18]

Smith explicitly linked the overriding sadness of the poems to the circumstances of her own life, and in their exploration of the effects of melancholy they are certainly autobiographical. *The Elegiac Sonnets*, however, are more than simply an obsessive account of Smith's own psychic state; rather, she uses the overwhelming quality of that emotion to explore the relationship between authorship, affect, and the literary tradition. Smith's *Elegiac Sonnets*, in fact, question the capacity of sympathy to alleviate individual woe. Indeed, paradoxically, their engagement with sympathy most often takes the form of attempting to delineate a state outside of emotion – a condition she usually calls "oblivion." This is a mental state available to lunatics, the dead, and other such beings; but it is a condition the poet herself can only "envy." Observing the dead of the "Church-yard at Middleton in Sussex" (*Sonnet XLIV*) she concludes (in what seems to be a direct rejoinder to Gray's *Elegy*) that "They hear the warring elements no more:/While I am doom'd – by life's long storm opprest,/To gaze with envy on their gloomy rest" (ll. 12–14).[19] In *Sonnet LXX*, "On Being Cautioned Against Walking on a Headland Overlooking the Sea, Because it was Frequented by a Lunatic," the poet claims to see the lunatic "more with envy than with fear" because "He has no nice felicities that shrink/From giant horrors; wildly wandering here,/He seems (uncursed with reason) not to know/The depth or the duration of his woe" (ll. 10, 11–14). The lines define the poet's own "cursed" state of reason, or awareness of time and emotional engagement, against the irrational, timeless existence of the lunatic. Her envy is almost the opposite of sympathy, in that she can imagine the emotion*less* state of the lunatic, but cannot feel it with him, cannot empathize with it; she is radically *disconnected* from the object of her desired identification.

Smith's concern with the feelings of others penetrates not only the themes of her sonnets, but also their rhetorical structure and form. Many of the poems in the volume are written in the voice of characters Smith has "borrowed" from other authors – such as Goethe's Werther – or from her own fiction. Even in sonnets seemingly written in the poet's own voice, she consistently alludes to other literature. For example, the sonnet entitled *To Oblivion* uses three allusions in the final nine lines:

> Oblivion! Take me to thy quiet reign,
> Since robb'd of all that gave my soul delight,
> I only ask exemption from the pain
> Of knowing "such things were" – and are no more;
> Of dwelling on the hours for ever fled,
> And heartless, helpless, hopeless to deplore
> "Pale misery living, joy and pleasure dead":
> While dragging thus unwish'd a length of days,
> "Death seems prepared to strike, yet still delays." (ll. 6–14)

Smith herself footnotes the second two phrases in quotation marks: the first (l. 12) is from a sonnet by Sir Brooke Boothby (1796); the second (l. 14) is a paraphrase of a line from Thomas Warton's *Ode to Sleep*. The words in quotation marks in line 9 (marked but not given a specific referent by Smith) are from *Macbeth*, from MacDuff's lament for his murdered wife and children. Here, it seems that the only language that can convey Smith's own sadness comes from others – oblivion may be the force that rescues her from both literary history and personal misery. Smith's heavy use of allusion seems to signal her awareness of her own immersion in a literary tradition, an immersion that dictates that her revival of the sonnet is not so much a reinvention as it is a self-conscious revision. Adela Pinch has argued that this rhetorical strategy also problematizes the individuality of the "personal" feelings Smith overtly explores:

> If quotation involves incorporation of someone else's expressions, perhaps writing makes one miserable because writing always involves taking in, reproducing, other people's expressons of feelings. However, I do not think we should take the affective dimension of this formulation, this misery, as the sign of a woman poet's defeat at the hands of a patriarchal literary tradition, her depression at being always already written: rather, this gloominess is a sign and medium...of a successful literary transmission.[20]

That is to say, Smith's use of other's voices is not an admission of poetic inadequacy, but rather a poignant and illuminating exploration of the intersection of the history of poetic genre with the voice of an individual author.

We have seen, then, the different ways that the ideals of civility and sentimentality could organize heterogeneous communities and help lay down the conventions by which their members could interact. But in late eighteenth-century sentimental poetry, we can also see the way sentimentality acknowledges unbridgeable differences between persons and the incommunicability of certain psychic states. Smith's poetry does this, and so does the poetry of her contemporary and correspondent, William Cowper. Cowper was one of the most popular poets of his day (and beyond: he was Jane Austen's favorite poet, for example), and yet, like Thomas Gray, he was an isolated and profoundly troubled person, who could never embrace public fame. After suffering a mental breakdown early in life, and being reborn as an evangelical Christian, Cowper retreated into the country, living with friends. He wrote many short, lyric sentimental poems celebrating his household pets and a long poem, *The Task*, which, in its introspective focus, many critics have seen as a precursor to Wordsworth's *Prelude*.

Cowper's very late poem, *The Castaway*, however, exemplifies the difficulty of using imaginative identifications as a way to communicate and share mental states. The poem begins by recounting a story Cowper drew from Anson's *Voyage Around the World*, 1740–4. As with much sentimental literature, the vision of a sailor drowning is framed by its description in another text – the poem describes the experience of reading about his death in the pages of a book, rather than actually being there. After a poignant description of the sailor's anguish in facing death, and his ship-mates' pain in watching him die, the poem tells us that the sailor's suffer-ings mirror something in the poet's own condition. In a snapshot of the identificatory process, the poet tells us that "misery ... delights to trace / its semblance in another's case." But the poem's last lines, with a brutal poi-gnancy, tell us that the poet's own mental suffering is worse than the physi-cal suffering the sailor has undergone.

> No voice divine the storm allay'd,
> No light propitious shone;
> When, snatch'd from all effectual aid,
> We perish'd, each alone:
> But I beneath a rougher sea,
> And whelm'd in deeper gulfs than he. (st. 11)

So the comparison between poet and sailor finally serves to show us that both are finally isolated – from fellow human beings and from God. And, while we are given copious detail about events that lead to the sailor's death, we are given no information about the conditions that make the poet's metaphorical "seas" rougher and deeper. The poem is challenging and unusual in its insistence that psychological suffering can be worse that physical suffering.

Both Smith and Cowper, then, perhaps the two most popular sentimen-tal poets of the later eighteenth century, underline the difficulties of sen-timental identification, and of sympathy as a way of building community, in their poetry. Both look forward to the Romantic era in their sense that individual psychic states may be impossible to communicate or share.

Trade and Travel

Introduction

My imagination is so captivated upon these occasions, that I seem to partake with the navigators, in all the dangers they encountered. I lose my anchor; my main-sail is rent into shreds; I kill a shark, and by signs converse with a Patagonian, and all this without moving from the fire-side. The principal fruits of these circuits, which have been made around the globe, seem likely to be the amusement of those that stayed at home.

William Cowper to John Newton, October 6, 1783

Of the many sources of eighteenth-century literature, none may be as important as the vast reservoir of travel literature produced during the period. These texts include ocean voyages, expeditions to faraway kingdoms, and dissertations on the languages and customs of foreign cultures. Such accounts had a tremendous impact not simply on the content of eighteenth-century literature but also on its forms. They generated new styles of writing by imitating conventions like the exactitude of seafaring and the fables of the near east. Writers often enjoyed writing about exotic locations for the opportunity it afforded of looking back on Britain with a critical eye. Foreign countries, real or imagined, could serve as experimental spaces to imagine new possibilities for society or the self.

The great joint stock companies, with the exception of the East India Company, were formed in the decades after the Restoration. The vast expansion in trade routes and goods enabled by these companies established Britain's mercantile empire, often called its first empire. This empire sought the accumulation of valuable goods that could be traded for profit, rather than dominion over territories that could be settled in the name of the crown. Thus, Britain's interest in China had to do with how much porcelain, tea, and silk it could export, its interest in Indonesia was based on the value of spices and mahogany, and its interest in India, through most of the eighteenth century, was spurred by the desire for fabrics and other commodities. The resulting importation of all these goods to Britain reshaped Britons' understanding of themselves and their country. In 1711, for instance, Addison described British culture's growing reliance on imported products:

> Nature seems to have taken a particular Care to disseminate her Blessings among the different Regions of the World, with an Eye to this mutual Intercourse and Traffick among Mankind, that the natives of the several Parts of the Globe might have a kind of Dependence upon one another, and be united together by their common Interest. Almost every *Degree* produces something peculiar to it. The Food often grows in one Country, and the Sauce in another. The Fruits of *Portugal* are corrected by the Products of *Barbadoes*: The infusion of a China Plant sweetened with the Pith of an Indian Cane: the *Phillipick* Islands give a Flavour to our *European* Bowls. The single Dress of a Woman of Quality is often the Product of a hundred Climates. The Muff and the Fan come together from the different Ends of the Earth. The Scarf is sent from the Torrid Zone, and the Tippet from beneath the Pole. The Brocade Petticoat rises out of the Mines of *Peru*, and the Diamond Necklace out of the Bowels of *Indostan*.[1]

Addison here praises the Royal Exchange, and the merchants who run it, as the site at which all these goods can come together and combine for the pleasure and well-being of British consumers: food, clothing, furniture were all transformed by the influence of this trading empire. And so was the British economy as a whole: trade came to form the tax base of the British state, and merchants supplied a large portion of the funds for long-term government borrowing.[2]

If the British voyaged abroad on trading routes in pursuit of profits, they also did so in quest of knowledge. In 1768, for example, the Royal Society commissioned Captain James Cook to go to Tahiti to observe the Transit of Venus; Cook was accompanied by the botanist and collector Joseph Banks. They eventually made landfall in several places on the continent that became known as Australia, one of which Banks christened Botany Bay for the wealth of specimens he collected there. Banks, one of the foremost naturalists of his day, went on to found and stock the Royal Botanical Gardens at Kew – bringing a bit of the exotic inside England – and to head the Royal Society for over forty years. Delighting in this exploration, Edmund Burke said, "The great Map of Mankind is unrolled at once, and there is no state or gradation of barbarism, and no mode of refinement which we have not at the same moment under our view."[3] This desire to map other cultures, to have them entirely under view, led George Sale to translate the Koran in 1734, and the great "orientalist" scholar

William Jones to learn Sanskrit, write an "Essay on the Poetry of the Eastern Nations" (1772), and found the Asiatic Society in 1784.

British respect and admiration for the empires of the East was real, yet, at the same time, the desire to master and control representations of other cultures paved the way for the later military and political conquest of Africa, India, and the Near East.[4] As Mary Louise Pratt has written of eighteenth-century scientific and topographical accounts of Africa, "the landscape is written as uninhabited, unpossessed, unhistoricized, unoccupied even by the travelers themselves":

> "The European improving eye produces subsistence habitats as 'empty' landscapes, meaningful only in terms of a capitalist future and of their potential for producing a marketable surplus. From the point of view of their inhabitants, of course, these same spaces are lived as intensely humanized, saturated with local history and meaning, where plants, creatures and geographical formations have names, uses, symbolic functions, histories, places in indigenous knowledge formations."[5]

Britain's quest for knowledge led not only to faraway countries, but also to its European neighbors and their classical pasts. The tradition of the Grand Tour became thoroughly entrenched during the period. Well-born young men like Horace Walpole and Thomas Gray journeyed to France, Italy, Germany, and even Greece to view historic sites, impressive ruins, and beautiful pieces of art as part of their education. Yet, while the Grand Tour certainly broadened the horizons of many men (and some women), it was also viewed as a form of laziness, a way of escaping responsibility at home. In Pope's *Dunciad*, for instance, a young man's activity is described as having "saunter'd Europe round":

> And gather'd ev'ry Vice on Christian Ground;
> Saw ev'ry Court, heard ev'ry King declare
> His royal Sense, of Op'ra's or the Fair;
> The Stews and Palace equally explor'd,
> Intrigu'd with glory, and with spirit whor'd;
> Try'd all hors-d'oeuvres, all liqueurs defin'd.
> Judicious drank, and greatly-daring din'd;
> Dropt the dull lumber of the Latin store,
> Spoil'd his own language, and acquir'd no more;
> All Classic Learning lost on Classic ground;
> And last turn'd Air, the Echo of a sound! (Book IV, ll. 311–21)

Here, travel is reduced to an excuse for vice; the young man quite literally dissipates his learning, "dropping" it until he is left with nothing but a knowledge of arias, or "air." The same effect could be achieved without ever leaving the island, of course, and Britons also traveled more within their own country, cataloging its important historical and aesthetic sites, and documenting the strange practices of the modern age. Thus, as tantalizing as travel could be, Britons also distrusted the effect it could have on the traveler.

The volume of texts generated by travel produced new, highly self-conscious representational forms. Travel writing was valuable in part because it gave accounts of things and places British readers had never heard of before, introducing new scenes and concepts to the reading public. Yet both authors and readers were aware that appeasing the desire for novelty could easily lead to fantasy; or, conversely, that real stories and images would be so new, they would be taken for inventions. Thus, travel writers trod a thin line between tantalizing readers with novelty, and assuring them of the writers' unwavering commitment to truth. Often, that commitment to truth is manifested through an outpouring of details and through the reiterated claim that the author was an eyewitness of the persons and places recounted. The authority of the eyewitness implied that those who had not traveled should not question the amazing scenes they read about. As Horace Walpole said of his description of crossing the Alps: "This sounds too bombastic and too romantic to one that has not seen it, too cold for one that has."[6] We might propose, then, that the wealth of empirical detail and dominance of first-person narration so central to the eighteenth-century novel is derived in part from the conventions of travel narratives.[7]

Travel writers also had to decide whether to emphasize the differences between Britain and the rest of the world, or the similarities. On the one hand, emphasizing the similarities had the effect of rendering foreign lands comprehensible to the British reader, and thus travel writers often drew comparisons between British life and other cultures, making the strange familiar. When Mungo Park, in the course of his best-selling account of his adventures in Africa (1799), sees "the long sought for majestic Niger, glittering in the morning sun," he describes it as being "as broad as the Thames at Westminster."[8] This comparison has the effect of allowing readers to picture the river in question more easily. Assimilating foreign cultures to British forms of understanding, however, reduces them to a simple mirror of British life, lessening the impact of their strangeness. On the other hand, emphasizing the differences between cultures can have the effect of estranging readers from the basic humanity of other cultures, making it easier to think of them as barbarians or savages. The African Association, which funded Park's journey, for example, describes Africa only in terms of its own savagery: "As the great continent of Africa, amidst its seas of sand, occasionally shows its Oasis...so in analogy to the face of the country, does the blank and torpid mind of its people, display occasionally notes of intelligence and philanthropy, rich spots of genius, and partial scenes of improved social establishment."[9] This rhetoric isolates Africa from any interaction with Europe or the rest of the world, eliding the complex socioeconomic relations between the two regions during the period.[10]

Yet, even as the travel narrative helped secure Britain's perception of its superior place in the world, it also made possible some innovative forms of social criticism and satire of British life. And, while imagining distant scenes as mirrors of British life occluded the particularities of other cultures, it also allowed writers to imagine exotic social structures and persons in an allegorical relation to British life. The distance and difference between the reader and the world described made it possible to mount critiques without launching a direct attack. The heroic dramatists of the Restoration often use this strategy, as does Swift in his descriptions of the fictional Lilliput. And, even as some writers used comparison to render the strange familiar, others reversed the technique for critical purposes, making familiar things seem newly strange. Thus, the eyewitness account of exotic locales inspired some writers to reverse the dynamic, and, following Montesquieu's *Persian Letters*, to invent travelers to England who write letters home about what they find there, their wonder and naivety emphasizing the foibles and folly of eighteenth-century British life. A popular example of this genre was Goldsmith's *Citizen of the World* (1760–7). Capitalizing on British fascination with Chinese goods and customs during the eighteenth century, Goldsmith invented a Chinese traveler to England, Lien Chi Altangi, who writes a series of letters home examining British life. Commenting on British provincialism from the broader perspective of "the world," Altangi laments:

> Wherever I come, I raise either diffidence of astonishment; some fancy me no Chinese, because I am formed more like a man than a monster; and others wonder to find one born five thousand miles from England, endued with common sense. Strange, say they, that a man who has received his education at such a distance from London, should have common sense; to be born out of England, and yet have common sense! Impossible! He must be some Englishman in disguise; his very visage has nothing of the true exotic barbarity.[11]

Here, the techniques of travel narratives are used to satirize their readers. These Englishmen have read enough accounts of China to expect exoticism and barbarity; instead, their prejudices are exposed and punctured by the measured tones of a dispassionate traveler.

The texts discussed in this section evidence the ways in which travel literature transformed both the form and content of eighteenth-century British literature. The avenues opened by trade allowed a flood of information about distant lands that influenced every genre of the period, from drama to the novel. Such writing shaped and managed Britons' understanding of the outside world, but also broadened their horizons by exposing them to images of otherness. The conventions of empirical eyewitness accounts generated by sea voyages and land explorations, for example, allowed Mary Wortley Montagu to construct a special kind of feminine rhetorical authority based on her access to hitherto unseen parts of Turkish life. Like Goldsmith, however, both Swift and Smollett tweak just such conventions to satirize both the eyewitness's claim to veracity, as well as the British "common sense" and clarity such accounts seem to exemplify. Tracing the interaction between travel writing and various forms of fiction from Dryden to Beckford also demonstrates a shift in Britain's understanding of its place in the world. If the Moghul Empire, for Dryden, provides a parallel to the British Empire through which he can explore the perils of tyrannical power, for William Beckford, the Near East is a repository of arcane knowledge and a place to explore fantasies of individual freedom. By the end of the eighteenth century, Britain increasingly came to see the rest of the world as an arena to be dominated by both military power and scientific knowledge.

Dryden, *Aureng-Zebe*

Dryden's last rhymed heroic drama (1676) tells the story of the last Moghul Emperor, Aurangzeb, and his ascension to power over his father, Shah Jahan. The play is unusual in that it represents a contemporary monarch; the real Aurangzeb was still alive when the play was first produced, and lived until 1707, actually clashing with East India Company forces in 1688–91. Dryden alters some aspects of the history, however, in order to allow Aureng-Zebe to conform to the ideals of a British hero, and adds a virtuous heroine, Indamora, a captive Kashmiri princess. The historical Aurangzeb allied with one of his brothers to defeat the forces of the other two, after (false) rumors of his father's death. Emerging victorious from this civil war, he executed his brothers (including the legitimate successor) and kept his father under house arrest. In contrast, Dryden's Aureng-Zebe remains loyal to his father, the old Emperor, despite many provocations, including his father's desire to possess Indamora, and forgives the brothers who revolt against him. He gains his kingdom through military acumen and domestic virtue. "In short," notes Balachandra Rajan, "to avoid being hissed off the Restoration stage, the fictional character would have to totally disavow the real one."[12]

Heroic drama has long been thought to be concerned primarily with questions of monarchical power and succession, using exotic settings and characters to explore analogies to the complicated politics of Restoration England. *Aureng-Zebe*, for example, criticizes the old Emperor's use of arbitrary power and susceptibility to lust in a way that seems to reflect on the practices of Charles II. Says the hero:

> To some new Clime, or to thy native Sky,
> Oh friendless and forsaken Virtue flie.
> The Indian Air is deadly to thee grown:
> Deceit and canker'd malice rule thy Throne.
> Why did my Arms in Battel prosp'rous prove,
> To gain the barren praise of Filial love?
> The best of Kings by Women is misled,
> Charmed by the Witchcraft of a second Bed. (I, i).

Aureng-Zebe himself is a model of restraint, deliberation and loyalty, who finally receives the "just rewards of Love and Honour" (V, i).

More recently, however, critics have paid attention to the way heroic drama of the period used information gleaned from travel narratives and other accounts of faraway places to comment on England's expanding empire. *Aureng-Zebe*, for example, displays what Bridget Orr identifies as a double concern with the empires of the East: "[Such] 'Indic' courts were easily seen as parallels to the Stuarts', but . . . they also answered to a pervasive curiosity about the Asian states where the English had significant trade interests."[13] British contact with India had gradually increased over the course of almost two centuries at the time Dryden wrote his play. It began in 1600 when Elizabeth I granted a charter to a group of merchants who incorporated themselves as the East India Company in 1600. This company was given monopoly privileges over all trade with the East Indies. The Company's first ship arrived at the port of Surat in 1608, and by 1615 they had been given the right to establish a factory there by the Moghul Emperor Jahangir. During the next century, sizable English communities developed in the trading centers of Calcutta and Madras. When Charles II married Catherine of Braganza, she brought Bombay with her as part of her dowry, establishing British rule there as well. Thus, when Dryden wrote *Aureng-Zebe*, the British public was aware of India as an important trading destination and the source of desirable goods. The king issued another charter to the East India Company the year the play was produced. As Samuel Johnson wrote, *Aureng-Zebe* was "a tragedy founded on the actions of a great prince then reigning, but over nations not likely to employ their criticks upon the transactions of the English stage. If he had known and disliked his own character, our trade was not in those times secure from his resentment."[14] Many of the details of Dryden's play are taken from a seventeenth-century account, Bernier's *History of the Late Revolution of the Empire of the Great Mogol* (1671), and show the influence of such narratives on literary representations of the period.

Over the course of the next two centuries, Britain's relationship with India became the more explicitly colonial one with which we are more familiar. At the battle of Plessey in 1757, the East India Company army, under the command of Robert Clive, defeated the Nawab of Bengal and gained the right to collect revenue for the Moghul Emperor, a right that it used to plunder the province. After this event, England began to dominate the territory politically as well as through trade. In 1773, the Regulating Act allowed the British government more power over political decisions and instituted the dual rule of company and crown. By 1784, Pitt's India Act gave the crown full power to guide Indian politics, and the Permanent Settlement agreement allowed the perpetual collection of revenues. In 1858, the East India Company was dissolved and the British government assumed full responsibility for the administration of India: India had become a colony. It is hard to read Dryden from this perspective and not see in *Aureng-Zebe* the seeds of a way of thinking that would allow Britain to assume colonial power. It is worth remembering, however, that in the late seventeenth century England was unsure about the direction its empire, built primarily on trade, would take, and regarded the Moghul Empire as a fascinating and intriguing example of the uses and abuses of power, one from which Britain could learn by comparing itself. The play considers the Moghul Empire as a parallel experiment in empire building, and even as a potential threat to its own existence.[15] Trade, as exemplified by the East India Company, brought such examples, and such exotic characters and tales, within the purview of the audience at home.

As several critics have pointed out, the struggle in Dryden's play, along with other representations of India of the period, is between assimilating the Moghuls to European paradigms and viewing them as examples of radical otherness. The most striking example of this ambivalent relationship to the practices of the East is Melesinda's, Aureng-Zebe's brother's wife, accomplishment of sati, a widow's self-immolation on her husband's funeral pyre, in Act V. Dryden draws on the many representations of sati circulating in the seventeenth century for his account, although he does transfer the Hindu ritual to a Muslim princess.[16] Following her husband into death, despite the fact that he has been disloyal to both her and the Emperor, Melesinda calmly announces:

> Now I am pleas'd; my jealousies are o'r:
> He's mine; and I can lose him now no more.
> [...]
> My love was such, it needed no return;
> But could, though he suppli'd no fuel, burn[.]
> [...]
> I'll seek his breast, and kindling by his side,
> Adorned with flames, I'll mount a glorious bride. (V, i)

Her words paint a portrait of female nobility, and she is considered virtuous and heroic by the other characters in the play – a striking contrast to the horror and incredulity lavished on sati in later periods by English observers.[17] Dryden seems to have realized that this character and her actions would be intriguing and provocative (he keeps the funeral pyre offstage), as he discusses her in his dedicatory letter to the play.

> That which was not pleasing to some of the fair Ladies in the last Act..., as I dare not vindicate, so neither can I wholly condemn, till I find more reason for their Censures... I have made my *Melesinda*, in opposition to *Nourmahal*, a Woman passionately loving of her Husband, patient of injuries and contempt, and constant in her kindness, to the last: and in that, perhaps, I may have err'd, because it is not a Virtue much in use. Those *Indian* Wives are loving Fools, and may do well to keep themselves in their own Country, or, at least, to keep company with the *Arria's* and *Portia's* of old Rome: some of our Ladies know better things.[18]

Here, Dryden compares Indian women to both classical Roman heroines and contemporary British women, as if he were setting up a transnational and transhistorical standard for female virtue against which English women do not measure well. At the same time, however, he isolates and distances Indian women, saying they should stay in their own country, carrying on practices that he can neither "vindicate" nor "condemn." This sense that Indians are radically different than Europeans, critics have argued, paved the way for a colonial ideology that justified their subjugation by the British in the following centuries.

Aureng-Zebe was the last play Dryden wrote in heroic couplets. He has grown "weary of his long lov'd Mistris, Rhyme," he confesses in the prologue: "Passion's too fierce to be in Fetters bound, / And Nature flies him like Enchanted Ground." Dryden associates rhyme with both formalist fetters and stale love, and one suspects those associations were cemented for him by using his last rhymes to paint a picture of the Moghul court as ritualistic and ruled by lust. Even in his earlier defense of rhyme for drama, in *An Essay of Dramatic Poesy* (1668), Dryden attributes the origins of rhyme to the barbarian conquest of Rome and the influence of the East:

> Now measure alone in any modern Language, does not constitute verse; those of the Ancients in *Greek* and *Latine*, consisted in quantity of words, and a determinate number of feet. But when, by the inundation of the *Goths* and *Vandals* into *Italy* new languages were introduced, and barbarously mingled with the *Latine*... a new way of Poesie was practiced; new, I say in those Countries, for in all probability it was that of the Conquerours in their own Nations: at least we are able to prove, that the Eastern people have us'd it from all Antiquity... This new way consisted in measure and number of feet and rhyme, the sweetness of Rhyme, and observation of Accent, supplying the place of quantity of words, which could neither exactly be observed by those Barbarians who knew not the Rules of it.[19]

In casting off rhyme, Dryden perhaps casts off these associations; his next play, *All For Love*, was written in blank verse.

Jonathan Swift, *Gulliver's Travels*

Perhaps the best-known fictional rendering of travel literature in the eighteenth century is *Gulliver's Travels* (1726). In this wildly popular work, Swift recounts the voyages and discoveries of a humble ship's surgeon and (eventual) captain as he encounters people remarkably small (the Lilliputians), people remarkably large (the Brobdingnagians), people who live on a floating island (the Laputans) and speaking horses who dominate debased humans (the Houyhnhnms and Yahoos). Through these voyages of discovery, Swift constructs a complex satire of British customs and Britain's place in a new world of global commerce, while at the same time exploring the possibilities of intercultural contact.

Sea voyages, both real and imagined, were one of the most popular forms of eighteenth-century travel literature, and, as Michael McKeon has documented, they generated their own rhetorical conventions, geared to underscoring the veracity of their exotic claims. "The fundamental trope of this antirhetorical style," McKeon notes, "is the self-reflexive insistence on its own documentary candor, as well as on the historicity of the narrative it transparently mediates."[20] Indeed, the Royal Society issued sets of instructions to travelers to guide them in recording their findings and shaping them into a readable narrative.[21] Such narratives were characterized by voluminous empirical detail, a convention Swift parodies at the outset of *Gulliver's Travels*. Its fictional publisher notes that:

> The style is very plain and simple; and the only fault I find is, that the author, after the manner of travelers, is a little too circumstantial.... This volume would have been at least twice as large, if I had not made bold to strike out innumerable passages relating to the winds and tides, as well as variations and bearings in the several voyages; together with minute descriptions of the management of the ship in storms, in the style of sailors.[22]

Yet it is the detailed nature of the text that generates the "air of truth" that the publisher also claims for it, something important in an age when travelers' discoveries arrived at such a furious rate that it was hard to distinguish the real from the imaginary. As one traveler remarked: "The Histories of Peru, Mexico, China, &c. were at first taken for Romances by many, but time has shewed since that they are verities not to be doubted of."[23] Swift's tales of wondrous beings inhabiting lands not yet charted by European maps exploit the fine line between truth and fiction in early modern travel narratives for satirical effect.

He does so by creatively reimagining the culture clash that many European travelers actually confronted. Whereas Dryden imagines the world of the Moghul Emperors without the presence of Europeans, Swift persistently stages the scene of encounter, mining it for satiric effect. He is particularly adept at using the meeting of unlike cultures to turn the familiar strange and cast a critical light back on English culture. For example, when the diminutive Lilliputians capture Gulliver on his first voyage, they write a careful inventory of all the objects they find on him, including,

> a great silver chain, with a wonderful kind of engine at the bottom. We directed him to draw out whatever was at the end of that chain; which appeared to be a globe, half silver, and half of some transparent metal: for, on the transparent side we saw certain strange figures circularly drawn, and thought we could touch them, until we found our fingers stopped by that lucid substance. He put this engine to our ears, which made an incessant noise like that of a watermill. And we conjecture it is either some unknown animal, or the god that he worships: but we are more inclined to the latter opinion, because he assured us (if we understood him right, for he expressed himself very imperfectly) that he seldom did any thing

without consulting it. He called it his oracle, and said it pointed out the
time for every action of his life. (pp. 28–9)

The Lilliputians' enquiry defamiliarizes an everyday object – a watch – and
thus neatly satirizes at least two aspects of British life: the slavish reliance
on mechanical time pieces (as if they were gods); and scientific, proto-
anthropological investigation itself, which promises to reveal the secrets of
new discoveries through exhaustive empirical research, yet so often takes
a wrong turn in explanation.

Like Dryden, then, Swift often uses other cultures as a screen upon
which to project versions of the vices of British culture. In Lilliput, for
instance, an elaborate account of the political importance of rope dancing
satirizes the superficiality of court life:

> This diversion is only practiced by those persons who are candidates for
> great employments, and high favour, at court. They are trained in this art
> from their youth, and are not always of noble birth, or liberal education.
> When a great office is vacant either by death or disgrace (which often
> happens), five or six of those candidates petition the emperor to entertain
> his Majesty and the court with a dance on the rope, and whoever jumps
> the highest, without falling, succeeds in the office. (p. 31)

Yet Swift also uses voices from other cultures to criticize British culture
more directly. When Gulliver tries to explain the social and political structure of his country to the King of Brobdingnag, the King concludes "the
bulk of your natives to be the most pernicious race of little odious vermin
that nature ever suffered to crawl upon the surface of the earth" (p. 107).
Gulliver tries to distance himself from this judgment – "Nothing but an
extreme love of truth could have hindered me from concealing this part
of my story...I was forced to rest with patience while my noble and
beloved country was so injuriously treated" (p. 107) – but his very commitment to the principles of travel writing, including veracity, "force" him to
include it.

Yet the ambiguity of Gulliver's stance in these encounters – couldn't he
have just lied to the King of Brobdingnag? – has led many readers to suspect
that Gulliver himself is an object of satire, a gullible dupe. He does, after
all, come to believe in the superiority of all the countries he visits, ignoring
their faults and prejudices. The most extreme example of Gulliver's capacity to renounce British culture comes after his visit to Houyhnhnmland.
Convinced that the intelligent horses live in a perfect society, even after
they find him to be a true Yahoo and expel him, Gulliver rejects all human
society on his return to England.

> As soon as I entered the house, my wife took me in her arms, and kissed me, at which, having not been used to the touch of that odious animal for so many years, I fell into a swoon for almost an hour. At the time I am writing, it is five years since my last return to England: during the first year, I could not endure my wife or children in my presence; the very smell of them was intolerable; much less could I suffer them to eat in the same room. To this hour they dare not presume to touch my bread, or drink out of the same cup, neither was I ever able to let one of them take me by the hand. (p. 234)

Instead, Gulliver associates with horses, who understand him "tolerably well." This radically antisocial behavior can be read in two different ways. If Swift means us to accept that the rational, peaceable world of the Houyhnhnms is indeed a utopia, then Gulliver's misanthropy is an appropriate response to a degraded human world. However, if Swift means us to find fault with the rigid apartheid of Houyhnhnm–Yahoo culture – a world devoid of passions, including love – then Gulliver has been driven mad by his travels, by his very ability to absorb different cultures.[24] In providing this unsatisfactory choice, the satire seems to give up its capacity to reform society, leaving us with the untenable options of madness or isolation.

Yet, even though much of *Gulliver's Travels* can be read as a commentary on eighteenth-century British culture, Swift also seems genuinely interested in the otherness of foreign lands: interested, at least, in the venue they provide for exploring comic or grotesque sexuality. During his time among the giant women of Brobdingnag, for example, one of the Queen's maids of honor, "a pleasant, frolicsome girl of sixteen, would sometimes set me astride one of her nipples, with many other tricks, wherein the reader will excuse me for not being over particular" (p. 96). The possibility of a sexual encounter between a European and a woman from an exotic culture, a possibility often toyed with in actual travel narratives, is here given a disturbing edge by being pushed to the limits of physical possibility. The sexual potential in intercultural encounters has an even darker tone in Gulliver's experience with a female Yahoo. One day, while swimming naked in a river:

> It happened that a young female Yahoo, standing behind a bank, saw the whole proceeding, and inflamed with desire...came running with all speed, and leaped into the water within five yards of the place where I bathed. I was never in my life so terribly frighted...She embraced me after a most fulsome manner; I roared as loud as I could, and the nag [Gulliver's protector] came galloping towards me, whereupon she quitted

her grasp, with the utmost reluctancy, and leaped upon the opposite bank, where she stood gazing and howling all the time I was putting on my clothes. (p. 215)

As Laura Brown has shown, Swift's depiction of the Yahoos draws heavily on contemporary accounts of Africans, and this encounter momentarily collapses the difference between human and Yahoo, African and European, since afterwards Gulliver can "no longer deny that [he] was a real Yahoo in every limb and feature" (p. 215).[25] This use of images of Africans from travel narratives also puts the events of *Gulliver's Travels* in implicit relation to Britain's growing concern with colonial and mercantile expansion.

The curiosities and souvenirs that Gulliver collects also bring the countries he visits out of a self-enclosed allegorical space and into a synchronic relationship with England. He takes a number of tiny animals back from Lilliput, hoping to make a profit on them, and bargains for his voyage home from Brobdingnag with a collection of body parts:

[I] showed [the Captain] the small collection of rarities I made in the country from which I had been so strangely delivered. There was the comb I had contrived out of the stumps of the king's beard, and another of the same materials, but fixed into a paring of her Majesty's thumb nail, which served for the back...I showed him a corn that I had cut off with my own hand from a maid of honour's toe; it was about the bigness of a Kentish pippin, and grown so hard, that when I returned to England, I got it hollowed into a cup and set in silver....

I could force nothing on him but a footman's tooth, which I observed him to examine with great curiosity, and found he had a fancy for it. (pp. 118–19).

The status of these objects is ambiguous: are they objects of scientific interest, aesthetic beauty, or are they useless and indeed slightly perverse? Swift raises the question here, as in other places in the text, of the value of goods as they move from one culture to another, just as more and more commodities were making similar incursions into the British Empire. This point is raised most acutely when Gulliver uses Yahoo skins to make the boat with which he escapes from Houyhnhnmland (p. 227). No longer content to accumulate and display the human resources of other cultures, he begins to treat those bodies as raw materials to be transformed. If we see Gulliver himself as a potential object of Swift's satire, we can read his callousness here as an implicit critique on the burgeoning trade in human bodies from Africa, in the service of imperial expansion.[26]

Lady Mary Wortley Montagu, *Turkish Embassy Letters*

While Dryden and Swift relied on tales brought back by other travelers, Lady Mary Wortley Montagu was an eyewitness to the scenes of Turkish life she recounted. Born into a prominent aristocratic family, Montagu educated herself by reading in her father's library and teaching herself Latin. She had a wide literary acquaintance throughout her life, including a difficult friendship with Alexander Pope. When her husband, Edward Wortley, was appointed ambassador to Turkey in 1716, she accompanied him on his journey, recording her travels for posterity in a series of letters to a variety of friends. Montagu fiercely believed in women's intelligence, and protested their exclusion from formal learning; she resented the fact that "the same studies which raise the Character of a Man should hurt that of a woman. We are educated in the grossest ignorance, and no art omitted to stifle our natural reason."[27] She was ambivalent, however, about the propriety of a person of her class entering the print market: "it is not the business of a Man of Quality to turn author...he should confine himself to the applause of Friends, and by no means venture on the press," she wrote (p. 243). Nevertheless, she seems to have carefully prepared her poems and letters for posthumous publication. When the *Turkish Embassy Letters* (written 1716–18) were published in 1763, they were extremely popular, going through a number of editions and garnering praise from major figures of the day.

Acutely conscious of her place in a generic and political history of writing about the Levant, Montagu often addresses the difficulties facing a traveler writing about her own experiences. "We travelers are in very hard circumstances," she complains, "If we say nothing but what has been said before us, we are dull and we have observed nothing. If we tell anything new, we are laughed at as fabulous and romantic" (To [Montagu's sister] Lady Mar, Pera of Constantinople, March 10, 1718, p. 110). Nevertheless, she presents herself as a reliable eyewitness, working to refute the inventions of earlier writers. In an earlier letter to her sister, she proclaims: "Thus you see...the manners of mankind do not differ so widely as our voyage writers would make us believe. Perhaps it would be more entertaining to add a few surprising customs of my own invention, but nothing seems to be so agreeable as truth, and I believe nothing so acceptable to you" (Adrianople, April 1, 1717, p. 97). This letter suggests that Montagu believes in a universal ideal of humanity and virtue – "the Turkish ladies don't commit one sin the less for not being Christians," she ironically notes – but other letters convey her enjoyment in finding that the rules of behavior can differ so much between different countries. Visiting Vienna on her way to the Levant, Montagu documents her pleasurable discovery that "gallantry and good breeding are as different in different climates as morality and religion," particularly when it comes to gender roles:

> [In Vienna] A woman till five and thirty is only looked upon as a raw girl and can possibly make no noise in the world till about forty... 'tis a considerable comfort to me to know there is upon earth such a paradise for old women, and I am content to be insignificant at present in the design of returning when I am fit to appear nowhere else... that perplexing word reputation has quite another meaning here than what you would give it in London, and getting a lover is so far from losing, that 'tis properly getting, reputation, ladies being much more respected in regard to the rank of their lovers than that of their husbands. (To Lady Rich, Vienna, September 20, 1716, pp. 85, 84).

Here we can see the feminist potential of Montagu's observations. Recognizing that sexual relations can be worked out quite differently than they are in England allows her to imagine a "paradise for old women" – a possibility that, despite her ironic tone, carries a utopian charge.

Montagu's musing on gender roles across cultures coincides with her ambition to contribute to travel writing about the Levant as she finds opportunities to venture into spaces of Turkish life in which only women are allowed. While Bernier, Dryden's main source for *Aureng-Zebe*, describes many aspects of Eastern life, he cannot describe the enclosure of the harem: "I now wish I could lead you about in the Seraglio, as I have done the rest of [the Fort at Delhi]: but who is the Traveller that can speak of that as an eye-witness?"[28] Lady Mary Wortley Montagu is that traveler and that witness. She visits women who live secluded inside the Harem, and the more physically intimate and revealing space of the women's bath, and everywhere tries to overturn the prurient and negative stereotypes of "Oriental" women. Elizabeth Bohls has noted that previous male travelers, of whom Montagu was aware, "unanimously present Turkish women as wanton or hypersexual."[29] One such writer hints at the sexual perversions to which isolated groups of women were thought to be susceptible: "if they have the will to eat radishes, cucumbers, gourds or such like meats, they are sent into them sliced, to deprive them of the means of playing the wantons."[30] Montagu's description of the women's baths in Sofia clearly aims to counter such speculations, presenting the female bathers as beautiful, gracious, and chaste:

without any distinction of rank by their dress, all being in the state of nature, that is, in plain English, stark naked, without any beauty of defect concealed, yet there was not the least wanton smile or immodest gesture amongst 'em. They walked and moved with the same majestic grace which Milton describes of our General Mother. There were many amongst them as exactly proportioned as ever any goddess was drawn by the pencil of Guido or Titian, and most of their skins shiningly white, only adorned by their beautiful hair divided into many tresses hanging on their shoulders, braided either with pearl or riband, perfectly representing the figures of the Graces. (To Lady ___. Adrianople, April 1, 1717, p. 91).

Montagu celebrates the scene in terms that were to influence many visual representations, including Ingres's *Le Bain turc* (1862). Her descrip-tion is characterized by comparisons between a scene that would have been exotic to her readers and well-known markers of European culture and beauty: Milton's Eve, Guido and Titian, the Graces. These comparisons accomplish many things. As Bohls points out, they defuse the erotic charge of a scene that had attracted much lascivious interest from earlier European commentators.[31] The comparisons also bring the Turkish women into a recognizable aesthetic framework for English readers; in contrast to Swift, Montagu makes the strange familiar. And, finally, such references increase Montagu's own authority – she is not merely a woman among women, but an educated, tasteful, and discriminating observer. These allusions reassure the reader that Montagu speaks as an English woman, rather than "going native."

Indeed, the climax of the scene occurs when Montagu is invited to relinquish her status as observer and to fully join the women in the baths by taking off her clothes. This last intimacy she refuses:

I excused myself with some difficulty, they being all so earnest in persuad-ing me. I was at last forced to open my skirt and show them my stays, which satisfied them very well, for I saw they believed I was so locked up in that machine that it was not in my own power to open it, which contriv-ance they attributed to my husband. (p. 91)

Montagu's light ironic tone here allows her to again glean multiple mean-ings from the moment. On the one hand, her refusal to disrobe saves her from any imputations of immodesty or even prurience. On the other hand, while the Turkish women's horror at Montagu's imprisonment in her stays might be read as a sign of their ignorance or barbarism, it also gives the reader an outsider's perspective on the confinement of British women. Montagu makes the familiar strange for just a moment and generates a subtle critique of English culture.

As her determination to keep her clothes on in the bath indicates, Montagu was very conscious of the power of clothes to determine identity. She was not alone in her reluctance to let go of this external marker of status. A young German noble describes encountering dancing girls at one of the residencies of the East India Company who ask him, too, to strip: "but perceiving I was unwilling to do it, and withal that I made some difficulty to accept of the profers they made to strip themselves naked, and doe any thing I would expect from persons of their sex and profession, they seem'd to be very much troubled, and so went away."[32] Yet Montagu, characteristically, also admires the very different identity shaped by Turkish clothes. The voluminous clothes of this culture allow women great freedom, she imagines: "You may guess how effectually this disguises them, that there is no distinguishing the great lady from her slave, and 'tis impossible for the most jealous husband to know his wife when he meets her, and no man dare either touch or follow a woman in the street" (p. 96). It is a "perpetual masquerade" (p. 97).

In the end, Montagu was as interested in imitating the way Turkish women dressed as she was uninterested in joining them naked. She brought back several suits of clothing and had herself painted in those costumes many times. Yet Montagu's borrowings from Turkish culture were not entirely superficial. She also brought back with her the practice of inoculating children against smallpox. "I am patriot enough," she wrote, "to take pains to bring this useful invention into fashion in England" (To Sarah Chiswell, Adrianople, 1 April 1717). Montagu had been scarred by the disease and thus had a personal stake in preventing its spread. She inoculated her own children and may have convinced the Princess of Wales to do the same – eventually the practice took hold in England. Her interest in the technique, however, sets up an interesting parallel between the physical practice of introducing a bit of disease into the body to protect it and the cultural practice of introducing a bit of exoticism into a country's self-understanding in order to avoid being assimilated completely. Thus, Srinivas Aravamudan argues that the letters themselves perform a kind of inoculation: "Travel narrative, after flirting with cultural crossover, acknowledges the superiority of returning home."[33] And this Montagu does, albeit with her customary diffidence and irony: "there is no perfect enjoyment of this life out of Old England. I pray God I may think so for the rest of my life, and since I must be contented with our scanty allowance of daylight, that I may forget the enlivening sun of Constantinople" (p. 118). She thus explores the consequences of the importation of otherness and change, through the body, or through writing. God did not grant

Montagu's prayer, however; she was not able find "perfect enjoyment" in England for the rest of her life. She eloped to Italy in 1739.

Tobias Smollett, *The Expedition of Humphry Clinker*

As much as Britons were intrigued by travel outside their national borders during the eighteenth century, they were also fascinated by travel within Great Britain. First-person accounts of visits to sites of particular historical, natural, or political interest proliferated, including works of aesthetic or political import, such as William Gilpin's *Observations, relative chiefly to Picturesque Beauty, made in the year 1772 on several parts of England, particularly the mountains and lakes of Cumberland and Westmoreland* (1786), and Arthur Young's *A Tour in Ireland; with general observations on the present state of the Kingdom* (1780). A vast improvement in the number and quality of roads allowed greater intercourse, both commercial and cultural, between rural and metropolitan areas. Nevertheless, large areas of Great Britain, especially Scotland, were still inaccessible to most travelers, and thus provided exotic subject matter for readers at home in texts such as Samuel Johnson's *Journey to the Western Isles of Scotland* (1775). Smollett's last and best-loved novel, *Humphry Clinker* (1771), draws on these new genres, even as it reinvigorates the epistolary novel, to provide a broad-ranging account of Britain in the last third of the eighteenth century. Rather than waxing appreciative or philosophical about the state of Britain, however, Smollett's novel paints a satirical picture almost Swiftian in the force of its disgust.

Humphry Clinker concerns the travels of an unconventional family grouping, consisting of two brother–sister pairs – Matthew Bramble, a misanthropic hypochondriac, and his sister Tabitha, a materialistic spinster; and Jerry Melford and his sister Lydia, Matthew's nephew and niece. They travel accompanied by their servants, including the eponymous Humphry Clinker, and the occasional friend or fellow traveler. The Bramble party sets out from their home in Wales on a twofold mission: to restore the health of Matthew (and since the novel was written during Smollett's last illness, the accounts of Matthew's sufferings, real or imagined, are vivid), and to rescue Lydia from an unsuitable admirer. They journey to Bath and a number of other spa towns, to London, and eventually to the far northern reaches of Scotland, before turning homewards. In contrast to that other well-known comic novel of family travel, Goldsmith's *The Vicar of Wakefield* (1766), in which the Primrose family is driven hither and yon by bad luck and economic necessity before finally arriving at a shared vision of home and happiness, the movements of the Bramble family are voluntary and their views of events agonistic. The plot, interspersed by powerful descriptive set pieces, works towards the marriages of Tabitha Bramble and Lydia Melford, although Matthew Bramble is also cured along the way. Importantly, both cure and husbands are encountered through travel, as Bramble concludes:

> I begin to think I have put myself on the superannuated list too soon, and absurdly sought for health in the retreats of laziness – I am persuaded that all valetudinarians are too sedentary, too regular and too cautious – we should sometimes increase the motion of the machine, to unclog the wheels of life; and now and then take a plunge amidst the waves of excess, in order to harden the constitution. I have even found a change of company as necessary as a change of air, to promote a vigorous circulation of the spirits, which is the very essence and criterion of good health.[34]

In a trope that echoes throughout the novel, Bramble links the psychic and physiological benefits of travel.

While novels like Richardson's *Clarissa* and Burney's *Evelina* draw on the epistolary form to mine the complexity of individual characters and relationships, *Humphry Clinker* uses letters to provide multiple perspectives on the scenes it visits. All the characters, only excepting Clinker himself, write to their friends at home, including Tabitha's maid Winifred Jenkins, creating what Eric Rothstein has called a "compound eye."[35] We often receive several versions of the same event or environment, and character is developed through differences of perception, rather than introspection. At times, the Bramble party almost seems to take it as a duty to explore different aspects of a person or place. As Jerry Melford explains, regarding their visit to the Scottish capital: "While Mr Bramble holds conferences with the graver literati of the place, and our females are entertained at visits by the Scottish ladies, who are the best and kindest creatures upon earth, I pass my time among the bucks of Edinburgh; who, with a great share of spirit and vivacity, have a certain shrewdness and self-command that is not often found among their neighbours, in the high day of youth and exultation" (p. 222). The letters thus provide a kaleidoscopic view on the places the Bramble party visits; this both broadens the range of the information conveyed and emphasizes the role of individual perspective in understanding new places. Matthew Bramble describes this effect most clearly with regard to Scotland:

> The first impressions which an Englishman received in this country, will not contribute to the removal of his prejudices; because he refers everything he sees to a comparison with the same articles in his own country,

and this comparison is unfavourable to Scotland in all its exteriors, such as the face of the country in respect to cultivation, the appearance of the bulk of the people, and the language of conversation in general. (p. 231)

Yet Bramble, perhaps echoing the feelings of Smollett, himself a Scot, concludes by saying, "I am so far from thinking it any hardship to live in this country, that, if I was obliged to lead a town life, Edinburgh would certainly be [my] headquarters" (p. 235). The novel thus seems to assert that, although prejudice and comparison may initially blind the traveler, he or she is still capable of being changed by experience.

For these reasons, the novel is interested in border crossing, particularly the borders between different parts of Great Britain – England, Scotland, and Wales. The Bramble party's passage into Scotland, for example, is brought into relief by their encounter with a figure who has been notably scarred by his experience of travel: Captain Lismahago, a Scottish soldier who has been transformed by his service in the Seven Years' War, and his resultant captivity by Native Americans. Lismahago has been "wounded at Ticonderoga": "a party of Indians rifled him, scalped him, broke his scull with the blow of a tomahawk, and left him for dead on the field of battle" (p. 189). Although he recovers from his wounds, "the scull was left naked in several places, and these he covered with patches." Lismahago regales the Bramble party with the story of his time among the Miami Indians, and eventually marries Tabitha Bramble – a union of grotesques the novel milks for farce. Lismahago tells his story just as the Bramble party crosses into Scotland, and the juxtaposition triangulates Scotland, England, and the American colonies, to the benefit of Scotland. As Robert Crawford argues: "The Scotland to be presented to these Welsh visitors appears all the more refined by contrast with the account of the Amerindian" barbarity in Lismahago's tale.[36] This threefold comparison reminds us that conceptions of travel within Great Britain during this period could not be divorced from ideas about more distant places and trajectories.

As it is for Lismahago in America, the experience of travel within England is often very visceral indeed in *Humphry Clinker*. The metropolitan and cultural centers that the Bramble party visit are invariably characterized by the intermingling of classes, professions, and ethnic groups:

> Every upstart of fortune, harnessed in the trappings of the mode, presents himself at Bath, as in the very focus of observation – Clerks and factors from the East Indies, loaded with the spoil of plundered provinces; planters, Negro-drivers, and hucksters from our American plantations, enriched they know not how; agents, commissaries and contractors, who

have fattened in two successive wars, on the blood of the nation; usurers, brokers and jobbers of every kind, men of low birth and no breeding. (p. 36)

The mixture of these various groups in Bath is not merely social, according to Bramble, but physical as well: "it is very far from being clear to me," he says, "that the patients in the Pump-room don't swallow the scourings of the bathers...In that case, what a delicate beveridge is every day quaffed by the drinkers; medicated with the sweat, and dirt, and dandriff, and abominable discharges of various kinds, from twenty different diseased bodies" (p. 45). In London, too, Bramble finds social classes swapping spit: "It was but yesterday that I saw a dirty barrow-bunter in the street, cleaning her dusty fruit with her own spittle; and who knows but some fine lady of St James parish might admit into her delicate mouth those very cherries, which have been rolled and moistened between the filthy and, perhaps, ulcerated chops of a St Giles huckster" (p. 120).

Travel, then, can change not only the traveler's mind, but also his or her body. Bramble's (and Smollett's) explanation for the disgusting porousness of bodies – their tendency to exchange fluids without actually intending to – is the rising "tide of luxury," which exposes all parts of Britain to the desire for new goods and pleasures. Travel, in this novel, is spurred both by the desire for luxury – as in all those visitors to Bath – and by the desire to find relief from luxury – as it is for Matthew Bramble and his family; local travel can be seen as a complicated response to Britain's new place in the world of global trade.

William Beckford, *Vathek*

Beckford's extravagant "oriental tale" recounts the history of the Caliph Vathek as he is drawn by his voracious appetites for wealth and pleasure to a hideous fate in the hellish "Halls of Eblis." His adventures along the way give Beckford and his annotators the opportunity to deliver a good deal of information about the goods, customs, and literary history of the Near East: the explanatory notes were at least half as long as the tale itself when *Vathek* was first published in 1786. Beckford wrote *Vathek* in French when he was only twenty-one. His former tutor, the Rev. Samuel Henley, published a translation in England, along with his own notes to the text, in 1786. The novel was warmly reviewed, although it did not become a best seller. The *Monthly Review* declared that it "preserves the peculiar character of the Arabian Tale, which is not only to overstep nature and probability, but even to pass beyond the verge of possibility, and suppose things, which cannot be for a moment conceived."[37] It made an impression on the following generation of writers, especially Byron, who wrote in a note to *The Giaour*: "For correctness of costume, beauty of description, and power of imagination, *Vathek* far surpasses all European imitations; and bears such marks of originality, that those who have visited the East will find some difficulty in believing it to be more than a translation."[38] He, like others, was struck by Beckford's interest in representing life in the Near East not just in the content of his text but also by adopting an "oriental" style.

Both before and after the publication of *Vathek*, William Beckford was himself a notorious figure. He inherited vast wealth from his father's West Indian plantations at age nine, lived in European exile for a number of years in his youth after a scandal over an adolescent boy, became a famous collector of books and paintings, and turned the family home, Fonthill Abbey, into an extraordinary example of (faux) gothic architecture. When he composed *Vathek*, Beckford was involved in two complex entangle-ments: his cousin's wife, Louisa Beckford, had fallen in love with him; and he himself was in love with William Courtenay, the thirteen-year-old son of Lord Courtenay. Following Beckford himself, critics have often tied the composition of *Vathek* to an extravagant Christmas party at Fonthill House (not yet Abbey) in 1781 that included Louisa Beckford along with a number of other young people of both sexes. The house was decorated for the occasion by the theatrical designer Philip de Loutherbourg. Beckford recorded his memory of that party in 1838:

> Immured we were "au pied de la lettre" for three days following – doors and windows so strictly closed that neither common day light nor common place visitors could get in or even peep in – care worn visages were ordered to keep aloof – no sunk-in mouths or furroughed [sic] foreheads were permitted to meet our eye. Our societe was extremely youthful and lovely to look upon.... Delightful indeed were these romantic wanderings – delightful the straying about this little interior world of exclusive happiness surrounded by lovely beings, in all the freshness of their early bloom, so fitted to enjoy it. Here, nothing was dull or vapid – here, nothing resembled in the least the common forms and usages, the "train-train" and routine of fashionable existence – all was essence – the slightest approach to same-ness was here untolerated – montony of every kind of banished.... It was, in short, the realization of romance in its most extravagant intensity. No wonder such scenery inspired the description of the Halls of Eblis.[39]

The "extravagant intensity" of the scene seems to reside in its endless novelty, aesthetic pleasure, indulgence of individual whim and desire, and freedom from the demands of everyday life – qualities Beckford's novel strives to reproduce. Interestingly, however, the description of the Halls of Eblis with which *Vathek* ends emphasizes the dark side of this scene: its solecism and emotional loneliness. Like Beckford's memory of this event, both the form and the content of *Vathek* explore a complex attraction to and repulsion from this sort of isolation.

Nigel Leask has argued that *Vathek* represents "a watershed between the old and new styles" of British depictions of the East, and the differences between Beckford's novel and an earlier fictional account, like *Aureng-Zebe*, are instructive.[40] While Dryden has a keen interest in Moghul manners and mores, he is more centrally concerned with two things: how his heroes and villains might embody abstract or general virtues – courage, loyalty, lust, etc.; and how their actions might be put into an allegorical relationship with current events in England. Beckford has two contrasting aims: to represent the history and culture of the Near East as particularly and exactly as possible; and to use Vathek's world as a place to examine the extremes of individual fantasy and psychology. The drive for exactitude is carried out primarily in the elaborate footnotes that accompany the text. Like writers before them, including Dryden, Beckford and Henley drew on earlier travel narratives in constructing their tale – texts like *The Present State of the Ottoman Empire . . . translated from the French Manuscript of Elias Habesci* (1784), by Alexander Ghiga. They also borrowed from the immensely popular translations of the Arabian Nights Entertainments, and from a growing body of books on the customs of the "Orient," such as Barthélemy d'Herbelot de Molainville's *Bibliothèque Orientale, Ou Dictionnaire Universel Contenant tout ce qui fait connoître les Peuples de l'Orient* (Paris, 1697). While earlier writers simply assimilated earlier accounts into their own, rarely signaling their presence, Beckford highlights his own erudition by directing the reader to further information on the costumes and customs displayed in his text. Eastern culture is thus depicted not as something roughly equivalent to Western culture – its structure and motivations basically similar – but as radically other, the object of Western specialist inquiry. As Leask says of the relationship between narrative and notes in *Vathek*: "Here the fictional *narrative* transcribes otherness whilst the notes translate it into the ethnological or historiographical discourse of the same. But the exotic image or allusion in the poetic narrative and the explanatory footnote, running like a parallel text alongside, beneath, or after [it], exist in a kind of intimate co-dependency."[41]

Just what kind of object the oriental world is in *Vathek* seems to vary considerably. The intellectual distancing provided by the scholarly apparatus of the footnotes allows the imagined world to be sometimes one of intense mystery and attraction, and sometimes a set of conventions vulnerable to parody. Compare, for example the depiction of the harem in Beckford's novel to Montagu's reverent description. In Beckford's novel, Nouronihar and the other sultanas trick the eunuch, Bababalouk, into a swing they set going over the bath, "with such unremitted assiduity, that at length, the cord which had secured it, snapt suddenly asunder; and Bababalouk fell, floundering like a turtle, to the bottom of the bath."[42] Trying to explain his humiliation to Vathek, Bababalouk exclaims: "with what gracious damsels doth the place...abound! Fancy to yourself how they have soaked me like a burnt crust; and made me dance like a jack-pudding, the live-long night through, on their damnable swing" (p. 59). But Vathek only laughs "immoderately" at the event (p. 60). Carathis, Vathek's mother, is at once a fantasy of amorality, and a joke about it:

> [She] never lost sight of her great object, which was to obtain favour with the powers of darkness...[She] made select parties of the fairest and most delicate ladies of the city: but in the midst of their gaiety, she contrived to introduce vipers amongst them, and to break pots of scorpions under the table. They all bit to a wonder, and Carathis would have left her friends to die, were it not that, to fill up the time, she now and then amused herself in curing their wounds, with an excellent anodyne of her own invention: for this good Princess abhorred being indolent. (pp. 38–9)

Scenes like this allow Beckford to play out extremes of sadism, while also treating that behavior ironically as a form of "oriental" excess with no relation to European practice.

Freeing the narrative of *Vathek* from any expectation of alignment or correspondence with contemporary England thus provided Beckford with an opportunity to explore the vagaries and limits of individual desire. Since it has no ambitions towards political or public allegory, but rather, as Beckford's later note indicates, desires to retreat from the outside world, the narrative concentrates on potentials of the unrestrained self. These desires most frequently are depicted as exaggerated appetites. Vathek is always hungry, always thirsty, and his appetite for wealth is writ large on the landscape when he hurls fifty young boys into a chasm to appease the Giaour.

> Vathek, who was...standing on the edge of the chasm, called out, with all his might: – "Let my fifty little favourites approach me, separately; and let them come in the order of their success. To the first, I will give my diamond bracelet; to the second, my collar of emeralds; to the third, by

aigret of rubies; to the fourth, my girdle of topazes; and to the rest, each a part of my dress, even down to my slippers."

This declaration was received with reiterated acclamations; and all extolled the liberality of a prince, who would thus strip himself, for the amusement of his subjects, and the encouragement of the rising genera- tion. The Caliph, in the meanwhile, undressed himself by degrees; and, raising his arm as high as he was able, made each of the prizes glitter in the air; but, whilst he delivered it, with one hand, to the child, who sprung forward to receive it; he, with the other, pushed the poor innocent into the gulph; where the Giaour, with a sullen muttering, incessantly repeated, "more! more!" (pp. 26–7)

The iteration of particularized like objects – here jewels – and the repetitive action of feeding an insatiable appetite – here the Giaour's appetite for boys, and Vathek's for the promised treasure – are characteristic of the novel.

Yet, as a number of critics have noted, *Vathek* can be considered a moral tale, since the Caliph's desires meet with a hideous punishment, rather than the eternal indulgence he expects. As Vathek and his entourage, including Nouronihar and Carathis, complete their quest to enter the Halls of Eblis, they first see the promised wealth and magnificence. They then discover the fate of those who have found "immortality" there:

> In the midst of this immense hall, a vast multitude was incessantly passing; who severally kept their right hands on their hearts; without once regard- ing anything about them. They had all, the livid paleness of death. Their eyes, deep sunk in their sockets, resembled those phosphoric meteors, that glimmer by night, in places of interment. Some stalked slowly on; absorbed in profound reverie: some shrieking with agony, ran furiously about like tigers, wounded with poisoned arrows; whilst others, grinding their teeth in rages, foamed along more frantic than the wildest maniac. They all avoided each other; and, though surrounded by a multitude that no one could number, each wandered at random, unheedful of the rest, as if alone on a desert where no foot had trodden. (pp. 109–10)

Here, the proliferation of goods and persons that powers earlier parts of the novel becomes a tableau of misery. The repetition of a single fate creates not a community of pleasure, but rather atomization and incoher- ence. The isolation from the world that Beckford was later to eulogize becomes an overpopulated and poignant solitude.[43]

Indeed, in a novel that focuses so much attention on the power of indi- vidual appetite and will, the only happy state turns out to be one without will: to be a child. The young boy Gulchenrouz escapes not only the confines of gender – when he "appeared in the dress of his cousin, he seemed more feminine that even herself" (p. 66) – but also of desire. When, through various twists of plot, Gulchenrouz believes himself to be dead, he enjoys a life "Remote from the inquietudes of the world, the impertinence of harems, the brutality of eunuchs, and the inconstancy of women...the genius, instead of burdening [him] with perishable riches and vain sciences, conferred upon [him] the boon of perpetual childhood" (pp. 97–8). This subject position was one that appealed to Beckford himself. Shortly before writing *Vathek*, he wrote of himself: "I am like one of those plants which bloom in a sequestered crevice of the rocks, and which few are destined to discover"[44]; and similarly, "I am now approaching the Age when the World in general expect me to lay aside my dreams, abandon my soft illusion and start into public Life. How greatly are they deceived how firmly I am to be a Child forever."[45] George Haggerty reads the novel's doubled view of isolation – a potential paradise or hell – in relation to Beckford's inability to articulate his own homosexuality: "Metaphorically, this novel may attempt to assert the supremacy of private experience, but the contexualizing force of the novel form itself answers that hope with the bitter reality of the self's isolation in a world of public meaning."[46] If the East functioned as a mirror for writers of the early eighteenth century, for Beckford, and those following, it provided an escape to an imaginary world of experimentation, even as the "real" Orient was ever more mapped, colonized, and put under academic scrutiny.

Colonialism and Slavery

While the previous chapter dealt with representations of trade and travel during the eighteenth century, and thus principally with Britain's mercantile interest in the Near and Far East, this chapter considers arenas in which Britain's territorial control was more complete and more violent: its colonies – places where the only government was the British crown. In Britain's trading empire, government officials and entrepreneurs attempted to negotiate with local leaders, and overt and violent coercion was kept to a minimum. In the colonies, however, British rule was maintained, if need be (and it usually was) by force. During the eighteenth century, Britain's colonial holdings were concentrated in North America and the Caribbean. Although its North American holdings were extensive during this period, Britain's most valuable – and most troubling – colonies were the sugar-producing Caribbean slave colonies. These colonies were bound to both Africa and North America by the immensely profitable "triangle trade" of slaves, rum, sugar, and cod and other provisions – forming a circum-Atlantic culture and economy. Some scholars have argued that the hierarchical, racialized, coercive relationships that characterized the Atlantic during the eighteenth century were prefigured and paralleled in the peripheral territories of "Great Britain" – Ireland and Scotland – labeling such arenas "internal colonies."

As was the case with regard to its mercantile empire, Britain went through different stages of thinking about itself as a colonizing power during the eighteenth century. Generally speaking, the period from the Restoration to the end of the Seven Years' War was a time of enormous growth and confidence as Britain expanded its North American holdings and increased its investment in the slave trade. Within this long period of sustained growth, however, there was an uneven transition between thinking of the unexplored world as already inhabited (as we have seen in *Gulliver's Travels*, for instance, or will see in *Oroonoko*) to imagining it as empty and in need of settlement, as in texts like *Robinson Crusoe*. After the global conflict of the Seven Years' War (1757–65), and especially after the loss of the North American colonies in 1783, the metropolis increasingly mistrusted colonial ventures, worrying that new territories would drain both economic and moral resources from the metropolis. This anxiety about colonization characterized the period from the end of the American War of Independence to the end of British slavery in 1833, after which Britain's imperial drive was renewed in the "Second Empire" of Africa, India, and the Far East which it established during the nineteenth century.

Slavery and colonialism were thus deeply intertwined during the eighteenth century; in the controversies about slavery during this period, we can chart the fate of colonialism. If England, and especially London, came to seem the "mart of the world" during the eighteenth century, as much of this wealth probably came from the profits of slave production and the slave trade as it did from trade in silk, china, or spices. England assumed the Assiento, an agreement granting it a monopoly over the transatlantic slave trade in 1713, as part of the Treaty of Utrecht that ended the War of Spanish Succession. Although Britain had used slave labor in the Caribbean since the early sixteenth century, this event marked the beginning of its greatest involvement in the trade: "annual shipments of slaves by the British probably tripled over the eighteenth century, rising from 12,000 to 14,000 before 1720 to 42,000 during the 1790s."[1] For a long time, this profitable practice gave very few moral qualms to British subjects but, by the 1770s and 1780s, more and more Britons had grown dissatisfied with the economic and moral structures that governed the slave trade and plantation culture, and agitation to abolish the trade and emancipate the slaves began to swell. Nevertheless, propositions to end Britain's involvement in the trade were defeated in parliamentary debates in 1791 and 1792, and, despite promises to the contrary, the trade was not abolished until 1807. It took another thirty years for complete emancipation to take effect: West Indian slaves were not granted their freedom until 1833 and many continued to be bound in "apprenticeship" until 1838.

The emergence of the British antislavery movement is one of the great puzzles of Enlightenment historiography; its eventual success is even less explicable. At the beginning of the eighteenth century, almost all Britons regarded chattel slavery as an unpleasant but necessary requirement for enjoying the fruits of an overseas empire. By the end of the same century, that same broad segment regarded slavery as a moral outrage that could not be tolerated in a modern nation. From a contemporary perspective, the story is puzzling on two counts. How could so many people have cared so little about the horrors of slavery for so long? But, if that was indeed the case, why did so many people change their ethical ideals so completely in such a relatively short amount of time? Until the second half of the twentieth century, historians most often drew on a Whiggish narrative of progress and enlightenment to explain the abolition of the British slave trade. The "Saints" theory of antislavery argued that, led by the spiritual insights of Evangelicals, Britons gradually came to see slavery as a moral wrong.[2] Later scholars proposed, by way of puncturing this narrative, that economic self-interest rather than morality drove the abolitionists, or that their idealism simply masked the sociocultural imperatives of the industrial revolution.[3] More recently, historians have focused on the spread of anti-slavery sentiments through popular culture, and tended to ignore the actions of governmental authorities and parliament.[4] To these explanations – moral, economic, ideological – Christopher Leslie Brown's recent book, *Moral Capital*, has added one firmly anchored in the political.[5] Brown argues that abolitionism achieved its moral dominance through the complex political negotiations that characterized transatlantic relationships during the eighteenth century – not least the fierce conflicts over the meaning of "liberty" during the American Revolution.

No matter which explanation of the triumph of antislavery one sub-scribes to, however, it is clear that an important way in which Britons re-evaluated the moral legitimacy of slavery was through literary representations of it. From Behn's depiction of the "royal slave" Oroonoko to Equiano's autobiography, such images helped readers decide whether slaves were human and whether slave production was a tenable road to national prosperity. Some writers, like the poets Hannah More, Ann Yearsley, and Anna Barbauld, and Equiano himself, took on a more direct role of advocacy, writing poems against the slave trade during the parliamentary debates of the 1790s.

One thing that shaped both the persistence of slavery and its destruction was the emergence of the concept of "race" as a way of differentiating and hierarchizing groups of people. Modern ideas about race were not firmly in place at the beginning of the eighteenth century. While both philosophers and ordinary people were likely to regard Africans and other "savage" peoples as inferior, they were more likely to believe that such inferiority resulted from a lack of maturity and civilization, rather than from insurmountable biological difference. This view is often called "cultural racism" because it is rooted in an idea of the mutability of culture, rather than a belief in the immutability of biology. Subscribers to cultural racism believed that such peoples could, with benevolent guidance, achieve levels of Christian domestic happiness and capitalist industriousness equal to those of Europeans. Paradoxically, they were often taken aback when subaltern people actually demanded the equality implied by this suggestion. Nor was skin color the only, or even the primary, determinant of difference for eighteenth-century Britons. Roxann Wheeler argues that "throughout the eighteenth century older conceptions of Christianity, civility and rank were more explicitly important to Britons' assessment of themselves and other people than physical attributes such as skin color, shape of the nose, or texture of the hair."[6] Thus, it is not accurate to say that racism "caused" slavery. And yet slavery was enabled by the practice of creating hierarchies based on visible differences among people. By the time slavery ended, the idea that racial hierarchies were rooted in biology was becoming more entrenched: although British slavery ended in 1833, racism had only just begun.[7]

If we understand racism as synonymous with the imposition of brutal hierarchies based on arbitrary distinctions between social groups, then it has a longer and a broader history than simply the division between black and white in the new world, and was foreshadowed by relationships internal to Great Britain. The four British territories of England, Wales, Scotland, and Ireland became a "united kingdom" only gradually over the course of the eighteenth century. While Wales had formally become part of England in 1536, an Act of Union only officially joined Scotland and England in 1707, and an Act of Union between Ireland and England did not occur until 1801. Scotland kept its own parliament, different legal and educational systems, and more religious freedom throughout most of the century. The Union offered some benefits for Scotland, particularly in terms of colonial emigration, which had previously been prohibited, and in terms of trade. In particular, many Scots were able to enter, and to distinguish themselves in, the British army. The Scottish situation, however, was complicated by the two Jacobite rebellions of the eighteenth century. Both uprisings in support of the deposed Stuart kings, in 1715 and 1745, were carried out with the support of Scottish leaders – particularly the Highland clan chieftains. After the more successful uprising of 1745, in which Jacobite forces came within 125 miles of London, was put down, England retaliated with a series of laws designed to strip traditional leaders of their power: arms were banned, as were clan plaids, and the "heritable jurisdictions," which gave local lairds legal power within their own territories, were dismantled. These sanctions had the added effect of creating two distinct regions within Scotland: Edinburgh and the lowlands enriched themselves by becoming great trading centers, while the Highlands became more and more impoverished and depopulated as lairds, reduced now to the status of ordinary landowners, raised rents, cleared villages, and encouraged emigration.

While Ireland's entry into the United Kingdom did not occur until the beginning of the nineteenth century, the depth of its colonial status was arguably of longer standing and greater intensity. England had increased its colonial interest in Ireland during Elizabeth I's reign and had tried to use military force to subdue the territory. This attempt had not been particularly successful, and the only parts firmly under English control by the mid-seventeenth century were "the pale" around Dublin and the plantations in Ulster, which were settled under James I.[8] Scholars such as Nicholas Canny have argued compellingly that representations of plantations in the New World were haunted by the history of earlier seventeenth-century plantations in Ireland.[9] England tried a bit more successfully for military domination under Cromwell's Protectorate – a campaign that included brutal massacres at Wexford and Drogheda in 1649. Cromwell paid his soldiers in land confiscated from the Catholic Irish. While Catholics owned 60 percent of the land in Ireland in 1641, by 1660 they held only 8 or 9 percent of it, and that mostly in the far western part of the country. After the Restoration in 1660, and especially after the Glorious Revolution in 1688 (the last, and only major battle of which – the Battle of the Boyne – was fought in Ireland), England's plan for subjugating Ireland moved from being primarily military to primarily economic. The crown passed a number of extremely restrictive economic policies, prohibiting, among other things, direct Irish trade with British colonies and the export of cattle, raw wool, and woolen manufacture from Ireland to England (collectively known as the "Navigation Acts"). In addition, Irish Catholics were constrained by "penal laws" – in force between 1727 and 1829 – that barred them from being members of parliament, bearing arms, running a school in Ireland, voting, and receiving degrees from the University of Dublin. The social geography of Ireland was more complicated than the simple opposition between Catholic and Protestant implies, however. At least four different communities jostled for social and legal status during the period: the Old English – Catholic landowners, some Anglo-Norman, resident since before the days of Elizabeth; the "native Irish" – Catholic, native inhabitants, primarily poor, often Gaelic-speaking; the Anglo-Irish – post-Cromwellian, Protestant settlers, often merchants (a group that included Swift and Goldsmith); and the "Scotch-Irish" – Scottish Presbyterians settled by James in those Ulster plantations, many of whom were Presbyterians, and who as dissenters were themselves discriminated against by the Church of Ireland. Many from this last group emigrated to the North American colonies in the eighteenth century.

These conditions of variegated subalternity in both Ireland and Scotland have led later historians to dub the situation "internal colonialism."[10] This term usually refers to the idea that the native inhabitants of Scotland and Ireland had been colonized, and were treated as second-class colonial citizens, by Great Britain. It further implies that England practiced, rehearsed, and to some degree perfected its colonial techniques in Ireland and Scotland before moving on to the New World. One hallmark of internal colonialism in both Ireland and Scotland was that it created a situation in which empty land became more valuable than the people who had labored on the land, as the territory was converted from subsistence farming to pasture. Profitable sheep and cattle replaced people who were then vulnerable to being moved (through clearances, emigration, empressment into the army, etc.) in a dynamic that was similar, though not of course identical, to the transatlantic movements of slavery.[11] Another way of thinking about internal colonialism is as forced underdevelopment: the British government used its power to create conditions under which most groups in Ireland and Scotland could not accrue the benefits of Britain's expanding trade and colonial empire.

Long ignored by scholars more interested in the progressive, liberalizing aspects of the Enlightenment, questions about the role of colonized people and places in shaping eighteenth-century literature have produced an explosion of new work in the last three decades. Scholars have argued for the generative force of New World contexts on eighteenth-century literature, pointing out that texts long central to the traditional canon of eighteenth-century literature are inseparable from their New World settings. They have suggested that it is no simple coincidence that new forms of literature and full-blown colonialism emerged at the same time in British culture. Some have drawn connections between the experience of colonial exploration and the new *formal* elements of British literature during this time, suggesting, for example that the insistence on empirical description in eighteenth-century literature, particularly the novel, derives from travelers' descriptions of the New World.[12] Others argue that the dynamics of the global market influenced the strategies of eighteenth-century fiction. The rise of contractual relations, Elizabeth Dillon claims, produced a "shift toward a belief in probability – not simply toward empiricism, but toward a kind of deliberative intelligence oriented toward navigating future (and thus fictive) possibilities."[13] Scholars have also seen insistent and resonant topoi emerging from circum-Atlantic historical experience – themes that "circulate" through both literature specifically set in colonial arenas and literature concerned with the metropolitan/domestic spaces of Britain. Nancy Armstrong and Leonard Tennenhouse, for example, argue that the trope of captivity works its way "back" from the narratives of British settlers to domestic novels such as *Pamela*, and that "one has to go to America...to understand where novels come from."[14] Laura Doyle proposes that a narrative of seduction and trauma that "entails...a deracinating but ultimately racialized and triumphant Atlantic crossing" characterizes both narratives of transatlantic passage, like *Oroonoko*, and domestic novels by writers like Eliza Haywood.[15]

Joseph Roach has dubbed the arena in which such creativity took place the "circum-Atlantic world": a world that "resembled a vortex in which commodities and cultural practices changed hands many times."[16] Such a concept, Roach argues, "insists on the centrality of the diasporic and genocidal histories of Africa and the Americas, north and south, in the creation of the culture of modernity. In this sense, a New World was not discovered in the Caribbean, *but one was truly invented there.*"[17] All of the texts discussed below are often invoked as exemplars of transatlantic literature. This new understanding of canonical texts such as *Robinson Crusoe* has remade our experience of eighteenth-century culture.

Aphra Behn, *Oroonoko*

Many firsts have been attributed to Aphra Behn's *Oroonoko* (1688). It has been called the first novel by a woman, the first American novel, and sometimes even the first novel written in English. It is certainly the first fictional representation of a slave rebellion in British literature. Its author was herself a remarkable person. Aphra Behn came to prose narrative late, after enjoying one of the most successful careers of any Restoration playwright, man or woman. The new rules governing the Restoration stage made it possible for playwrights to earn a good living, and Behn exploited this possibility as well as any, becoming one of the first professional woman writers. In *A Room of One's Own*, Virginia Woolf famously says of her, "All women together ought to let flowers fall upon the tomb of Aphra Behn...for it is she who earned them the right to speak their minds." In the 1680s, however, the market for the kind of bawdy comedy at which Behn excelled dried up a bit, as did the public admiration for ardent royalists such as herself, and Behn drew on what was probably first-hand knowledge of the seventeenth-century Caribbean to write *Oroonoko*, published posthumously the year of her death. Although not much is known of Behn's biography, it does seem to be true that she traveled to Surinam, as the English slave colony on the

Caribbean coast of South America was then known (the area is now Guiana), with her family. Left alone with her mother and sister after her father's death (he was probably a functionary for Cromwell), the young Behn may have witnessed the kind of slave revolt her novel depicts. Or, she may have gleaned her accounts from travel literature and other sources. In any case, the canny author presents the story as an eyewitness account of a female narrator, fashioning a mythic narrative of race relations in the sugar colonies that influenced many generations of thinking about slavery and slaves. *Oroonoko* long seemed a kind of curiosity, of more sociopolitical than literary interest. The past three or four decades, however, have seen an explosion of scholarship about the text, spurred by interest in both women authors and colonial contexts, as well as renewed engagement with the generic precursors to the novel form.

Behn's novel tells the story of an African warrior prince, Oroonoko, caught in a battle with his king (and grandfather) over the woman they both love, Imoinda. Furious at what he perceives as their betrayal, the king sells first Imoinda and then Oroonoko into New World slavery. Both survive the Middle Passage, and are reunited in the sugar plantations of Surinam. After coming close to being reconciled to his fate, Oroonoko is spurred to rebellion by Imoinda's pregnancy. But he and his group of fol-lowers are subdued, and Oroonoko himself spectacularly executed – both dismembered and burnt at the stake. The unnamed female narrator returns to England chastened by what she has seen. This horrifying story is juxta-posed to a proto-anthropological description of the native people of Surinam. The novel thus gives us an almost unique vision of the varied inhabitants of the colony: British colonizers, transported West African slaves, and the native (noble) "savages."

Oroonoko shows us clearly that these three disparate groups occupy very different positions with regard to colonial production and to the valuing of colonial territory. With the native people, the British participate in the same kind of accumulation of valuable curiosities from foreign lands we have seen described by Pope and others, collecting the types of luxuries displayed on Belinda's dressing table. The feathers, skins, and artifacts such as headdresses acquired from the native peoples of Surinam are not quite commodities, since they attain their value through a personal relationship with the place in which they originate, rather than through exchange value. As Roach points out, feathers are "both exotic tokens of otherness and the polychromatic markers of its alarming copiousness and confu-sion."[18] Such objects are what Nicholas Thomas has described as curiosi-ties.[19] The African slaves, on the other hand, are involved in the production of raw materials in plantation labor – here, and most often in the Caribbean, that product was sugar. This was a labor system that many have seen as proto-industrial. Although this scene of labor is clearly central to the novel – why else would slaves be necessary? – it is never represented.

But *Oroonoko* is as important for its generic innovations as for its historical context. Indeed, it is the intersection of New World contexts with new narrative strategies that has generated so much of the interest in the novel. Readers have long noted the way the text seems to shift back and forth between two different genres or ways of telling a story, between an empirical eyewitness account and the kind of language and imagery associated with Romance. The former is associated with the New World, the latter with Oroonoko's previous life in Africa. The empirical style is introduced in the opening paragraphs in which the narrator disavows the idea that hers is a "feign'd *Hero*": "there being enough of Reality" to support her story, "and to render it diverting, without the Addition of Invention."[20] Like the writers of travel narratives, she claims to be an "Eyewitness" to the events related, and the recipient of eyewitness accounts of those events which she did not see. And, indeed, the first few pages of the novel give a kind of proto-ethnographic account of the native people of Surinam – their dress, customs, and manufactures. This description, while admiring, is relentlessly material, documenting the empirical world rather than an interior one of personalities or emotions. In the portion of the novel set in Africa, however, the narrative takes on the distinctive, exaggerated cadences of seventeenth-century heroic Romance. When Oroonoko falls in love with Imoinda, "he told her with his Eyes, that he was not insensible of her Charms; while Imoinda, who wish'd for nothing more than so glorious a Conquest, was pleas'd to believe she understood that silent Language of new-born Love; and from that moment put on all her additions to Beauty" (p. 15). Here, in contrast, overpowering internal forces make empirical details irrelevant.

Yet the project of writing a heroic romance about Africans does strange things to the discursive conventions of that tradition. For example, when we are first introduced, through the narrator's eyes, to Oroonoko's extraordinary physical presence, we can see the conventional modes of describing heroic beauty in tension with European assumptions about Africans:

> He was pretty tall, but of a Shape the most exact that could be fancy'd: the most famous Statuary cou'd not form the Figure of a Man more admirably turn'd from head to foot. His face was not of that brown rusty Black which most of that Nation are, but of perfect Ebony, or polished Jett. His Eyes were the most awful that cou'd be seen, and very piercing; the White

of them being like Snow, as were his Teeth. His Nose was rising and Roman, instead of African and flat. His Mouth the finest shaped that could be seen; far from those great turn'd Lips, which are so natural to the rest of the Negroes. The whole Proportion and Air of his Face was so nobly and exactly form'd, that, bating his Colour, there could be nothing in Nature more beautiful, agreeable and handsome.[21]

This description aptly illustrates the difficulties a non-European hero posed for British writers. Oroonoko is compellingly beautiful – his physicality symbolizes his intelligence, honor, and bravery – and yet the narrator stumbles over his physical difference. Even though his color differs from the "rusty Black" of most Africans, it is that which stands in the way of his being the *most* "beautiful, agreeable and handsome" man she has seen. Even more clearly, the description exemplifies the system of comparison upon which racial hierarchies are built: "Roman" noses are compared to "African" noses, Oroonoko's mouth and skin color compared to those of other Africans. By glorifying his characteristics, the narrator implicitly denigrates the other half of the comparison, while, as Laura Brown notes, at the same time assimilating Oroonoko to a European ideal of masculine beauty.

The transposition of such heroism to the world of plantation slavery brings its own problems. For a while, Oroonoko is uneasily reconciled to a life of slavery, his anger assuaged by finding Imoinda still alive and the fact that the other slaves still regard him as their king. Imoinda's pregnancy, however, pushes him towards rebellion: "this new Accident made [Oroonoko] more Impatient of Liberty...and [he] offer'd either Gold, or a vast Quantity of Slaves which shou'd be paid before they let him go." His sudden drive for freedom springs from the fact that the birth of Imoinda's child into slavery would signify Oroonoko's loss of sovereignty over his family – "all the breed is theirs to whom the parents belong." The emotional upheaval caused by even the possibility that Imoinda will bear a child into slavery reminds us of the especially vexed position of slave women, who were valuable as workers in the plantation as reproducers of the labor force but often treated as sexual objects as well by their owners. For Oroonoko, the possibility of losing not just himself but also his child into perpetual servitude signifies the final, unforgivable, loss of autonomy – his loss of control over his own family and patrimony.

And yet this episode ends not with the violence of a slave uprising, as one might expect, but with an extraordinary scene of intrafamilial brutality. After the rebellion fails, Oroonoko plans revenge against his overseers, but decides first to kill Imoinda so that she will not be "ravished by every

Brute; exposed first to their nasty Lusts, and then a shameful Death" (p. 71). Imoinda agrees to the necessity of her own death, and so: "The lovely, young and ador'd Victim lays her self down before the Sacrificer; while he, with a hand resolved and a heart-breaking within, gave the fatal Stroke, first cutting her Throat, and then severing her yet smiling Face from that delicate Body, pregnant as it was with the Fruits of tenderest love" (p. 72). Oddly enough, all of Oroonoko's resistance to the horrors of slavery is channeled into this violence against the person he loves best. Odder still, Imoinda's death seems to sap his remaining energy for rebellion, and he stays motionless by her body until he is recaptured. Even then, he does not assault his captors, but "cut[s] a piece of flesh from his own Throat" and "rip[s] up his own Belly, and [takes] his Bowels, and pull[s] them out, with what strength he [can]" (p. 75) – the sites of his self-mutilation eerily recalling Imoinda's severed head and terminated pregnancy. He can only demonstrate his heroism and strength through self-mutilation. The narrative evokes the social violence at the heart of slave culture by raising the possibility of rebellion, only to channel it back into the family, back into "romance." This is a violence we are supposed to read as love.[22]

The narrative ends with another episode of supererogatory brutality, as Oroonoko is executed.

> He had learn'd to take Tobacco; and when he was assur'd that he should die, he desir'd they would give him a Pipe in his Mouth, ready lighted; which they did. And the Executioner came, and first cut off his Members, and threw them into the Fire; after that, with an ill-favour'd Knife, they cut off his Ears and his Nose, and burn'd them; he still smoak'd on, as if nothing had touched himl then they hack'd off one of his Arms, and still he bore up, and held his Pipe; but at the cutting off of his other Arm, his Head sunk, and his Pipe dropt and he gave up the Ghost without a Groan or a Reproach. (p. 77)

According to Laura Brown, this remarkable scene bears a complex relationship to the execution of Charles I.

> The "Spectacle . . . of a mang'd King," then . . . when Oroonoko is quartered and his remains are distributed around the colony, evokes with surprising vividness the tragic drama of Charles Stuart's violent death. The sense of momentous loss that Behn's narrative generates on behalf of the "royal slave" is the product of the hidden figuration in Oroonoko's death of the culminating moment of the English revolution.[23] (p. 58)

Both Charles I and Oroonoko die violently, Brown argues, in the wake of the triumph of "anti-absolutist mercantile imperialism" – the very forces produced both Britain's new constitutional monarchy and the colonial riches of the slave trade. The transition to modernity is a violent one, Behn shows.

Oroonoko is a story of world historical proportions, but it is carefully shaped for its readers by its self-consciously female narrator. Hewing closely to the emergent conventions of realism, this narrator painstakingly tells us which events she has been a witness to and which were related to her by others. She laments Oroonoko's misfortune of falling into an obscure world, with only a female pen to record his fate. Interestingly enough, she seems quite concerned that we read the novel as a love story. For example, as Oroonoko readies himself to kill Imoinda, the narrator remarks that "the eternal leave-taking of two such Lovers, so greatly born, so sensible, so beautiful, so young and so fond, must be very moving, as the Relation of it was to me afterwards" (p. 72). And after the political resonance of Oroonoko's death, she drags us back to the love story, hoping that "the Reputation of my pen is considerable enough to make his glorious Name to survive to all Ages, with that of the brave, the beautiful, and the constant Imoinda" (p. 78). Critics have noted the complex relationships between Oroonoko, his African wife, Imoinda, and the white female narrator. Some, like Catherine Gallagher, have emphasized the narrator's identification with Oroonoko whose injustly subordinate status can be read as a mirror to that of a female writer; others, like Margaret Ferguson, have noted the implicit competition between the two women in the text – in that one must die to provide the story for the other to tell.[24] But it is precisely the narrative's oscillation between the historical and the romantic, between questions of race and questions of love, which have made it so resonant for contemporary readers.[25]

Daniel Defoe, *Robinson Crusoe*

There is no more iconic text of eighteenth-century literature than *Robinson Crusoe*. It is one of those narratives, like *Frankenstein*, of which everyone knows the story, whether they have read it or not. From the moment it was published in 1719, Defoe's story was tremendously popular, going through five additional editions in that year alone. The number of retellings it continues to produce demonstrates its enduring resonance. Some of the more recent of these include: J. M. Coetzee's novel, *Foe* (1986), which reimagines the story from its occluded viewpoints, including Friday's; the Tom Hanks movie, *CastAway* (2000), in which Friday becomes a volley ball; even the television shows *Survivor* and *Lost*, with their fascination with (versions of) deserted islands. But even though it was enjoyed for a long time as a rousing story of British courage, masculine ingenuity and spiritual renewal, *Robinson Crusoe* is also a story of imperialism, impossible to understand outside the context of Britain's conquest of the New World.

The novel begins with Crusoe's defiance of his father's wishes in setting out to make his fortune at sea. Although his father urges him, in words that have become a standard description of middle-class identity, to stay home and enjoy "the middle State, or what might be called the upper Station of Low Life, which he has found by long Experience was the best State in the World,"[26] Crusoe cannot resist his "rambling Thoughts" (p. 4). He then experiences a number of adventures before his famous sojourn on the island, including being captured and held as a slave himself by Moors. Eventually, he makes his way to South America and begins a successful career as a sugar plantation owner. In the novel's most memorable episode, however, Crusoe, on his way from his Brazilian plantation to buy new slaves in Africa, is shipwrecked on a Caribbean island. All alone for many years, he learns to make and grow all the things he needs. Eventually, he meets and recruits as a companion a native he names Friday. Together, they defend themselves against Friday's cannibal fellow tribesmen and are eventually rescued.

Unlike *Oroonoko*, the narrative voice of *Robinson Crusoe* remains consistently, vehemently, empirical, never veering into the more hyperbolic and fantastical discourse of romance. Its language is relentlessly referential and circumstantial – detailing the collections of the things Crusoe collects and makes. For this reason – what has been celebrated as its consistent realism – Defoe's 1719 text is still deemed by many critics to be the first English novel. Critics have seen it as the first example of a new genre arising from the types of nonfictional narratives popular at the time. It certainly owes a great debt to travelogues and captivity narratives. Britain was fascinated by stories of shipwrecked sailors, and Crusoe's narrative seems to have been particularly inspired in part by the numerous accounts of the sailor Alexander Selkirk, shipwrecked for four years on the island of Juan Fernandez, along with the numerous other shipwreck narratives that circulated at the time. But the narrative structure of his tale, in which a repentant older self retrospectively recounts the failings and strivings of his younger self, also takes the genre of spiritual autobiography as its model. Even as he details his experiences, Crusoe consistently tries to place them in an overarching divine plan – or to at least understand them as God's punishment for his sinful ways. As Michael McKeon says, "Robinson's island conversion depends upon a new-found ability to spiritualize his situation, to detect and interpret the signs of God's presence in his life on the island."[27] Defoe asserts that it is this quality – the capacity of earthly experience to provide spiritual revelation – that justifies his publication of Crusoe's tale. As he explains in the preface: "The Story is told with Modesty, with Seriousness, and with a religious Application of Events to the Uses to which wise Men always apply them (viz.) to the instruction of others by this Example" (p. 3). This tension between the cluttered details of "real life" and the organization of divine planning is a hallmark of Defoe's novel, although readers and critics disagree over which side of this tug-of-war prevails.

During his time on the island, Crusoe establishes himself as a paradigm of industriousness and self-sufficiency. Marx famously says of him: "Despite the variety of his productive functions, he knows that they are but various forms of the activity of one and the same Robinson Crusoe, and are therefore nothing but different manifestations of human labour... The relations between Robinson and the things which comprise the wealth he has created are... simple."[28] Away from the increasingly complicated divisions of labor in the metropolis, Crusoe encounters no needs he cannot meet himself; he controls the means of production as well as the conditions of consumption. His world on the island is very different, too, from the Caribbean society Behn depicts in *Oroonoko*. In Crusoe's solitary world, there is no commodification of goods or labor; there is no coercion of labor, either, since the only laborer, through most of the novel, is himself. Crusoe's accomplishments are based on his own hard work, rather than accorded to him by privilege or inheritance, and this is what has allowed the novel to be read as an expression of an emergent middle-class identity in the eighteenth century. And yet this avatar of middle-class identity enjoys thinking of himself as a king. "I was Lord of the whole Manor," he says, "or if I please'd, I might call my self King, or Emperor over the whole Country which I had Possession of. There were no Rivals. I had no Competitor, none to dispute Sovereignty or Command with me" (p. 94). He calls the dwelling he builds his "Castle" (p. 112). The suture here between industrious self-sufficiency and an ideal of absolute power reveals one of the ideological building blocks of colonialism: the island is Crusoe's by right of hard work, but, once he has it, he is the absolute monarch of it.

Crusoe's island is thus both realistically described and powerfully symbolic. We might begin to explore its symbolic qualities by noting how different this space is than Behn's Surinam: it is deserted, rather than being inhabited by multiple antagonistic groups: uncultivated, rather than already devoted to a proto-industrial mode of production. As Peter Hulme notes, such empty spaces were rare, even in the seventeenth- and eighteenth-century Caribbean. Hulme argues that

> the realistic detail of the text obscures elements of the narrative that...would have to be called mythic, in the sense that they have demonstrably less to do with the historic world of the mid-seventeenth-century Caribbean than they do with the primary stuff of colonialist ideology – the European hero's lonely first steps into the void of savagery[.][29]

Crusoe's island differs from home most dramatically when we discover, halfway through the narrative, that the island has other visitors, and that those visitors are cannibal tribesmen. When Crusoe first understands that he is not, after all, alone on his island, his first reaction is utter terror. Seeing "the Print of a Man's naked Foot on the Shore," he reacts as "one Thunderstruck, or as if I had seen an Apparition" (p. 112). He flees to his shelter "like one pursued...for never frighted Hare fled to Cover, or Fox to Earth, with more Terror of Mind than I to this Retreat" (p. 112). Crusoe here imagines himself as the attacked native – a reversal of the actual situation in most of the region. When Crusoe later sees "the shore spread with Skulls, Hands, Feet and other Bones of human Bodies," and realizes he has found the place where "the Savage Wretches had sat down to their inhumane Feasting upon the Bodies of their Fellow Creatures," he tells us that: "I turn'd away my Face from the horrid spectacle; my Stomach grew sick, and I was just at the point of Fainting, when Nature discharg'd the Disorder from my Stomach; and having vomited with uncommon Violence, I was a little relieved." This array of body parts recalls the dismembered body of the "royal slave" that is one of the final images of *Oroonoko*. Here, of course, the violence has been perpetrated by natives against other natives, but it does remind us of the colonial brutality endemic to the region in Defoe's time: a kind of cruelty that has more or less been excluded from the narrative up until this point. In both cases, the New World dismembers bodies, redistributing them over new territories. Crusoe's nausea also seems exaggerated. But Peter Hulme suggests that this "paradigmatic manifestation of cannibalism finally allows Crusoe to clearly distinguish himself from others. He finally knows who he is; although only after vomiting symbolically voids him, producing that impossible 'pure' body, alimentarily chaste."[30]

We've now seen two competing myths of the Caribbean: the gentle natives of *Oroonoko*, and the warlike cannibals of *Robinson Crusoe*. And yet, Crusoe's "pure" solitude is altered by his relationship with one of these cannibals. He initiates this relationship by saving one native from cannibals who seem ready to eat him, and adopts him as servant and companion. Their attempts to communicate across cultural and linguistic difference are instructive with regard to the greater colonial project.

> [H]e came running to me, laying himself down again upon the Ground, with all the possible signs of an humble, thankful Disposition, making many antic Gestures to show it: At last he lays his Head flat upon the Ground, close to my Foot, and sets my other Foot upon his Head, as he had done before; and after this; made all the Signs to me of Subjection, Servitude and Submission imaginable, to let me know, how he would serve me as long as he liv'd. I understood him in many Things, and let him know, I was very well pleas'd with him; in a little Time I began to speak to him and teach him to speak to me; and first I made him know that his Name should be *Friday*, which was the Day I sav'd his Life; I call'd him so for the Memory of the Time; I likewise taught him to say *Master*, and then let him know, that was to be my Name. (p. 149)

We see their communication through Crusoe's perspective, of course, but the leaps in his interpretation of Friday's gestures are still apparent. He seems eager to translate Friday's gestures of gratitude as willingness to enter perpetual servitude. Yet he might also just be imposing his will on a linguistic and cultural gulf, since Friday's perpetual servitude is also just what Crusoe desires. Crusoe's Adamic desire to name also reveals his desire to shape the world to his own linguistic/conceptual framework. Rather than trying to ascertain Friday's original name, he imposes a name that arises out of Crusoe's own actions, and that refers to a European system of ordering time (much as Oroonoko is given the slave name of Caesar, or Equiano is given the slave name of Gustavus Vassa – both names out of European history). And, whereas Friday's name derives from a singular event, the name Crusoe gives himself in this context – *Master* – is not his given name, but a definition of his powerful position. Scholars have seen this drive to rename the New World as part of the colonialist project – a kind of linguistic conquest.

In many ways, then, Friday holds the position of Crusoe's slave, and yet the novel is careful to differentiate him from the kind of plantation slaves we have seen in *Oroonoko*. The narrative takes pains to distinguish him physically from both native Caribbeans and Africans:

> His hair was long and black, not curl'd like Wool . . . The Colour of his Skin was not quite black, but very tawny; and yet not of an ugly yellow nauseous tawny, as the Brasilians and Virginians, and other Natives of America

are; but of a bright kind of a dun olive Colour, that had in it something very agreeable; tho' not very easy to describe. His Face was round, and plump; his nose small, not flat like the Negroes, a very good Mouth, thin Lips, and his fine Teeth well set, and white as Ivory. (p. 149)

Like Oroonoko, Friday is beautiful *because* he differs from his countrymen, as well as from those others who occupy the same subjugated status: African slaves. Crusoe's relationship to Friday is conflict-free and enormously satisfying – "perfectly and completely happy, *if any such Thing as compleat Happiness can be form'd in a sublunary State*," Crusoe says (p. 159). It is also a fantasy of what relations between Europeans and native people would look like if all resistance and coercion were edited out, or transmuted into personal gratitude and loyalty. Still, the introduction of Friday does take the novel in some unexpected directions. As in *Gulliver's Travels*, including an outsider's viewpoint puts the inconsistencies of English culture into sharp relief, as when Friday questions Crusoe about the relationship between his God and the Devil (p. 158).

The end of the novel surprisingly reveals that Crusoe has been making money the whole time he was on the island. Hulme points out that Crusoe's discovery of this money on his return is as disturbing as his first encounter with the cannibals – it precipitates a physical collapse. This is because "it marks the discovery of the secret of capital itself, that it accumulates in magical independence from the labor of its owner"; Crusoe profits off his colonial holdings even as he is living a moral and self-sufficient life on his island.[31] Finally, then, do we read *Robinson Crusoe* as a founding text of colonialism or as a founding text of middle-class British identity? The truth is that it is both. As James Joyce said, we can see in Crusoe the "true prototype of the British colonist": "The manly independence, the unconscious cruelty; the persistence; the slow yet efficient intelligence; the sexual apathy; the practical, well-balanced religiousness; the calculating taciturnity" (p. 323). Crusoe thus shows us that aspects of emerging ideas of virtue and national identity could not be disassociated from the skills necessary to conquer large swathes of the world.

Internal Colonialism: Swift, "A Modest Proposal," and Samuel Johnson, *A Journey to the Western Isles*

Swift's notoriously brutal satire of Irish poverty, "A Modest Proposal," published a decade after *Robinson Crusoe*, also employs the dynamic of cannibalism as a way of describing the violence of the colonial arena. As in *Gulliver's Travels*, Swift creates a distinctive persona for the voice of "A Modest Proposal." Usually known simply as "the Proposer," since he doesn't name himself in his text, this figure is as self-confident, close-minded, and mathematically inclined as Gulliver is gullible and open to wonder. The Proposer is entranced by what was called at the time political arithmetic, the practice of assigning commercial values to bodies. He proposes that a solution to Ireland's problems would be possible if the poor could be convinced to sell their children as food. The existence of a "prodigious Number of Children"[32] living in poverty "is in the present deplorable State of the Kingdom, a very great additional Grievance" (p. 439). And so the Proposer suggests that the majority of them "be offered in Sale to the Persons of Quality and Fortune through the Kingdom...A Child will make two Dishes at an Entertainment for Friends, and when the Family dines alone, the fore or hind Quarter will make a reasonable Dish" (p. 441). This will make "these Children Sound and Useful Members of the Common-wealth" (p. 444). The scheme is laid out in precise detail in a way that simultaneously satirizes the poor, the Anglo-Irish Ascendancy, and the emergent discourse of socioeconomic calculation.

Swift also draws here on a long running association between Ireland and cannibalism, dating back to at least the Elizabethan era. He was familiar with Thomas Sheridan's exploration of the topic in the *Intelligencer* (no. 18, November 1728), in which Sheridan summarizes Fynes Morrison's account of the aftermath of Tyrone's Rebellion (1617):

> [A] poor widow of *Newry*, having six small children, and no food to support them, shut up her Doors, Died through despair, and in about three or four Days after, her children were found Eating her Flesh...at the same time, a discovery being made of Twelve Women, who made a practice of stealing Children, to Eat them, they were all burned by order of Sir *Arthur Chichester*, then Governour of the *North* of *Ireland*.[33]

This, like most of the best-known accounts of Irish cannibalism, comes out of the Elizabethan conqest of Ireland, which follow a "scorched earth" policy of devastation in order to "deprive the Irish of food, succour and recruits," and aimed to "make Ireland 'a razed table' upon which the Elizabethan state could transcribe a neat pattern" – the era, in other words, that made a subjugated Ireland part of the British Empire.[34] Swift's eighteenth-century invocation of Irish cannibalism thus both reinforces an idea of the savagery of the Irish, and reminds us of the consequences of colonial conquest. "A Modest Proposal" collapses the temporal distance between the "savage" world England labored to subdue in the sixteenth and seventeenth centuries, and the "civilized" world of Ascendancy culture. In this way, Swift suggests that the seemingly progressive strategies of the Proposer are in fact regressive – and will eventuate in the degeneration of Irish culture.

There is something historically specific about the plight of the eighteenth-century Irish poor, however. As the odd dynamics of Ireland's relationship to England made it more profitable for landlords to turn land into pasturage than to keep it tilled, they created a system in which livestock became more valuable than people. Decrying the laws which made it illegal for Ireland to export wool products, or raw wool anywhere but England, Swift wrote in another of his "Irish Tracts":

> [T]here is something so monstrous to deal in a Commodity (further than for our own Use) which we are not allowed to export manufactured, or even unmanufactured, but to one certain Country, and only to some few Ports in that Country; there is, I say, something so sottish, that it wants a Name, in our Language to express it by: and the Good of it is, that the more Sheep we have, the fewer human Creatures are left to wear the Wool or eat the Flesh. Ajax was mad when he mistook a flock of Sheep for his Enemies: but we shall never be sober, until we have the same way of thinking.[35]

Swift inveighs against the paradoxes of colonial production under mercantilist laws here, but he also implicitly comments on the way these conditions affect perceptions of the colonized subject. Placed in competition with sheep, the native Irish are rendered almost indistinguishable from them. As Irvin Ehrenpreis notes with regard to "A Modest Proposal": "treated as cattle, and as passive as cattle, the Irish are figuratively reduced to pieces of beef."[36] Swift probably never fully identified himself with or even sympathized with the native Irish, but his images of them can be read as depicting degradation rather than a natural condition.

In the Irish economy, the absurd reversals continue. Sheep and cattle occupy land that should belong to people and their crops, and, since livestock cannot be exported, people themselves take on the qualities of portable goods. In other words, the Irish themselves become the valuable raw material on offer, exportable for profit. In a pamphlet written the year before "A Modest Proposal" called "Maxims Controlled for Ireland," Swift meditates on how Ireland might profit by this export of raw materials.

> It is an undisputed Maxim in government, that people are the riches of a nation, which is so universally granted, that it will hardly be pardonable to

bring it into doubt. And I will grant it to be so far true, even in this island, that if we had the African custom, or privilege, of selling our useless bodies for slaves to foreigners, it would be the most useful branch of our trade, by ridding us of a most unsupportable burthen, and bring us money in the stead.[37]

This situation, in which the Irish poor are only valuable as exportable commodities, underlies the opening paragraph of "A Modest Proposal," which decries the fate of infants "who, as they grow up, either turn Thieves for want of Work or leave their dear native Country to fight for the Pretender in Spain, or sell themselves to the Barbadoes": they either live outside the law, that is, or export themselves as mercenaries or indentured servants. By turning these children into meat to be eaten, however, "we can incur no Danger in disobliging England. For this kind of Commodity will not bear exportation, the Flesh being of too tender a Consistence to admit a long Continuance in Salt, although perhaps I could name a Country which would be glad to eat up our whole Nation without it." Cannibalism, in other words, will keep a valuable commodity at home. We can think of "A Modest Proposal" as a pre-Malthusian satire of excess population.

According to both Louis Landa and George Wittkowsky, Swift had a long-standing interest in the mercantile maxim he satirizes in "Maxims controlled for Ireland": "people are the riches of the nation."[38] In the Irish context, this principle has often been associated with the work of William Petty, an originator of "political arithmetic" – the practice of trying to calculate the financial value of human bodies.[39] In his work surveying Ireland for Cromwell after his seventeenth-century conquests, Petty sought to quantify the value of Irish land and Irish people, so as to facilitate the payment of English investors and soldiers. Considering the losses of the "late rebellion," Petty calculates:

> The value of people, Men, Women and Children in England, some have computed to be 70 L. per Head, one with another. But if you value the people who have been destroyed in Ireland, as Slaves and Negroes are usually rated, viz. at about 15 l. one with another; Men being sold for 25 L. and Children 5 L each; the value of the people lost will be about 10,355,000 L.[40]

Thus, Swift's suggestion that the native Irish might be valued in the same way as African slaves has some historical precedent. As Wittkowsky remarks, Swift certainly wrote "A Modest Proposal," with its interest in the dehumanization and commodification of bodies, with the aide of the "muse of political arithmetic."[41]

One remarkable subtext of the pamphlet, however, is its recognition of the global context of colonialism in which this dehumanization and commodification occurs. Only from an international perspective could a comparison between Irish and African bodies make any sense. Toward the end of "A Modest Proposal," the Proposer compares Ireland unfavorably to several other societies thought to be cannibalistic. The Irish, he contends, "have failed in learning to love their Country, wherein [they] differ even from LAPLANDERS, and the inhabitants of TOPINAMBOO." This comparison reiterates the Proposer's claim that the misery of his country is unique, and the extremity of his scheme suits "this one individual Kingdom of IRELAND, and . . . no other that ever was, is, or ever can be upon Earth" (p. 445). Yet, even as this formulation insists on Irish exceptionalism, it simultaneously makes available the connections between Ireland and other 'savage' landscapes. Swift's purpose is clear; he is arguing that Ireland should be rescued from such comparisons, restored to a condition of equality with England. Yet the comparisons collapse spatial distance in much the same way that the treatment of cannibalism collapses temporal distance, creating suggestive links between Ireland and the colonial periphery. We do not have to posit Swift's identification or even sympathy with the native Irish to see the anticolonial implications of the text.

With Johnson's *Journey to the Western Isles*, also a description of the vagaries of internal colonialism, we move from Ireland in the 1720s to Scotland in the 1770s, a very different political situation. The restrictive laws put into place after the suppression of the 1745 rebellion changed the socioeconomic conditions of the Highlands and Islands in particular. Deprived of their hereditary rights over legal decisions, the Highland Lairds became landlords rather than tribal leaders – their wealth measured not in the number of men they could keep, but in what their land could produce. As Johnson puts it, "The chiefs, divested of their prerogatives, necessarily turned their thoughts to the improvement of their revenues, and expect more rent, as they have less homage."[42] As such landowners realized that sheep farming might be a better source of revenue than the rents of impoverished tenants, rural people who had hitherto been subsistence farmers were pushed to the edges of large sheep runs, or to the unpredictable fishing trade on the coasts. Brutal clearances and evictions of such people, such as those that took place in Sutherland in the second decade of the nineteenth century, were not the norm; still, the poverty and general misery of the Highlanders increased during this period. One remedy for their situation seemed to be emigration to the New World.

Thus, these conditions precipitated a crisis in ideas about the virtues of emigration, as Highland Scots, like the Irish before them, were rendered less valuable than livestock on the land they had traditionally inhabited. Between 1763 and 1775 twenty thousand Highlanders and islanders emigrated.[43] This process fostered two, complementary, anxieties about the effects it would have on Britain as a whole – worries Johnson articulates admirably. On the one hand, such emigration depletes and depopulates the British nation: as Johnson says, "all that go may be considered as subjects lost to the British crown; for a nation scattered in the boundless regions of America resembles rays diverging from a focus. All the rays remain, but the heat is gone. Their power consisted in their concentration: when they are dispersed, they have no effect" (p. 128). The "boundless" regions of America absorb England's strength. Yet, on the other hand, Johnson also entertains the possibility that America might collect and reorganize that strength: "The numbers which have already gone ... are very great, and such as if they had gone together and agreed upon any certain settlement, might have founded an independent government in the depths of the western continent" (p. 362). Emigration thus seemed pernicious both because it threatened to depopulate England itself and because it seemed to foster American independence. If Swift was concerned about the perils of overpopulation, Johnson is concerned with the perils of depopulation. The effects of internal colonialism can be seen here too in the problem of newly mobile bodies: the Scots moving through the circuits of empire to the New World are as yet an unknown quantity.

Johnson journeyed to the Highlands with his younger, Scottish, friend, James Boswell. Boswell, who was from Edinburgh, convinced Johnson to come to Scotland with him. The journey to the Highlands was very difficult at the time, rarely attempted by Englishmen and lowland Scots. Johnson, furthermore, was an elderly man by eighteenth-century standards – he was 63 to Boswell's 32 – although he was surprisingly hardy. What Johnson struggles to represent once he reaches the Highlands is a disappearing culture. He eloquently expresses his own ambivalence about this process:

> There was perhaps never any change of national manners so quick, so great, and so general, as that which has operated in the Highlands, by the last conquest, and the subsequent laws. We came hither too late to see what we expected, a people of peculiar appearance, and a system of antiquated life ... Of what they had before the late conquest of their country,

> there remain only their language and their poverty. Their language is
> attacked on every side...Such is the effect of the late regulations, that a
> longer journey than to the Highlands must be undertaken by him whose
> curiosity pants for savage virtues and barbarous grandeur. (pp. 73–4)

Here, Johnson reveals the partly voyeuristic motive of his journey – satisfying his curiosity about "savage virtues and barbarous grandeur" – while
also both admitting that conquest has destroyed that culture and proposing
that "subjection" has some pleasing aspects.

And yet describing that culture means trying to make visible something
that has already disappeared. In a particularly evocative allusion, Johnson
ironically compliments Boswell for his ability to see things that aren't there.
Referring to Hamlet's ability to see his father's ghost, while his mother sees
only "vacancy," Johnson compares the attempt to "see" Scottish culture in
a deserted landscape to the ability to see ghosts. Britain's political and
economic policies since the "conquest" have fostered emptiness, Johnson
argues:

> To hinder insurrection, by driving away the people, and to govern peace-
> ably, by having no subjects, is an expedient that argues no great profundity
> of politicks. To soften the obdurate, to convince the mistaken, to mollify
> the resentful, are worthy of a statesman; but it affords a legislator little
> self-applause to consider, that where there was formerly an insurrection,
> there is now a wilderness. (p. 103)

The same holds true for the new Scottish agricultural practice: "to make
a country plentiful by diminishing the people, is an expeditious mode of
husbandry; but that abundance, which there is nobody to enjoy, contrib-
utes little to human happiness" (p. 96).

The frustration and poignancy of Scottish Highland culture, for Johnson,
is not simply that it is disappearing but also that it can leave no permanent
record behind. Evoking the same vocabulary of emptiness, he notes that
each person who emigrates leaves "a lasting vacuity" as no one will come
to take their place. The oral culture of the Highlanders is, to Johnson,
devastatingly ephemeral. "The traditions of an ignorant and savage
people," he opines, "have been for ages negligently heard, and unskillfully
related" (p. 69). Written records are superior because:

> Books are faithful repositories, which may be a while neglected or forgot-
> ten; but when they are opened again, will again impart their instruction:
> memory, once interrupted, is not to be recalled. Written learning is a fixed
> luminary, which, after the cloud that had hidden it has past away, is bright

in its proper station. Tradition is but a meteor, which, if once it falls, cannot be rekindled. (p. 113)

Johnson articulates the eighteenth-century belief that a culture is sustained by its permanent records.

Yet, paradoxically, the emptiness of the Highlands has unexpected benefits for the writer, particularly in the way it opens things up for imagination. For Johnson, that emptiness is linked to its literariness – the space it opens for imagination. Although he decries an empty land, he also enjoys the intellectual/literary opportunities opened up by that emptiness. Johnson's account of the ruins on the island of Iona exemplifies the powerful effects of formerly inhabited places:

> To abstract the mind from all local emotion would be impossible, if it were endeavoured, and would be foolish, if it were possible. Whatever withdraws us from the power of our senses; whatever makes the past, the distant, or the future predominate over the present, advances us in the dignity of thinking beings. Far from me and from my friends, be such frigid philosophy as may conduct us indifferent and unmoved over any ground which has been dignified by wisdom, bravery or virtue. That man is little to be envied, whose patriotism would not gain force upon the plain of Marathon, or whose piety would not grow warmer among the ruins of Iona. (pp. 140–1)

Like Swift, Johnson draws attention to the particularity of a place – the "local emotion" it can generate – while also making connections between that place and other parts of the world. However, it is the very emptiness of the place, rather than its overfullness, that generates those emotions.

Colonialism did not only happen far away in the eighteenth century. As both Swift and Johnson's texts remind us, just as Britain was exploring – and often conquering and exploiting – the colonial periphery, it was also exploring and describing the British Isles themselves – partly because the means of transportation were improving, partly by way of consolidating a national identity through assimilating otherness, and partly as an attempt to discover an "older," more authentic Britishness that seemed to be vanishing under the onslaught of colonial capital. Such expeditions were also encouraged by a proto-ethnographic interest in cataloging human nature – in discovering the archetypal characteristics of human community. It was ironic, to say the least, that the English developed an intellectual and sentimental interest in such "primitive" communities just as they were disappearing.

The Interesting Narrative of the Life of Olaudah Equiano, or Gustavus Vassa, The African, Written by Himself

Although, as we have seen, African and Amerindian characters appear in British literature throughout the eighteenth century – Oroonoko and Friday are only two of the most famous – the first widely read narrative in English written by a person of African descent is Olaudah Equiano's autobiographical text, published in 1786. This was one of the most important texts of the early antislavery movement in Britain. Although it was the most popular, Equiano's was not the first text published by an African writer during this period. The narrative of James Albert Ukawsaw Gronniosaw appeared in 1772; in 1773 Phyllis Wheatley's poems arrived in print; Ignatius Sancho's letters were published posthumously in 1782, followed, in 1785, by the narrative of John Marrant, and in 1787 by a polemic against slavery by Ottobah Cugoano.

Equiano's text is neither polemic nor poetry, however. Instead, he tells the story of his life – his remarkable journey from a happy infancy in Africa into slavery, and then out of slavery to a career as a sailor and then a political activist and shopkeeper in England. As he tells it, Equiano was born in West Africa, but was kidnapped and sold into slavery as a young child in Barbados but then resold to a British naval officer who took him to England, where he learned to read. After serving aboard ship during the Seven Years' War, Equiano was sold into slavery again: this time to a merchant trading between the Caribbean and North American colonies. In this position, however, he managed to make enough money on the side to eventually buy his freedom. After being freed, he continued to work on merchant ships – eventually sailing to the Arctic, the Mediterranean, and to Central America. He converted to Anglicanism, and was involved with the Sierra Leone settlement project. After he published his narrative, which went through nine editions, Equiano settled in England, where he became an important part of the early antislavery movement. He married an English woman and had two daughters with her before dying in 1797.

Like his fictional predecessors, Oroonoko and Friday, Equiano went by many names during his lifetime, as he traversed a number of places and cultures. Oluadah Equiano is the name he tells us he was given at birth – and most contemporary readers use it, giving precedence to its originary status. When he is enslaved, his captors give Equiano several English names, including Michael and Jacob. The naval officer, Pascal, renames him yet again: Gustavus Vassa, a hero of sixteenth-century Swedish independence. While Equiano resents these names, he came to use Gustavus Vassa more than his birth name, incorporating it as part of the title of his memoir, signing letters and legal documents with it. His many names, and his oscillation between them according to circumstances, mark both the instability and the tenuousness of Equiano's status, as well as his subordination.

Although Equiano's story is not fiction, he draws on many of the same generic conventions as Behn and Defoe. Like them, he relies on the empirical discourse of travel narratives, providing numerous material details of the various persons and places he encounters. If Defoe mimics the structure of spiritual autobiography in *Robinson Crusoe*, Equiano provides a heartfelt version of the real thing in his memoir, recounting his conversion aboard ship in poignant detail. As an African writer, Equiano needs to muster all the narrative authority he can. As in Johnson's representation of Scotland, there is a clear hierarchy between written and oral culture. Henry Louis Gates has pointed out that Enlightenment Europe took African illiteracy to be a damning sign of inferiority. In response, "the narrated, descriptive 'eye' was put into service as a literary form to posit both the individual 'I' of the black author as well as the collective 'I' of the race." And yet, Gates asks, "how could the black subject posit a full and sufficient self in a language in which blackness is a sign of absence? Can writing, with the very difference it makes and marks, mask the blackness of the black face that addresses the text of Western letters[?]"[44] In order to communicate his predicament to English readers, the African or Afro-British subject must first prove his literacy – but the underlying assumption of African inferiority is so strong that such literacy is always open to question. Later editions of Equiano's narrative were published with letters testifying to his truthfulness and his authorship; apparently even the most articulate of African writers needed the veracity of his words bolstered. Recently, the question of the accuracy of Equiano's narrative has surfaced again. Vincent Carretta has uncovered evidence that suggests that Equiano was born in South Carolina, rather than Africa.[45] If this is true, then the idyllic scenes of an African childhood he recounts are as fictional as those in Behn's and Defoe's novels. It is hard to know how much this information should affect our reading of the text – but it does demonstrate how much of the memoir's power derives from its claim to be a record of lived experience. It is also interesting to consider why Equiano thought he would be a more effective antislavery advocate if he claimed to be born in Africa rather than North America.

His seemingly paradoxical status as a literate African puts Equiano in a difficult position with regard to fashioning his authorial voice. As he moves between Africa, America, and England, he tries to find a way to represent his experience of slavery – an experience that has been heretofore almost invisible to most English readers – conveying its newness while still using a language that English readers can understand. We can see the problems his split position poses from the very beginning of the narrative. As he puts it in the first paragraph of the memoir:

> I believe there are few events in my life, which have not happened to many: it is true the incidents of it are numerous; and did I consider myself an European, I might say my sufferings were great: but when I compare my lot with those of most of my countrymen, I regard myself as a particular favorite of Heaven, and acknowledge the mercies of Providence in every occurrence of my life.[46]

The sentence does a remarkable job of tracing out the paradoxes of Equiano's narrative voice, while simultaneously driving home the cruelty of slavery to his readers. He writes as the representative of a group (most of what has happened to him has "happened to many" others who live in slavery). And yet, rather than being a typical member of that group, he is unusual: his "sufferings," while "great," are mild in comparison to what happens to most slaves. He has found his way to freedom and has found a way to communicate his experiences. His very eloquence underlines the problem of exemplarity: paradoxically, Equiano is able to represent other slaves and former slaves precisely because his experience has been so unrepresentative. He reminds his English readers, albeit in a cautious subjunctive mode, that, though the cruelties of his life are nothing to that of most slaves, they dwarf those of most Europeans. Thus economically sketching comparisons between himself and both Africans and Britons, Equiano balances his life story precariously between exemplarity and novelty, between voiceless Africans and British rhetoric. He himself implicitly raises the question of whether he belongs primarily to the community of English readers whom he addresses, or to the voiceless (to British ears) population of African slaves out of which he has emerged/freed himself. Or whether he belongs to no community at all, but writes only as an "interesting" and unique individual, whose story reveals only a single, unrepeatable set of circumstances. The effect, which recurs throughout the narrative despite its sincerely empirical tone, is vertiginous.

For all these reasons, books play an important role in Equiano's story – they are almost magical conveyers of status and legitimacy. In a trope that Henry Louis Gates has identified as central to the emergent genre of the slave narrative, Equiano at first believes that books are magical objects.

> I had often seen my master and Dick employed in reading; and I had a great curiosity to talk to the books, as I thought they did; and so to learn how all things had a beginning: for that purpose I have often taken up a book, and have talked to it, and then put my ears to it, when alone, in hopes it would answer me; and I have been very much concerned when I found it remained silent. (p. 48)

Gates argues that in imagining that books can speak, Equiano, and other slaves who recount similar experiences, recognize something important about the place of the literary in determining the hierarchy of the Atlantic world. "Making the book speak, then, constitutes a motivated and political engagement with and condemnation of Europe's fundamental sign of domination, the commodity of writing, the text and technology of reading."[47] Later, Equiano turns the authoritative voices of books to his own uses. As did many late eighteenth-century authors who were not of African descent, Equiano bolsters his narrative authority through allusion. His narrative is studded with references to the emerging canon of English literature, to works like *Paradise Lost*, and, even more importantly, the Bible. Like his recourse to the structure of spiritual autobiography, these allusions are probably an important way in which Equiano drew his eighteenth-century audience into his narrative. Look, he seems to be implying, I have read the same books as you have; grant me the same capacity for intelligence and spiritual integrity.

After many schemes and adventures in the West Indies, Equiano puts together enough money to buy his own freedom. For reasons that should now be apparent, he includes the text of his manumission document as proof and corroboration of his story. Unfortunately, however, he finds that racism is a broader problem than slavery in the American colonies.

> Hitherto I had thought only slavery dreadful; but the state of a free negro appeared to me now equally so at least, and in some respects even worse, for they live in constant alarm for their liberty; and even this is but nominal, for they are universally insulted and plundered without the possibility of redress; for such is the equity of the West Indian laws, that no free negro's evidence will be admitted in their courts of justice. In this situation is it surprising that slaves, when mildly treated, should prefer even the misery of slavery to such a mockery of freedom? (p. 91)

Equiano finds that slavery and racism are not exactly synonymous. And the effort in his book extends to both.

The power of Equiano's narrative is that it is simultaneously a life history and an antislavery polemic. In the course of relating the events of his life, he also deploys a myriad of arguments against slavery. The primary one, of course, derives from the evidence of injustice and suffering in his own life. But at times he also speaks more directly to the reader about the evils of slavery. "O, ye nominal Christians!" Equiano implores, after describing slaves being separated from their families,

> "might not an African ask you, learned you this from your God, who says unto you, Do unto all men as you wish men should do unto you? Is it not enough that we are torn from our country and friends to toil for your luxury and lust of gain? Must every tender feeling be likewise sacrificed to your avarice?" (p. 43).

This is an argument based on Christian doctrine and the eighteenth-century sentimental ideal of empathy: Africans are human beings too, and it is a sentimental failure on the part of Europeans not to understand the sufferings caused by slavery. Despite the evidence of growing racism all around him, Equiano grounds his appeal in the idea that the differences between Africans and Europeans are cultural rather than biological: "Let the polished and haughty European recollect that his ancestors were once, like the Africans, uncivilized, and even barbarous. Did Nature make them inferior to their sons? And should they too have been made slaves? Every rational mind answers, No" (p. 31). Thus, Equiano finds hope for Africa's (and Africans') future in modernity, not a return to an edenic African past evoked by the early chapters of the narrative. Instead, he hopes that the abolition of the slave trade, and the instigation of free trade will bring both continents into a kind of free market utopia:

> A commercial intercourse with Africa opens an inexhaustible source of wealth to the manufacturing interests of Great Britain, and to all which the slave trade is an objection.... Population, the bowels and surface of Africa, abound in valuable and useful returns; the hidden treasures of centuries will be brought to light and into circulation. Industry, enterprise and mining, will have their full scope, proportionably as they civilize. In a word, it lays open an endless field of commerce to the British manufactures and merchant adventurer. The manufacturing interest and the general interest are synonymous. The abolition of slavery would be in reality an universal good. (p. 177)

During the eighteenth century, much of the Caribbean and North America was colonized by the British Empire, while Ireland and Scotland were treated in similar ways closer to home. The native inhabitants of these places suffered accordingly. But the fact of conquered territory doesn't fully explain the significance of the slave trade and slavery, nor does it explain the contours of the broader category of subalternity – the condition of being subordinated – during this period. As the stories of the Middle Passage, and of the problems of emigration and global circulation in Britain's internal colonies, remind us, subalternity in the eighteenth century involved coerced mobility. Persons who were subjected to being moved from their natal places had to invent new voices, new identities. Out of this transatlantic circulation, eighteenth-century literature emerged.

Notes

Introduction

1 John Brewer, *Sinews of Power: War, Money and the English State, 1688–1783* (New York: Alfred A. Knopf, 1989).
2 See also Mary Poovey, *Genres of the Credit Economy: Mediating Value in Eighteenth- and Nineteenth-Century Britain* (Chicago: University of Chicago Press, 2008).

Chapter 1 National Identity and a National Literature

1 Laurence Sterne, *A Sentimental Journey through France and Italy* (1768) (London: Penguin Books, 1986), p. 114.
2 Linda Colley, *Britons: Forging the Nation, 1707–1837* (London: Pimlico, 1994), p. 11.
3 On this subject see Paul Langford, *Englishness Identified: Manners and Character 1650–1850* (Oxford: Oxford University Press, 2000).
4 Gerald Newman, *The Rise of English Nationalism: A Cultural History 1740–1830* (New York: St Martin's Press, 1987), pp. 52–3. "The term 'nationalism' was used for the first time in 1798 by Augustin Barruel when, in a history of Jacobinism, he recalls that 'Nationalism, or the love of nation, took the place of the love of mankind in general'" in Antony Easthope, *Englishness and National Culture* (London and New York: Routledge, 1999) p. 49.
5 Ernest Renan, "What is a Nation?" translated by Martin Thom, in Homi K. Bhabha (ed.), *Nation and Narration* (London and New York: Routledge, 1990), pp. 19, 11.
6 Homi Bhabha, "DissemiNation: Time, Narrative, and the Margins of the Modern Nation," in *Nation and Narration*, p. 311.
7 Quoted in Roy Porter, *Enlightenment: Britain and the Creation of the Modern World* (London: Allen Lane/Penguin, 2000), p. 43.
8 Catholics in Britain were awarded full political rights by the Catholic Emancipation Act of 1829, Jews by the Jewish Emancipation Act of 1858. The Test and Corporation Acts, which prevented non-Anglicans from holding public office or attending Oxford or Cambridge, were repealed in 1828.
9 Frances Burney, *The Wanderer* (1814) (Oxford: Oxford University Press, 1991), p. 855.
10 Colley, *Britons*, p. 6.
11 Kathleen Wilson, *The Sense of the People: Politics, Culture and Imperialism in England, 1715–1785* (Cambridge: Cambridge University Press, 1998), p. 283.
12 See John Barrell, *English Literature in History, 1730–80: An Equal, Wide Survey* (London: Hutchinson, 1983).
13 Jonathan Kramnick, *Making the English Canon: Print-Capitalism and the Cultural Past, 1700–1770* (Cambridge: Cambridge University Press, 1998), p. 4.
14 Easthope, *Englishness and National Culture*, p. 55.
15 Howard Erskine-Hill, *The Augustan Idea in English Literature* (London: Edward Arnold, 1983), p. 216. For a contrasting view, see Howard Weinbrot, *Britannia's Issue: The Rise of British Literature from Dryden to Ossian* (Cambridge: Cambridge University Press, 1993).

16 Samuel Johnson, *Lives of the English Poets*, ed. George Birkbeck Hill (Oxford: Clarendon Press, 1905), vol. 1, p. 469.

17 *The Works of John Dryden* (Berkeley: University of California Press, 1956–2000), ed. Edward Hooker, Edward Niles and H. T. Swedenberg, Vol. 1, p. 112 ("Preface to Ovid's Epistles"). See James Anderson Winn, *John Dryden and His World* (New Haven: Yale University Press, 1987), p. 331.

18 Paul Hammond, "Classical Texts: Translations and Transformations," in Steven N. Zwicker (ed.), *The Cambridge Companion to English Literature, 1650–1740* (Cambridge: Cambridge University Press, 1998), p. 159.

19 Claudia N. Thomas, *Alexander Pope and His Eighteenth-Century Women Readers*, (Carbondale and Edwardsville: Southern Illinois University Press, 1994), p. 34.

20 Johnson, *Lives*, 3, p. 240.

21 Quoted in Joseph M. Levine, "The Battle of the Books and the Shield of Achilles," *Eighteenth-Century Life* 9 (1984): 49.

22 Joseph M. Levine, "Ancients and Moderns Reconsidered," *Eighteenth-Century Studies* 15(1) (Fall 1981): 83.

23 Howard Weinbrot, *Britannia's Issue: The Rise of British Literature from Dryden to Ossian* (Cambridge: Cambridge University Press, 1993), pp. 276–81.

24 On the use of this trope, see Earl Wasserman, *The Subtler Language: Critical Readings of Neoclassical and Romantic Poems* (Baltimore: Johns Hopkins University Press, 1959), p. 82.

25 Weinbrot, pp. 288–9.

26 Maynard Mack, *Alexander Pope: A Life* (New Haven and London: Yale University Press; New York and London: W. W. Norton, 1985), pp. 71–5; Donna Landry, "Alexander Pope, Lady Wortley Montagu, and the Literature of Social Comment," in Steven N. Zwicker (ed.), *The Cambridge Companion to English Literature 1650–1740* (Cambridge: Cambridge University Press, 1998), pp. 317–20.

27 E. P. Thompson, *Whigs and Hunters: The Origins of the Black Act* (New York: Pantheon, 1975).

28 Laura Brown, *Alexander Pope* (Oxford: Basil Blackwell, 1985), p. 30.

29 Erskine-Hill, *The Augustan Idea*, pp. 240–1.

30 Brown, *Alexander Pope*, p. 31.

31 Quoted in Edwin Jones, *The English Nation: The Great Myth* (Gloucestershire: Sutton, 1998), p. 154.

32 Quoted in Langford, *Englishness Identified*, p. 96.

33 Levine, "The Battle of the Books and the Shield of Achilles," p. 87.

34 Mark Salber Phillips, *Society and Sentiment: Genres of Historical Writing in Britain, 1740–1820* (Princeton: Princeton University Press, 2000), p. xii.

35 Karen O'Brien, *Narratives of Enlightenment: Cosmopolitan History from Voltaire to Gibbon* (Cambridge: Cambridge University Press, 1997), p. 13.

36 Salber Phillips, *Society and Sentiment*, p. 37. For a discussion of Hume's political allegiances, see Wooten, n. 41.

37 Quoted in O'Brien, *Narratives of Enlightenment*, p. 59.

38 Catharine Macaulay, *The History of England from the Accession of James I to That of the Brunswick Line*, 8 vols. (London, 1763–83), Vol. 1, pp. 1, 2.

39 Edward Gibbon, *The Decline and Fall of the Roman Empire*, ed. Dero A. Saunders (Harmondsworth: Penguin, 1981).

40 Porter, *Enlightenment*, p. 231.

41 David Wooten, "David Hume, the Historian," in David Fate Norton (ed.), *The Cambridge Companion to Hume* (pp. 281–313) (Cambridge: Cambridge University Press, 1993), p. 293.

42 David Hume, *History of England*, Vol. V. (Boston: Phillips, Sampson, and Company, 1856), pp. 382, 374.

43 Hayden White, *Metahistory: The Historical Imagination in Nineteenth-Century Europe* (Baltimore: The Johns Hopkins University Press, 1973), p. 55.

44 Natalie Zemon Davis, "History's Two Bodies," *American Historical Review* 93(1) (1988): 1–30, 9.

45 See Bridget Hill, *The Republican Virago: The Life and Times of Catharine Macaulay, Historian* (Oxford: Clarendon Press, 1992).

46 Langford, *Englishness Identified*, p. 528.

47 Quoted in Davis, "History's Two Bodies," p. 7.

48 Catharine Macaulay, *The History of England*, Vol. 7, p. 446.

49 Susan Wiseman, "Catharine Macaulay: History, Republicanism, and the Public Sphere," in Elizabeth Eger, Charlotte Grant, Cliona O'Gallchoir, and Penny Warburton (eds), *Women, Writing and the Public Sphere, 1700–1830* (Cambridge: Cambridge University Press, 2001), pp. 181–99, p. 193.

50 Thomas Percy, *Reliques of Ancient English Poetry* (1765) (London: George Routledge and Sons, 1857), p. lxxv.

51 Samuel Johnson, *Lives of the English Poets*, ed. Geroge Birkbeck Hill (Oxford: Clarendon Press, 1905), vol. 3.

52 The committee concluded that Macpherson

> was in use to supply chasms, and to give connections, by inserting passages which he did not find, and to add what he conceived to be dignity and delicacy to the original composition, by striking out passages, by softening incidents, by refining the language, in short by changing what he considered too simple or too rude for a modern ear, and elevating what in his opinion was below the standard of good poetry (quoted in Davis, "History's Two Bodies," p. 89).

53 *The Poems of Ossian*, trans. J. McPherson, vol. 1 ("Fingal") (Edinburgh: printed by Thomas Oliver, 1805), p. 185.

54 Katie Trumpener, *Bardic Nationalism: The Romantic Novel and the British Empire* (Princeton: Princeton University Press, 1997), pp. 71, 75.

55 Leith Davis, *Acts of Union: Scotland and the Literary Negotiation of the British Nation, 1707–1830* (Stanford: Stanford University Press, 1998), p. 84.

56 Adam Potkay, "Virtue and Manners in Macpherson's *Poems of Ossian*," *PMLA* 107(1) (1992): 121.

57 See Nick Groom, "Fragments, Reliques, & MSS: Chatterton and Percy," in Nick Groom (ed.), *Thomas Chatterton and Romantic Culture* (New York: St Martin's Press, 1999), pp. 188–210.

58 *The Letters of Horace Walpole, Fourth Earl of Orford*, ed. Paget Jackson Toynbee (Oxford: Clarendon Press, 1903–5), Vol. 6, p. 447.

59 Maurice Morgann, *Shakespearean Criticism*, ed. Daniel A. Fineman (Oxford: Oxford University Press, 1972), p. 170. Quoted in Michael Dobson, *The Making of the National Poet: Shakespeare, Adaptation and Authorship, 1660–1769* (Oxford: Clarendon Press, 1992), p. 228.

60 Dobson, *The Making of the National Poet*, p. 219.

61 See Deidre Shauna Lynch, *The Economy of Character: Novels, Market Culture, and the Business of Inner Meaning* (Chicago: University of Chicago Press, 1998), pp. 133–8.

62 Laura Rosenthal, "(Re)Writing Lear: Literary Property and Dramatic Authorship," in John Brewer and Susan Staves (eds), *Early Modern Conceptions of Property,* (London and New York: Routledge, 1995), p. 323.

63 Rosenthal, "(Re)Writing Lear," p. 329.

64 Lewis Theobald, *Shakespeare Restored* (London, 1726; repr. 1971), p. v. Quoted in Simon Jarvis, *Scholars and Gentlemen: Shakespearean Textual Criticism and Representations of Scholarly Labour, 1725–1765* (Oxford: Clarendon Press, 1995), p. 64.

65 Jarvis, p. 104.
66 Margreta de Grazia, *Shakespeare Verbatim: The Reproduction of Authenticity and the 1790 Apparatus* (Oxford: Clarendon Press, 1991), pp. 179, 205.
67 November 1758. Quoted in Dobson, *The Making of the National Poet*, p. 182.
68 Porter, *Enlightenment*, p. 93.
69 Jane Austen, *Mansfield Park* (1814) (Oxford: Oxford University Press, 1970), p. 306.

Chapter 2 Print Culture and the Public Sphere

1 Isaac Watts, *The Improvement of the Mind* (London: Printed for James Brackstone, 1741), p. 340.
2 William Law, *A Serious Call to a Devout and Holy Life* (London: Printed for William Innys, 1729), p. 71.
3 See Nigel Smith, *Perfection Proclaimed: Language and Literature in English Radical Religion, 1640–1660* (Oxford: Clarendon Press, 1989); and N. H. Keeble, *The Literary Culture of Nonconformity in Later Seventeenth-Century England* (Athens: The University of Georgia Press, 1987).
4 The foremost theorist of this development is Jürgen Habermas. See *The Structural Transformation of the Public Sphere: An Inquiry into a Category of Bourgeois Society*, trans. Thomas Burger with the assistance of Frederick Lawrence (Cambridge, MA: The MIT Press, 1995).
5 Benedict Anderson, *Imagined Communities: Reflections on the Origins and Spread of Nationalism* (London: Verso, 1991), p. 35.
6 See Joan Landes, "The Public and the Private Sphere: A Feminist Reconsideration," in Johanna Meehan (ed.), *Feminists Read Habermas: Gendering the Subject of Discourse* (London: Routledge, 1995), pp. 91–117; and Nancy Fraser, "Rethinking the Public Sphere: A Contribution to the Critique of Actually Existing Democracy," in Craig Calhoun (ed.), *Habermas and the Public Sphere* (Cambridge: The MIT Press, 1992), pp. 109–43.
7 John Brewer, *The Pleasures of the Imagination: English Culture in the Eighteenth Century* (New York: Farrar, Strauss, Giroux, 1997), p. 35.
8 Peter Stallybrass and Allon White, *The Politics and Poetics of Transgression* (Ithaca: Cornell University Press, 1986), p. 97.
9 On women's public activities, see Amanda Vickery, *The Gentleman's Daughter: Women's Lives in Georgian England* (New Haven and London: Yale University Press, 1998); and Lawrence Klein, "Gender and the Public/Private Distinction: Some Questions about Evidence and Analytic Procedure," *Eighteenth-Century Studies* 29(1) (Fall 1995): 97–111.
10 John Dryden, *Religio Laici* (1682), ll. 400–1; quoted in Brewer, *The Pleasures of the Imagination*, p. 36; Olivia Smith, *The Politics of Language, 1791–1819* (Oxford: Clarendon Press, 1984), p. 161.
11 Hester Chapone, *Letters on the Improvement of the Mind* (1773), *Female Education in the Age of Enlightenment*, Vol. 2 (London: Pickering and Chatto, 1996), p. 205.
12 Habermas, *The Structural Transformation of the Public Sphere*, p. 43.
13 Terry Eagleton, *The Function of Criticism: From* The Spectator *to Post-Structuralism* (London: Verso, 1984), pp. 21, 22.
14 Kathryn Shevelow, *Women and Print Culture: The Construction of Femininity in the Early Periodical* (London: Routledge, 1989), p. 3.
15 Erin Mackie, *Market a la Mode: Fashion, Commodity and Gender in "The Tatler" and "The Spectator"* (Baltimore: Johns Hopkins University Press, 1997), p. 5. See also Mackie's excellent introduction to *The Commerce of Everyday Life: Selections from "The Tatler" and "The Spectator"* (Boston: Bedford/St Martins, 1998).
16 Samuel Johnson, *Selected Writings* (edited by Patrick Cruttwell) (Penguin: London, 1986), pp. 432, 433.

17 Quoted in Paula McDowell, *The Women of Grub Street: Press, Politics and Gender in the London Literary Marketplace, 1678–1730* (Oxford: Clarendon Press, 1998), pp. 243–4.

18 See Catherine Gallagher, *Nobody's Story: The Vanishing Acts of Women in the Marketplace, 1670–1820* (Berkeley: University of California Press, 1994), p. 131.

19 Some readers have seen Astrea as a reference to Aphra Behn, who adopted this name. See Ros Ballaster, *Seductive Forms: Women's Amatory Fiction from 1684 to 1740* (Oxford: Clarendon Press, 1992).

20 Delarivier Manley, *The New Atalantis*, edited and with an introduction by Ros Ballaster (London: Penguin Books, 1991), p. 13.

21 Manley had a personally rancorous relationship with Steele, who seems to have refused to lend her money at a particularly low point in her life. They later reconciled.

22 McDowell, *The Women of Grub Street*, 1998, p. 232.

23 For discussion of the keys, see Gallagher, *Nobody's Story*, pp. 125–7.

24 On the former, see Gallagher, *Nobody's Story*; on the latter, William Warner, *Licensing Entertainment: The Elevation of Novel Reading in Britain, 1684–1750* (Berkeley: University of California Press, 1998), pp. 97–111.

25 Marshall McLuhan, *The Gutenberg Galaxy* (University of Toronto Press, 1962) pp. 304, 309.

26 *Poetry and Prose of Alexander Pope*, ed. Aubrey Williams (Boston: Houghton Mifflin, 1969), p. 304.

27 Pope, Swift, Gay, Arbuthnot, Thomas Parnell, and the Tory politician Lord Oxford formed the Scriblerus Club in 1713. They invented a pedantic modern writer named Martin Scriblerus. Although the club disbanded in 1714, Pope used the Scriblerus character to write the introduction to *The Dunciad* and some of its fake footnotes.

28 Colley Cibber, *A Letter from Mr Cibber to Mr Pope, Inquiring in the Motives that might induce him in his Satyrical Works, to be so frequently fond of Mr Cibber's name* (London: 1742).

29 Emrys Jones, "Pope and Dulness," *Proceedings of the British Academy* (1998) 54: 231–63.

30 Alexander Pope to John Arbuthnot, 2 August 1734, *Correspondence*, ed. George Sherburn (Oxford: Clarendon Press, 1956), p. 423.

31 Joseph Levine, "Ancients and Moderns Reconsidered," *Eighteenth-Century Studies* 15 (1981): 82.

32 Richard Bentley (1662–1742) was a noted classical scholar and the master of Trinity College, Cambridge. He was much ridiculed for publishing a version of *Paradise Lost* in which he set off in brackets many passages he did not think Milton could have written.

33 See Robert DeMaria, *Johnson's Dictionary and the Language of Learning* (Chapel Hill: University of North Carolina Press, 1986); and Allen Reddick, *The Making of Johnson's Dictionary 1746–1773* (Cambridge: Cambridge University Press, 1990).

34 *Samuel Johnson, Selected Poetry and Prose*, ed. and Introduction by Frank Brady and W. K. Wimsatt (Berkeley: University of California Press, 1977).

35 For the significance of this association, see John Barrell, *English Literature in History, 1730–80: An Equal, Wide, Survey* (New York: St Martin's Press, 1983).

36 See Deirdre Lynch, "'Beating the Track of the Alphabet': Samuel Johnson, Tourism, and the ABCs of Modern Authority," *ELH* 57(2) (Summer 1990): 357–405; Martin Wechselblatt, "The Pathos of Example: Professionalism and Colonization in Johnson's 'Preface' to the Dictionary," *Yale Journal of Criticism* 9(2) (Fall 1996): 381–403; Rajani Sudan, "Lost in Lexicography: Legitimating Cultural Identity in Johnson's Preface to the Dictionary," *The Eighteenth Century: Theory and Interpretation* 39(2) (Summer 1998): 127–46.

Chapter 3 The City

1 M. Dorothy George, *London Life in the Eighteenth Century* (Harmondsworth: Penguin Books, 1925, 1965), p. 74.

2 John Graunt, *Natural and Political Observations made upon the Bills of Mortality*, edited and with an introduction by Walter F. Wilcox (Baltimore: The Johns Hopkins University Press,

1939), p. 35. For information about Graunt's methodology, see Philip Kreager, "New Light on Graunt," *Population Studies* 42 (1988): 129–40.

3 Gregory King, *Two Tracts: Natural and Political Observations upon the State and Condition of England* (London: 1696), p. 44.

4 Roy Porter, *London: A Social History* (London: Penguin Books, 1996), p. 134.

5 Corbyn Morris, *Observations on the Past Growth and Present State of the City of London* (London: 1758), p. 88.

6 Richard Price, *Observations on Reversionary Payments. To which are added four essays, on different subjects on the Doctrine of Life Annuities and Political Arithmetic* (Dublin: 1781), p. 158.

7 See Neil McKendrick, John Brewer, and J. H. Plumb, *The Birth of a Consumer Society: The Commercialization of Eighteenth-Century England* (London: Europa, 1982).

8 See Laura Brown, *Ends of Empire: Women and Ideology in Early Eighteenth-Century Literature* (Ithaca: Cornell University Press, 1993).

9 Saunders Welch, *"A Proposal To render effectual a Plan, To remove the Nuisance of Common Prostitutes from the Streets of the Metropolis"* (London: 1758), p. 17. Paraphrased in Paul Langford, *A Polite and Commercial People: England 1727–1783* (Oxford: Oxford University Press, 1992), p. 144.

10 Roy Porter, *English Society in the Eighteenth Century* (London: Penguin, 1990), p. 135.

11 Paul Langford, *A Polite and Commercial People: England 1727–1783*, p. 156.

12 E. P. Thompson, *Whigs and Hunters* (New York: Pantheon, 1975), p. 258.

13 Ian Watt, *The Rise of the Novel* (Berkeley: The University of California Press, 1957), p. 32.

14 Daniel Defoe, *Moll Flanders* (New York and London: W. W. Norton, 2004).

15 From Captain Alexander Smith, *The History of the Lives of the Most Noted Highway-Men, Foot-pads, House-Breakers, Shoplifts, and Cheats of both Sexes... for above fifty years last past*, 2nd edn (London, 1714). Included in the Norton Critical Edition of *Moll Flanders*.

16 See, for example, Wayne C. Booth, "Troubles with Irony in Earlier Fiction," in *The Rhetoric of Fiction* (Chicago: The University of Chicago Press, 1961); and Maximillian E. Novak, "Defoe's 'Indifferent Monitor': The Complexity of 'Moll Flanders'," *Eighteenth-Century Studies* 3.3 (Spring 1970): 351–9.

17 On Moll's experience in Newgate, see John Richetti, *Defoe's Narratives: Situations and Structures* (Oxford: Oxford University Press, 1975): "What matters about Newgate is not its concrete existence as a wretched habitation but its power to suppress and transform the self" (p. 134).

18 Virginia Woolf, *The Common Reader*, First Series (New York: Harcourt, Brace & World, 1925), pp. 89–97.

19 On the incest episode, see Ellen Pollak, "'Moll Flanders', Incest, and the Structure of Exchange," *The Eighteenth-Century: Theory and Interpretation* 30(1) (1989): 3–21.

20 As the moral and literary climate changed in the mid-eighteenth century, Haywood wrote more morally instructive novels, most famously *The History of Miss Betsy Thoughtless* (1751).

21 See Ros Ballaster, *Seductive Forms: Women's Amatory Fiction from 1684–1740* (Oxford: Oxford University Press, 1998); Catherine Gallagher, *Nobody's Story: The Vanishing Acts of Women in the Market Place, 1670–1820* (Berkeley: University of California Press, 1994); William Warner, *Licensing Entertainment: The Elevation of Novel-Reading in Britain, 1684–1750* (Berkeley: University of California Press, 1998); on romance, see Michel McKeon, *The Origins of the English Novel, 1600–1740* (Baltimore: The Johns Hopkins University Press, 1987).

22 Eliza Haywood, "Fantomina: Or, Love in a Maze (1724)," in Robert Demaria Jr, *British Literature 1640–1789* (Oxford: Blackwell, 1996), pp. 786–803.

23 Terry Castle, *Masquerade and Civilization: The Carnivalesque in Eighteenth-Century English Culture and Fiction* (Stanford: Stanford University Press, 1986), pp. 2, 28.

24 Swift also famously dubbed the play a "Newgate pastoral." For the play's relationship to the conventions of the pastoral, see William Empson, *Some Versions of Pastoral* (New York: New Directions, 1974).

25 See Bertrand Goldgar, *Walpole and the Wits: The Relation of Politics to Literature 1722–1742* (Lincoln: University of Nebraska Press, 1976).

26 On this subject, see Michael Denning, "Beggars and Thieves: The Ideology of the Gang," *Literature and History* 8 (1982): 41–55.

27 For more on the negotiation of identity in Boswell's *London Journal*, see Felicity Nussbaum, *The Autobiographical Subject: Gender and Ideology in Eighteenth-Century England* (Baltimore: The Johns Hopkins University Press, 1989).

Chapter 4 The Countryside

1 Raymond Williams, *The Country and the City* (London: Chatto and Windus, 1973), p. 9.

2 Donna Landry, *The Invention of the Countryside: Hunting, Walking and Ecology in English Literature, 1671–1831* (New York: Palgrave, 2001), p. 1.

3 E. P. Thompson, *Whigs and Hunters: The Origins of the Black Act* (New York: Random House, 1975), p. 197. For other interpretations of the significance of the Black Act, see Pat Rogers, "The Waltham Blacks and the Black Act," *Historical Journal* 17 (1974): 465–86, which argues that the act was necessary to curb rural unrest; and Eveline Cruikshanks and Howard Erskine-Hill, "The Waltham Black Act and Jacobitism," *Journal of British Studies* 24 (1985): 358–65, which argues for the real relationship between the disguised "Blacks" and Jacobites.

4 See John Allen Stevenson, "Black George and the Black Act," *Eighteenth-Century Fiction* 8(3) (April 1996): 355–82.

5 See Peter King, "Legal Change, Customary Right, and Social Conflict in Late Eighteenth-Century England: The Origins of the Great Gleaning Case of 1788," *Law and History Review* 10(1) (Spring 1992): 1–31, 5.

6 Roy Porter, *English Society in the Eighteenth Century* (Penguin Books, 1982).

7 Arthur Young, *Inquiry into the Propriety of Applying Wastes to the Better Maintenance and Support of the Poor* (Bury: Printed by J. Rackham, 1801, p. 51.

8 J. M. Neeson, *Commoners: Common Right, Enclosure and Social Change in England, 1700–1820* (Cambridge: Cambridge University Press, 1993), p. 12.

9 Quoted in Neeson, *Commoners*, p. 292.

10 Greg Laugero, "Infrastructures of Enlightenment: Road-making, the Public Sphere, and the Emergence of Literature," *Eighteenth-Century Studies* 29(1) (1996): 45–67, 50.

11 Roy Porter, *English Society in the Eighteenth Century* (London: Allen Lane, 1982), p. 217.

12 Jane Austen, *Northanger Abbey* (New York: W. W. Norton, 2004), p. 136.

13 Elizabeth K. Helsinger, *Rural Scenes and National Representation: Britain 1815–1850* (Princeton: Princeton University Press, 1997), p. 13.

14 Maynard Mack, *The Garden and the City: Retirement and Politics in the Later Poetry of Pope* (Toronto: University of Toronto Press, 1969), p. 82.

15 Williams, *The Country and the City*, p. 38.

16 Andrew Marvell, *The Garden* (1681), ll. 41–8.

17 See, for example: Elizabeth Wahl, *Invisible Relations: Representations of Female Intimacy in the Age of Enlightenment* (Stanford: Stanford University Press, 1999); Harriette Andreadis, *Sappho in Early Modern England: Female Same-Sex Literary Erotics, 1550–1714* (Chicago: Chicago University Press, 2001).

18 The first passage is from *Winter Night* (ll. 253–9), the second from *Winter: A Poem* (ll. 74–9), though they appear in slightly revised form in the expanded version of *The Seasons* in "Autumn" (ll. 1030–4).

19 Johnson, "Life of Gay," in George Birkbeck Hill, *Lives of the English Poets*, Vol. II (Oxford: Oxford University Press, 1905), p. 269.

20 John Barrell, *The Dark Side of the Landscape: The Rural Poor in English Painting 1730–1840* (Cambridge: Cambridge University Press, 1980), p. 57.

21 Crabbe's poem has been called an anti-pastoral.

22 See John Sekora, *Luxury: The Concept in British Thought, Eden to Smollett* (Baltimore: Johns Hopkins University Press, 1977).

23 Alfred Lutz, "'The Deserted Village' and the Politics of Genre," *Modern Language Quarterly* 55(2) (1994): 149–68, 155.

24 Barrell, *The Dark Side of the Landscape*, p. 78.

25 Barrell, *The Dark Side of the Landscape*, p. 78.

26 Barrell, *The Dark Side of the Landscape*, p. 37.

27 Karen O'Brien, "Imperial Georgic, 1660–1789," in Gerald MacLean, Donna Landry, and Joseph P. Ward, *The Country and the City Revisited* (Cambridge: Cambridge University Press, 1999), pp. 160–80, p. 163.

28 Donna Landry, *Muses of Resistance: Laboring Class Women's Poetry in Britain, 1739–1796* (Cambridge: Cambridge University Press, 1990), p. 22.

29 O'Brien, "Imperial Georgic, 1660–1789," p. 161.

30 O'Brien, "Imperial Georgic, 1660–1789," p. 160.

31 *Samuel Johnson: Selected Poetry and Prose*, ed. and Introduction by Frank Brady and W. K. Wimsatt (Berkeley: University of California Press, 1977), p. 642.

32 Roger Lonsdale, *The Poems of Thomas Gray, William Collins, Oliver Goldsmith* (London and New York; Longman, 1969).

33 John Guillory, *Cultural Capital: The Problem of Literary Canon Formation* (Chicago and London: The University of Chicago Press, 1993), p. 86.

34 There have been some interesting discussions of the effect of Gray's probably-never-acted-upon homosexuality on his poetry recently. See, for example, George Haggerty, "O Lachrymarum Fons: Tears, Poetry and Desire in Gray," *Eighteenth-Century Studies* 30(1) (1996): 81–95; and Robert Gleckner, *Gray Agonistes: Thomas Gray and Masculine Friendship* (Baltimore: Johns Hopkins University Press, 1997).

35 William Empson, "Proletarian Literature," from *Some Versions of the Pastoral* (New York: W. W. Norton, 1938), p. 4.

36 For an interesting account of the New Critics' engagement with the poem, see William H. Epstein, "Counter Intelligence, Cold War Criticism and Eighteenth-Century Studies," *ELH* 57(1) (1990): 63–99.

37 Donna Landry, *The Muses of Resistance: Laboring-Class Women's Poetry in Britain, 1739–1796* (Cambridge: Cambridge University Press, 1990), p. 130.

38 William Wordsworth, "At the Grave of Burns" (1803), ll. 34–6.

Chapter 5 Individuality and Imagination

1 Laurence Sterne, *The Life and Opinions of Tristram Shandy* (Harmondsworth: Penguin Books, 1986).

2 Charles Taylor, *Sources of the Self: The Making of Modern Identity* (Cambridge: Harvard University Press, 1989), p. 172.

3 Anthony Collins, *An Answer to Mr Clarke's Third Defense to His Letter to Mr Dodwell* (1708), p. 66. Quoted in Roy Porter, *Enlightenment: Britain and the Creation of the Modern World* (Penguin: London, 2000), p. 167.

4 Isaac Alogist, *Mechanical Essay on the Operations of the Mind* (1729). Quoted in Dennis Todd, *Imagining Monsters: Miscreations of the Self in Eighteenth-Century England* (Chicago: University of Chicago Press, 1995), p. 137.

5 Todd, *Imagining Monsters*, p. 138.

6 Maria Edgeworth's *Belinda* recounts such a story, as does Elizabeth Inchbald's *Nature and Art*, and Bernadin de Saint-Pierre's *Paul and Virginie*.

7 C. B. McPherson, *The Political Theory of Possessive Individualism: Hobbes to Locke* (Oxford: Clarendon Press, 1962), p. 3.

8 Walter Chernaik, *Sexual Freedom in Restoration Literature* (Cambridge: Cambridge University Press, 1995), p. 4.

9 John Brewer, *The Pleasures of the Imagination: English Culture in the Eighteenth Century* (New York: Farrar, Strauss, Giroux, 1997), p. 108.

10 Ian Watt, *The Rise of the Novel* (Berkeley: University of California Press, 1955), p. 206.

11 N. H. Keeble, *The Literary Culture of Nonconformity in Later Seventeenth-Century England* (Athens: University of Georgia Press, 1987), p. 78.

12 John Bunyan, *Grace Abounding to the Chief of Sinners* (Harmondsworth: Penguin Books, 1987), p. 2.

13 Chernaik, *Sexual Freedom in Restoration Literature*, p. 2.

14 See Paul Hammond, "Censorship in the Manuscript Transmission of Restoration Poetry," *Essays and Studies 1993: Literature and Censorship*, ed. by Nigel Smith (Cambridge: The English Association, 1993): 39–63.

15 William Empson, "Rochester," in *Argufying: Essays on Literature and Culture*, ed. John Haffenden (London: Hogarth Press, 1988), p. 275.

16 Thomas Sprat, *The History of the Royal Society*, 1667, Part Two, Section XX, excerpted in Geoffrey Tillotson, Paul Fussell, and Marshall Waingrow, *Eighteenth-Century Literature* (New York: Harcourt Brace Jovanovich, 1969), p. 27.

17 There was a tradition of poems on this topic, including Behn's *The Disappointment*. See Leo Braudy, "Remembering Masculinity: Premature Ejaculation Poetry of the Seventeenth Century," *Michigan Quarterly Review* 33 (1994): 177–201.

18 Carole Fabricant, "Rochester's World of Imperfect Enjoyment," *Journal of English and Germanic Philology* 73 (1974): 38–50.

19 See Terry Castle, *Clarissa's Ciphers: Meaning and Disruption in Richardson's Clarissa* (Ithaca: Cornell University Press, 1982); Terry Eagleton, *The Rape of Clarissa: Writing, Sexuality and the Class Struggle in Samuel Richardson* (Cambridge: Basil Blackwell, 1982); William Warner, *Reading Clarissa: The Struggles of Interpretation* (New Haven: Yale University Press, 1979). See also Sandra MacPherson, "Lovelace, Ltd," *ELH* 65.1 (Spring 1998): 99–121.

20 James Boswell, *Life of Samuel Johnson* (April 6, 1772).

21 Letter to Richardson, January 1749. Quoted in John Mullan, *Sentiment and Sociability: The Language of Feeling in the Eighteenth Century* (Oxford: Clarendon Press, 1988), p. 109.

22 For the idea that Clarissa is a captivity narrative, see Nancy Armstrong, "Reclassifying *Clarissa*: Fiction and the Making of the Modern Middle Class," in *Clarissa and Her Readers: New Essays for the Clarissa Project*, edited and introduced by Carol Houlihan Flynn and Edward Copeland (New York: AMS Press, 1999), pp. 19–45.

23 See Christopher Hill, "Clarissa Harlowe and Her Times," *Essays in Criticism* 5 (1955): 315–40.

24 Frances Ferguson, "Rape and the Rise of the Novel," *Representations* 20 (Fall 1987): 88–112, 99.

25 Samuel Richardson, *Clarissa: or, the History of a Yong Lady* (Harmondsworth: Penguin, 1985).

26 *Critical Review* 9 (January 1760): 73. Quoted in Ian Campbell Ross, *Laurence Sterne: A Life* (Oxford: Oxford University Press, 2001), p. 13.

27 Quoted in Ross, *Laurence Sterne*, p. 18.

28 Quoted in Ross, *Laurence Sterne*, p. 204.

29 Thomas Keymer, *Sterne, the Moderns and the Novel* (Oxford: Oxford University Press, 2002), pp. 49–63.

30 *The Monthly Review* 32 (Feb. 1765): 125–6. Quoted in John Mullan, *Sentiment and Sociability: The Language of Feeling in the Eighteenth Century* (Oxford: Clarendon Press, 1988), p. 152.

31 Dennis Todd, *Imagining Monsters: Miscreations of the Self in Eighteenth-Century England* (Chicago: University of Chicago Press, 1995), p. 136.

32 Thomas Keymer, *Sterne, the Moderns and the Novel*, p. 211.

33 Jonathan Lamb, *Sterne's Fiction and the Double Principle* (Cambridge: Cambridge University Press, 1989), p. 68. Lamb argues that Sterne rejects Locke's idea of mental processes guided by reason and self-reflection in favor of the more radically contingent models of associationism formulated by Hume and Hartley.

34 Quoted in Lamb, *Sterne's Fiction*, p. 65.

35 Keymer, *Sterne, the Moderns and the Novel*, p. 86.

Chapter 6 Religious Experience

1 Christopher Hill, *The Century of Revolution, 1603–1714* (London: Routledge, 1980), p. 211.

2 Paula McDowell, "Enlightenment Enthusiasms and the Spectacular Failure of the Philadelphian Society," *Eighteenth-Century Studies* 35(4) (2002): 515–33, 518.

3 McDowell, "Enlightenment Enthusiasms and the Spectacular Failure of the Philadelphian Society," p. 518.

4 J. Paul Hunter, *Before Novels: The Cultural Contexts of Eighteenth-Century English Fiction* (W. W. Norton, 1990), p. 134.

5 Harriet Guest, *A Form of Sound Words: The Religious Poetry of Christopher Smart* (Oxford University Press, 1989), p. 6.

6 John Sitter, *Literary Loneliness in Mid-Eighteenth-Century England* (Ithaca: Cornell University Press, 1982), p. 68.

7 *Journal of George Fox, Being an Historical Account of the Life, Travels, Sufferings, Christian Experiences and Labour of Love in the Work of the Ministry...* (London: W. and F. G. Cash, 1852).

8 Katharine Evans, *A Brief History of the Voyage of Katharine Evans and Sarah Cheevers, to the Island of Malta* (London: J. Sowle, 1715).

9 Phyllis Mack, *Visionary Women: Ecstatic Prophecy in Seventeenth-Century England* (Berkeley, CA: University of California Press, 1992), p. 274.

10 Margaret Fell, *Women's Speaking Justified* (1667), The Augustan Reprint Society, Publication Number 194 (Los Angeles: The William Andrews Clark Memorial Library, 1979), p. 1.

11 "For Fell, woman's inspired speech is not distinct from her gendered identity but rather emerges from her femininity to offer itself and female difference to the broad community of believers" (Teresa Feroli, "Margaret Fell's *Women's Speaking Justified* and Quaker Ideas of Female Subjectivity," unpublished MS, p. 244).

12 *An Old-spelling Critical Edition of Shaftesbury's Letter Concerning Enthusiasm and Sensus Communis: An Essay on the Freedom of Wit and Humor*, ed. Richard B. Wolf (New York: Garland Publishing, Inc, 1988), p. 54.

13 See Phillip Harth, *Swift and Anglican Rationalism* (Chicago: University of Chicago Press, 1961).

14 Jonathan Swift, "A Tale of a Tub," in *Gulliver's Travels and Other Writings* (Boston: Houghton Mifflin, 1960), p. 299.

15 Warren Montag, *The Unthinkable Swift: The Spontaneous Philosophy of a Church of England Man* (Verso: London, 1994), p. 94.

16 Donald Davie, *The Eighteenth-Century Hymn in England* (Cambridge: Cambridge University Press, 1993), p. 32.

17 Samuel Johnson, *Lives of the English Poets*, Vol. III, edited by George Birkbeck Hill (Oxford: Clarendon Press, 1905), p. 306.

18 Quoted in Richard Arnold, *The English Hymn: Studies in a Genre* (New York: Peter Lang, 1995), p. 67.

19 For the former view, see Elie Halevy, *The Birth of Methodism in England*, trans. Bernard Semmel (Chicago: Basic Books, 1971); and E. P. Thompson, *The Making of the English Working Class* (Harmondsworth: Penguin, 1968); for the latter, see Bernard Semmel, *The Methodist Revolution* (New York: Basic Books, 1973).

20 James Boswell, *The Life of Samuel Johnson* (New York and Scarborough: New American Library, 1968), p. 132.

21 Lecture IV in John Drury, *Critics of the Bible 1724–1873* (Cambridge University Press, 1989), p. 71.

22 Christopher Smart (trans.), "Preface" to *The Works of Horace, Translated into Verse with a Prose Interpretation, for the Help of Students* (London: W. Flexney, Johnson & Co., T. Casion, 1767). Four vols, 1: xii.

23 Northrop Frye, "Towards Defining an Age of Sensibility," *Fables of Identity: Studies in Poetic Mythology* (New York: Harcourt, Brace and World, 1963), p. 137.

24 Patricia Meyer Spacks, *The Poetry of Vision: Five Eighteenth-Century Poets* (Cambridge: Harvard University Press, 1967), p. 126.

25 Quoted in William Robert, *Memoirs of the Life and Correspondence of Mrs. Hannah More*, 2 vols (New York, 1835), I, p. 281. Quoted in Paula Feldman (ed.), *British Women Poets of the Romantic Era: An Anthology* (Baltimore: The Johns Hopkins University Press, 1997), p. 470.

26 Thomas Laqueur, *Religion and Respectability: Sunday Schools and Working Class Culture, 1780–1850* (New Haven: Yale University Press, 1976), p. xi.

27 The Reverend James Dore, *A Sermon Preached (on Isaiah XXXIX: 12) at Maze Pond, Southwark, Sept. 27, 1789, for the Benefit of the Society for the Support and Encouragement of Sunday Schools (1789)*. Quoted in Laqueur, *Religion and Respectability*, p. 9.

28 Quoted in Olivia Smith, *The Politics of Language, 1791–1819* (Oxford: Clarendon Press, 1984), p. 94.

Chapter 7 Female Sexuality and Domesticity

1 John Gibson Lockhart, *Memoirs of the Life of Sir Walter Scott* (Boston and New York: Houghton Mifflin, 1902), pp. 596–7.

2 Frances Burney, *Evelina*, ed. Stewart J. Cooke (New York and London: W. W. Norton, 1998), p. 65.

3 "The Blazing World" in Sylvia Bowerbank and Sara Mendelson (eds), *Paper Bodies: A Margaret Cavendish Reader* (Peterborough, Ont.: Broadview Press, 2000), p. 242.

4 Dr John Gregory, *A Father's Legacy to his Daughters* (printed for W. Strahan, T. Cadell in the Strand and W. Creech in Edinburgh, 1774), p. 26.

5 Mary Poovey, *The Proper Lady and the Woman Writer: Ideology as Style in the Works of Mary Wollstonecraft, Mary Shelley and Jane Austen* (Chicago: University of Chicago Press, 1984), pp. ix, 6.

6 Thomas Laqueur, "Orgasm, Generation and the Politics of Reproductive Biology," *Representations* 14 (Spring 1986): 3. See also Laqueur, *Making Sex: Body and Gender from the Greeks to Freud* (Cambridge: Harvard University Press, 1990).

7 Laqueur, "Orgasm, Generation and the Politics of Reproductive Biology": 18, 19.

8 Nancy Armstrong, *Desire and Domestic Fiction: A Political History of the Novel* (Oxford: Oxford University Press, 1987), p. 3.

9 Dr Gregory, quoted in Armstrong, *Desire and Domestic Fiction*, p. 90.

10 See Charlotte Sussman, "Women's Private Reading and Political Action, 1649–1838," in Timothy Morton and Nigel Smith (eds), *Radicalism in British Literary Culture, 1650–1830* (Cambridge: Cambridge University Press, 2002), pp. 133–51.

11 On women's limited access to the public sphere, see Joan Landes, "The Public and the Private Sphere: A Feminist Reconsideration," in Johanna Meehan (ed.), *Feminists Read Habermas: Gendering the Subject of Discourse* (London: Routledge, 1995), pp. 91–117; and Nancy Fraser, "Rethinking the Public Sphere: A Contribution to the Critique of Actually Existing Democracy," in Craig Calhoun (ed.), *Habermas and the Public Sphere*, pp. 109–43 (Cambridge, MA: MIT Press, 1992). The rigidity of the distinction between public and private has been questioned by Amanda Vickery in "Golden Age to Separate Spheres?"

Historical Journal 36 (1993): 383–415; and by Lawrence Klein, "Gender, Conversation and the Public Sphere in Early Eighteenth-Century England," in Judith Still and Michael Worton (eds), *Textuality and Sexuality: Reading Theories and Practices* (New York: St Martin's Press, 1993), pp. 100–16.

12 See Leonore Davidoff and Catherine Hall, *Family Fortunes: Men and Women of the English Middle Class, 1780–1850* (Chicago: University of Chicago Press, 1987).

13 Laura Rosenthal, "Introduction," to *Nightwalkers: Prostitute Narratives from the Eighteenth Century* (Ontario: Broadview Press, 2008), p. xii. See also Rosenthal's *Infamous Commerce: Prostitution in Eighteenth-Century British Literature and Culture* (Ithaca: Cornell University Press, 2006).

14 Valerie Rumbold, *Women's Place in Pope's World* (Cambridge: Cambridge University Press, 1989), p. 58.

15 Tita Chico argues that many commentators associate "cosmetics with the degradation of the social order. Underlying this view is the belief that women are, by nature, simultaneously deceitful and alluring. Thus an artificially beautiful woman turns masculine desire into impotence when her disguise is revealed, and her enjoyment of the entire process confirms her narcissism and danger to the male hegemony" (p. 7). "The Arts of Beauty: Women's Cosmetics and Pope's Ekphrasis," *Eighteenth-Century Life* 26(1) (Winter 2002): 1–23.

16 See, for example, Felicity Nussbaum, *The Brink of All We Hate: English Satires on Women, 1660–1750* (Lexington: University of Kentucky Press, 1984), which argues for Pope's sympathy with Belinda; and Ellen Pollak, *The Poetics of Sexual Myth: Gender Ideology in the Verse of Pope and Swift* (Chicago: University of Chicago Press, 1985), who argues for Pope's objectification of Belinda.

17 Laura Brown, *Alexander Pope* (Oxford: Basil Blackwell, 1985), pp. 9, 23.

18 Michael Seidel, *Satiric Inheritance: Rabelais to Sterne* (Princeton: Princeton University Press), pp. 12–13.

19 Pope was translating the *Iliad* at the same time as he was writing *The Rape of the Lock*, and there is a great deal of intertextuality between the two works.

20 Armstrong, *Desire and Domestic Fiction*, p. 98.

21 Ian Watt, *The Rise of the Novel: Studies in Defoe, Richardson and Fielding* (Berkeley: University of California Press, 1957), p. 161.

22 William Warner, *Licensing Entertainment: The Elevation of Novel Reading in Britain, 1684–1750* (Berkeley: University of California Press, 1998).

23 Samuel Richardson, *Pamela* (Boston: Houghton, Mifflin, Harcourt Riverside edition, 1971), p. 6.

24 Kristina Straub, "Reading the Domestic Servant Woman in *Pamela*," in Lisa Zunshine and Jocelyn Harris (eds), *Approaches to Teaching the Novels of Samuel Richardson* (New York: MLA, 2006).

25 Armstrong, *Desire and Domestic Fiction*, p. 116.

26 Michael McKeon, *The Origins of the English Novel, 1600–1740* (Baltimore: The Johns Hopkins University Press, 1987), p. 378.

27 Helen Thompson, *Ingenuous Subjection: Compliance and Power in the Eighteenth-Century Domestic Novel* (Philadelphia: University of Pennsylvania Press, 2005).

28 William Warner, *Licensing Entertainment: The Elevation of Novel Reading in Britain, 1684–1750* (Berkeley: University of California Press, 1998). See also Tassie Gwiliam, *Samuel Richardson's Fictions of Gender* (Stanford: Stanford University Press, 1993).

29 See Charlotte Sussman, "'I wonder whether poor Miss Sally Godfrey be living or dead': The Married Woman and the Rise of the Novel," *Diacritics* 20(1) (Spring 1990): 88–104.

30 McKeon, *The Origins of the English Novel*, p. 373.

31 Henry Fielding, *Joseph Andrews, with Shamela and Related Writings* (New York and London: W. W. Norton, 1987), p. 283.

32 See Paula McDowell, "Why Fanny Can't Read: Joseph Andrews and the (Ir)relevance of Literacy," in *A Companion to Eighteenth-Century English Novel and Culture*, ed. Paula Backscheider and Catherine Ingrassia (Cambridge: Blackwell, 2005), pp. 167–91. See also Judith Frank, "Literacy, Desire and the Novel: From *Shamela* to *Joseph Andrews*," *Yale Journal of Criticism* 6 (1993): 157–74.

33 Rosenthal, "Introduction," p. xiv.

34 See Bradford Mudge, *The Whore's Story: Women, Pornography, and the British Novel, 1684–1830* (Oxford: Oxford University Press, 2000).

35 John Cleland, *Fanny Hill; or, Memoirs of a Woman of Pleasure* (1748–9), (Harmondsworth, Middlesex, England: Penguin Books, 1985), p. 62.

36 Lisa Moore, *Dangerous Intimacies: Towards a Sapphic History of the British Novel* (Durham, NC: Duke University Press, 1997), p. 56.

37 On the relationship between Leapor and other female poets and Swift, see Margaret Doody, "Swift Among the Women," *Yearbook of English Studies* 18 (1988): 68–92.

38 See Laura Mandell, "Demystifying (with) the Repugnant Female Body: Mary Leapor and Feminist Literary History," *Criticism* 38(4) (Fall 1996): 551–82.

39 On the topic of women poets' satirical depiction of the quotidian world, see Doody, "Swift among the Women."

40 Donna Landry, *The Muses of Resistance: Laboring-Class Women's Poetry in Britain, 1739–1796* (Cambridge: Cambridge University Press, 1990), p. 114.

41 *Maria, or the Wrongs of Woman* (Oxford: Oxford University Press, 1976), p. 83.

42 *Maria*, p. 83.

43 *Maria*, pp. 84–5.

44 Frances Burney, *Evelina*, ed. Stewart J. Cooke (New York, London: W. W. Norton, 1998), p. 70. Of course, the joke here is that there were any number of conduct books, yet none would truly prepare Evelina for the situations she encounters – indeed most seem to offer no behavioral solutions at all, other than silent suffering.

45 Poovey, *The Proper Lady*, p. 21.

46 James Fordyce, *Sermons to Young Women* (London: Printed for D. Payne, 1766).

47 The phrase is Poovey's.

48 Margaret Doody notes that Burney uses "shopping" as a verb for the first time in English. On this topic in Burney, see Elizabeth Kowaleski-Wallace, *Consuming Subjects: Women, Shopping and Business in the Eighteenth Century* (New York: Columbia University Press, 1997).

49 Armstrong, *Desire and Domestic Fiction*, p. 48.

50 Kristina Straub, *Divided Fictions: Fanny Burney and Feminine Strategy* (Lexington: Kentucky University Press, 1987).

Chapter 8 Wit and Sensibility

1 See Peter Stallybrass and Allon White, *The Politics and Poetics of Transgression* (Ithaca: Cornell University Press, 1986).

2 Peter Holland, *The Ornament of Action: Text and Performance in Restoration Comedy* (Cambridge: Cambridge University Press, 1979), pp. 19–54.

3 Norman N. Holland, *The First Modern Comedies: The Significance of Etherege, Wycherley and Congreve* (Cambridge: Harvard University Press, 1959), p. 103.

4 Peter Hynes, "Richard Steele and the Genealogy of Sentimental Drama: A Reading of *The Conscious Lovers*," in *Papers on Language and Literature* 40(2) (2004): 142–66, p. 150.

5 Lisa Freeman, *Character's Theater: Genre and Identity on the Eighteenth-Century English Stage* (Philadelphia: University of Pennsylvania Press, 2002), p. 96.

6 Quoted in Hynes, "Richard Steele and the Genealogy of Sentimental Drama," p. 147.

7 Sir Richard Steele, "The Conscious Lovers," in David W. Lindsay (ed.), *The Beggar's Opera and Other Eighteenth-century Plays* (London: J. M. Dent, 1993), p. 97.

8 Freeman, *Character's Theater*, p. 196.

9 Janet Todd, *Sensibility: An Introduction* (London, New York: Methuen, 1986), p. 4.

10 Northrop Frye, "Towards Defining an Age of Sensibility," in *Fables of Identity: Studies in Poetic Mythology* (New York: Harcourt, Brace and World, 1963), p. 131.

11 Sterne, 1768, quoted in John Mullan, *Sentiment and Sociability: The Language of Feeling in the Eighteenth Century* (London: Clarendon Press, 1988), p. 158.

12 Laurence Sterne, *A Sentimental Journey through France and Italy* (Harmondsworth: Penguin, 1986), p. 141.

13 Mullan, *Sentiment and Sociability*, p. 61.

14 Lynn Festa, *Sentimental Figures of Empire in Eighteenth-Century Britain and France* (Baltimore: The Johns Hopkins University Press, 2006), p. 74.

15 Robert Markley, "Sentimentality as Performance: Shaftsbury, Sterne and the Theatrics of Virtue," in Felicity Nussbaum and Laura Brown (eds), *The New Eighteenth Century: Theory, Politics, English Literature* (New York: Methuen, 1987), pp. 210–11, 223.

16 Markman Ellis, *The Politics of Sensibility: Race, Gender and Commerce in the Sentimental Novel* (Cambridge: Cambridge University Press, 1996), p. 217.

17 Frye, "Age of Sensibility," p. 135.

18 Markham Peacock, *The Critical Opinions of William Wordsworth* (Baltimore: Johns Hopkins University Press, 1950), p. 351 (from a letter of 1835).

19 I discuss these themes in greater depth in "The Art of Oblivion: Charlotte Smith and Helen of Troy," *Studies in Eighteenth-Century Culture* 27 (1998): 131–47.

20 Adela Pinch, *Strange Fits of Passion: Epistemologies of Emotion, Hume to Austen* (Stanford, CA: Stanford University Press, 1996), p. 63.

Chapter 9 Trade and Travel

1 *Spectator* No. 69 (Saturday, May 19, 1711). In Erin Mackie (ed.), *The Commerce of Everyday Life: Selections from "The Tatler" and "The Spectator"* (Boston: Bedford/St Martins, 1998), p. 205.

2 Linda Colley, *Britons: Forging the Nation 1707–1837* (London: Pimlico, 1992), p. 65.

3 Quoted in Roy Porter, *Enlightenment: Britain and the Creation of the Modern World* (London: Allen Lane, 2000), p. 354.

4 Edward Said, *Orientalism* (New York: Penguin, 1978).

5 Mary Louise Pratt, *Imperial Eyes: Travel Writing and Transculturation* (London and New York: Routledge, 1992), pp. 51, 61.

6 Quoted in Chloe Chard, *Pleasure and Guilt on the Grand Tour: Travel Writing and Imaginative Geography 1600–1830* (Manchester: Manchester University Press, 1999), p. 4.

7 See Percy G. Adams, *Travel Literature and the Evolution of the Novel* (Lexington: Kentucky University Press, 1983); Michael McKeon, *The Origins of the English Novel, 1600–1740* (Baltimore: Johns Hopkins University Press, 1987).

8 Quoted in Pratt, *Imperial Eyes*, p. 71.

9 Quoted in Pratt, *Imperial Eyes*, p. 74.

10 Thus, Europe and other places seem to occupy not only two different places, but also two different times. See Johannes Fabian, *Time and the Other: How Anthropology Makes its Object* (New York: Columbia University Press, 1983).

11 Oliver Goldsmith, *The Citizen of the World*, letter XXXIII (1760), in Arthur Friedman (ed.), *Collected Works of Oliver Goldsmith*, Vol. II (Oxford: Clarendon Press, 1966). On Goldsmith's use of chinoiserie, see David Porter, *Ideographia: The Chinese Cipher in Early Modern Europe* (Stanford: Stanford University Press, 2001), pp. 138–41.

12 Balachandra Rajan, *Under Western Eyes: India from Milton to Macaulay* (Durham: Duke University Press, 1999), p. 71.

13 Bridget Orr, *Empire on the English Stage 1660–1714* (Cambridge: Cambridge University Press, 2001), p. 16.

14 Samuel Johnson, "Dryden," in George Birkbeck (ed.), *The Lives of the English Poets*, in *The Works of Samuel Johnson, LL.D*, 3 vols (Oxford: Clarendon Press, 1905), Vol. 1, p. 360.

15 Bernier, Orr points out, considered the weakness of the Moghul Empire to be its disregard for private property.

16 See Kate Teltscher, *India Inscribed: European and British Writing on India 1600–1800* (Delhi: Oxford University Press, 1995), pp. 51–68.

17 See Lata Mani, "The Production of an Official Discourse on Sati in Early Nineteenth-century Bengal," in Francis Barker et al. (eds), *Europe and its Others*, 2 vols (Colchester: University of Essex Press, 1985), pp. i, 107–27; and Gayatri Spivak, "Can the Subaltern Speak?," in Patrick Williams and Laura Chrisman (eds), *Colonial Discourse and Post-Colonial Theory: A Reader* (Hemel Hempstead: Harvester Wheatsheaf, 1993).

18 "John Dryden, *Aureng-Zebe*," in Vinton A. Dearing (ed.), *The Works of John Dryden*, Vol. 12 (Berkeley: University of California Press, 1994), pp. 155–6.

19 John Dryden, "An Essay of Dramatic Poesy," in Samuel Holt Monk (ed.), *The Works of John Dryden*, Vol. XVII (Berkeley: University of California Press, 1971), p. 71.

20 Michael McKeon, *The Origins of the English Novel 1600–1740* (Baltimore: The Johns Hopkins University Press, 1987), p. 105.

21 McKeon, *The Origins of the English Novel 1600–1740*, p. 103.

22 Jonathan Swift, *Gulliver's Travels and Other Writings* (Boston: Houghton Mifflin, 1960), p. 7.

23 Quoted in McKeon, *The Origins of the English Novel*, p. 111.

24 James Clifford, "Gulliver's Fourth Voyage: 'Hard' and 'Soft' Schools of Interpretation," in Larry S. Champion (ed.), *Quick Springs of Sense: Studies in the Eighteenth Century*, Vol. 18 (Athens, GA: University of Georgia Press, 1974).

25 Laura Brown, *Ends of Empire: Women and Ideology in Early Eighteenth-Century Literature* (Ithaca: Cornell University Press, 1993), pp. 193–9.

26 I make this argument in greater detail in *Consuming Anxieties: Consumer Protest, Gender and British Slavery, 1713–1833* (Stanford: Stanford University Press, 2000), ch. 2.

27 Lady Mary Wortley Montagu, *The Selected Letters of Mary Wortley Montagu*, ed. Robert Halsband (Harmondsworth: Penguin Books, 1986), p. 246.

28 Quoted in Teltscher, *India Inscribed*, p. 42.

29 Elizabeth Bohls, *Women Travel Writers and the Language of Aesthetics, 1716–18* (Cambridge: Cambridge University Press, 1995), p. 29.

30 Quoted in Bohls, *Women Travel Writers*, p. 30.

31 Bohls, *Women Travel Writers*, p. 28.

32 John Albert de Mandelso, "The Voyages and Travels of J. Albert de Mandelso," in *The Voyages and Travels of the Ambassadors sent by Frederick Duke of Holstein, to the Great Duke of Muscovy, and the King of Persia*, trans. John Davis (London, 1662), p. 27. Quoted in Teltscher, *India Inscribed*, p. 49.

33 Srinivas Aravamudan, *Tropicopolitans: Colonialism and Agency, 1688–1804* (Durham: Duke University Press, 1999), 184.

34 Tobias Smollett, *The Expedition of Humphry Clinker* (Oxford: Oxford University Press, 1966), p. 339.

35 Eric Rothstein, *Systems of Order and Inquiry in Later Eighteenth-Century Fiction* (Berkeley: University of California Press, 1975), p. 110.

36 Robert Crawford, *Devolving English Literature* (Oxford: Oxford University Press, 1992), p. 70.

37 May 1787 (lxxvi, 450). Quoted in Roger Lonsdale, "Introduction," in *William Beckford, Vathek* (Oxford: Oxford University Press, 1970), p. xix.

38 Quoted in Nigel Leask, "'Wandering through Eblis': Absorption and Containment in Romantic Exoticism," in Tim Fulford and Peter J. Kitson (eds), *Romanticism and Colonialism: Writing and Empire, 1780–1830* (Cambridge: Cambridge University Press, 1998), pp. 165–189, 180.

39 Quoted in Lonsdale, "Introduction," pp. x–xii.

40 Leask, "Wandering through Eblis," p. 180.

41 Leask, "Wandering through Eblis," p. 181.

42 Lonsdale, *William Beckford, Vathek*, p. 58.

43 Aravamudan says of this scene: "We thereby witness in Beckford's orientalist gothic a transition from early modern despotism, as seen in Vathek's and Carathis's grotesque menagerie of one-eyed Africans, deaf-mutes, eunuchs and cripples, to the bureaucratic fantasy of the disciplined body, underground but in a vast space, where all prisoners are formally indecipherable because all are morally equivalent" (*Tropicopolitans*, p. 218).

44 Quoted in Lonsdale, "Introduction," *William Beckford, Vathek*, p. ix.

45 Quoted in George Haggerty, "Literature and Homosexuality in the Late Eighteenth Century: Walpole, Beckford, and Lewis," *Studies in the Novel* 18(4) (Winter 1986): 341–52, 346.

46 Haggerty, "Literature and Homosexuality," p. 348.

Chapter 10 Colonialism and Slavery

1 David Richardson, "The Slave Trade, Sugar, and British Economic Growth, 1748–1776," in Barbara Solow and Stanley Engerman (eds), *British Capitalism and Caribbean Slavery: The Legacy of Eric Williams* (Cambridge: Cambridge University Press, 1987), p. 106. See also Philip D. Curtin, *The Atlantic Slave Trade: A Census* (Madison, WI: The University of Wisconsin Press, 1969); and Paul E. Lovejoy, "The Volume of the Atlantic Slave Trade: A Synthesis," *Journal of African History* XXIII (1982): 474–500.

2 See, for example, Frank J. Klingberg, *The Anti-Slavery Movement in England: A Study in English Humanitarianism* (New Haven, CT: Yale University Press, 1926).

3 For the former, see Eric Williams, *Capitalism and Slavery* (Chapel Hill, NC: University of North Carolina Press, 1944); for the latter, see David Brion Davis, *The Problem of Slavery in the Age of Revolution, 1770–1823* (Ithaca, NY: Cornell University Press, 1975).

4 See Seymour Drescher, *Capitalism and Antislavery: British Mobilization in Comparative Perspective* (New York, NY: Macmillan, 1987).

5 Christopher Leslie Brown, *Moral Capital: Foundations of British Abolitionism* (Chapel Hill, NC: The University of North Carolina Press, 2006).

6 Roxann Wheeler, *The Complexion of Race: Categories of Difference in Eighteenth-Century British Culture* (Philadelphia: The University of Pennsylvania Press, 2000), p. 7.

7 See Nancy Stepan, *The Idea of Race in Science: Great Britain 1800–1960* (Hamden, CT: Archon Nooks, 1982); Nicholas Hudson, "From 'Nation' to 'Race': The Origin of Racial Classification in Eighteenth-Century Thought," *Eighteenth-Century Studies* 29(3) (1996): 247–64. More generally, see Henry Louis Gates, Jr, "Writing 'Race' and the Difference it Makes," in Henry Louis Gates, Jr (ed.), *"Race," Writing and Difference* (Chicago: University of Chicago Press, 1987), pp. 1–21. For a different account of the initial importance of physical difference to English settlers in North America, see Joyce Chaplin, *Subject Matter: Technology, the Body, and Science on the Anglo-American Frontier, 1500–1676* (Cambridge, MA: Harvard University Press, 2001).

8 James I cleared six of the nine counties of Ulster in Northern Ireland, moving both tenants and landowners south, and transported in English and Scottish landowners and settlers to create "a mixed plantation of British and Irish, that they might grow together in one nation."

9 Nicholas Canny, "The Ideology of English Colonization: From Ireland to America," *William and Mary Quarterly* 30 (October 1973): 575–98; *Kingdom and Colony: Ireland in the Atlantic World* (Baltimore, MD: Johns Hopkins University Press, 1987).

10 Michael Hechter, *Internal Colonialism: The Celtic Fringe in British National Development, 1536–1966* (Berkeley, CA: University of California Press, 1975).

11 See Charlotte Sussman, "The Colonial Afterlife of Political Arithmetic: Swift, Demography, and Mobile Populations," *Cultural Critique* 56 (Winter 2004): 96–126.

12 See, for example, William Spengemann, *New World of Words: Redefining Early American Literature* (New Haven, CT: Yale University Press, 1994).

13 Elizabeth Dillon, "The Original American Novel, or, The American Origin of the Novel," in Paula R. Backscheder and Catherine Ingrassia (eds), *A Companion to the Eighteenth-Century English Novel and Culture* (Oxford: Blackwell, 2005), pp. 235–61, p. 246.

14 Nancy Armstrong and Leonard Tennenhouse, *The Imaginary Puritan: Literature, Intellectual Labor, and the Origins of Personal Life* (Berkeley, CA: University of California Press, 1992), p. 199.

15 Laura Doyle, *Freedom's Empire: Race and the Rise of the Novel in Atlantic Modernity, 1640–1940* (Durham, NC: Duke University Press, 2008), p. 4.

16 *Cities of the Dead: Circum-Atlantic Performance* (New York: Columbia University Press, 1996), p. 4. See also Paul Gilroy's important discussion in *The Black Atlantic: Modernity and Double Consciousness* (Cambridge, MA: Harvard University Press, 1993); David Armitage, *Greater Britain: 1516–1776: Essays in Atlantic History* (Aldershot: Ashgate, 2004); and Ian Baucom, *Specters of the Atlantic: Finance Capital, Slavery and the Philosophy of History* (Durham NC: Duke University Press, 2005).

17 Roach continues, "Newness enacts a kind of surrogation – in the invention of a new England or a new France out of memories of the old – but it also conceptually erases indigenous populations." *Cities of the Dead*, p. 4.

18 *Cities of the Dead*, p. 125.

19 Nicholas Thomas, *Entangled Objects: Exchange, Material Culture and Colonialism in the Pacific* (Cambridge: Harvard University Press, 1991).

20 Aphra Behn, *Oroonoko* (New York: W. W. Norton, 1997), p. 8.

21 Behn, *Oroonoko*, p. 13.

22 For a more detailed version of the argument in these two paragraphs, see Charlotte Sussman, "The Other Problem with Women: Reproduction and Slave Culture in Aphra Behn's *Oroonoko*," in Heidi Hutner (ed.), *Rereading Aphra Behn: History, Theory, and Criticism* (Charlottesville and London: University Press of Virginia, 1993), pp. 212–33.

23 Laura Brown, "The Romance of Empire: *Oroonoko* and the Trade in Slaves," in Laura Brown and Felicity Nussbaum (eds), *The New Eighteenth Century* (New York: Methuen, 1987), pp. 41–61.

24 Catherine Gallagher, *Nobody's Story: The Vanishing Acts of Women Writers in the Marketplace, 1670–1820* (Berkeley and Los Angeles: University of California Press, 1994); Margaret Ferguson, "Juggling the Categories of Race, Class and Gender: Aphra Behn's *Oroonoko*," *Women's Studies* 19 (1991): 159–81.

25 On contemporary critics' obsession with the text, see Srinivas Aravamudan, *Tropicopolitans: Colonialism and Agency 1688–1804* (Durham, NC: Duke University Press, 1999).

26 Daniel Defoe, *Robinson Crusoe*, ed. Michael Shinagel (New York and London: W. W. Norton, 1994), p. 5.

27 Michael McKeon, *The Origins of the English Novel, 1600–1740* (Baltimore: The Johns Hopkins University Press, 1987), p. 323. See also J. Paul Hunter, *The Reluctant Pilgrim* (Baltimore: The Johns Hopkins University Press, 1966).

28 Karl Marx, *Capital*, Vol. 1, trans. Eden and Cedar Paul (London: Dent, Everyman's Library, 1930, Rpt. 1978), p. 42.

29 Peter Hulme, *Colonial Encounters: Europe and the Native Caribbean, 1492–1797* (London and New York: Methuen, 1986), p. 186.

30 Hulme, *Colonial Encounters*, p. 196.

31 Hulme, *Colonial Encounters*, p. 220.

32 Jonathan Swift, *Gulliver's Travels and Other Writings* (Boston: Houghton Mifflin, 1960), pp. 439.

33 Jonathan Swift and Thomas Sheridan, *The Intelligencer*, No. 18, ed. James Wooley (Oxford: Clarendon, 1992), p. 198.

34 R. F. Foster, *Modern Ireland: 1600–1972* (London and New York: Penguin, 1989), pp. 34–5.

35 Jonathan Swift, "An Answer to a Paper called a Memorial of the Poor Inhabitants, Tradesmen, and Labourers of the Kingdom of Ireland." *Irish Tracts 1728–1733*. Ed. Herbert Davis (Oxford: Basil Blackwell, 1955), p. 19.

36 Irvin Ehrenpreis, *Swift: The Man, His Works, and the Age. 3 vols* (Cambridge: Harvard University Press, 1983), Vol. 3, p. 630.

37 Swift, *Irish Tracts*, p. 60.

38 Louis Landa, "A Modest Proposal and Populousness," *Modern Philology* 40 (1942): 161–70; George Wittkowsky, "Swift's Modest Proposal: The Biography of an Early Georgian Pamphlet," *Journal of the History of Ideas* 4(4) (January 1943): 75–104. See also Charlotte Sussman, "The Colonial Afterlife of Political Arithmetic: Swift, Demography and Mobile Populations," *Cultural Critique* 56 (Winter 2004): 96–126.

39 See Mary Poovey, "The Social Constitution of 'Class': Toward a History of Classificatory Thinking," in Wai Chi Dimock and Michael T. Gilmore (eds), *Rethinking Class: Literary and Social Formations* (New York: Columbia University Press, 1994), pp. 15–56.

40 William Petty, *The Political Anatomy of Ireland*, in Charles Henry Hull (ed.), *The Economic Writings of Sir William Petty*, Vol. 1 (Cambridge: Cambridge University Press, 1899), p. 52.

41 George Wittkowsky, "Swift's *Modest Proposal*: The Biography of an Early Georgian Pamphlet," *Journal of the History of Ideas* 4 (1943): 75–104.

42 Samuel Johnson and James Boswell, *A Journey to the Western Islands of Scotland AND The Journal of a Tour to the Hebrides* (Harmondsworth: Penguin Classics, 1984), p. 102.

43 See Bernard Bailyn, *Voyagers to the West: A Passage in the Peopling of America on the Eve of the Revolution* (New York: Knopf, 1986).

44 Henry Louis Gates, Jr, "Writing 'Race' and the Difference it Makes," in Henry Louis Gates Jr (ed.), *"Race," Writing, and Difference* (Chicago and London: The University of Chicago Press, 1986), pp. 1–21, p. 12.

45 Vincent Carretta, *Equiano, The African: Biography of a Self-Made Man* (Athens: University of Georgia Press, 2005).

46 *The Interesting Narrative of the Life of Olaudah Equiano, or Gustavus Vassa, The African, Written by Himself.* Ed. Werner Sollers (New York: W. W. Norton, 2001), p. 19.

47 Gates, "Writing 'Race' and the Difference it Makes," p. 12.

Index

violence 21, 22, 108, 123
and colonialism 241, 242, 246, 248–55
to women 166, 176, 182
Virgil 15, 16, 71, 98, 102
Virginia Company 5
virtue 51, 84, 101, 155, 191, 193, 194–200
female 126–9, 156, 157–9, 163–70, 175, 178, 179–84, 213, 219–21
and social class 182–3, 198–9

Wales/Welsh 11, 13, 30, 64, 235
Walpole, Horace 35, 106, 207, 208
Walpole, Robert 54, 81–2
War of Spanish Succession 4, 19, 233
Warton, Thomas, *Ode to Sleep* 202
Watts, Isaac 41, 147–8
wealth 67, 196, 198, 233, 245, 252, 260
Welsted, Leonard 192
Wesley, John and Charles 138, 148–9
West, Benjamin 19
Westminster Paving Act 64
Wexford 236
Wheatley, Phyllis 256
Whigs 43, 49, 53
Whitefield, George 138, 148
Wilberforce, William 138, 154
William III (William of Orange) 2, 5
Wilmot, John, Earl of Rochester *see* Rochester, Earl of (John Wilmot)
wisdom 18, 146–7
wit 185–204

Wollstonecraft, Mary, *Maria* 178–9
women 49, 67, 84, 156–84, 219, 220–1
and beauty 156–7, 160–3, 176–7, 180, 273
and domesticity 48, 96, 158–9, 164, 169–70
female body 80, 122, 157, 168–9, 180, 181
female identity 51, 128, 164, 180, 222, 271
and propriety 139, 176, 180–2, 192
readers 17, 43–4, 45, 48
and religion 139, 140–1, 145, 147–8
and satire 176, 183–4
and sexual desire 52, 77–80, 157
and sexuality 6, 53, 97, 156–84, 220–1
and social class 48, 158–9, 165, 174–5, 178
and social interaction 44, 51, 96–7
and the theater 2, 37, 187
violence to 166, 176, 182
and virtue 126–9, 156, 157–9, 163–70, 175, 178, 179–84, 213, 219–21
writers 29, 42, 50, 175–6, 180, 238
Woolf, Virginia 76, 238
Wordsworth, William 35, 111, 201, 203
writing, professional 56–8, 62

Yearsley, Ann 109–11, 113, 234
Young, Arthur 93, 223